D1569950

# Ceremonial Splendor

# Ceremonial Splendor

Performing Priesthood in Early Modern France

Joy Palacios

**PENN**

UNIVERSITY OF PENNSYLVANIA PRESS

PHILADELPHIA

Published by
University of Pennsylvania Press
Philadelphia, Pennsylvania 19104-4112
www.upenn.edu/pennpress

Printed in the United States of America on acid-free paper
10  9  8  7  6  5  4  3  2  1
Hardcover ISBN: 9781512822786
eBook ISBN: 9781512822779

A catalogue record for this book is available from the
Library of Congress

*For my parents*

# CONTENTS

# NOTE ON TRANSLATIONS

Unless otherwise indicated, all translations are my own. My English translations use modernized punctuation where this is helpful for comprehension. For the most part, I have preserved the early modern spelling and capitalization in the original French for quotes and for the titles of works, except that I have added missing letters where the manuscript used abbreviations. For example, where a manuscript uses "ō" to indicate "on," I have transcribed it as "o[n]."

# Priestly Performance, 1630–1730

In sacristies throughout Paris during the second half of the seventeenth century, a mirror hung on the wall near where clergymen put on their vestments and prepared the ornaments before conducting Mass. This mirror, however, was made not of glass but rather of paper. It took the form of a large broadsheet summarizing a thirty-seven-page pamphlet entitled *Miroir des prestres et autres ecclesiastiques* (Mirror of priests and other churchmen), which in turn summarized longer volumes that contained instructions on the way churchmen should carry out their liturgical and pastoral duties. Designed for frequent self-evaluative consultation, the text invited—or rather commanded—its readers to use its pages as a looking glass: "But in the same way that to discover the stains on your face you look willingly into the mirrors that are presented to you and do not fail to quickly wipe yourself carefully, look at this one which is presented to your soul."[1] A clergyman who stopped to read the "mirror" while putting on his robes or who carried the pamphlet version in his pocket was reminded that he conducted his priestly tasks before watchful eyes, both divine and human, whose judgment he should avoid and approval he should seek. "Unless you had lost your mind," argues the mirror's text, "you would not want to publicly undertake the functions of your order with stains on your face that render you deformed in the eyes of the attendees; you are without doubt even more rash and senseless if you tolerate [stains] on your soul that render you criminal, or even a little disagreeable in the eyes of God."[2] Whether clergymen were out and about in the parish or in the church preparing to administer the sacraments, the premise of a text like the *Miroir des prestres et autres ecclesiastiques* was that because clergymen enacted their profession in full view of others they should pause, look at themselves, and compare their behavior to an external standard so as to improve their performance.

Although the *Miroir des prestres et autres ecclesiastiques* and texts like it do not use the term "performance," the metaphor of the mirror has evoked image making, representation, and theater since Plato's *Republic* and Aristotle's *Poetics*.[3] Antoine Furetière's (1619–1688) *Dictionnaire universel*, published in 1690, foregrounds the process of representation in his explanation of the way moral discourses use the mirror metaphor: "*Mirror* is used figuratively in moral terms for that which represents something, or which places it before our eyes."[4] In seventeenth-century French terms, therefore, a text and a person could be considered a "mirror" insofar as they represented something else. With this metaphor in mind, the founders of France's Counter-Reformation seminaries fully understood that the project of training priests involved representation. Ideally, once he began his ministry, a priest functioned as a mirror for his parishioners by representing a moral standard toward which they should strive, prompting them to compare their own behavior against his example. Spanish and Italian Catholic reformers from the sixteenth century whose writings inspired France's seventeenth-century renewal of priestly training had made the clergyman's representational function explicit. "The priest is a mirror and a light," declared a French translation from 1658 of Juan de Ávila's treatise on the dignity of the priesthood, "in which people must look at themselves to know the darkness in which they walk and to reflect within themselves, saying 'Why am I not as good as this priest?'"[5] In order to become like a mirror a clergyman needed to engage in a series of other representational practices. He needed to watch and learn from those with more experience, submit himself to their evaluation of his skills, practice the rites and sacraments over and over, and play the role of priest before he actually occupied it.

In contemporary theoretical terms, the varied processes evoked in early modern ecclesiastical handbooks by the mirror metaphor coalesce in the concepts of performance and performativity. Richard Schechner, who helped create the field of performance studies, defines performance as "showing doing" or the act of "pointing to, underlining, and displaying" an action, a definition that captures the idea that priests were to bracket and examine their own behavior so as to then display the right actions to others.[6] The skills and habits taught in France's early seminaries resulted in an identity that certainly on many occasions framed itself in a Schechnerian sense and displayed its "doing" to a public, thereby crystalizing as a performance with a more or less identifiable beginning and end, such as a sermon or a Mass.

Priestly performance, however, as the mirror metaphor conveyed, entailed more than framing clerical actions or setting priests apart. The ideal priest, which

seminary texts referred to as the *vray ecclésiastique*, or true churchman, consci-
entiously copied ecclesiastical models on the one hand while scrupulously serving as a model for other people. His precision in imitating models and representing
them to others derived, according to seminary handbooks, from a clergyman's
efforts to achieve perfection. A "true" churchman was synonymous with a "perfect" churchman, in the sense of one who mastered and continually demonstrated
"ecclesiastical discipline."[7] A handbook on priestly practice entitled *Le Parfaict
ecclesiastique, ou diverses intructions sur toutes les fonctions clericales* (The perfect
churchman, or diverse instructions on all the clerical functions), for example,
lauds France's bishops as "the perfect models that churchmen must imitate, the
living books they must study," and then goes on to present the handbook as a
manifestation of their perfect models, which will in turn produce "the perfect
churchman."[8] In performance theory terms, the churchman who imitated ecclesiastical models "cited" a dynamically evolving set of behaviors, each of which,
in the words of W. B. Worthen, contributed to "an elaborate reiteration of a
specific vision of social order."[9] When a seventeenth-century French clergyman
seemed to his peers and parishioners like a "true" or "perfect" churchman, his
citational behavior so thoroughly encompassed each aspect of his bodily movements, speech, and thought that those who interacted with him could find little
to no difference between the self he presented and the models he represented.

Priestly identity, therefore, arose less from instances of framed "doing" than
from repeated citational practices of the kind Judith Butler analyzes in her work
on the construction of gender.[10] In much the way a coherent gender identity, according to Butler, results from "words, acts, gestures, and desire" that "produce
the effect of an internal core or substance," so too the vray ecclésiastique, to the
extent that any individual clergyman conformed to this ideal, possessed "no ontological status apart from the various acts which constitute[ed] its reality."[11] Like
gender identity, priestly identity was performative. Butler chooses the term "performative" to describe the way the "acts, gestures, and enactments" that express
an identity perceived as essential in fact "manufactu[re]" and "sustain" that identity.[12] In her effort to reveal the cultural operations that produce gender, in her
early work Butler figures the performative expressions of gender as "*fabrications*,"
arguing that gender has "no ontological status apart from the various acts which
constitute its reality."[13] Its constructedness, though, does not make gender false.
Gender has social substance and real effects. So, too, the priestly identities crafted
by individual clergymen who aspired to the ideal of the vray ecclésiastique. By
analyzing priestly identity as performance, I do not mean that churchmen
were just pretending or hypocritical, although seventeenth-century Catholic

reformers and laity did worry about that possibility. Rather, in its construction through the citation of behavioral norms and standardized practices, seventeenth-century priestly identity had material consequences for French parishioners, most notably by influencing when and how they received sacraments and which individuals found themselves excluded from the Catholic Church's rites and ceremonies.

This book uses theories of performance and performativity to examine the emergence in Counter-Reformation France of a variation of priestly identity organized around the idea of the vray ecclésiastique and elaborated by France's early seminaries between approximately 1630 and 1730. Although I focus on the long seventeenth century and the decades immediately after Louis XIV's reign, the vray ecclésiastique structured priestly identity in France until the French Revolution. Historians have traced the basic contours of this figure's institutional development in works like Antoine Degert's *Histoire des séminaires français jusqu'à la révolution* (1912), Paul Broutin's *La Réforme pastorale en France au XVIIe siècle* (1965), Jeanne Ferté's *La Vie religieuse dans les campagnes parisiennes (1622–1695)* (1962), and, more recently, Joseph Bergin's *Church, Society and Religious Change in France, 1580–1730* (2009). In early modern theater studies and seventeenth-century French literary studies, this type of priest makes cameo appearances in scholarship on antitheatrical sentiment, since a strong correlation exists between the priests involved in France's Counter-Reformation movement and the clergymen who preached against the theater, attacked plays like Molière's *Tartuffe*, and refused to administer sacraments to actors unless they renounced their profession as stage players.[14]

Given that the theater was so important for France's ascendance as Europe's early modern cultural center, French studies has perceived Counter-Reformation priests who took a stand against the theater as enemies of France's national heritage. Scholarship on *la querelle de la moralité du théâtre*—the name given in French studies to early modern debates about the theater's moral status—often portrays the Catholic Church and its representatives as backward looking or as obstacles to French greatness.[15] Priests and their devout converts contested the theater, rejected arguments that presented it as a positive moral force, and persecuted actors by refusing to give them the sacraments. In an analytical framework that takes theater as early modernity's preeminent cultural product, the Catholic Church's polemical stance toward the stage and its players aligns religion with the past.

From a history of Christianity perspective, however, France's seventeenth-century Catholicism represents the mature flowering of a two-century process in which the Catholic Church reformed itself for the modern age. In *The Spirit of the Counter-Reformation,* H. Outram Evennett argues that the Counter-Reformation was "the total process of adaptation to new world conditions which Catholicism underwent in the first two centuries of the post-medieval age," a "modernisation" that culminated toward the end of Louis XIV's reign.[16] From a strictly French perspective, the seventeenth century's religious creativity matched that of its theatrical developments, fostering "an admirable religious re-naissance" and an age "in which holiness abound[ed]."[17] In terms of its religious inventiveness, France's seventeenth-century church cannot be figured as a strictly conservative force bent on suppressing new cultural forms that contained the seeds of modern social life. To the contrary, the Catholic Church, too, propelled France toward forms of organization essential to its *Grand Siècle.*

A new approach to the relationship between the church and the theater in early modern France is therefore needed. Rather than starting from the theater, I begin from the church, building on scholarship in religious studies and the history of Christianity and on archival research from France's early seminaries, which trained and influenced many of the clergymen who attacked the theater. In taking the church as my starting point, I begin from the premise that France's seventeenth-century priests were thoroughly modern figures in the sense given to this term by Bruno Latour, by which I mean that priestly identity was hybrid and produced by mixing repertoires from a range of domains to create something distinctive.[18] The process of becoming a priest who bore the marks of a vray ecclésiastique required craft, discipline, and even art and consequently deserves the kind of sustained analysis that has more often been directed toward theatrical production in seventeenth-century France. Only by reconstructing the inner dynamics of early modern priestly performance will the way churchmen responded to the theater and its players shed light on the broader range of performance innovations, in addition to and alongside the theater, which contributed to France's cultural dominance in the seventeenth century.

The complexity of priestly performances means that what Marc Fumaroli has called the "'ecclesiastical reaction' against the theater," and French antithe-atrical sentiment more broadly, must be studied not only through an analysis of theological and philosophical arguments waged against the theater by its clerical opponents but also through an analysis of the religious practices that gave rise to clerical identity in the first place.[19] Whereas a robust literature examines early modern discourses for and against the theater, studies on French antitheatrical sentiment have yet to consider the church's rites and ceremonies as performances in their own right; that is to say, as behaviors carried out in the presence of others in a designated space and time, often in conformity to a script or tradition, frequently involving a display of skill, and constitutive of social roles as well as communal identities.[20] Among the many performance genres in which priests engaged, preaching has received the most study. Certainly, preaching accounted for an important aspect of priestly performance, and more scholarship on early modern preaching is needed.[21] Nonetheless, France's Catholic reformers believed that the liturgy outweighed the pulpit in importance. Without the sacraments, in particular the Eucharist, sermonic oratory counted for naught. In acknowledgment of the liturgy's fundamental relation to early modern priestly identity, I therefore concentrate on the way France's seventeenth-century churchmen learned and enacted the ceremonies of the mass, the sacraments, and such related rites as blessings and burials, as well as the way they acquired the modes of embodiment and self-presentation appropriate for liturgical action. Through an analysis of the components of priestly performance, this book offers a new angle from which to understand the danger that early modern priests believed that the theater posed to the social order and a framework for the examination of physical interactions between churchmen and stage players. In doing so, the study of priestly performance details the way iterative practices carried out by thousands of clergymen in unremarkable times and places across the kingdom—the dining hall, the dormitory, the chapel, the classroom, the road to the parish church—enacted concepts of personhood and established liturgical publics strong enough to sustain an institution, the Catholic Church, that faced external opposition from Protestants, was grappling with internal divisions between Jansenists and Jesuits as well as between ultramontanist and Gallican visions for French Catholicism, and that perceived secular modes of popular culture, such as the theater, as detrimental to a Christian society.

## Priestly Performance and the Parish

Parish life provided the horizon in which most clergymen negotiated the distance between the ideal of the vray ecclésiastique and the concrete challenges of providing liturgical services and pastoral care to seventeenth-century French Catholics. As René Taveneaux explains, materially the parish consisted of a "collection of houses grouped around a church and a cemetery," while administratively the parish served as the basic unit of civic organization.[22] Many parishes dated from as early as the eleventh century, but parish boundaries fluctuated over time and could be quite porous.[23] Catholic reform efforts and the Council of Trent's insistence that priests reside in the parishes where they held benefices reinforced the parish as central to religious belonging and practice, a process that was well under way by the middle of the seventeenth century in France.[24] Discursively, ecclesiastical handbooks reflected the parish's importance by representing the *bon curé*, or good parish priest, as a privileged manifestation of the "true" or "perfect" churchman. Manuals aimed at improving the clergy, such as *Le Parfaict ecclesiastique*, cited above, conflated the perfect churchman and the good parish priest by including multiple chapters on the dignity and duties of the bon curé.[25] As a horizon for clerical action, the parish meant that the vray ecclésiastique carried out the framed and the iterative aspects of his identity in a variety of settings that included the church building as well as the streets, houses, and public squares that composed the parish.

Epitomized in the bon curé, the ideal of the vray ecclésiastique consequently applied to a specific category of priest, the *prêtre séculier*, or secular priest. For anyone not familiar with Catholic terminology, the notion of a "secular" priest sounds like an oxymoron. Defined in opposition to "regular" priests, or those who belong to religious orders, the term "secular" signals a clergyman's status as someone who lives among the laity, while connoting the public and outward-turning nature of his pastoral responsibilities. For example, in seventeenth-century parlance, a priest who did not belong to a religious order, or one who left his monastery, "lived secularly in the world."[26] By contrast a regular priest, in principle if not always in practice, set himself apart from worldly life. Upon joining an order, the regular clergy swore solemn vows, typically of poverty, chastity, and obedience, and committed to live by the "rule" (*règle*), or code of life, shared by all the members of their order.[27] Even if a physical cloister did not separate a regular priest from the world, his observation of a rule—from which the term "regular" is derived—did. The distinction between secular and regular priests therefore entailed the idea that priests who did not belong to a religious order lived their lives in full view of the faithful. Indeed, although some regular priests interacted frequently with laypeople, became bishops, or served as parish priests, the great majority of parish priests and local clergymen belonged to the secular clergy. Secular churchmen cultivated the religious ideas and habits of lay French Catholics, who relied on them for baptisms, burials, marriages, weekly masses, and the required doctrinal classes known as catechism.

Ecclesiastical canons refer to the parish priest's pastoral and liturgical responsibilities as the "cure of souls." From the Latin *cūra*, in old French cure meant *soin*, or care, such that in modern parlance the parish priest has "care of souls."[28] A *curé*, or curate, is thus "a priest endowed with a cure."[29] A cure of souls entailed and continues to entail both instructional and ceremonial duties. These duties involve "the instruction, by sermons and admonitions, and the sanctification, through the sacraments, of the faithful in a determined district, by a person legitimately appointed for the purpose."[30] As Nicole Lemaître explains, discussions about the secular clergy's care of souls stretch back to the thirteenth century, matured at the end of the fifteenth century, and bifurcated at the beginning of the sixteenth century when Protestant and Catholic reformers articulated divergent views about the spiritual care provided by clergymen.[31] Whereas Protestants emphasized the clergyman's relationship to God's Word expressed in sermons through the pulpit, Catholics emphasized the clergyman's reiteration of Christ's sacrifice at the altar. Circa 1520–1530, argues Lemaître, Catholic authors of ecclesiastical handbooks "invert[ed] the hierarchy pastor / man of the mass" by developing a sacerdotal theology that "orient[ed] the function of the priest toward the sacrament of the sacraments: the Eucharist."[32] Without denying the priest's function as preacher, the churchmen gathered at the Council of Trent (1545–1563) privileged a Eucharistic vision of the Catholic priest.[33] For Catholic reformers after Trent, priesthood found its legitimation and clearest manifestation in the liturgy.

Theological articulations of the Catholic priest's eucharistic dignity did not, however, quickly translate into Masses that were well run at the parish level. In France, prior to the foundation of seminaries in the 1640s, most secular clergymen lacked formal training and the ceremonial skills such training would cultivate by the end of the seventeenth century.[34] Ordination requirements during the sixteenth century and the early seventeenth century were minimal and did not include practical preparation for administering the sacraments. The most prohibitive condition, imposed by the Edict of Blois in 1561, required candidates for the priesthood to demonstrate they had property worth a minimum sum, usually one hundred *livres*; an amount roughly equivalent to a laborer's annual earnings.[35] Someone aiming for the priesthood then had to present testimony to the bishop or his auxiliaries from the priest of his home parish certifying his moral uprightness.[36] To attain the preliminary stage of ordination, candidates also had to take a short test to ensure they knew some Latin. Although an additional test preceded each successive ordination on the way toward the priesthood—a process that entailed seven stages—and each test required progressively greater doctrinal knowledge, the tests called for rudimentary knowledge and did little to prevent cheating.[37] Even in larger cities like Paris, where many men entering the priesthood had earned university degrees, possessed a more refined Latin, and perhaps had a theological background, candidates received no training specifically related to the ceremonial duties they would assume as secular clergymen.

Consequently, liturgical practices varied greatly from diocese to diocese. From the perspective of the seventeenth-century's Catholic reformers, this diversity diminished the liturgy's expressive power and the secular clergy's legitimacy. Vincent de Paul (1581–1660) lamented in 1659, "Oh, if you had seen . . . the diversity in the ceremonies of the mass forty years ago, it would have made you ashamed! It seems to me that there was nothing uglier in the world than the diverse ways it was celebrated."[38] In the worst cases, like that of a vicar near Marseilles who admitted in 1627 that "he didn't understand anything about the administration of the sacraments" and could not even name all of them, liturgical ignorance threatened the faith, diluted the apologetic force of ceremonies, and opened the clergy to Protestant critiques of corruption and ignorance.[39] Liturgical handbooks from the second half of the seventeenth century abound with references to the secular clergy's poor ceremonial practices and the corresponding degradation of ceremonies in the previous century. The preface to *Le Parfaict ecclesiastique* contrasts a seventeenth-century rebirth of "a truly ecclesiastical spirit" characterized by "an extraordinary science concerning matters of church discipline," such as ceremonies, with a previous period in which "the ecclesiastical condition (*estat*) was extremely degraded."[40] Although a widespread ceremonial knowledge among secular priests spread more slowly than the author of *Le Parfaict ecclesiastique* wanted to believe, Bruno Restif's analysis of Tridentine reforms at the parish level in Haute-Bretagne leads him to conclude that by the second half of the seventeenth century "the model of the good priest no longer merely corresponded to an ideal, but also, in a nonnegligible number of cases, to a reality."[41] Little by little, the institutional structures created during the seventeenth century to facilitate clerical reform, which I discuss below, developed methods for connecting embodied practices to the Counter-Reformation's discursive formulation of a priestly ideal.

As France's secular clergy gradually acquired ceremonial skills over the course of the seventeenth century, their liturgical expertise reinforced a separation of the priesthood and the laity begun in the twelfth century.[42] "The priest is a mediator," writes Lemaître in her analysis of the way medieval theologies of the priesthood shaped future clerical practice, "set apart for the ministry of the Eucharist and forgiveness."[43] Their separateness, ritually enacted through ordination and reiterated each time they administered the sacraments to their parishioners, made priests visible in their parish communities.[44] Meanwhile, transformations in church architecture following the Council of Trent placed the secular priest's liturgical action on display in a way it had not been during the medieval period. Whereas parish Mass during the twelfth through sixteenth centuries unfolded in an enclosed area called the chancel accessible only to churchmen and separated from the laity by a wall or screen called a *jubé*, in France the destruction wreaked by religious wars combined with Catholic reform efforts initiated a slow restructuring of ecclesial spaces in the middle of the sixteenth century.[45] Between approximately 1560 and the end of the eighteenth century, French churches removed their jubés, creating what Bernard Chédozeau calls "a new church, the *Tridentine church*."[46] The process of modifying a parish church's architecture to open the chancel and make liturgical ceremonies visible to the laity could take decades. In the Parisian parish of Saint-Sulpice, the process took more than ninety years.[47] Nonetheless, France's seventeenth-century secular clergymen possessed an acute awareness of the outward-turned, public-facing nature of their liturgical responsibilities. Separation from the laity, ceremonial expertise, and open chancels positioned the seventeenth-century secular priest as a man with many eyes upon him.

The increased visibility of the secular priest in the seventeenth century has led historians to conceive of his sacerdotal position in theatrical terms. Lemaître writes that "the Council of Trent and especially the French School of Spirituality knew how to place this new priest on stage, make him valuable in the eyes of the faithful."[48] Philippe Martin gives fuller expression to this metaphor by titling his history of the Mass from the sixteenth to the twentieth century *Le Théâtre divin*, or the divine theater, a conception of the Mass that really only became possible in France in the seventeenth century.[49] Prior to this period, a priest in a pulpit might provoke theatrical anxiety but rarely a priest at the altar. Early modern jokes and anecdotes regularly compared *prédicateurs*—preachers—to actors and theatrical entertainments. Pierre de L'Estoile, for example, an acute observer of sixteenth-century affairs, gauged the size of crowds drawn to actors by comparing them to the crowds drawn by preachers. In his journal for the year 1577, L'Estoile records that on Sunday, May 19, the Italian acting troupe *li Gelosi* began performing comedies at the Hôtel de Bourbon in Paris. "They took as pay four *sous* per head from all the French who wanted to see them play," writes L'Estoile, "and there was such a crowd of people that the four best preachers in Paris did not have the same crowd altogether when they preached."[50] L'Estoile's use of the preacher-actor comparison implied that preachers offered a sought-after spectacle. So much so that the public attracted by preachers served as a recognizable measure against which to gauge the size of other audiences, including theatrical ones. By the seventeenth century, the preacher-actor binary evolved into a mainstay of antitheatrical discourses. In their writings, the theater's adversaries frequently opposed, in Sylviane Léoni's words, "the ruses and lies of the histrion to the sincerity of the sacred orator."[51] Such comparisons served not only to vilify actors but also to denigrate bad preachers.

After the 1640s, poor ceremonial performance, much like bad preaching, could appear empty to worshippers as well. A liturgical manual published in 1679 by the Congregation of the Mission warned priests that if they did not conduct the ceremonies of the Mass correctly, divine services would devolve into entertainment. Composed as a letter to God, the manual's preface exclaims: "LORD, some of your ministers . . . neglect almost entirely this holy exercise of ceremonies; they no longer know either the laws or the methods [of the ceremonies], and if they still practice something of it, it is with so little order and so much irreverence that the People . . . lose the respect that they should have for holy things, with the result that the honor of your Churches and the sanctity of your divine offices is nothing more for many than an occasion for babbling and a site for entertainment."[52] The terms used here to warn priests about what Mass could but should not become—an occasion for babbling and entertainment—belonged to the seventeenth century's antitheatrical vocabulary. Steeped in an Augustinian tradition suspicious not only of plays but also of harmonious melodies and fancy turns of speech, representatives of this school of early modern thought considered entertainments incompatible with religious practice.[53] Seminary rules instructed the clergyman, for example, to "remove from his mind all ideas of entertainment" before reciting the breviary or saying the rosary.[54] After his conversion to Catholicism, Molière's former protector, the Prince de Conti, drew on the same vocabulary to declare that the theater "is not an innocent entertainment" in his 1666 treatise against plays.[55] By suggesting that Mass could become a mere entertainment if not conducted properly, the manual placed pressure on seventeenth-century priests to become better performers, so as to safeguard the authority and perceived authenticity of liturgical ceremonies.

As parish priests gained ceremonial skills, as church buildings evolved to place these skills on display, and as post-Tridentine discourses emphasized the sacraments as channels for divine grace, secular clergymen went on the defensive against a range of people and practices whose activities challenged the type of social bond forged through the sacraments. Actors, stage playing, and theatergoing were not the only people and practices to come under fire. In fact, many priests, even if they embraced Saint Augustine's conviction that the theater corrupted those who performed in and watched it, did not bother harassing actors. For one thing, few parishes could boast a theater in the seventeenth century. Other people and practices—banking, prostitution, drunkenness, magic, and witchcraft, for example—received more ecclesiastical attention in France than acting did because these practices were carried out throughout the kingdom. Given the relatively small number of actors who lived and worked in France as compared to the number of prostitutes or pub owners, the fact that priests worried about stage players makes the secular clergy's antitheatrical tendencies even more significant and reveals the tensions churchmen faced in constructing their own professional identities. Priests who wanted to conform to the model of the vray ecclésiastique both admired and feared actors. On the one hand, actors provided a model for ceremonial preparation and good liturgical performance. On the other hand, actors established a connection with their audiences that was inimical to the communion created through sacraments. Whereas sacramental bonds reinscribed early modern France's hierarchical relations, theatrical identification did not.

The treatment of actors in the parish of Saint-Sulpice during the mid-seventeenth century demonstrates the correlation between liturgical reform among the secular clergy and ecclesiastical action against stage players. Between 1642 and 1651, Jean-Jacques Olier (1608–1657), the parish's curate and the founder of the Seminary of Saint-Sulpice, gave a series of conferences on the Mass in which he emphasized the importance of éclat, or ceremonial splendor.[56] The first recorded refusal of sacraments to an actor dates from the same period, occurring in his parish in 1647.[57] In the same way the imperative of ceremonial perfection placed pressure on priests to monitor their liturgical performance, a desire for ceremonial splendor went hand in hand with a more rigorous approach to plays and players. One parish does not, of course, represent an entire kingdom. Ecclesiastical attitudes toward actors varied from diocese to diocese. And yet, developments in the parish of Saint-Sulpice, home to what would become one of France's most influential institutions for training its secular clergy, quietly helped shape the way priests responded to the theater far beyond the capital. Rituals, or liturgical manuals issued by bishops for use in their diocese that contained instructions for all the sacraments, bear witness to this spread. Between 1649 and 1713, bishops in nineteen French dioceses plus Quebec issued Rituals that explicitly excluded stage players from some combination of Communion and the last rites by classifying them as pécheurs publics, or public sinners, a status that also barred them from marriage and from serving as a godparent.[58] In a culture where sacramental participation granted social recognition, the status of public sinner imposed a sort of civic death. For actors, the rivalry between altar and stage had serious consequences. In relation to the history of priestly performance, the secular clergy's treatment of actors offers a lens through which to analyze the citational structure of clerical identity in early modern France as enacted at the parish level.

## Priestly Performance and Seminaries

Even with a pamphlet like the *Miroir des prestres* in hand, a parish priest who tried to craft himself in the model of the vray ecclésiastique had little chance of succeeding on his own. The external standard to which secular clergymen were to hold themselves was not easy to define or summarize. Rather than try to paint an image of an ideal priest, the *Miroir* gives a list of seventy paragraph-length questions clergy were to ask themselves, all starting with "if": "If you are capable of your office," "If you allow your Church to be dirtier than your bedroom," "If you celebrate the holy mass having passed almost all the previous day drinking and eating without necessity."[59] Each question implicitly conveyed a norm, without explicitly articulating it. To correct his own behavior, a clergyman would need to convert the questions into instructions. After doing so, he would still be left with a long list of actions and little sense of how they fitted together to form a whole.

For a sense of the whole, a clergyman needed community. He needed to learn from, and ideally live with, other clergymen who were equally committed to perfecting themselves and were more experienced in doing so. To learn how to properly fulfill his obligations, the *Miroir des prestres* suggests a clergyman should go to seminary. "This mirror is thus to make clergymen see several points . . . that they do not usually think about," states the anonymous author's notice to the reader, adding in parentheses that the clergymen it targets are those "who do not have the spirit of their profession, or who have not had the happiness of being instructed in the seminaries."[60] The *Miroir*'s second question reiterates the importance of attending seminary, or of at least obtaining guidance from other priests. Any clergyman who finds himself incapable of administering the sacraments, giving a sermon, or enacting any of his other functions the *Miroir* urges to "have yourself taught as soon as possible in a seminary, or with some other people of the same profession capable of making you aware of your obligations and of teaching them to you through practice."[61] By overwhelming its readers with a seventy-item assessment of their flaws, the *Miroir* and other pamphlets like it nudged clergymen toward the conclusion that self-evaluation was not enough and that they needed to submit to the evaluation of others. They needed seminary training.

Seminaries provided the French church's primary vehicle for shaping the secular clergy's priestly identity. In their mature form, France's seminaries were educational institutions in which priests trained aspiring priests while living together in community. They offered vocational training in a format that blended elements from a range of ecclesiastical and secular domains, including *collèges*, universities, monasteries, court society, and the theater. The result produced an environment in which priests and priests-in-training learned and practiced the interlocking activities that forged priestly identity and the ceremonial building blocks essential to an early modern understanding of religion.

After almost a century of fits and starts, a flurry of seminaries sprung up in the early 1640s once this practice-oriented model for seminary training took hold.[62] According to Joseph Bergin's count, France welcomed thirty-six new seminary foundations between 1642 and 1660, fifty-six between 1660 and 1682, and twenty-five between 1683 and 1720.[63] He notes that "only six of the smallest southern dioceses never had a seminary of their own."[64] Paris alone boasted eleven seminaries by 1715.[65] Four of the seminaries founded in Paris in the early 1640s exerted a particularly strong influence over the standard features of clerical formation and liturgical training in France for the next 150 years. They are the Seminary of Saint-Sulpice (1642), founded by Olier and run by the priestly society he instituted for this purpose; the Seminary of Saint-Lazare (1642), founded by Vincent de Paul (1581–1660) and run by his Congregation of the Mission; the Seminary of Saint-Magloire (1642), founded by the bishop of Paris and entrusted to the French Oratory; and the Seminary of Saint-Nicolas du Chardonnet (1644), founded by Adrien Bourdoise (1584–1655) and run by the community of priests out of which the seminary grew.[66] These seminaries shaped the way France's secular clergymen dressed, ate, thought, carried themselves, interacted with parishioners, and conducted the church's rites and sacraments.

The seminaries founded in the 1640s by Catholic reformers such as Bourdoise and Olier grew out of an approximately eighty-year period during which Catholic authorities experimented with ways to enhance clerical preparation. Liturgical books, from which simplified pamphlets and posters like the *Miroir des prestres* ultimately derived, constituted part of this effort. In a move toward greater liturgical and pastoral standardization, the Council of Trent (1545–1563) issued a catechism in 1566, a new Roman Missal in 1570, and a Ritual in 1614.[67] Together, these publications provided a framework for what a clergyman should know and do. The catechism outlined basic Catholic doctrine, the missal contained all that a priest should say, read, or sing during the eucharistic rite throughout the church year, and the Ritual provided instructions for all the sacraments and rites a priest would administer, excluding those given in the Missal or reserved for a bishop.[68] In a signal of the standardizing function represented by such books, Pope Pius V published a bull along with the Missal making the revisions it contained mandatory unless a local version of the Mass had been in use for more than two hundred years.[69] Such texts helped establish shared expectations for priestly practice across Catholic Europe.

Political and practical difficulties, however, limited the Roman Missal's effectiveness as a tool for liturgical standardization in France. Critically, the French king and parliaments, protective of what they perceived as the rights of the Crown and the liberties of the Gallican Church, refused to officially accept the Council of Trent, which prevented its pronouncements from having the force of law in France.[70] They worried that the council's decrees would increase the pope's authority within France's borders.[71] Although the Assembly of French Clergy formally embraced the council's decisions, they did not do so until 1615.[72] This considerably slowed any homogenizing effect of Pope Pius V's Missal. Even where French bishops chose to adopt the Roman Missal as the official text for their dioceses, this did not mean that local parish priests began using it. In the words of historian Robin Briggs, once ordained, "most clerics learned their trade—for this was how they and their parishioners commonly saw it—through apprenticeship to an existing priest, very often a relative."[73] Older parish priests, though, frequently insisted on remaining faithful to local usages, however nonstandard, insufficiently ancient, or idiosyncratic they might appear to outsiders.[74] In 1605–1606 the Assembly of Clergy decided, wanting to foster liturgical unity, to distribute copies of the Roman Missal to parishes that did not have one. Especially in poor or remote parishes where the parish priest could barely read, this was, in historian René Taveneaux's opinion, likely to have done little more than create confusion.[75] Consequently, although liturgical books helped define norms for ceremonial performance and the Counter-Reformation precipitated a marked increase in their publication, at the beginning of the seventeenth century the Catholic Church in France had as yet no mechanism for directly influencing liturgical practice.[76] When evaluated according to the Council of Trent's criteria, France's secular clergymen performed ceremonies poorly and the French church had a performance problem.

Seminaries gradually helped rectify this situation. Like the upsurge in liturgical books, France's seminaries received their initial impetus from the Council of Trent, which passed a decree in 1563 called *Cum adolescentium aetas.*[77] It obliged every bishop to found a seminary near his cathedral to educate and train young clerics from his diocese for the priesthood.[78] The bishop was supposed to fund his seminary by taxing the revenue of all the chapters, abbeys, priories, and other benefices in the diocese, using the money to build new facilities if necessary, pay instructors, and cover the expenses of poor students, to whom the seminaries were to give preference. The seminaries envisioned by the decree strongly resembled the collèges, or grammar schools, that had begun to spring up all over Europe under the management of religious orders like the Jesuits. Students would start at the age of twelve, the decree suggested, complete coursework in grammar and other liberal arts, and then receive specific training for the priesthood, attending Mass every day all the way through.[79] In the words of Antoine Degert, author of the most comprehensive history of French seminaries covering the years between the Council of Trent and the French Revolution, *Cum adolescentium aetas* "set in place the principles and sketched the plans" that would guide all future seminary efforts.[80]

It proved difficult, however, to found seminaries in precise accordance with the Council of Trent's specifications. Even bishops who wanted to comply with the council's decree had a terrible time figuring out how to finance such a large and expensive undertaking, since benefice holders resisted the new tax.[81] A seminary also needed capable instructors, which were difficult to find in some dioceses, especially in those without a large university. As a result, seminaries started sporadically and assumed a range of configurations into the early seventeenth century—some bishops tried a seasonal format, some entrusted their seminaries to religious orders, some attempted to found seminaries like those outlined by the decree but ran out of funds—but none of these experiments evolved into a lasting institution.[82] The fact that in France the decrees of the Council of Trent did not have the force of law opened a very wide margin for experimentation. Through trial and error, the seminaries that met with success did so by moving away from a grammar school model and admitting seminarians at a much older age, typically between twenty and thirty.[83] They also tended to develop at some remove from the bishop's supervision, even if they espoused a high theological view of his authority. As Vincent de Paul said of the obligation to report directly to the bishop, "Although the thing seems reasonable . . . this has unfortunate results."[84] Finally, the model for seminary education that proved successful shifted the emphasis from, in Vincent's words, the ecclesiastical "sciences" to "the usage of these."[85] In performance terms, French seminaries shifted their emphasis from theory to practice.

Derived from the Latin word for a seed bed, the term "seminary" implied a kind of education that not only transferred knowledge but also imparted a way of being and a style of embodiment, what Pierre Bourdieu calls a habitus.[86] Olier defined a seminary as "a place destined for giving the seeds and the first fruits of the ecclesiastical spirit to all the subjects of the clergy."[87] Liturgical ceremonies constituted a central part of the curriculum in the seminaries of the mid-seventeenth century. The letter at the beginning of *Le Parfaict ecclesiastique* described seminaries as places "where a great many capable men labor with incredible care to form workers worthy to serve at the Altar."[88] At the time, this was a revolutionary idea. Vincent de Paul identified Bourdoise as "the first whom God had inspired to make a seminary for teaching all the rubrics," or instructions for conducting the sacraments.[89] Degert notes that Bourdoise placed so much emphasis on learning liturgical ceremonies that contemporaries often concluded his seminary's primary objective was to train priests to celebrate Mass.[90] "Before him," continued Vincent de Paul, addressing priests at his own seminary, "we hardly knew what it was [to administer the sacraments], there was not any particular place where one taught them. A man, after his theology, after his philosophy, after the least bit of studies, after a bit of Latin, went off to his parish and administered the sacraments in his own fashion."[91] As Bergin observes, Vincent "was as well placed as anyone" to evaluate the early seminaries.[92] France's seventeenth-century seminaries flourished by specializing in character formation and practical skills.

The model of priestly training developed by Vincent de Paul and Bourdoise and subsequently adopted throughout France relied on a division of labor between collèges and universities on the one hand and seminaries on the other. Rather than teaching grammar, philosophy, and theology as prescribed by the Council of Trent, French seminaries either required students to have completed these studies at a collège or university upon entry or, in university cities like Paris, arranged the schedule so that some seminarians could attend classes at the Sorbonne or the Collège de Navarre twice per day.[93] Not until after the reign of Louis XIV did French seminaries begin to create chairs in subjects like philosophy and seek recognition as academic establishments.[94] Focused on the physical and vocational aspects of priestly training, seminary directors and seminary-trained clergymen saw themselves in conflict with institutions, like the theater, that fostered modes of embodiment contrary to liturgical enactment. Thanks to their emphasis on gestures, behaviors, and technical skills, by the end of the seventeenth century seminaries had largely standardized ceremonial practices and priestly self-presentation among the secular clergy.

These developments in priestly performance facilitated the "emergence and consolidation" of the secular clergy as a professional group, a process common to parish priests across Europe in both Protestant and Catholic confessions between the sixteenth and eighteenth centuries.[95] Although not without critiques, the "professionalization thesis," as Wietse de Boer calls it, argues that Trent brought about "the formation of a compact, well-trained, socially distinctive and culturally cohesive body of 'pastoral workers,' endowed with a professional ethos and collaborating within an efficient hierarchy towards the creation of a new Catholic identity."[96] De Boer goes on to dispute this thesis by showing how the stories of individual priests could diverge from Tridentine prescriptions for clerical behavior. In France, seminary founders recognized such disparities. Bourdoise exclaimed in his maxims, "Those who only judge by the surface of things say that the people and the clergy have never been better, but those who penetrate more deeply cry to see that that both are so far from their perfection, and despair to see them ever achieve it given how much is left to do and to hope for."[97] Bourdoise's maxim conveys an impression at the middle of the seventeenth century that priestly behavior had indeed changed during his lifetime. Bourdoise simultaneously insists that neither priests nor the Catholic laity conform entirely to the ideals of the Counter-Reformation. In other words, the particularities of individual experience do not negate a general shift in clerical behavior and standards, even if those standards remain aspirational.

Despite the inevitable divide between prescription and action, the progress of the French secular clergy's emergence as a professional group during the seventeenth century can be broken into three phases, which correspond to the creation and institutionalization of France's early seminaries. The period from approximately 1610 to 1642 represented a phase of collaborative experimentation during which the ideal of the vray ecclésiastique and the practices that expressed it animated the activities of a relatively small circle of Catholic reformers among France's secular clergy, which in turn influenced a broader network of churchmen in their immediate spheres of influence. Two endeavors exerted a shaping influence in this period, the foundation of the French Oratory in 1611 by Pierre de Bérulle (1575–1629) and Vincent de Paul's ordination retreats. When considered together, they elaborated the spiritual vision and organizational structures out of which France's mid-seventeenth-century seminary foundations would grow.

Henri Bremond deemed Bérulle's contribution so extraordinary that he named the spirituality fostered by the French Oratory the French School of Spirituality.[98] Although Bérulle published very little, through letters, spiritual

direction, talks, and sermons his spiritual theology proposed "a Pauline and pa-
tristic image of the Church as the 'mystical body' of Christ" and an "extremely
elevated conception of the ministerial priesthood."[99] This spiritual vision of the
priesthood's holiness called for the secular clergy to live together in shared houses
in the way that priests in religious orders did.[100] Inspired by Bérulle's model, his
followers, spiritual directees, and the reform-minded clergymen in their circles
adopted and promoted the idea that priestly perfection went hand in hand with
communal life. Olier, Jean Eudes (1601–1680), and—although further removed
from Bérulle—Bourdoise all made communal living in one form or another central to their respective methods for training France's secular clergy.

Before the establishment of what Degert calls the *grands séminaires* of the
mid-seventeenth century, Vincent de Paul's ordination retreats disseminated an
elevated view of the priesthood to a broader segment of France's clerical population, introduced them for a short period of time to communal life, and extended
professionalization beyond a narrow circle by raising standards for ordination.
At the request of the bishop of Beauvais, in 1628 Vincent welcomed his first group
of candidates for ordination—men who wanted to receive one of the seven grades
leading to the priesthood—for an eight-day retreat.[101] The goal was to "take great
care to not admit anyone to Holy Orders who did not have the necessary science
and the other marks of a true vocation" while at the same time "working toward
those that one would like to admit, to render them capable of their obligations
and to make them acquire the ecclesiastical spirit."[102] In the mornings, the ordinands learned essential doctrinal matters, and in the afternoons they acquired
practical skills, such as how to pray, to prepare for confession, to conduct the sacraments, and to undertake the duties that would be theirs after receiving the
ecclesiastical rank into which they would soon be ordained.[103] After the initial
retreat, which the bishop of Beauvais considered a great success, subsequent retreats were extended to ten days and made mandatory in the diocese of Beauvais. From Beauvais, the idea spread across France. The archbishop of Paris, with
Vincent de Paul's help and in collaboration with Bourdoise, instituted obliga-
tory ten-day ordination retreats in his diocese in 1631, after which so did the archbishops of Poitiers, Angoulême, Rheims, Chartres, and many others.[104]

Ordination retreats had extensive reach and made an important contribution to the emergence of the secular clergy as an identifiable group. Six ordinations took place per year until 1643, after which the frequency was reduced to
five, with as many as ninety or more ordinands each time, such that by the end
of Vincent de Paul's life in 1660 an estimated twelve thousand churchmen had
participated in the retreats in Paris alone.[105] By 1668, the retreats had fallen out

of use, mostly because they had habituated France's clergy to the idea that ordination required a stay in a seminary, which most scholars agree developed out of the retreats.[106] Although, as Degert rightly notes, a ten-day retreat was not enough to turn a man into a priest, the ordination retreats made France's secular clergy aware of the Council of Trent's ideals for the priesthood as refracted through Bérulle's mystical theology and the broader movement that would come to be known as the French School of Spirituality.[107]

With the first wave of enduring seminary foundations established from 1642 to 1660, the churchmen who attended them had more time to absorb the priestly ideals associated with the vray ecclésiastique and learn the embodied practices required to manifest that ideal. Some seminaries, like that founded by Bishop Alain de Solminihac (1593–1659) in the diocese of Cahors, developed directly out of retreats, gradually extending the stay required before each ordination.[108] After 1643, students were required to stay for a total of six months, which was then extended to one year, the minimum Vincent de Paul thought necessary.[109] At Saint-Nicolas du Chardonnet as well the average stay was one year.[110] By 1655, a group of bishops who had gathered in Paris to discuss priestly training agreed that two years in a diocesan seminary should be required.[111] In addition to extending the time clergymen spent in seminaries, during the period from 1642 to 1660 reform-minded churchmen reinforced the secular clergy's professionalization through a number of factors: increased coordination between bishops and seminary directors, episcopal efforts to codify the secular priest's appearance and duties, a proliferation of handbooks and pamphlets like the *Miroir des prestres* aimed at prescribing the secular clergy's gestures and routines, the involvement of seminarians in parish ministry, and the creation of ecclesiastical conferences to foster ongoing discussion and training among parish priests. At the end of this period, the death of the first generation of seminary founders marked the achievement of vocational expectations and legibility for the secular clergy. By the time Bourdoise died in 1655, Olier in 1657, and Vincent de Paul in 1660, the secular clergy had a clear understanding of its distinctive qualities in relation to regular clergymen on the one hand and the laity on the other. Henri Bremond goes so far as to say that when Louis XIV began his personal reign in 1661, "our great priestly reform was almost complete."[112] The essential features of seventeenth-century priestly performance were in place.

From 1660 until the end of the long seventeenth century in 1715 stretched a period of codification and expanded influence for seminary training. Not only did the number of seminaries grow, France's secular clergy spent longer periods of time living and studying in seminaries, while seminaries standardized and codified the training they offered.[113] After 1660, the average stay in a seminary gradually increased from one year to approximately fifteen months to two years by 1710, giving secular clergymen more time to absorb the ideal of the vray ecclésiastique.[114] In terms of codification, as seminaries transitioned to a second and third generation of leadership, they began to publish and circulate their house rules, specifying in greater detail the comportment expected of incoming seminarians. The Seminary of Saint-Nicolas du Chardonnet, for example, published a pamphlet-form, thirty-five-page *abrégé*, or summary, of its house rules in 1672 and 1677. Internally, an interlocking set of *registres*, or book-form manuscripts, provided more detailed rules for each office and function within the seminary, from the prefect, who had his own four-hundred-folio registre, to the seminarian whose turn it was to wash the dishes and whose tasks were detailed in a one-folio *règlement* in a separate 305-folio registre entitled *Livre dans lequel sont escrits tous les reglements de chaque office, et exercice du seminaire* (Book in which are written all the rules for each office and exercise of the seminary). Similarly, the manuscript règlements from the Seminary of Saint-Sulpice date from approximately 1682 and 1710.[115] Such efforts at standardizing the behavior learned by secular clergymen and extending their seminary training contributed to the crystallization of a priestly type that, by the end of the seventeenth century, was the subject of explicit parody and critique. Saint-Simon ridiculed the "dirty beards of Saint-Sulpice"—a reference to their modesty—and grouped "seminary directors" among the devout Catholics he thought encircled Madame de Maintenon with a "sea of frivolous, illusory, annoying, always misleading . . . childishness which leads normally to nothing."[116] The availability of stereotypes for the secular clergy during the second half of the seventeenth century signaled their progress in establishing themselves as a recognizable group, whether we accept the framework of professionalization for understanding this process or not.

The second half of the long seventeenth century further reinforced the ideal of clerical perfection by extending seminary training to France's poorest clergy, on the one hand, while on the other hand seminary-trained secular clergymen occupied an ever-greater number of positions of ecclesiastical authority from which they could propagate the expectations and comportment associated with the image of the vray ecclésiastique and the figure of the bon curé. Clergymen from poorer families had received attention from seminary founders from the earliest phase of the chronology I am sketching here. Vincent de Paul's ordination retreats in the dioceses of Beauvais and Paris, as well as the retreats they inspired throughout France, were financed by the bishop or by wealthy patrons, making them accessible to churchmen of modest origins.[117]

In a similar vein, founders of Paris's grands séminaires recognized the importance of making seminary training accessible, hence the creation of scholarships like the *bourse cléricale* at the Seminary of Saint-Nicolas du Chardonnet, which enabled 118 clergymen from poor families to attend the seminary between 1637 and 1642.[118] Even the seminarians at Saint-Nicolas who did not receive a scholarship lacked wealth and rank.[119] After 1680, however, the education of poorer clerics took on greater importance as France's grands séminaires opened petits séminaires, "small" seminaries in which donations from nobles and bishops paid the students' expenses with the idea that these clergymen, once trained, would undertake the church's more arduous tasks by becoming priests in rural communities, schoolmasters, and missionaries.[120]

At the elite end of the spectrum, the Seminaries of Saint-Magloire and Saint-Sulpice gained reputations for training the aristocratic members of France's secular clergy.[121] In Dominique Julia's estimation, by the end of the long seventeenth century the Seminary of Saint-Sulpice had become "the true national school for the training of future bishops."[122] The numbers support this view. According to Louis Bertrand, between 1642 and 1790, 250 of France's bishops had spent time at the Seminary of Saint-Sulpice, representing one-third of the French episcopate.[123] Whether of humble background or high rank, by the end of the seventeenth century France's secular clergy shared an ideal of priestly perfection supported by a repertoire of daily practices and bodily habits understood as constitutive of the vray ecclésiastique. Although not without internal tensions and polemics, this shared set of expectations, skills, and behaviors made the secular priest an identifiable figure at the end of the century in a way he had not been at the beginning.

## Priestly Performance and Religious Authority

The story of how France's secular clergy emerged as an identifiable group during the second half of the seventeenth century enfolds a related inquiry into the authority this emergence generated for parish churchmen. Scholarship on the theater's relationship to the Catholic Church in seventeenth-century France treats the clergy's authority as a given.[124] This stance makes sense given that priests like Olier who make appearances in theater-history accounts possessed benefices, ran seminaries, and managed a large corps of other clergymen. In other words, priests who were in a position to refuse sacraments to actors or preach against the theater enjoyed institutional supports that stage players and theater troupes did not.

Priests, however, did not always perceive their authority as assured in advance, if authority means, as Max Weber proposed, "the probability that a specific command will be obeyed."[125] Institutional supports such as a clergyman's title were not enough to make most parishioners obey commands against a whole range of behaviors prohibited by the church, from performing in plays to dueling to wearing clothing that exposed too much skin or displayed too much wealth. Rather, following Bruce Lincoln's argument, "authority is the effect produced by a specific conjunction" of factors, including "the right speech and delivery, the right staging and props, the right time and place, and an audience whose historically and culturally conditioned expectations establish the parameters of what is judged 'right' in all these instances."[126] Or, as Laura Feldt puts it, "authority is always a matter of performance."[127] In order to "produce attitudes of trust, respect, docility, acceptance, even reverence" among parishioners in the moment a specific command was given, France's secular clergy had to foster and maintain an extensive ritual system on which their authority hinged.[128]

Ceremonies held this system together, connecting bodies, objects, people, and places through gestural patterns, such as bowing, genuflection, and processions. In religious studies, ritual theory points to the way these kinds of patterns create insiders and outsiders and set certain places and things aside as sacred. Émile Durkheim's famous definition of religion as "a unified system of beliefs and practices relative to sacred things . . . which unite into a single moral community called a church, all those who adhere to them" synthesizes these two features of ritual practice: sacrality and belonging.[129] Critiques of Durkheim notwithstanding, the "most commonly cited outcome of rituals" continues to be "the sense of unity and shared identity they create among co-participants."[130] As secular priests consolidated their presence at the parish level, their ceremonial specialization and enforcement of ceremonial norms among the laity certainly reinforced the altar's sacrality and demarcated Catholics from non-Catholics.

In the attention that ritual theory pays to spaces and objects, however, it misses an important insight into the construction of religious authority: the boundaries of religious authority function in a way that is opposite the dynamics constitutive of sacred space. Whereas sacred space is created by using ritual practices that separate it from the profane, religious authority is produced by blurring the boundaries between the individual who possesses authority and his or her surroundings. In seventeenth-century France, for example, parish priests enhanced the chancel's sacred status by tightly regulating who could enter and exit and under what conditions. Taboos and prohibitions made the chancel's boundaries clear. By contrast, the secular clergyman's religious authority grew to the extent that the edges of his priestly identity remained obscured, on the one hand by dissolving the line between his individual particularity and his office and, on the other hand, by stretching the boundaries of his public self to encompass the members of the Catholic community for whom he served as sacramental intermediary.

This means that religious authority's power and legitimacy derive from its elaboration as what performance theorists understand as a production. "A performance is not an entity that exists atemporally for the spectator," writes David Román; "rather, the spectator intersects in a trajectory of continuous production. A production is generally composed of a series of performances."[131] Applied to the phenomenon of priestly identity, Román's insight suggests that religious authority arises not from one discrete instance of ceremonial enactment but rather from the larger "trajectory of continuous production" in which a religious figure engages over time. Authority's maintenance depends on weaving each instance of its exercise into the next, such that each moment of authority's performative iteration remains embedded in the moments that precede and follow it. Should an instance of religious authority's construction through performance come into view *as* performance, as an event set apart from other expressions of authority in authority's continual production, that framed moment jeopardizes the legitimacy of the whole. For a secular priest in seventeenth-century France, this meant that the edges of any particular performance of his authority had to be deferred, folded into the next instance of authority's expression, so that he did not draw too much attention to himself, either for an excellent performance or for elements of his person not aligned with the ideal of the vray ecclésiastique.

Although my book traces the contours of priestcraft from the early seventeenth century to the end of Louis XIV's reign, my goal is not to isolate each discrete stage of change in the larger story of transformation the book unearths. Other works have already taken chronological approaches to France's Counter-Reformation seminaries and their impact on priestly training. Instead, I undertake a performance analysis of the trajectory of continuous production that generated and sustained the priestly identity of France's seminary-trained secular clergymen so as to better understand the fabric and the fragility of the authority they possessed and, by extension, the practical reasons why reform-minded parish priests were likely to oppose the theater. My analysis focuses especially on the seminaries of Saint-Sulpice and Saint-Nicolas du Chardonnet, for several reasons. First, they pioneered hands-on pastoral and liturgical training for priests in France, exerting a lasting influence over what and how churchmen learned in French seminaries of the *ancien régime*. Second, a substantial collection of primary documents remains from these two seminaries, providing detailed information about the content and methods of instruction and the norms for ceremonial practice. Finally, churchmen associated with these seminaries either used theater-based pedagogical techniques, as was the case at the Seminary of Saint-Nicolas du Chardonnet, or regularly interacted with theater performers, as was the case in the Parish of Saint-Sulpice, where Molière's former troupe settled after his death in 1673. In their proximity to theater practice and stage players, the seminaries of Saint-Nicolas du Chardonnet and Saint-Sulpice offer a privileged glimpse of the structure of priestly performance and its often-contentious relationship to theatrical representation.

The sources on which this book is based offer a wealth of information, but only of a certain kind. Even at their most vivid, the sources examined in the book rarely give us direct access to the sustained details of any single French churchman's story. What they do provide, though, is a portrait of the aggregate norms, expectations, and obligations that structured individual actions and choices. They are primarily prescriptive sources, such as seminary rules and manuals, liturgical handbooks, ecclesiastical pamphlets, and episcopal conferences and edicts, which outline what churchmen were supposed to do. To these can be added letters, spiritual journals, memoires, parish registers, and hagiographic accounts, which inscribe traces of what churchmen did do or describe what they are said to have done. Like the prescriptive sources, though, these descriptive sources reflect the ideals of the perfect churchman and the bon curé. The actions they record therefore frequently reveal more about the way those ideals shaped the narrative representation of priestly identity than about material facts. Although my analysis of priestly identity does not focus on gender but rather focuses on the ceremonial construction of priestly personhood, one of Butler's recent formulations for analyzing gender's performative structure provides a way to understand what type of information prescriptive and descriptive sources give us. In *Undoing Gender*, Butler proposes that gender is "a practice of improvisation within a scene of constraint."[132] According to this conception, the norms and models produced and circulated by France's Catholic reformers and the seminaries they founded formed the constraints within which an individual clergyman needed to improvise to enact his identity as a vray ecclésiastique, or true churchman, in any given situation. This book therefore studies the codes that made clerical improvisation possible in seventeenth-century France.

In examining sources from France's early seminaries, in addition to paying attention to features such as content, author, circulation, and style, I read for moving bodies.[133] In doing so, I apply to ecclesiastical sources the spatial sense used by students and scholars of theater and performance studies when they read a play and imagine its onstage action, asking questions like: What were people doing with their bodies, and why? Where were they? Who was looking? What could they see? What were they meant to see? How did these interactions convey, create, or destroy each person's power, authority, complicity, or alienation in relation to the other people in the interaction? The gestural substrate that comes to the surface through this type of reading makes an important contribution to studies of priesthood and to studies of antitheatrical sentiment, since the ceremonial repertoires that constituted the secular clergy's priestly identity were largely shared across sectarian boundaries within the Catholic Church. Jansenist-leaning churchmen like Nicolas Pavillon (1597–1677), the bishop of Alet, or Jean-Baptiste de la Croix de Chevrières de Saint-Vallier (1653–1727), the bishop of Quebec, may have emphasized certain aspects of the sacramental system over others—for example, by refusing absolution to Catholics for a broader range of public sins—but they shared with their less radical colleagues a conviction that ceremonies mattered and that secular priests needed to conduct them correctly.[134] A liturgical approach to priestly identity and its repercussions for clerical attitudes toward the theater has the advantage of bringing to light motivations derived less from theological debates that fractured the Catholic Church internally during the seventeenth century than from a more broadly shared set of sacramental practices that evolved during the same period.

In relation to the Catholic Church's seventeenth-century internal divisions, the sources on which my book relies were created by priests whom historians have identified as *dévot* for their commitment to instituting the Council of Trent's reforms, as ultramontanist in their support of papal authority, and as Augustinian in their conviction that Catholic reform should entail rigorously disciplined Christian practice aspiring toward moral and spiritual perfection at both the ecclesiastical and the lay level.[135] These categories differ from those used by the priests themselves, who focused on preparing able clergymen for service in France's parishes. Despite their usefulness for mapping theological alliances, such classifications at times obscure the aspects of Catholic reform that France's clergymen shared amid their debates. Although some priests who worked closely with Vincent de Paul, Olier, and Bourdoise in the early efforts to organize ordination retreats and to found seminaries later allied themselves with Jansenism, the Augustinianism that characterized seminary education in places like Saint-Sulpice remained distinct from Jansenism.[136] As Anthony Wright concludes, "Catholic rigorism in later seventeenth- and eighteenth-century

France was arguably a phenomenon which was pervasive but not uniform" and was "not the preserve of committed Jansenists alone."[137] Reform-minded clergymen, whether influenced more by François de Sales's humanism, an Augustinian rigorism, or Port-Royal's Jansenism, were invested in teaching priests to do the same kinds of things. Even if their doctrines of grace differed, they cared deeply about proper ceremonial comportment. Seminary founders and Jansenist leader Jean Duvergier de Hauranne, abbé of Saint-Cyran (1581–1643), thus shared, underneath their frequent theological differences, an outlook that was "less interested in the ideas themselves than in their application, spontaneously turned toward pastoral care, works, morals, or rules for living."[138] The fact that orthodox reformers like Olier and Jansenist bishops like Pavillon both rose to prominence thanks to mentorship from the same circle of Counter-Reformation leaders demonstrates a shared liturgical repertoire and mutual interest in clerical discipline that persisted alongside doctrinal differences.

This more or less shared ceremonial substrate suggests an alternative explanation for Catholic opposition to the theater in early modern France.[139] Whereas most scholarship on antitheatrical activity in early modern France accepts some version of the thesis that Jansenist ideas drove clergymen to reject the theater, I propose that the post-Tridentine liturgy's internal logic with its ceremonial dynamics and their relation to priestly identity also motivated ecclesiastical responses to the stage and stage players, possibly outweighing Jansenist ideas.[140] Ceremonies shaped polemics about the theater in more than one way. Liturgical training entailed a sacramental outlook toward representation, inclining clergymen to consider stage plays a threat to the church's ritual bonds. At the same time, the issue of the theater's place in public life prompted churchmen to enact ceremonial responses that asserted the Catholic Church's vision of the social order. Rather than a strictly philosophical debate or theological polemic, France's early modern quarrels about the theater reveal cultural transformations in the gestural repertoires for community and belonging.

In what follows, I examine ceremonial practices as they radiate outward from the priest's body to consider what was at stake for the Counter-Reformation liturgy when faced with theatrical representation. My book does not attempt a complete record of all the ceremonial practices in which secular priests engaged, nor is its central goal to trace the development of specific features of the liturgical repertoire, such as genuflection, unless evidence suggests that those features reveal a broader shift in priestly identity or in the way the Catholic Church's ceremonies sought to create communal bonds. Rather, my main interest concerns the way the ceremonial practices that were emphasized in seminary rules and handbooks leveraged such dynamics as seeing, being seen, patterned behavior, evaluation, the display of skill, and role-playing to elaborate a form of clerical identity suited to the liturgical goals of the Counter-Reformation church in France. What I offer, then, is a performance analysis of priestly identity as expressed through liturgical ceremonies and represented in seminary sources. My hope is that this new, but necessarily limited, view of France's secular clergy will prompt further research on the intersections between ecclesiastical practice and cultural realms such as the court and theater. Although many of the ceremonial practices examined in this book continue to be practiced weekly by Catholic priests and laity around the globe, in analyzing my sources I have chosen to use the past tense to acknowledge the historical specificity of the form these ceremonies took during the long seventeenth century and to avoid making transhistorical claims about priestly identity or Catholic liturgy.

Clothing served as the most visible marker of the secular clergyman's priestly identity, whose long, black robe, called a soutane, distinguished him from the laity and from priests in religious orders. Episcopal orders had tried since the thirteenth century to impose the soutane on secular priests, with variable success. By 1664, when Molière staged his controversial play *Le Tartuffe, ou l'hypocrite*, which featured a main character whose robes suggested a soutane, two decades of seminary foundations had firmly associated the soutane with the seminary-trained clergyman. Chapter 1 takes Tartuffe's first costume and the polemic it elicited as a starting point from which to examine the way the secular clergyman's priestly identity intersected practices from three performance cultures, that of regular priests, of courtiers, and of actors. By staging poor priestly performance, *Tartuffe* foregrounds the secular priest as a modern figure constructed through hybridization and purification whose religious authority depended on his continuous iteration of ceremonial practices that fused the monastic, courtly, and theatrical aspects of his identity.

Chapter 2 turns to the secular priest's gestures, which became increasingly codified between the 1640s and 1680s. Together with a secular clergyman's robes, these gestures produced clerical modesty, which seminary manuals imagined as communicative in its own right, calling it a form of preaching without words. The vrai ecclésiastique's modesty guaranteed his authenticity. Yet, modesty could be acquired only through techniques that churchmen shared with the theater. To learn modest comportment, seminarians imitated models, worked hard to perform up to a standard, and practiced ceremonial skills in sacramental rehearsals. The way in which secular clergymen learned to embody modesty reveals the performative structure of priestly identity and shows how the ceremonialization

of everyday behaviors made the boundaries of priestly performance more difficult to see.

Modest comportment was a prerequisite for liturgical enactment. A secular clergyman's gestural discipline enabled the ceremonies of the Mass to operate, as Olier would put it, as "preaching for the eyes." Chapter 3 examines the
way secular priests conducted liturgical ceremonies. It shows how in sacramental contexts, particularly in the Eucharist, the gestural habits and codes learned
through seminary training elaborated ceremonial patterns that positioned the
priest as a node in a ritual agent greater than himself. This corporate ritual agent,
created through coordinated liturgical action, manifested Christ's presence in
the consecrated Eucharist by generating *éclat*, or ceremonial splendor, which
seventeenth-century French Catholics understood as the sign of kingly presence. In its ceremonial constitution, the secular clergyman's priestly identity consequently helped secure post-Tridentine theologies of the Mass, which
raised the stakes of priestly performance and its interruptions. Poor ceremonial
enactment and liturgical disruptions therefore threatened not just an individual priest's local religious authority but also the doctrine of transubstantiation
and the broader ritual system that supported it.

The secular clergyman's sacramental obligations made him a *personne publique*, or public person, a status further enhanced by his involvement in the production of liturgical éclat. Public personhood implied power and influence—magistrates
and nobles enjoyed similar status—but entailed risks. Priestly mistakes or miscon-
duct, combined with exposure to the laity's gaze and parishioners' judgement,
could plunge clergymen into the category of public sinner, the category into
which many reform-minded bishops placed actors. Chapter 4 considers the ceremonial practices that sustained the priest's positive publicness and offers performance definitions of public personhood and public sin.

It was in his quality as a liturgically constituted personne publique that the
secular priest confronted the actors in his parish, withholding sacraments from
them until they renounced the stage. Chapter 5 presents a microhistory from the
Parisian parish of Saint-Sulpice to demonstrate how churchmen used liturgical
ceremonies to contest the growing cultural preeminence enjoyed by the theater
between approximately 1640 and 1730. Saint-Sulpice presents an ideal case study
because it housed, in close quarters, a church, a seminary, a monastery, a seasonal
fair where acrobats, tightrope dancers, marionette players, and, after 1673,
Molière's former troupe performed. As demonstrated by a reconstruction of the
way seminary-trained priests used the last rites, the goal of sacramental refusals was
not exclusion but rather absorption. By reabsorbing actors into the liturgical

community, parish priests highlighted the importance of ceremonies, extended the church's liturgical space into the surrounding neighborhood, and performed a symbolic victory over the stage by transforming an actor's dying body into a central element of the church's own ritual display.

The sacramental exclusion and ceremonial reabsorption of actors point to the force that performance repertoires exert over human action at the improvisational moment in which a person must decide how to respond to a lived situation. Theological and philosophical arguments for and against the theater aside, the Counter-Reformation liturgy's spatial organization and internal logic provided reasons for priests to counteract the theater and its players, especially given the ceremonial constitution of the priest's own professional identity. The closing chapter offers a theoretical framework for analyzing seventeenth-century liturgical enactment and theatrical representation as distinctive performance regimes that mobilized the same cultural and material elements but distributed and connected those elements in divergent ways. Whereas the liturgy's internal logic sought to link bodies and objects in its all-encompassing extension, the theatrical repertoire tended to concentrate and mark off time and space in framed unities. Thus, even when a play or performer offered no direct threat to church doctrine or theology at the level of content, the theater's way of organizing bodies and objects had the capacity to disrupt and erode liturgical relations.

## CHAPTER I

# Clothing

In May 1664, Louis XIV organized eight days of festivities at his sumptuous palace outside Paris, the Château de Versailles. On the second-to-last day, Molière (1622–1673), already well on his way to becoming France's premier comic dramatist and actor, presented a new play to Louis's guests, a comedy in three acts called *Le Tartuffe, ou l'hypocrite*. The play staged the story of a man whose outward expressions of piety gained him entry to a bourgeois home, where he dispensed spiritual advice while proceeding to try to seduce the master's wife and steal the master's property. Tartuffe, the title character's name, almost immediately entered the French language as a synonym for hypocrisy, and ecclesiastical authorities condemned *Tartuffe* quickly after its début.[1] In a letter to the king, the curate of the parish of Saint-Barthélemy demanded that Molière "suppress and tear up, stamp out and burn" his play, on the grounds that the play threatened to "ruin the Catholic religion" by "blaming and playing [the church's] most religious and holy practice, which is the direction of souls and of families by wise guides and pious directors."[2] Within a week, under pressure from the archbishop of Paris and the Company of the Blessed Sacrament, the king issued a prohibition against the play's performance in the kingdom's public theaters.[3]

When the actor who played the first Tartuffe—Philibert Gassot (1626–1695), known as Du Croisy—stepped onto the stage at Versailles on 12 May 1664, scholars believe he wore a costume that helped provoke the scandal that engulfed the play.[4] Although none of the extant versions of the dramatic text refers to Tartuffe as a clergyman, as Georges Couton persuasively argues the venom with which pious Catholics in Paris greeted Molière's play derived in part from the character's attire, which evoked the clothing worn by men who sought a career in the church.[5] A description Molière gives of the way he modified the title character's attire so as to make him more worldly for the 1667 version of the play

allows Couton to deduce that the first Tartuffe's costume entailed the following elements: "large hat, short hair, small collar, no sword, robe without lace."[6]
This ensemble, and in particular its small collar, in fact conformed to the
clothing worn in the mid-seventeenth century by men enrolled in the seminaries that had been founded in the 1640s by France's leading counter-reformers.
Tartuffe's initial costume and the outrage it elicited highlight that priestly performance was changing and reveals that for seventeenth-century French churchmen the stakes of this transformation were serious enough to compel men of
wealth and influence to attack a play that, when the polemic began, had been
performed only once, at an event not open to the general public. For the purposes of this book, *Tartuffe* therefore condenses the processes of priestly transformation the rest of my study unfolds and foregrounds the stakes of priestly
performance in seventeenth-century France.

Tartuffe's clerical-like attire elicited debate because it disrupted a chain of
signification leading from a priest's clothes and body to the Catholic Church's
authority and ultimately to the perceived truthfulness of Christ's divine presence
in the Eucharist.[7] For Catholics, in other words, questions about clerical robes
cut to faith's heart and to the foundation for the institutional church's legitimacy.
A set of beliefs and practices known as investiture held fast many of the signify-
ing links that connected priestly clothing to core Catholic doctrines. The term
"investiture" refers to the idea that rites leading to and including the sacrament
of ordination endowed a priest with a new character, expressed by his robes, such
that outer clothes reflected an inner reality. In the seventeenth century, investiture belonged to a larger project of professionalizing the secular priesthood,
meaning priests who did not belong to religious orders. Molière's play played with
investiture. In doing so, Tartuffe's original costume threatened to undo twenty
years of work France's counter-reformers had done to elevate the ecclesiastical and
social standing of secular priests.

The clerical robes evoked by Tartuffe's costume and promoted by seminaries tell the story of how Catholic reformers reworked and recombined practices
from a range of cultural domains, both religious and secular, to craft a new priestly
identity, that of the vray ecclésiastique, or true churchman. As Tartuffe's first costume and the polemic to which it contributed illustrate, the Counter-Reformation
priest's identity intersected practices from three performance cultures, that of
regular priests, of royal courtiers, and of stage actors. When blended together,
these disparate practices produced a priest whom his peers and superiors would
consider divinely called to his office, and whose presentation of self would in-
vest the priestly role, rather than the individual man, with authority. As the

next chapter shows, the task of integrating practices from disparate cultural domains required performance techniques and skills, such as role-playing and rehearsal, to which not all clergymen had access, that took time and discipline to master, and that seminaries helped clergymen incorporate. Since the Counter-Reformation ideal of the vray ecclésiastique required a delicate balance of behaviors derived from relatively restricted communities, its embodiment posed a challenge at the individual level by requiring clergymen to learn patterns of behavior that might be foreign to their previous cultural experiences. Furthermore, the failure to properly integrate any of the composite practices threatened to delegitimize not just a particular person but rather an entire institution. Molière's play represented an incompletely integrated priestly identity. In doing so, it rattled something much larger than any individual priest's personal reputation. By staging the incomplete mixing of the monastic, courtly, and theatrical practices a vray ecclésiastique needed to incorporate into a seamless whole, *Tartuffe* inverted investiture, turning it into a disguise. *Tartuffe* thus provides a broken mirror through which to examine the Counter-Reformation's ideal clergyman.

## The Costume

When Tartuffe appeared on stage in 1664, the physical appearance of what seminary manuals referred to as the vray ecclésiastique had acquired a precise form, even if seminary directors felt that many secular clergymen failed to live up to it. The portraits of Adrien Bourdoise (Figure 1) and Jean-Jacques Olier (Figure 2)—founders of the Seminaries of Saint-Nicolas du Chardonnet and of Saint-Sulpice, respectively—clearly depict two of the exterior features that by the mid-seventeenth century had become essential to the secular clergy's public appearance: small collars and short hair. In Bourdoise's portrait a third key feature, the soutane, or dark clerical robe, is also discernible near his hands and neck, although covered by a white surplice—or short, liturgical robe worn when performing the sacraments. By evoking a small collar, short hair, and a plain robe in Tartuffe's first costume, Molière's play cited vestiary norms that seminaries in Paris had spent two decades promoting as signs of the authenticity of a clergyman's vocation.

Of the three elements, the small collar carried the strongest connotation of seminary-trained, reform-minded secular clergymen. Seminary rules, like those of the Seminary of Saint-Nicolas du Chardonnet in Paris, required seminarians

Figure 1.  Adrien Bourdoise (1584–1655), founder of the Seminary of
Saint-Nicolas du Chardonnet in Paris, engraving, late 1650s (Archives
nationales de France MM 472, fol. 11).

Figure 2. Jean-Jacques Olier (1608–1657), founder of the Seminary of
Saint-Sulpice, engraving, late seventeenth century, from Charles Hamel,
*Histoire de l'Église de Saint-Sulpice*, 2nd ed. (Paris: Librairie Victor Lecoffre,
J. Gabalda, 1909), 118–19, courtesy of the Archives of Saint-Sulpice (Paris).

to wear just such a collar. "The use of collars in the Community of Saint Nicolas," reads the seminary's *coutumier*, or rule book, "has been since the beginning
of its establishment to wear them modest and very simple as to their style."[8] Not
only does Bourdoise's portrait display this small collar, the seminary's rules even
included a pattern titled "Le veritable models des rabats du seminaire" (The true
model of seminary collars), according to which all seminarian collars had to be
made.[9] By the end of the seventeenth century, conformity among clerics trained
in or influenced by seminaries had turned the small collar into a trope for involvement in the Counter-Reformation. According to Antoine Furetière's *Dictionnaire universel*, "One calls 'Little Collar' a man who has joined himself to
the reform, to devotion, because out of modesty people of the Church wear small
collars, whereas people of the world wear big ones adorned with points and lace."[10]
At the same time, by the end of the century the phrase "little collar" also doubled as slang for hypocrisy. Furetière notes that "sometimes it is said in a bad way
of hypocrites who assume modest manners, especially by wearing a small collar."[11]
Tartuffe's first costume seems to have played upon the small collar's simultaneous reference to reform-minded clergymen and artifice.

Tartuffe's short hair and plain robe, too, evoked seminary garb. As the manuscript minutes of an episcopal conference on the subject of priestly dress held
in approximately 1656 or 1657 confirm, by the mid-seventeenth century ecclesiastical ideals called for clergymen to keep their hair cut short, and they were to
wear the soutane, which was an ankle-length, long-sleeved black robe.[12] Documentary evidence does not indicate that the first Tartuffe wore the tonsure, the
shaved circle at the crown of the head worn by clergymen. His short hair, however, would have been enough to signify intention to join the clerical state. The
path to priesthood began with a tonsure ceremony in which the bishop symbolically clipped the candidate's hair.[13] Among other signs of readiness for clerical
status, to participate in the ceremony candidates were supposed to present themselves before the bishop "with their hair short and even."[14] For secular clergymen who did not belong to religious orders, short hair represented what Victor
Turner would call their liminal status in between the full renunciation of a monk
and a layperson's complete engagement "dans le siècle" (in the century), as seminary directors put it.[15] In a handbook written for tonsure candidates by Bourdoise,
an excerpt from the Italian Catholic reformer Cardinal Bellarmin (1542–1621)
explains that the tonsure candidate's short hair signified "that one must leave
behind all superfluous thoughts and desires, like those for worldly things, riches,
honors, pleasures, and other similar things."[16] Short hair thus denoted withdrawal
from the world. At the same time, short hair did not represent full renunciation.

The rules for the Seminary of Saint-Nicolas du Chardonnet included an entry entitled "Cheveux" (Hair), which explained that the requirement to wear short hair reminded clergymen to care neither too much nor too little for the physical world: "It is recommended to priests to not shave their hair, nor to nourish their hair, but only to clip it to a certain length to teach them that they must not totally apply themselves to the care of external things, nor entirely abandon them, but apply themselves with moderation . . . to the degree required by pure necessity, charity, or obedience."[17] A secular clergyman's short hair announced to the world that he was in it but not of it. With or without a tonsure, Tartuffe's short hair would have triggered ecclesiastical associations for the audience.

Tartuffe's plain garments would have further augmented the clerical impression made by his collar and hair. From the earliest decades of the seventeenth century, episcopal edicts, ecclesiastical pamphlets, and seminary rules unanimously reminded clergymen to wear the soutane, or ankle-length, long-sleeved robe that constituted the clerical garment par excellence. One of many such pronouncements, an episcopal letter issued by the bishop of Paris, Henri de Gondi, in 1620 declared, "We order . . . that all the priests residing in our diocese . . . will be always dressed in the long, honest, and decent soutane."[18] Made of "simple cloth in a simple style," as a set of rules drawn up by seminary directors in Paris put it, the garment was typically secured in the front with buttons that ran from the neck down to the waist, at which point rules called for a fully closed seam all the way to the hem.[19] Since the thirteenth century, black had gained favor as the color for the soutane, becoming normative in France in the sixteenth century.[20] Evidence does not indicate whether the first Tartuffe wore black. As Maureen Miller points out, however, in practice one would have seen the soutane in a range of dark colors, given that sunlight and frequent use would cause black fabric to fade.[21] As long as the first Tartuffe's robe was long, plain, dark, and closed, audiences would have interpreted it as a sign of clerical status.

In constructing the identity of the vray ecclésiastique, the soutane made members of the secular clergy visible as a class, differentiating them from the laity on the one hand and monks on the other. In his maxims, published posthumously, Bourdoise expressed the soutane's differentiating function by comparing it to the leaves that make a tree recognizable: "One knows each thing by its exterior; one knows the diversity and distinction of the species of the trees by their flowers, leaves, and fruits. An apple tree never borrows the leaves of a pear tree. Each tree keeps the form of its God-given species. Only churchmen who are not content with their exterior and who despise the robe that the Church has given them and required of them, disguise themselves by taking clothes of whatever fashion and color pleases them."[22] According to Bourdoise's parable, the soutane serves as the leaves that distinguish a clerical "tree" from a lay one. Clearly, Bourdoise's maxim, along with the frequently repeated edicts and instructions that mandated the clergyman's use of the soutane, indicate that some churchmen flouted the church's vestiary rules. Bishops and seminary directors would not have needed to reiterate the rules so often and at such length if the rules were consistently obeyed. Nonetheless, the soutane set the cleric apart from the lay person. As the secular clergyman's distinctive "street wear," the soutane, writes Miller, served "to indicate clerical status."[23] Wearing a soutane signaled a man's priestly identity.

In addition to differentiating clerics from laymen, the soutane also distinguished secular clergymen from priests in religious orders. Dress in religious orders had its own history filled with conflicts and transformations.[24] Since at least the twelfth century, the general population knew that what Alejandra Concha Sahli calls a "grammar" of vestments encoded the differences between orders and among members within orders.[25] During the second half of the seventeenth century, interest in this grammar of clothing prompted the publication of volumes that presented brief histories of each religious order alongside an engraving of its robes.[26] These compendiums help twenty-first-century readers imagine secular clergymen in the context of the ecclesiastical diversity on daily display in seventeenth-century French streets, where one would have seen, among others, the Carthusians in their white robes and black hoods (Figure 3), the Fueillants in their long hoods of heavy, white cloth (Figure 4), the Augustinians (known in Paris as the Jacobins) in their wide-sleeved, black tunics and white undergarments (Figure 5), and the Capuchins with their pointed hoods and rough robes belted with a twisted cord (Figure 6).[27] Adrien Schoonebeek's *Histoire des ordres religieux de l'un & de l'autre sexe*, first published in 1695 and re-edited in 1700, proves especially useful because it represents the secular clergyman at the end of the process of professional transformation that Molière's *Tartuffe* threatened in 1664. A full engraving of a priest in a soutane and small collar appears in Schoonebeek's volume alongside the entry for the Priests of the Oratory, a congregation of secular priests first founded in Italy circa 1550 and then brought to Paris in 1611 by Pierre de Bérulle, who influenced seminary founders like Olier. Schoonebeek says of the Priests of the Oratory, "They are dressed as secular priests, without other modification" (Figure 7).[28] His confidence in the soutane and small collar as distinctive of the secular clergy attests to the achievements of the seminary movement by the end of the century.

Carthusianus.

73

Figure 3. Depiction of a Carthusian's robes, from Adrien Schoonebeek,
*Histoire des ordres religieux de l'un et de l'autre sexe* (Amsterdam, 1695), 73,
courtesy of the Bibliothèque nationale de France.

Monachus Fuliensis.

*84*

Figure 4. Depiction of the robes of the Fueillants, from Adrien
Schoonebeek, *Histoire des ordres religieux de l'un et de l'autre sexe*
(Amsterdam, 1695), 84, courtesy of the Bibliothèque nationale de France.

Auguſtinianus.

98

Figure 5.  Depiction of the robes of the Augustinians, from Adrien
Schoonebeek, *Histoire des ordres religieux de l'un et de l'autre sexe*
(Amsterdam, 1695), 98, courtesy of the Bibliothèque nationale de France.

Capucinus.

Figure 6. Depiction of the robes of the Capuchins, from Adrien
Schoonebeek, *Histoire des ordres religieux de l'un et de l'autre sexe*
(Amsterdam, 1695), 122, courtesy of the Bibliothèque nationale de France.

Sacerdos Oratorii S.<sup>ti</sup> Philippi Nerii.

14

Figure 7. Depiction of the Oratorians, representative of secular priests at
the end of the seventeenth century, from Adrien Schoonebeek, *Histoire des
ordres religieux de l'un et de l'autre sexe* (Amsterdam, 1695), 14, courtesy of
the Bibliothèque nationale de France.

Like Schoonebeek's compendium of robes, Bourdoise's maxims present the soutane as a garment that distinguished secular clergymen from priests in religious orders, with the difference that Bourdoise's aphorisms provide a glimpse of the struggle seminary directors undertook to impose the soutane as the secular clergy's normative dress. When Bourdoise was actively in ministry, between approximately 1612 and 1655, the effort to standardize the secular clergy's use of the soutane was still in progress, as his maxim reveals by the way it reprimands the secular clergy for not holding their own robes in high esteem: "A churchman who would find it painful to wear the short hair, crown [tonsure], soutane, belt, and the rest of the modest clothes [of the secular clergy], does not find it strange at all, if he becomes a Capuchin, to be dressed in a manner entirely contrary and ridiculous according to the world. . . . What is the cause of this? Having never known the dignity of his clerical state, he did not love it, and thus it is not surprising that he despised all that which was part of his duty."[29] In Bourdoise's view, a clergyman would be willing to wear a Capuchin's less comfortable robes without complaint because he viewed the rough cloth and hood of the Capuchin's dress as the sign of a noble ecclesiastical state. Bourdoise wanted his seminarians to attribute the same dignity to the secular clergy's soutane. Although by the 1660s France's seminaries had begun to standardize the secular clergyman's appearance and the ecclesiastical identity it represented, as Bourdoise's acerbic tone testifies, they perceived their gains as precarious.

Indeed, the secular clergy's visibility was new. Although ecclesiastical authorities had prescribed certain kinds of dress for secular churchmen since the twelfth century, as Louis Trichet shows in his study of clerical attire, before the late sixteenth century in France these codes usually concerned only clergymen who had already attained the major orders by becoming subdeacons, deacons, or priests. Clergymen in minor orders—the first four ordinations leading toward the priesthood, namely, porter, lector, exorcist, and acolyte—wore a much wider variety of clothes.[30] In addition, the young men in minor orders did not necessarily remain clergymen, further compromising the secular clergy's visibility. In church historian Joseph Bergin's words, "Probably at no time in European history was the distinction between lay society and the clergy in the broad sense as blurred as in the fifteenth and sixteenth centuries."[31] During this period, families habitually had their preteen boys seek ordination in minor orders, making their sons eligible to receive benefices and enjoy legal exemption from secular courts.[32] In some dioceses, however, as many as ten clerics left the minor orders and returned to lay life upon reaching adulthood for every one cleric who became a priest.[33] Determining who did or did not belong to the secular clergy in the Middle Ages thus proved complicated. Adding to this difficulty, synodal ordinances suggest that clergymen in major orders either refused to wear their robes, dressing like laymen instead, or modified their robes to suit fashion trends.[34] As a result, in the late sixteenth and early seventeenth centuries, secular clergymen frequently blended in with their parishioners. Seminaries, by contrast, made France's secular churchmen easier to see by training them to assiduously wear their clerical robes. Without the effort exerted by France's early seminaries to promote the secular clergy's adherence to vestiary norms, a soutane-like garment onstage would not have elicited such ire from the likes of the curate of Saint-Barthélemy. A play like *Tartuffe* that seemed to invert and deconstruct the vray ecclésiastique leveraged the increased visibility of the secular clergy that resulted from greater conformity to the seminaries' vestiary rules.

## Investiture and Priestly Professionalization

Despite the resonances between Tartuffe's first costume and the secular clergy's dress, Tartuffe's small collar and the costume it crowned functioned differently onstage from the way clergymen claimed their own robes operated. Seminary directors asserted that their vestments did not merely adorn a man's body but rather shaped his person. In the words of the Council of Trent, during the sacrament of holy orders in which a man receives these robes "a character is imprinted, which can neither be effaced nor taken away."[35] Bourdoise's metaphor of the soutane as leaves reflects the idea that clerical robes effect an irreversible transformation, a view reinforced by the many ecclesiastical pamphlets and episcopal minutes that refer to priestly clothing as a "mark."[36] For example, a manuscript volume from the library of Louis Tronson (1622–1700), third superior general of the Seminary of Saint-Sulpice, bears the title "Marques de vocation à l'estat ecclésiastique" (Marks of vocation for the ecclesiastical state). It lists the experience of an inner movement toward the clerical life as the first mark of calling to the priesthood, which the soutane replicates outside the body: "The soutane is the robe of the religion of Jesus Christ by which we make profession externally that we are dressed internally in Jesus Christ's religion toward his father."[37] From a priestly perspective, ecclesiastical robes did not represent a character, they made one.

Since at least the fourteenth century in English and the late fifteenth century in French, the term "investiture" has designated this linking of clothing and character. The same word—"investiture"—refers simultaneously to the act of making a bishop and to the act of dressing the newly made bishop in the robes of his office.[38] During the medieval and early modern period, investiture practices secured a wide range of identities. A suzerain invested a knight by belting a sword around his waist and putting spurs upon his heels.[39] Judges were robed, nuns given a habit, and by the fourteenth century a lord clothed his men in livery that differentiated his followers from those attached to other lords.[40] Renaissance scholars Ann Rosalind Jones and Peter Stallybrass offer an excellent definition of investiture on the eve of the early modern period. "Investiture, the putting on of clothes," they write, "quite literally constituted a person as a monarch or a freeman of a guild or a household servant. Investiture was, in other words, the means by which a person was given a form, a shape, a social function, a 'depth.'"[41] By depth, Jones and Stallybrass mean "that clothes permeate the wearer, fashioning him or her within" in a way that "undoes the opposition of inside and outside, surface and depth."[42] This oneness of dress and essence, fabric and person, held the social order in place.

Although surprisingly little research examines the way clothing did or did not shape its wearers in early modern France, a robust scholarly literature on investiture exists for the early modern English context, inspired in part by Stephen Greenblatt's work on "self-fashioning" in the Renaissance.[43] Based on English evidence, the standard argument regarding investiture posits that early modern theater costumes eroded investiture, while the Catholic Church served as one of investiture's last bastions. Costumes eroded investiture because actors changed costumes from play to play, challenging the idea that clothes immutably constituted a person. Furthermore, actors frequently dressed above their stations, and theaters placed clothes in circulation by providing a venue in which spectators could display their own finery and by renting out stage clothes. The Catholic Church, by contrast, or so the argument goes, carried investiture forward into the present. Jürgen Habermas provides a good example of the idea that the Catholic Church preserved medieval practices for the representation of rank. Although he does not use the term "investiture," Habermas underlines the importance of clothing in the way medieval lordship made itself manifest, a process he describes as the "*publicness . . . of representation.*"[44] He then identifies the Catholic Church as the single domain capable of perpetuating investiture beyond the medieval and early modern periods: "In church ritual, liturgy, mass, and processions, the publicity that characterized representation has survived into our time."[45] According to these arguments, an initial hypothesis about the polemic that Tartuffe's original, small-collared, no-lace costume caused would propose that it subverted the link between clothing and identity. By undoing investiture, such an argument would go, Tartuffe's costume threatened the Catholic Church's hold on the past.

A broader analysis of seventeenth-century French theater practice and transformations in French liturgical ceremony, however, challenges the arguments inherited from the English context and reveals that for Catholic authorities the stakes concerned the future. Tartuffe did subvert investiture practices, but not in the way Habermas would have guessed. Rather than using the theater as a new medium to unravel the church's old investiture paradigm, Molière deployed the theater's own traditional investiture logic to trouble the Counter-Reformation church's efforts to reinvent investiture practices that had fallen into disuse during the previous two centuries. On the early modern French stage, costumes purported to depict noble characters with *vraisemblance*, or verisimilitude, thereby reinforcing the idea that certain types of clothes manifested a person's rank. Stage clothes therefore demonstrate how early modern French culture still subordinated fashion-as-change or self-invention—the type of fashion dangerous for investiture—to fashion as what Jones and Stallybrass call "deep making."[46] The best evidence for the degree to which a sense of deep making pervaded early modern costuming can be found in the fact that a separate vocabulary did not designate clothes for the stage. French authors writing about the theater referred to stage costumes simply as *habits*, or clothes.[47] Even stage clothes that would seem, from a twenty-first-century perspective, to break openly with norms imposed by early modern investiture in fact conformed quite closely to how kings and princes represented themselves on special occasions, if not to what kings and princes wore on a daily basis at court. The *habit à la romaine*, or Roman-like tunic and armor worn by actors depicting warriors and noblemen, corresponded to the type of dress monarchs assumed during triumphal entries or court masques as well as to the attire French elites frequently chose when sitting for a portrait.[48] Both in language and in practice, then, the French stage perpetuated the idea that a noble wears a certain kind of garment because such a garment manifests his or her royal birth. Tartuffe's costume, therefore, capitalized on the audience's investiture expectations to generate surprise and shock at the juxtaposition between Tartuffe's clothing and the character revealed by his actions.

At the same time, Molière's play capitalized on the still-ambiguous boundary between clergyman and layperson that seminaries had been working so hard to define since the 1640s. Whereas Habermas considered investiture a relic from the past, to secular clergymen during the first half of the seventeenth century investiture ceremonies would have felt new. The tonsure ceremony for which a

cleric first donned his soutane, discussed above, had inducted men into the secular clergy since the sixth century.[49] By the fifteenth and sixteenth centuries, however, large numbers of young men took the tonsure without thereafter becoming
priests, diminishing its investiture function and blurring the boundaries between
the laity and the clergy.[50] Furthermore, at the beginning of the seventeenth
century many young men participated in the ceremony in order to gain the priv-
ileges granted to clergymen—the right to hold ecclesiastical benefices and to
enjoy exemption from lay juridical authority, among others—but did not take
on any of the outer marks of their new identity, refusing to cut their hair short,
shave the crown of the head, or wear the soutane.[51] Bourdoise's handbook for tonsure candidates, published in 1623, attests to the tonsure rite's desuetude at the
beginning of the century. Composed as a dialogue between an experienced priest,
designated as the *Maître* (Master), and a young man who aspires to enter the
clergy, whom the text calls the *Désireux* (Desiring one), the master instructs
the Désireux to read an extract from an "old Pontifical" in which a bishop instructs tonsure candidates what to do before arriving at the church for the ceremony.[52] After reading the extract, the Désireux asks a series of questions about
the logistics of the ceremony, as if he had never seen one, or at least never seen
one that conformed to the pontifical. In response to a rubric that requires tonsure candidates to carry a surplice over one arm, for example, the Désireux re-
marks: "I have never seen clerics in our parish who carry the surplice over the
arm."[53] Thus, although technically the tonsure rite had a long history in France,
churchmen and laymen alike had all but extinguished its investiture function
during the late medieval period.

The tonsure ceremony's revival in the seventeenth century, along with
the tightening of dress codes for secular clergymen, together constituted a program to reassert an investiture paradigm in support of the identity of the vray ecclésiastique. Also referred to as *bon* (good) or *parfait* (perfect), the true, good, or
perfect churchman's identity blended fully into its institutional framework.
His soutane manifested the vray ecclésiastique's complete absorption into his
clerical office. Since the soutane stretched to the heels and the wrists, it left
only a clergyman's face and hands exposed.[54] In Olier's words, the soutane
"envelopes the entire body and leaves nothing to see except under a garment of
death."[55] A clergyman's pursuit of death-to-self meant always wearing the marks
of his ecclesiastical state so as to never allow others to see him as an individual
rather than a cleric. The house rules at the Seminary of Saint-Sulpice mandated this for its members: "We will always wear the soutane and belt and we
will have short, modest hair with the tonsure well-marked, and we will not even

go to the bedroom door in a bathrobe, and without a hat or *bonnet carré*."[56] Not even fellow seminarians were to see each other without their vestments. All these rules that imposed and enforced strict and continuous use of the soutane and related "marks" enacted the investiture paradigm that texts like Bourdoise's handbook associated with the reception of new robes in the context of liturgical ceremonies.

In their function of renewing an investiture paradigm, rules and ceremonies related to the secular clergy's robes also supported a professionalization project aimed at elevating the secular priest, in particular the curate, relative to priests in religious orders. Protestant and Catholic reformers had no shortage of criticism for regulars.[57] Reform began to sweep through France's religious orders in the fifteenth and sixteenth centuries, however, in some cases a full century or more before figures like Bourdoise and Olier founded the seminaries that would extend reform to the secular clergy.[58] Catholic reformers who focused on improving the secular clergy therefore perceived the regulars as possessing a reputation for spiritual superiority. Their emphasis on the soutane as the secular clergy's distinctive vestment belonged to a broader effort to reposition the secular clergy as an order submitted directly to Jesus Christ, rather than to a human founder or superior general. At Saint-Sulpice, the promotion of the soutane as "the robe of the religion of Jesus Christ," cited above, must be read in light of debates about dress within religious orders, such as the Capuchins, where members in opposing camps sought to demonstrate whether Saint Francis had established a rounded, square, or pyramidal hood.[59] By claiming Jesus Christ as the secular clergy's founder, secular clergymen sought to attribute to their ranks a spiritual dignity at once more universal and more foundational than that of the regulars. In a treatise Olier wrote in 1651 to outline for French bishops his vision for the importance and function of diocesan seminaries, he went so far as to reject the term "secular priest" in favor of the terms "Prêtre du Clergé" (priest of the clergy), "le S[aint] Clergé" (the holy clergy), or "Prêtres de JES[US] CH[RIST]" (priests of Jesus Christ).[60] In doing so, he figured the secular clergy as a sort of religious order. "The Holy Clergy is properly this powerful body that God has established in the Church to combat [the vices of] the century," wrote Olier, adding several pages later, "Thus this magnificent order of the holy clergy . . . has upon it the universal spirit of the Religion of Jesus Christ."[61] From Olier's perspective, the continuous use of the soutane, representing Christ's death and the clergy's death-to-self, gave visible expression to the secular clergy's special mission in comparison to priests in religious orders.[62] When Tartuffe donned a soutane-like robe in 1664, the play's ecclesiastical critics, most of whom belonged to the

secular clergy, saw a challenge to the still-tenuous revival of an investiture paradigm aimed at dignifying their ranks.

## Tartuffe and the Three Repertoires of Priestly Performance

Although scholarship has focused little on the way France's early seminaries
helped produce the ecclesiastical models on which critics have long speculated
that Molière crafted *Tartuffe*, the main character's resemblance to key figures in
the French Counter-Reformation has received ample attention. One of the oldest explanations for the ire incited by *Tartuffe* posits that the play aroused anger
not because it mocked religious doctrine but because it satirized religious identities. Molière himself advanced this argument in the second of three letters he
wrote to Louis XIV to request support in the face of his play's critics. His de-
tractors, Molière noted, had not said a word against other potentially scandalous comedies: "These other [plays] only attacked piety and religion, of which they
[Molière's critics] care very little; but this one here [*Tartuffe*] attacks and plays
them [his critics], and it is this that they cannot stand."[63] Molière's critics had
not really lashed out to defend religion, according to Molière, but because they
felt that *Tartuffe* placed them on the stage. In the early twentieth century, scholars pursued Molière's argument, proposing that Tartuffe represented a "type" or
"animated abstraction" of the devout Catholic.[64] Seventeenth-century responses
to the play certainly support the claim that *Tartuffe* attacked a specific style of
religious embodiment with which ecclesiastical authorities identified.

Criticism, however, has tended to treat this style of embodiment as a quirk
of specific individuals rather than as the function of a larger historical process.
Very early in the play's reception critics and scholars began treating the play as a
*livre à clef*, a text with a key that "stages real characters or makes allusion to real
people under imaginary or altered names."[65] Most guesses as to the true identity
of Tartuffe point toward members of the Company of the Blessed Sacrament.[66]
The Company of the Blessed Sacrament was a secret Catholic society composed
of clergy and devout laymen that operated from 1630 to 1666, promoting chari-
table and missionary projects that furthered the Catholic cause in the face of
Protestantism and also exerting political influence, as they did when they pushed
for prohibitions against performances of *Tartuffe*.[67] Some critics went so far as
to suggest specific individuals. In the seventeenth century, members of the court,
writers, and pamphleteers proposed, among others, Gabriel Roquette (c. 1623–
1797), who later became the bishop of Autun, the abbé de Pons, Desmarets de

Saint-Sorlin (1595–1676), Gaston de Renty (1611–1649), Antoine de Salignac, Marquis de La Mothe-Fénelon (c. 1620–1683), the Count d'Albon, and the Count de Brancas, all of whom had strong connections to the Company of the Blessed Sacrament.[68] In the twentieth century, Francis Baumal implicated Olier, before identifying a lay barber from Lyon named Jacques Cretenet as Tartuffe's model.[69] After taking stock of this list, Emanuel Chill rightly argues that all these individuals present "plausible resemblances" to Tartuffe.[70] Yet, their numerousness "suggests that Tartuffe was a real composite," a theatrical rendering of "what was currently plausible in religious circles" and of the "gestures and idioms of upper-class piety."[71] As a composite, Tartuffe defies categories. "The Tartuffe we know wears semiclerical dress and is priest-like without being a priest. He is austere without being unworldly," writes Chill.[72] Based on Tartuffe's indeterminate nature, Chill proposes that Tartuffe was a lay director of conscience.

In the same way, however, that membership in the Company of the Blessed Sacrament does not, in the end, prove sufficient to establish a historical figure as the blueprint for Molière's *Tartuffe*, neither does lay activity as a spiritual director capture the full range of categories that Molière's Tartuffe blurred to create the effect of priestlike character. Rather, Tartuffe's liminal quality—the way in which his character was at once clerical and lay, courtly and crude, theatrical and monastic—reflected the variety of performance repertoires a secular clergyman had to incorporate and reconcile to fulfill his role as a vray ecclésiastique. Tartuffe's bad behavior while wearing the small collar and plain robe upended the Counter-Reformation's reassertion of investiture by exposing the much broader range of mechanisms—beyond tonsure or ordination ceremonies and divine calling—that produced a good, true, or perfect churchman. Molière's title character confused the audience's conceptual categories and did so in a way that mirrored the Counter-Reformation project.

Although investiture supposedly belonged to the medieval world, the project of reinstituting investiture as a paradigm among the secular clergy in seventeenth-century France in fact demanded a very modern set of procedures. These procedures entailed a double move very similar to the paradoxical classificatory pattern Bruno Latour finds at the heart of modernity in his book *We Have Never Been Modern*. Moderns, Latour argues, engaged in what he calls "hybridization," creating "mixtures between entirely new types of beings, hybrids of nature and culture."[73] At the same time, moderns undertook a program of "purification," establishing strict conceptual boundaries between objects and activities that a century earlier had not seemed separate, differentiating nature from culture, humans from nonhumans, earth from heaven, and scientific power from political power.[74] According to Latour, this ontological purification in fact permitted and propelled the process of hybridization, enabling, for example, a natural philosopher like Robert Boyle to leverage penal law and biblical exegesis to invent the air pump.[75] The secular clergy's counter-reformers were not inventing a new machine, but they were inventing a new ecclesiastical type. This type resulted from a series of cultural translations as seminaries adopted and adapted cultural practices from the theater, the court, and the monastery, creating a hybrid. Even the investiture that served as this hybrid figure's sign constituted a mixing of opposed categories, the mystical mingling of human and nonhuman, flesh and fabric.

As in Latour's model, purificatory gestures made possible the cultural translations by means of which the secular clergy constructed this hybrid, thereby reinvigorating investiture. It is easiest to discern the cultural translations that constituted the Counter-Reformation's secular clergyman after identifying the purifications that made his creation possible. As we have already seen, reform-minded seculars engaged in purification by firmly defining the secular clergy in opposition to the laity on the one hand and the regulars on the other; both groups into which the seculars had blended during the late medieval period. "Being a priest and being a man are two almost incompatible things," declared Bourdoise regarding the difference between a layperson and a secular priest, placing them in what Latour might call "distinct ontological zones."[76] Meanwhile, Olier asserted the primacy of the secular clergy over the regulars by defining the seculars as "the order of Jesus Christ," a religious order founded by the divine savior rather than merely a saint and therefore of heavenly rather than earthly institution.[77] Ecclesiastical rules for ordination prohibited actors from becoming priests, while Counter-Reformation pamphlets on clerical dress renounced fashion-conscious priests as "courtiers, gamblers, and acrobats," all of which were presented as incommensurable with priesthood.[78] Over the course of the seventeenth century, the seculars carved out an ontological category for themselves by discursively setting themselves apart.

Meanwhile, the behaviors that signaled an intimate link between a secular clergyman's clothing and his character—the style of comportment that made his robes seem to reflect both a social role and an inner identity—required him to blend skills drawn from the very groups against which he defined himself. To achieve the affect that manifested what seminary founders called the "ecclesiastical spirit" and without which his robes would seem false, a secular clergyman had to master elements of a monk's asceticism, a gentleman's ceremonial gravitas, and an actor's preparation techniques.[79] The next chapter provides a more detailed examination of the gestures each of these repertoires entailed. Broadly, though, the vray ecclésiastique, as envisioned by seminary pamphlets and manuals, borrowed from the regular clergy by following a daily rule, wearing distinctive dress, and seeking to live in community. From the courtier, the true churchman adapted a codified form of bodily movement that expressed his place in a divine hierarchy imagined through the prism of French monarchical power. The vray ecclésiastique learned to bring these divergent repertoires together into a new and coherent whole by borrowing from actors the idea of role-playing and the technicalities of rehearsal. Tartuffe's behavior draws on these three repertoires and produces something audiences called hypocrisy by incompletely fusing the patterned behavior the ideal secular clergyman needed to incorporate from actors, courtiers, and monks. By leaving the hybrid nature of the secular clergyman unpurified, *Tartuffe* threatened to unravel the priestly identity France's Catholic reformers had spent several decades constituting through the renewal of investiture practices.

   Although the register kept by Molière's troupe indicates that they performed the first three acts of *Tartuffe* at Versailles in 1664, the text from that initial performance has not survived.[80] Before its eventual publication in 1669, the play underwent a series of rewritings, first for private readings between 1664 and 1667, when Tartuffe reappeared on stage under the guise of Panulphe, and then again between 1667 and 1669, when the final, softened version of *Tartuffe* met with "very lively and durable success" and Molière had the play printed.[81] An analysis of the text must rely on the 1669 version of the play. This version, nonetheless, retains, without fusing, traces of the three repertoires out of which a vray ecclésiastique constructed his identity. Most obviously, Tartuffe's quasi-clerical character derives from his deployment of behaviors associated with priests in religious orders. Indeed, when Tartuffe makes his first entrance in the play at the beginning of act 3, scene 2, his opening line suggests that he has just been engaged in self-mortification. Tartuffe says to his valet, "Laurent, lock up my scourge and hair shirt, too. / And pray that our Lord's grace will shine on you."[82] A hair shirt is a garment made of rough material, such as goat skin or sackcloth, worn against the skin as a form of penance and to help the wearer remember to fight against bodily temptations, while the scourge was used for self-flagellation.[83] Although used by lay people as well as clergy, in the Middle Ages hair shirts and the scourge were among the tools of self-mortification used by a monk to "make a martyr of himself through penance."[84] Tartuffe's reference to his hair shirt and scourge connect him not just to the priesthood but specifically to priests in religious orders and a medieval style of monasticism. To conform to the ideal type promoted by France's Counter-Reformation seminaries, a secular clergyman likewise needed to incorporate ascetic practices of the kind used in

religious orders into his way of being, "castigating his flesh and punishing especially those members [of his body] that had participated in sin."[85] By evoking
self-mortification, Molière astutely highlights the monastic elements of the
secular clergyman's hybrid identity.

Yet, *Tartuffe* foregrounds the wrong features of the monastic repertoire.
Rather than corporal penance, which the new and reformed religious orders of
the sixteenth and seventeenth centuries had reduced, the seminaries borrowed
communal living, silence, a daily examination of conscience, and, most important, submission to a rule from the regulars.[86] Although seculars were not clois-
tered, the act of living by a rule set them slightly apart from the world, which
gave social meaning to the symbolism Catholic reformers assigned to the secular clergy's robes. The soutane, they claimed, represented a man's death to the
world.[87] Several interlocking layers of rules gave shape to a clergyman's daily life.
While in seminary, he followed a house rule that indicated the hours for rising,
sleeping, meals, Mass, recreation, and prayer.[88] Each seminarian had a spiritual
director who made sure he followed even the smallest details in the house rules
while also from time to time assigning additional spiritual exercises.[89] And before leaving the seminary, each undertook a short spiritual retreat during which
he established a "life rule for the future," which the directors adamantly encouraged him to follow.[90] Whether a seminarian was hired as a chaplain by a wealthy
family, returned to his country parish, or stayed in the city and rented a room
where his neighbors might be, as one set of seminary rules put it, "libertines, heretics, atheists, gamblers, drunks, blasphemers, women, [or] girls," the rule structured the secular clergyman's behavior and helped ensure that his actions, as well
as his robes, differentiated him from his lay peers.[91] To make investiture work, a
secular clergyman had to be a bit of a monk. No matter how high up the hierarchy he was, though, a combination of rules and spiritual direction embedded the
ideal secular clergyman's monkishness in a set of social relations to which he was
accountable. Tartuffe, on the other hand, takes spiritual direction from no one
and follows no shared rule. Molière gives Tartuffe only a fragment of patterned
behavior—the hair shirt and the scourge—indicative of monastic piety without
situating him within the broader set of relations and practices that gave order to
that fragment in the life of a clergyman.

Only slightly less obvious than his citation of monastic behavior, Tartuffe
enacts fragments of the second repertoire on which secular clergymen drew: that
of courtly behavior. A secular cleric needed to display ceremonial decorum for his
vestments to convey an ecclesiastical spirit and thus fulfill their investiture function. Ceremonial decorum's importance derived from a Counter-Reformation

understanding of the chancel—or area around the altar—as God's royal chamber. Seminary directors therefore figured the clergymen who conducted Mass as servants attending a prince or courtiers advancing socially in the house of a sovereign.[92] Bourdoise exclaims, "Oh that God would be well honored in our churches if one behaved themselves in his presence like one behaves in the house of the great, or in their presence."[93] In a letter written in 1643 by Olier to a young cleric who had just entered the priesthood, Olier made the clergyman's courtly function even more explicit. "By entering the clergy, we have declared to you that you enter into [God's] house to render him service," wrote Olier, "being thereafter like one of his domestics who must attend continually to his person."[94] As I discuss in Chapter 3, this royal metaphor shaped the way seminarians applied decorum in the sanctuary. In order to enable secular clergymen to enact ceremonial reverence toward the altar, seminary training inculcated a set of behavioral norms for the expression and recognition of hierarchical difference that correlated strongly with the aristocratic ideals that informed Molière's comedies. James F. Gaines argues that "Molière's exemplary aristocrats are well-rounded, idealized versions of the New Nobility promulgated by the court of Louis XIV: respectful of authority, scrupulously moderate, conscious of the *souverain bien*."[95] Gaines continues, "Although they do not flaunt their superiority, they continually take part in the relentless comparison of the individual to the standards of what he should be."[96] For Molière and the secular clergy, courtly protocol represented a shared reference to a codified behavioral standard indicating moderation and respectful submission.

Tartuffe's use of the courtly repertoire displays itself most clearly in the first two acts of the play, when other characters discuss him before he makes his first stage entrance. Part of Tartuffe's charm derives from his use of courtly gestures in the context of worship. These gestures feature prominently in the description that Orgon, the bourgeois master of the house duped by Tartuffe, gives to his skeptical brother-in-law of their first meeting. "My brother," exclaims Orgon, "you would be charmed to know him.... Ha! If you had seen how I met him, you would have for him the same friendship I show him" (1.5.270, 281–82). Orgon continues:

> Each day he came to church, with a gentle air
> Right next to me, he would kneel on both knees.
> He attracted the eyes of the entire assembly
> By the ardor with which he exclaimed his prayers;
> He gave great sighs, and great pains,
> And humbly kissed the ground at each moment. (1.5.283–28)[97]

Four elements of courtly coded gestures used in worship are featured in Orgon's description of Tartuffe's behavior: Tartuffe genuflects with both knees, bows, kisses the ground, and conveys gentleness and humility, presumably through the positioning of his head and eyes.[98] These gestures belonged to the repertoire used in the presence of a king and in the presence of the consecrated Eucharist.

Again, however, Tartuffe extracts these coded gestures from the context in which a seminary-trained secular clergyman would use them. A seminary-trained clergyman learned to use ceremonial decorum to blend in with the rest of the clergy and orient the gaze of worshippers toward the altar. Tartuffe does the opposite, drawing attention to himself. In the context of liturgical services, Tartuffe also misdirects the reverence he pays to others. Seminaries taught secular clergymen to deploy ceremonial decorum toward each other, enacting and reinforcing the ecclesiastical hierarchy. A liturgical handbook from Vincent de Paul's Congregation of the Mission instructed clergymen to perform a medium inclination whenever they passed before a cardinal, an archbishop, a bishop, or a priest wearing sacramental vestments.[99] Tartuffe, by contrast, directs his courtly attention toward Orgon. Right after describing the kisses Tartuffe gave to the floor in his prayers, Orgon describes the deference Tartuffe showed to him: "And when he [Tartuffe] was leaving, he ran ahead of me, to meet at the door to offer me holy water" (1.5.289–90).[100] Even though the gesture described here does not appear in the seminary literature, by offering holy water Tartuffe places himself in the role of servant in a way analogous to the service offered by clergy at the altar. Tartuffe therefore deploys fragments of the same courtly repertoire taught in seminaries for use during liturgical ceremonies but enacts them at the wrong times, to the wrong degrees, toward the wrong objects.

In France's seventeenth-century seminaries, a third repertoire, that of the theater, enabled secular clergymen to fuse the patterned behaviors borrowed from monastics and courtiers. A long history of antitheatrical sentiment dating to the early church fathers equates the theater with duplicity. The titles Molière gave his play—Le Tartuffe, ou l'hypocrite and Le Tartuffe, ou l'imposteur—would seem to suggest that his central character stages an ecclesiastical use of the theater as a form of falsehood. This notion of theater would make role-playing, or pretending to be something one is not, central to the theatrical repertoire. But this is not the aspect of the theatrical repertoire the seminaries privileged, nor is it the feature of the theater that made Tartuffe such a threatening character to France's ecclesiastical authorities. Rather, in constructing a new priestly identity for the secular clergy the seminaries looked to the theater as a model of repetition and rehearsal. Whereas before the foundation of seminaries in the 1640s secular clergymen learned their profession haphazardly through informal apprenticeship-type relationships, the counter-reformers sought to standardize clerical behavior and liturgical practice. Performance expertise in sacramental situations was important to their efforts to reinvigorate an investiture paradigm because liturgical skill signaled that a clergyman qualified as one among what seminary directors called "true priests and pastors."[101] Only repetition of the required skills could make them seem like second nature.

Bourdoise's seminary helped pioneer the performance standards by which a "true" priest could be distinguished from a false one by developing pedagogical techniques that used role-playing and rehearsal to teach the sacraments. What Bourdoise admired about the theater, however, was not the way actors assumed characters but, instead, the way practice enabled them to perform without mistakes. Bourdoise's maxims, published posthumously, indicate he positioned actors very explicitly as one of the models for priestly preparation: "A Preacher would die of embarrassment if he had made a noticeable mistake in a Sermon. Likewise, an Orator lecturing before a Prince [or] an Actor on Stage; to this end they all study and prepare themselves and rehearse an infinity of times. . . . And (what is deplorable) no one worries himself one bit during the divine Office, which is recited before and in the presence of the divine Majesty, to make a hundred mistakes due to lack of preparation. Is there any faith among churchmen?"[102] Whatever the extent of Bourdoise's actual theater knowledge, the *règlements*, or rules, for the ceremonies instructor at Saint-Nicolas-du-Chardonnet—conserved at the Archives nationales de France—show that seminarians rehearsed the sacraments twice a week in a classroom and once a week in the parish church.[103] In the classroom, the instructor prepared a mise-en-scène by assembling props—like a doll and a "cushion for the infant's head" when practicing baptism—and assigning roles to the seminarians.[104] In addition to those slotted to play the priest and his clerical assistants, the instructor selected students to represent the laypeople who received the sacraments. These students played roles like godfather, godmother, sick person, and penitent.[105] By the end of the seventeenth century, sacramental rehearsal and role-playing enjoyed a fixed place in seminary curriculums across France.[106] In order for a secular clergyman to exhibit an ecclesiastical spirit, he had to rehearse like an actor.

Tartuffe, by contrast, never is shown in rehearsal. At least one of Molière's seventeenth-century critics reproached him for this, arguing that a devout person and a hypocrite look the same on the outside and that "it is necessary to show what the *dévot* does secretly, as well as the hypocrite."[107] The typical character type for the *faux dévot*, or false believer, in works prior to *Tartuffe* revealed the hypocrite's machinations through asides and overheard conversations.[108] Molière, however, does not stage the theatrical repertoire as role-playing or doubleness. Instead, in *Tartuffe* the audience meets only the smooth exterior honed through unseen repetitions. In the words of historian Emanuel Chill, "Tartuffe's special virtues are not cunning and deception but energy, will, virtuosity."[109] When Orgon's son catches Tartuffe trying to seduce his mother and denounces Tartuffe to Orgon, Tartuffe makes a true confession—"Yes, my brother," he tells Orgon, "I am evil, I am guilty"—thereby restoring Orgon's trust.[110] When Orgon at last witnesses Tartuffe seducing his wife and attempts to throw him out of the house, Tartuffe uses one of Orgon's true confessions against him. It turns out that Orgon had harbored a box of papers from a friend who had been declared an enemy of the state, making Orgon an accomplice. Tartuffe had reported this to the king and used it to confiscate Orgon's property. Switching adeptly between well-rehearsed repertoires, each unmasking reveals not a fraud but a new dimension of Tartuffe's persona. In Chill's words again, "To the very end Tartuffe retains, almost as a question of honor, the obvious grimace of virtue."[111] By hiding repetition and rehearsal, Molière thus presents the theatrical repertoire at work through its ability to produce a character with depth. Tartuffe, then, foregrounds that which terrified the counter-reformers most about the theater, even as they used theatrical strategies to train priests. Seminary directors believed the theater dangerous not for its role-playing but because it, they believed, excited and transmitted real passions with the power to transform both actors and audiences.[112] When theatrical repetition was directed toward the creation of priests who lived up to their robes, counter-reformers embraced it, but Tartuffe presented them with a nightmare vision of the real identities rehearsal could create.

## The Challenges of Performing Priesthood

In conclusion, Tartuffe's attire at the play's début in 1664 placed the performance repertoires and ritual practices that gave meaning to theater costumes and clerical robes in conversation. The comic situation proposed by the play derived in part from the way this conversation pitted two versions of investiture against each other, one version inherited from the Middle Ages and leveraged by theatrical conventions to create convincing on-stage worlds, and the other a newer version embraced—and perhaps created—by the Counter-Reformation church that used a combination of ontological purification (secular priests are totally different from regulars and lay people) and cultural hybridization (secular priests needed skills borrowed from actors, monks, and courtiers) to forge an ecclesiastical persona whose social identity would match his robes. In their aspect as a theater costume, Tartuffe's clothes provoked a reaction from devout Catholics precisely because stage clothes in the seventeenth century—despite their capacity to erode investiture by causing clothes to circulate across social boundaries—built their storytelling power on investiture's remains. Unless the content of a play clearly instructed otherwise, audiences did not consider theater costumes to be disguises. Rather, costumes revealed a character's social identity according to a logic native to investiture: if he wears a fine cloak, he is a prince; if he wears a small collar and plain robe, he is a cleric. Molière exploited the theater's medieval investiture logic to put his generation's Catholic reformers on stage.

It was precisely the theater's inherited investiture framework that enabled Molière to examine how the church's claim that clerical robes left a spiritual imprint was in fact premised on a paradigm that called for the creation of character through extensive training, repetition, and rehearsal. In its aspect as a clerical robe—whether in fact a soutane or merely a garment that suggested one—Tartuffe's attire critiqued Counter-Reformation investiture by staging an incomplete mixing of cultural practices upon which the clerical identity legitimized by investiture depended. This incomplete mixing or unpurified hybrid produced a mode of action whose effect was hypocrisy. Tartuffe's ambiguous identity betrays this incomplete cultural mixing. Scholars have long wondered whether he represented a Jesuit, a Jansenist, or specific members of the Company of the Blessed Sacrament, the secret organization that helped censure Molière's play. Tartuffe is better described as a secular clergyman in whom the skills of the actor, the gentleman, and the monk are incompletely hybridized and out of balance. His persuasiveness smacks of the theater, his charm of the court, and his asceticism of the monastery, and yet the spectator cannot quite reconcile these three strands of his identity. He thus makes visible the cultural repertoires incorporated by the secular clergy in their attempts at restoring investiture, and perhaps the impossibility of sufficiently fusing them to become a "true priest."

At the same time, Tartuffe's depth depicts the way the early modern church's reinvigoration of investiture paradoxically offered a platform for self-creation. Even though putting on new clothes did not necessarily transform a person—as seminary directors knew all too well—a pedagogical system that gave access to new cultural skills opened the door for personal reinvention. Tartuffe, who at the end of the play's five-act version almost gets away with expropriating Orgon's house, represents the upheaval to the social hierarchy that the Counter-Reformation's circulation of practices had the potential to unleash. The church's program for reinstating investiture empowered the individual—dangerously so, the play implies—even when it thinks it disciplines vestiary abuses.

In terms of priestly performance, Molière's play reveals the complex work an individual cleric needed to undertake to learn embodied repertoires from a range of cultural domains, incorporate them into his body, fuse them into a coherent whole through repetition, and fastidiously wear the outer marks of the vray ecclésiastique so as to participate in the investiture paradigm's presentation of priestly selfhood as divinely created the moment a clergyman receives his robes through the sacrament of ordination. In parodying the difficulties of this process, Molière did not tell seminary directors something they did not already know. Seminary directors recognized the extraordinary and continual labor required to enact the perfection they desired from each clergyman. Bourdoise railed that "there is almost not a single churchman in this century, however spiritual and such that he might be, whose life, clothes, and actions are in conformity with the rules and canons of the Church."[113] Rare were the secular priests, such as Vincent de Paul or François de Sales, who fused the necessary monastic, courtly, and theatrical skills with apparent effortlessness, thereby projecting a priestly ideal to which the clergymen of his period aspired. Even very saintly priests, like Bourdoise, failed to completely fuse the repertoires out of which the vray ecclésiastique's identity was composed. Despite his ceremonial strictness, Bourdoise lacked courtly grace, which left his monastic adherence to rules and his faithfulness to practice and rehearse too visible. Cardinal de Retz said of him, "Monsieur Bourdoise is much talked about because his zeal has too much ardor and not always enough prudence."[114] If not quite like Tartuffe's, Bourdoise's piety with insufficient courtliness definitely placed him among the "Little Collars," or petits collets, referenced by Tartuffe's initial costume, which shows not the hypocrisy of France's secular clergy but rather the enormity of the performance challenge they had taken upon themselves. For the Catholic Church as a whole, that challenge was to develop institutional supports to standardize, transmit, refine, motivate, evaluate, and enforce the adoption and proper integration of the behaviors necessary to produce the identity of the vray ecclésiastique. For the individual clergyman, the challenge was to discover through training, practice, and experiment how to blend and deploy to best effect the various repertoires at his disposal when faced with different publics—men or women, lay or clerical, secular or religious, noble or not, courtly or civilian, urban or rural—while avoiding the air of artifice.

CHAPTER 2

# Gestures

As the number and size of France's seminaries grew between the 1640s and the end of the long seventeenth century, the style of embodiment that signified a clergyman's conformity to the ideals of the vray ecclésiastique, or true churchman, became increasingly codified.[1] In much the way the soutane gained recognition as the secular clergy's distinctive vestment during the same period, seminary directors used the term "modesty" to denote the overall effect of the movements and gestures essential to the ideal secular clergyman. In the handbook he composed to guide seminarians through the various elements of their training, or "exercices" (*exercices*), Matthieu Beuvelet (1620–1657) of the Seminary of Saint-Nicolas du Chardonnet referred to modesty as "the form that they [churchmen] must observe in their exterior to conform themselves entirely to the spirit of the Church, as indicated by the holy Councils."[2] A clergyman's gestures, as Beuvelet's definition of modesty suggests, served as a proxy for gauging his inner disposition. Catholic reformers who wanted to ascertain whether an ordination candidate possessed or had acquired *l'esprit clérical* or *ecclésiastique*—a "clerical or ecclesiastical spirit"—could not see into an individual's heart and instead evaluated his bodily activities.[3] Does he say Mass too fast? Does he keep the altar and its ornaments clean? Does he allow parishioners to use the altars as benches, armrests, or closets by sitting on them or putting their cloaks and hats on them? Does he sing too fast during divine services? Does he ever avoid any of his liturgical duties, thinking them below his status?[4] Reform-minded priests trained in or influenced by France's seventeenth-century seminaries learned to read each other's bodies for clues regarding an individual's spiritual alignment with the Counter-Reformation's values.

Seminary directors imagined the modest clerical body as having special communicative powers. Louis Tronson, director of the Seminary of Saint-Sulpice in

Paris from 1657 to 1676, composed a series of devotional reflections for seminarians on ecclesiastical behavior in which he guided his readers to exclaim, "O, what beautiful preaching, to appear in modesty before the people."[5] Similarly, a *conférence ecclésiastique*—or instructional session for priests on a specific topic—from the diocese of Cahors circa 1656 described ecclesiastical modesty as "silent preaching."[6] Like a good sermon, modesty, as seminaries understood it, could capture people's attention and convey the church's core message. Modesty could preach without words. Whether or not the gestures that constituted modesty communicated as effectively as seminary directors thought, the metaphor of modesty as preaching reveals a shift in priestly performance that seminary training helped to accelerate. By ritualizing and theologizing the secular clergyman's gestures, the bodily movements and training practices that translated into modesty diminished the distinction between liturgical enactment in the context of the sacraments and pastoral practice in the homes, streets, and fields where secular clergymen ministered to the faithful. The ritualization of the secular clergyman's everyday comportment insulated his priestly identity against charges of artifice, theatricality, or tartuffery by erasing the boundary between an individual priest and the office he occupied, legitimizing the clergyman's status as a "true" or authentic churchman.

## Modesty

As France's seminaries expanded during the second half of the seventeenth century, their directors and professors published handbooks for use by seminarians and developed training materials in manuscript form, such as lectures called *conférences* and *entretiens*, guidelines for instructors, and guided meditations. These documents cover a broad range of topics, corresponding to the standard seminary curriculum, which according to Matthieu Beuvelet of the Seminary of Saint-Nicolas du Chardonnet included "exercises in silent prayer" and conferences on "piety, moral theology, the Roman catechism, the practice of the sacraments, the catechisms, ceremonies, plain chant."[7] Almost without exception, whether in the context of teaching pious behavior or liturgical ceremonies, seminary manuals devoted attention to modesty. In these texts, modesty constituted a foundational component of the "great progress toward perfection" that a stay in a seminary was designed to facilitate.[8] Although less important in the economy of clerical perfection than conducting all actions with "holy intentions and Christian dispositions," seminary texts presented modesty as absolutely essential.[9] In a series of entretiens, or lessons, given to new seminarians by Tronson, he explains that modesty is as important to perfection as the body is to the soul: "The interior is, in truth, that which is primary. It is the soul and the life such that without it, whatever beautiful appearances and whatever their external brilliance, they are dead, unfruitful, and without merit before God. As we have said, it is, however, absolutely necessary to regulate the exterior, too ... because although the exterior is only the body of the action it nonetheless serves the action just as the body serves the soul. . . . It is impossible that the exterior be disorderly and that the interior not suffer from it."[10] Without the visible signs of modesty in his outer comportment, a churchman could not achieve perfection.

As the preaching metaphors suggested, in addition to supporting a churchman's progress toward ecclesiastical perfection, seminary directors believed that modesty instructed and uplifted those who witnessed it. Tronson explained to his seminarians that not only a clergyman's own perfection but also kindness toward others made modesty essential. "Finally, even charity for our neighbor obliges it [modesty] upon us," wrote Tronson, "because we must edify him [our neighbor], we are obliged to give him an example and we would not know how to do that except by the exterior."[11] Unlike the harsh words that could fill a sermon, seminary manuals imagined modesty's voice as sweet. "Oh, what a beautiful thing is modesty," effused a guided meditation in a manuscript volume attributed to Tronson, "by its voice alone it attracts all hearts to imitate it."[12] To imitate modesty, seminary training further suggested, was to imitate Jesus Christ, whose modesty rendered him "both adorable and loveable in the eyes of angels and men."[13] Another meditation, or *examen,* in the volume attributed to Tronson led its readers to exclaim, "Let us adore Our Lord Jesus Christ, the true model of modesty, which was so remarkable and so charming in him."[14] By analogy, a modest priest could, like Christ, inspire others to goodness by his physical decorum alone, educating them in the way to holiness.

At the same time, seminary directors believed that modesty elevated the secular clergy by connecting their everyday behavior to their sacramental gestures, especially to the ceremonies of the Mass. Tronson's meditation exercises prompted seminarians to move in their reflections directly from modesty's edifying function to its capacity to make visible the secular clergy's saintly status. Tronson guided his readers to consider whether "we have so thoroughly followed the rule of modesty given us by Saint Augustine that there is nothing in our exterior that would not edify our neighbor, and that has not been in conformity with the holiness of our condition."[15] Condition, or *estat,* here refers to the quality of being a secular clergyman. Like his predecessors at the Seminary of Saint-Sulpice, Tronson believed in the secular clergy's unique role as the proprietors of what Jean-Jacques Olier, founder of the Society of Saint-Sulpice, called "the universal spirit of the religion of Jesus Christ," as opposed to the particular charisma of each religious order.[16] In his 1651 proposal to France's bishops for the foundation of seminaries, Olier had made the case that the secular clergy and the seminaries that trained them were more necessary to the Catholic Church than the monasteries and convents of the religious orders, "since the Church cannot subsist without these essential Ministers."[17] Outside the relatively narrow circle of reform-minded bishops and seminary directors, however, such was not the broadly accepted view of the secular clergy's status. Even Antoine Furetière's *Dictionnaire universel* notes, in the entry for the adjective "séculier" in the 1701 edition, "Regular priests assert that they are more perfect than secular priests."[18] By the 1660s and 1670s, when Tronson served as director of the Seminary of Saint-Sulpice in Paris, the secular clergy's reputation had improved enough for him to treat its saintliness as a fact in internal documents, but this still must be read as prescriptive rather than descriptive. Modesty therefore helped construct the sanctity it was meant to reveal.

This sanctity, as seminary training conceived it, established gestural continuity between a clergyman's quotidian actions and his liturgical office. A pamphlet published in 1658 by Pierre Trichard, a printer near the Seminary of Saint-Nicolas du Chardonnet, makes the connection between daily and liturgical gestures clear. Composed by sixteenth-century Spanish Catholic reformer Juan de Ávila (1499–1569), translated into French, and then carefully conserved in 1664 by the curate of the French parish of Gisors, the tract states: "The priest, who being outside the altar desires to walk with composure and with the gravity and the modesty suitable to his dignity, remembers the grandeur in which he has been placed, and how the business he has handled at the altar is great and important."[19] From Ávila's perspective, modest comportment in non-sacramental contexts referenced the eucharistic sacrifice. Without using the word "modesty," Beuvelet conveys a similar idea in his *Conduite*, or guide to seminary training. In a chapter on how to prepare to celebrate Mass, he writes that "the innocence of the holiness of the life" of the priest constitutes the first form of preparation, which involves treating every action as a preface to the Eucharist. "Relate there [in meditation] all the actions that one does as so many ways and dispositions for celebrating Mass well," urges Tronson, "in the same way that Our Lord related his entire life to the sacrifice he had to offer on the cross."[20] Seminaries thus taught that dignified behavior outside the chancel referred back to the

Eucharist's central importance, and that modest comportment should characterize liturgical and nonliturgical action alike. In the words of Vincent Ferrer (1350–1419), cited by Tronson in an entretien for seminarians on "actions in general," "Never undertake any action unless it is accompanied by modesty."[21] Like the soutane, which should never come off, modesty should have no end, no backstage, no rupture from altar to dormitory, from chancel to *champs*.

More than an abstract concept, modesty had a precise form, which seminary manuals clearly articulated. Tronson's collection of examens devotes ten meditations to modesty, painting a detailed picture of the gestures that contributed to modest comportment. After a meditation entitled "Modesty in General," the other nine address modesty in the way one holds one's head, the postures of the body, when speaking, when walking, in regard to clerical dress, when in the street, when in the dining hall, when at church, and when engaged in conversations and recreations.[22] As the opening meditation explains, "Modesty is a virtue that arranges, in accordance with Christian propriety and honesty, all the outer movements [of the body]: speech, walking, looking, postures, gestures, the bearing of the body and generally all our exterior."[23] Together, the descriptions of modest head movements, bodily postures, and gait convey the gestural norms for clerical comportment, which the meditations on modesty in specific contexts, such as the street or the church, reiterate.

For a novice clergyman, just learning how to properly hold the head would have demanded considerable effort. Instructions in the meditation gave seminarians guidelines for the position of the head as well as each detail of their facial expressions. In the meditation's words, "Modesty normally leads one to hold the head straight, without lifting it too high, without tilting it to one side or the other, and without turning it carelessly and on all occasions."[24] Modesty regulated the eyes as well, requiring that "one normally lowers the eyes" and that "one does not move them too swiftly."[25] Rather, modesty called for an expression in the eyes that could be described as "soft and benign and not atrocious and off-putting."[26] Finally, the forehead should be "serene," and the lips "neither too open nor too closed," so that the face gave no sign of "constraint, of severity, and of melancholy."[27] Whatever the situation and whatever his feelings, a secular clergyman's head and face were supposed to convey a joyful calm.

Guidelines for modest posture and modest walking likewise presented seminarians with myriad instructions for each part of the body. "Modesty makes one hold the body in a seemly posture," began the meditation on the topic.[28] A long list of dos and don'ts followed. Modesty "prevents one from leaning over too much and also from straightening up with too much effort."[29] It "does not tolerate that one changes position at every moment or that one leans first on one leg and then on the other."[30] Modesty did not allow a clergyman to hold his hands "behind his back like a horseman," to rest his head or chin in his hands, to cross his feet, put one leg over the other, touch the face unnecessarily, or "stretch out the arms and legs with too much dissolution."[31] When walking, modesty required that a secular clergyman neither hurry nor run, that he climb the stairs one at a time rather than taking them two by two, that he keep his shoulders relaxed, try not to waive his arms around, and avoid both stomping and tiptoeing.[32] The meditation advised that modesty "would rather tolerate . . . that someone suspects it of laziness than to exhibit the least carelessness in its steps."[33] In his bearing, his movements, and his gait, the clergyman who practiced modesty displayed measured self-control at all times.

Such absolute control of the body remained an elusive ideal. Each meditation ended with a short prayer asking for forgiveness and imploring God for help to do better. "My God, I recognize that I have not paid attention to most of these rules," read the prayer at the end of the meditation on modesty of the head, "give me the grace to observe them from now on."[34] Modesty's elusiveness served a theological function, suggested by meditations that preceded the ten devoted to modesty in the collection attributed to Tronson. Immediately before reflecting prayerfully on how to hold their heads and bodies, seminarians completed seven mediations on the mortification of the senses. The inevitable failure to manage the body perfectly therefore remade each movement of the head, arms, legs, hands, eyes, and forehead into an opportunity for self-mortification. Olier suggested as much in his *Projet de l'establissement d'un séminaire dans un diocèse* (Project for the establishment of a seminary in a diocese), where he presented the "universal modesty of vestments and the modest [*médiocre*] use of all things necessary for life" that should characterize the seminary experience as part of the greater task of "found[ing] these subjects [seminarians] in the mortification of all the natural appetites and mak[ing] them aspire to a perfect death from everything worldly."[35] Theologically, the secular clergyman's never-ending process of regulating his body according to modesty's norms supported his spiritual progress toward worldly renunciation.

Yet, modesty served a social function, too, which Olier acknowledges in his plan for diocesan seminaries. One challenge faced by seminary directors, Olier explained, was that seminary training brought the poor and the rich together in shared living quarters. Modesty, in his view, constituted a way to "obviate the inconvenience that exists in the type of life that one must create to satisfy the inequality of the people who could compose a seminary, and the diversity of their conditions."[36] Olier worried that in the case of poor students from the countryside, seminary food and clothes might "accustom them to comforts very contrary to the work and inconveniences of the countryside," while seminary living might "fatigue and repel" wealthier students, or "persons of condition," as Olier calls them.[37] Modesty in dress, food, and all other seminary activities promised to keep the poor from "flattering themselves in their sensuality" while pushing the rich to "cut away . . . the superfluities of their condition."[38] The modest embodiment promoted in France's early modern seminaries thus sought to create more than rigorously decorous individuals. Rather, seminary training aimed at constructing a new type, an identity that struck a balance between the norms, behaviors, and expectations of its poor and its rich, its rural and its urban, its peasant-born and its noble students.

## Modesty as Performance

Rhetorically, seminary manuals and meditations aligned modest gestures with natural movement, setting up an opposition between modesty and artifice. Modest bearing of the head and face, for example, "avoids feigned grimaces, fake expressions, and everything that smacks of any artifice."[39] A clergyman's gait, likewise, should not make it seem like he tried too hard, "studying his steps so much that they seem artificial."[40] Yet, to achieve modesty and make it look natural required frequent practice, enormous effort, and continuous attention, supported by an ongoing process of imitation and evaluation. If not artifice, priestcraft required art.

From an etic perspective, the process of learning to embody modesty engaged secular clergymen, and especially seminarians, in activities now associated with the term "performance." As performance theorist Marvin Carlson argues, "performance" does not mean the same thing in every context.[41] In some cases, performance refers to what Carlson calls "the display of skills," in others to "patterned behavior," and in still other settings to "keeping up a standard."[42] In an effort to transmit and naturalize the behaviors that signified modesty, seminary training deployed all three types of activity. As Chapter 3 discusses, when clergymen administered the sacraments, in particular the Eucharist, they performed in the sense that they publicly demonstrated their ceremonial skill. To the degree that learning to embody modesty required repeating "strips of behavior" that could be compared to "performance scores," modesty entailed a type of patterned behavior defined by Richard Schechner as "restored behavior."[43] Schechner thinks of these behaviors as "second nature."[44] They use the body and belong to the self while simultaneously remaining separate, "distant from 'me'," and modifiable.[45] Restored behaviors have the capacity to "be put on the way a mask or costume is" and worked on from the outside—in the way a seminary instructor might tell a young clergyman how to hold his hands or head—and so in ritual contexts these behaviors exist on a continuum with other artful modes of embodiment like dance and theater.[46] For seminarians, though, the most prominent performance activity would have been that of trying to carry out their ecclesiastical tasks and clerical gestures successfully "in light of some standard of achievement which may not itself be precisely articulated."[47] In the same way that, according to Carlson, the success of someone's linguistic or scholastic performance "is really framed and judged by its observers," a seminarian could not determine for himself whether he had achieved the status of vray ecclésiastique.[48] The responsibility of judging a seminarian's conformity to the norms that composed the abstract ideal of the perfect churchman rested with his superiors. Structurally, in fact, a secular clergyman never possessed the authority to judge his own perfection, only to identify his imperfections. To continue on the path toward perfection, he therefore needed to surround himself with other clergymen to help him observe and evaluate himself, whether by seeking a spiritual director or joining an ecclesiastical community. Performing priesthood meant perpetual evaluation in the light of a standard.

France's early seminaries afforded clergymen a condensed and prolonged encounter with the models and judges that constituted the post-Tridentine ideal of the vray or parfait ecclésiastique.[49] In addition to Jesus—the perfect churchman's perfect model—seminary training held an array of exempla before the seminarians' eyes. Chief among these, as demonstrated by the house rules for the Seminaries of Saint-Nicolas du Chardonnet and Saint-Sulpice, were the lives of saintly or recently canonized churchmen who had helped implement the reforms recommended by the Council of Trent in France, as well as in Italy and Spain, where reform had begun almost a century earlier. At Saint-Nicolas, seminarians were encouraged to own a copy of the life of Charles Borromeo (1538–1584), the archbishop of Milan from 1564 to 1584 and one of Italy's leading sixteenth-century Catholic reformers, as well as lives of France's own François de Sales (1567–1622), Vincent de Paul, Alain de Solminihac, and Pierre Fourier (1565–1640).[50] Seminary rules treated these stories as nourishment for the soul. At each meal, as seminarians ate in silence, a designated officer read passages from the Old and New Testaments, followed by an excerpt from the life of a saint.[51] Public readings from the spiritual and instructional writings of the sixteenth and early seventeenth centuries' great Catholic reformers supplemented the stories of the saints, translating their lives into applicable prescriptions that contributed to the model of clerical perfection. At Saint-Nicolas, on Mondays, Tuesdays, and Thursdays after the seminarians had had a short break following the recitation of the canonical hours at Nones or Vespers, the prefect read aloud from a short text deemed "more practical, moral or devout than doctrinal," and then led a brief discussion and prayer.[52] Favorite texts included the writings of François de Sales, treatises on the dignity of priests by Juan de Ávila and Spanish ascetic Antonio de Molina (c. 1550–1612), and catechisms or meditations by Paris's seminary founders, directors, and instructors, such as Olier, Bourdoise, and Beuvelet.[53] Morning, noon, and night, seminarians listened to the deeds and advice of Europe's clerical Counter-Reformation heroes, upon whom they were supposed to model their own behavior.

Alone, none of these readings could convey a complete picture of the perfect churchman. Rather, by weaving stories of exemplary churchmen into the daily routine, seminary directors sought to inspire in secular clergymen a desire for perfection. The master règlement kept by the prefect at the Seminary of Saint-Nicolas explained that public readings were necessary "because most of those who enter the seminary are individuals who are dry and sterile in their desire for perfection . . . and very little experienced in the practice of Christian virtues. . . . That is why they must often be excited, warmed, instructed, and nourished in these things by frequent readings."[54] Regular readings that exposed seminarians to models of ecclesiastical perfection had first and foremost an affective aim. The prefect at Saint-Nicolas thought they could "imprint some good feeling of piety," which the prefect fostered by "question[ing] a member of the group about the feelings he had had about the reading that had been done."[55] Models therefore represented the standard toward which seminarians were supposed to strive, but even more important was that the models incited—at least the seminary directors hoped—an affective state conducive to clerical training.

Obedience and submission were central to the affective state that produced modesty and led to behaviors in keeping with the norms for ecclesiastical perfection. Put simply, the desire for perfection that saintly models were supposed to inspire ideally led seminarians to willingly follow their superiors' instructions and to perceive other churchmen as authorized to observe and evaluate their conformity to clerical norms. Models doubled as and facilitated judges. Although none of the seminary documents explicitly articulate the relative authority of churchmen in their capacity to evaluate each other, seminarians would have deduced from the saint's lives, devotional readings, and seminary rules that, at the local level, bishops occupied the pinnacle of evaluative authority over the clergy in their diocese. According to canon law, of course, a priest received his ordination from the bishop. The bishop's "institution" of the priest, as one pamphlet called it, translated into oversight.[56] In his *Discours aux prestres* (Discours to priests), which the prefect's règlement at Saint-Nicolas considered a preferred text for the weekly public devotional reading, Juan de Ávila extoled the bishop's position as God-given guide to his clergy. "He [God] has placed us under the direction of a bishop who must be full of zeal to excite us to the perfection that we should have," writes Ávila, adding that Saint Peter "advises the clergy to be humble and obedient toward them [the bishops]."[57] The dedicatory letter at the beginning of *Le Parfait ecclesiastique* (The perfect churchman)—a posthumous collection of ecclesiastical pamphlets by Claude de la Croix (1598–1661), who taught liturgical ceremonies at the Seminary of Saint-Nicolas—expressed a similar view.[58] Addressed to France's bishops and archbishops and presented as a summary of the instructions they had given to the French clergy, the letter asked rhetorically of the collection, "To whom could it therefore better belong than to you, Messeigneurs, who imprint the character of the priesthood upon priests, who regulate all the actions of their lives . . . ?"[59] Placed by God over the clergy, in theory the bishop watched over and judged them.

In practice, however, as seminary directors pointed out, bishops could not train and evaluate all their clergy all at once. In his *Projet pour l'etablissement d'un séminaire dans un diocese* (Project for the establishment of a seminary in a diocese), Olier argued: "The Prelate, who is the Holy Spouse of his Church, and who must see to its needs, cannot be present to his entire diocese, to instruct and officiate, to offer and administer in person all the goods necessary for the salvation of his people."[60] Since a bishop was not omnipresent or all-seeing, he needed a seminary to provide him with worthy substitutes, ready to act as the bishop's "many mouths and many hands, many limbs and many ministers" in relation to his diocese.[61] Responsible for training the members of the bishop's extended body, seminary directors thus inherited the bishop's authority to evaluate his clergy. The bishop remained in principle "the true and only superior of the seminary," but seminary directors "manage[d] the house in the bishop's hand," acting on the bishop's behalf.[62] That which the bishop held in possession, the seminary directors oversaw. Seminary rules made the director's role as judge or evaluator very clear. The preface to the abbreviated version of rules published by the Seminary of Saint-Nicolas for incoming seminarians advised them to "consider it [the règlement] carefully so that by taking pleasure in following it they might attract Heavenly Blessings as they submit themselves perfectly to the orders of their directors."[63] Not only did seminary directors issue commands, they also evaluated and authorized all movements in and out of the seminary. Each time a seminarian entered or exited the building, whether upon first arrival to enroll or when going in and out on a regular basis to attend classes at the nearby Sorbonne, as some seminarians did, the rules required clergymen to present themselves to the superior and obtain his permission.[64] At Saint-Nicolas, the prefect held a brief meeting every Saturday afternoon to announce who would fulfill each ceremonial responsibility the following week, as well as to "give advice about the faults and failings that one could have noticed during the week."[65] A more personalized form of evaluation took place through periodic one-on-one meetings with the prefect during which each seminarian "gave him an account ... of the way he spent his time and of his faithfulness to the ... rules."[66] Seminary directors kept a watchful eye over the seminarians, evaluating their daily behavior in light of the rules spelled out in the house règlement and the standard of ecclesiastical perfection that inspired them.

A seminarian's spiritual director, his peers, and his own inwardly turned eye added increasingly intimate and constant layers of surveillance and evaluation to a clergyman's effort to achieve ecclesiastical perfection. Before entering the seminary, each incoming seminarian completed a short spiritual retreat under the guidance of a spiritual director, chosen for him by the community of priests who ran the seminary.[67] At the end of the retreat, the spiritual director gave the seminarian a personal règlement, or rule, to follow in addition to the seminary's general règlement. Afterward, the spiritual director doubled as the seminarian's confessor.[68] Although a strict schedule did not regulate the seminarians' interactions with their spiritual director, the director assigned daily readings and made himself available for confessions every Saturday morning and before each feast day from nine o'clock to eleven o'clock, as well as by appointment, and he was committed to being "always ready to help them in every meeting, when it concerns their spiritual advancement."[69] One of the spiritual director's central responsibilities toward his directees was to "often impose upon them faithfulness toward even the smallest seminary rules."[70] For their part, seminarians knew from the house rules that they were to "receive his [the director's] advice as if it were from God, communicate with him from time to time to give him an account of how faithful [they] had been in their resolutions, and tell him straightforwardly [their] pains and temptations."[71] Closer to the seminarian's daily actions than the seminary's superior or prefect and privy to the seminarian's view of his own faults, the spiritual director helped craft each seminarian's encounter with the models of clerical perfection and served as a privileged evaluator of the seminarian's success or failure in relation to those models.

A seminarian and his peers, too, had an important, although limited, authority to evaluate each other. At Saint-Nicolas du Chardonnet, the house rules instructed them, in relation to their fellow seminarians, "to tolerate their failings in a brotherly way and, if possible, pull them out of [their failings] gently."[72] Gentle correction might include "advice, instruction, and other means, as long as permitted by the rules," such that brotherly evaluation could not overstep the authority accorded to spiritual directors or seminary superiors.[73] When a seminarian noticed significant differences between the model of ecclesiastical perfection and a colleague's behavior, he was to refer his colleague to the seminary directors. The rules specified: "If the failings are glaring, and contrary to the edification of the public and the good order of the house, inform the prefect so that he can remedy them."[74] Seminarians thus watched and evaluated each other, without having full freedom to judge one another's conformity to the standard of the vray ecclésiastique.

Seminarians did, however, have a responsibility to observe and evaluate themselves. The rules "in respect to oneself" at Saint-Nicolas instructed the seminarian: "Make yourself very faithful, in God's sight alone, on the inside and outside in relation to all the advice and all the rules written herein," by reading the house rules at least once per month and the guide to seminary exercises carefully.[75] Daily moments for self-evaluation punctuated the seminary schedule. At both Saint-Nicolas du Chardonnet and Saint-Sulpice, everyone participated in an *examen particulier*, perhaps best translated as a "targeted self-evaluation," every day at eleven o'clock, during which all "listened attentively and on their knees" as someone read the theme for that day's reflection.[76] Each examen focused on "some virtue, some vice, or some imperfection, so as to make us aware of the principle mistakes we can make with the goal of avoiding these errors, facilitating in us the practice of virtue, and elevating us to Christian and ecclesiastical perfection."[77] These morning self-reflections treated the same theme for two days at a time, thereby enabling seminarians to perceive patterns in their behavior in relation to a specific aspect of clerical perfection.[78] Patterned failures came under further scrutiny in collaboration with the spiritual director. As the rules for the Seminary of Saint-Sulpice explained, "In addition to that [the examen particulier], it is necessary that everyone focuses for a much longer time, like a month or two, on a specific flaw or practice of virtue, for a length of time that will be decided by his director."[79] In the evening, a second self-examination, focused specifically on that day's failings, concluded the day, followed by a final prayer.[80]

Beuvelet, in his guide to each of the seminary's activities, makes the evaluative character of the examen clear. "Look inside yourself by the Faith of the divine Majesty, recognizing, detesting, judging, condemning, punishing your sins down to the very smallest," he advises in a chapter on how to do the examen.[81] Each individual was meant to be his own harshest critic.

His self-critiques then fed the larger system of evaluation of which he was part, as he revealed the faults he had perceived during the examen to his spiritual director in confession and as he felt moved, in response to the examen, to apologize to his fellows or his superiors. At the Seminary of Saint-Sulpice, the rules set aside time after the day's closing examen and prayer for this feedback loop, specifying that "those who have failed in relation to some part of the *Règlement* during the day and who have not yet apologized to Monsieur the Superior or to his substitute, must do so after the prayer before leaving the room."[82] The hierarchy of judges and models that sustained the process of keeping up a standard of clerical perfection therefore connected the least to the greatest, the tonsured cleric to the prelate, in an evaluative cycle in which each participant learned to watch himself as if he had the eyes of another.

Parishioners, and more generally the lay people to whom the secular clergy ministered, did not figure in seminary training as individuals authorized to evaluate a priest's conformity to the standard of ecclesiastical perfection. Handbooks such as Beuvelet's *Conduite* and La Croix's *Le Parfait ecclesiastique* barely mention the laity. Seminary rules and the examens, like those attributed to Tronson, likewise remain largely silent regarding the ways lay people might evaluate priests. In most cases, seminary texts evoke the laity indirectly by invoking the idea that a priest who adequately fulfills his functions "greatly edifies the people."[83] Metaphors like those discussed earlier that compared a clergyman's modest comportment to preaching came closer to depicting the laity as observers of priestly behavior, but they figured the laity as bedazzled witnesses. The examen on how to walk modestly, for example, directed seminarians to admire "the great Saint Francis walking with such modesty" that "each step was so many secret sermons and the radiance of this virtue that appeared in his walk was so surprising that it ... won thereby the world to Jesus Christ."[84] In this anecdote, lay people do indeed watch priests, but not as evaluators. Rather, what they see overwhelms and converts them.

Inversely, references to poorly performing priests depict the laity as passive victims, stuck in "ignorance and sin," who "moan incessantly" in longing for "true priests and pastors."[85] When seminary texts explicitly discuss parishioners, they represent the Catholic faithful as children or animals who must be led, instructed,

corrected, and lifted up, rather than as potential peers. Direct references to parishioners appear most frequently at the end of handbooks, where seminary directors provided advice to clergymen who were leaving the seminary to work as
parish priests, and in pamphlets akin to the *Miroir des prestres* (Mirror of priests)
that detailed a priest's obligations. One such pamphlet, *Les Principaux devoirs
d'un bon curé* (The principal duties of a good curate), included a section on a
priest's duties "toward his parishioners."[86] After spurring curates to "have great
zeal for the salvation of their [parishioners'] souls, to love them all intensely and
equally" and "to treat them with great gentleness of spirit and words," the pamphlet figures parishioners as children by enjoining the curate to "have the heart
of a mother for all, tolerating patiently the pains and difficulty he will encounter in elevating them to the perfection of the Christian life."[87] Like "the good
Shepherd," the pamphlet continues, the good curate "must feed his flock."[88] Although drawn directly from Jesus's parables and meant to connote the tender-
ness and love a clergyman should feel for his parishioners, these images nonetheless
excluded the laity from the evaluative cycle that constructed priestly identity.

Beuvelet's *Conduite*, in a closing chapter on best practices for a curate, accords parishioners a small degree of reciprocity in relation to their priests by ad-
vising a new curate to implore his parishioners, in his first sermon, to pray for
him.[89] The second thing Beuvelet counsels a new curate to ask for in his first sermon, however, is "a docility of spirit in everyone, so as to make themselves more
susceptible to the teaching and advice he will give them on behalf of God, whom
they must see in his person."[90] Conceptualized as God's vehicle, the priest occupied a plane of activity separate from his parishioners, who consequently had
no legitimate grounds from which to judge the priest's success or failure in ap-
proximating clerical perfection. Only fellow priests, especially ecclesiastical
superiors—with the help of a priest's own confessions—could judge priestly performance. The ideal of ecclesiastical perfection, with its constant interplay between saintly models and inter-clerical evaluation, positioned clergymen as
performers first and foremost for each other.


## Modesty's Theatrical Construction

In order to transmit the specific gestures that constituted modesty and expressed
ecclesiastical perfection, France's early seminaries designed exercises that trained
and shaped clerical bodies. Without the seminary's walls and the strict divisions
between insiders and outsiders that seminary rules imposed, these activities

would in many cases have seemed theatrical to seventeenth-century French Catholics, in the sense of an activity set aside or raised up so as to be watched by others. Five of the ten definitions Furetière gives in his *Dictionnaire universel* for *théâtre* entail the idea of a physical space for "performing representations" or "for putting on spectacles."[91] When used "figuratively in moral contexts," Furetière's examples for the word "théâtre" suggest even more strongly the sense of being watched. "Princes must be careful of their actions," writes Furetière, "because they are on a great stage (*théâtre*) and they are very carefully observed."[92] Although seminarians were not princes, their training brought together these two early modern meanings for the word "théâtre"—that of a space for representation and that of moral surveillance—by using techniques associated with the seventeenth-century French stage. Seminarians learned modest bodily comportment through rehearsals and role-playing.

The discursive framing of these exercises made it unlikely that a secular clergyman who participated in rehearsals and role-playing as part of his seminary training would have thought to himself, "I am like an actor." Rules at both the Seminary of Saint-Nicolas du Chardonnet and the Seminary of Saint-Sulpice prohibited seminarians from attending the theater or reading plays. In addition, the diocesan Ritual issued by the archbishop of Paris in 1654 had listed actors as public sinners, and, like other public sinners, they could not join the priesthood.[93] Nonetheless, theatrical techniques such as rehearsal and role-playing created situations in which clergymen intentionally engaged in behavior that Schechner describes as "'me behaving as if I am someone else' or as if I am 'beside myself,' or 'not myself,'" introducing the doubleness that, according to performance theory, links ritual to theater.[94] In Carlson's words, "The difference between doing and performing, according to this way of thinking, would seem to lie not in the frame of theater versus real life but in an attitude—we may do actions unthinkingly, but when we think about them, this brings in a consciousness that gives them the quality of performance."[95] Seminaries, by adopting theatrical methods to teach modest gestures, leveraged the theater-ritual spectrum with the intent of making clergymen extremely aware of their behaviors while within the seminary walls so that later, when outside the seminary walls, those behaviors would contain as little of the "consciousness" of performance as possible. Theatrical performance in the seminary served to generate naturalized embodiment outside in public.

Rehearsal and role-playing embedded the idea and practice of modesty—which clergymen were to enact at all times—within the more specialized gestural repertoire that priests needed to master in order to conduct the sacraments. The exact number of early modern French seminaries that adopted rehearsal as a pedagogical method remains unknown, but by the late seventeenth century churchmen who commented on seminary education regarded the use of rehearsal as widespread. The author of a *Vie* about the bishop of Geneva, Jean d'Aranthon d'Alex (1620–1695), describes how the bishop would visit the diocesan seminary between three and four o'clock in the afternoon to watch the seminarians rehearse the sacraments. Accompanied by an entourage of other clergymen and seated in an armchair, the bishop "took pleasure in seeing his seminarians, one playing the penitent and the other the confessor, so as to judge their capacity for the ... direction of souls."[96] According to the *Vie*'s author, this sort of exercise was "customary in seminaries," especially for the sacrament of penance.[97] Consequently, within the carefully controlled hierarchy of models and judges that stretched from bishop to seminary directors to lowly clergymen, the theatricalization of liturgical training situated seminarians as performers not only in relation to a standard but also in the sense that they represented pleasing scenes for spectators.

Bourdoise and the collaborators who helped him found the Seminary of Saint-Nicolas du Chardonnet pioneered the use of rehearsals to train priests. Bourdoise's maxims suggest that admiration for the discipline demonstrated by stage players contributed to the decision to make seminarians role-play their ceremonial duties. Like his fellow Catholic reformers, Bourdoise considered appalling the early seventeenth century's variance in ceremonial customs and skills from priest to priest and parish to parish. One way that Bourdoise expressed his disgust with priests who enacted liturgical ceremonies incorrectly or sloppily was by shaming them, which he did by comparing priests to professionals whose work required public display and who had a reputation for rigorous preparation even though their performances, in Bourdoise's view, were less dignified than the ceremonies. Whether priests rehearsing their sermons, which he considered necessary but dangerous, or actors rehearsing plays, which he deemed outright sinful, Bourdoise thought clergymen who conducted liturgical ceremonies should learn from the preparation methods of performers: "A preacher would die of embarrassment if he made a noticeable mistake in a sermon. Likewise, an orator lecturing before a prince [or] an actor on stage; to this end they all study and rehearse an infinity of times, etc., in order to be accepted and succeed according to their pleasure and honor. And (what is deplorable), no one worries himself one bit during the divine office, which is recited before and in the presence of the divine Majesty, to make a hundred mistakes for lack of preparation. Is there any faith among churchmen?"[98] Here, actors figure at the bottom of a list of increasingly suspect performers. How could men whose gestures rendered service to the King of Kings care less about their ceremonial skills than even lowly public sinners like stage players?

Although the preachers Bourdoise had in mind would have been Catholic clergymen, he considered sermons inferior to the liturgy and suspected preachers of seeking fame for themselves rather than salvation for their auditors. His maxims dismiss "most of the young preachers" as unconcerned with converting sinners and advise preachers to "keep quiet" unless their actions match those of Jesus.[99] For Bourdoise, preaching belonged to the church but bordered dangerously on the more secular forms of public speech represented by the orator and the actor. According to Furetière, the orator is someone "eloquent, who knows the rules of rhetoric well and puts them into practice," in the model of Cicero or Quintilian.[100] From the perspective of someone like Bourdoise, an orator played with moral fire by stirring up strong feelings in his listeners. "The principal objective of the orator," writes Furetière, "is to know how to excite the passions."[101] Within the Augustinian framework that infused France's early seminaries and characterized most antitheatrical discourses, activities that excited the passions led to sin. Pierre Nicole (1625–1695) and, later, Jacques-Bénigne Bossuet (1627–1704) rejected the theater as morally hazardous by arguing that actors incited passions in themselves, which they transmitted to the spectators, making stage plays "a school and an exercise in vice."[102] In Bourdoise's maxim, preachers, orators, and actors not surprisingly signify increasingly disparaging, because increasingly sin-prone, comparisons for priestly performance.

Yet, by associating preachers, actors, and orators along a spectrum, Bourdoise's maxim not only brings preachers down but also raises stage players up in terms of the esteem they deserved, at least in terms of their preparation. The maxim gave its hearers cause to consider entertainers as an example of the type of practice required to produce a "perfect" churchman able to embody modesty and execute liturgical ceremonies with a grace and skill that appeared natural.

Seminarians who studied at Saint-Nicolas du Chardonnet heard Bourdoise's maxims on a regular basis. His positioning of the actor as a model for priestly preparation thus had currency in seminary circles. Bourdoise's maxims figured among the books on the rotation of devotional texts read aloud during meals in the refectory, as well as on a much shorter list of books about ecclesiastical discipline that provided the material for a short reading every evening.[103] In addition, at least five editions appeared between 1660 and 1833, pointing toward a readership beyond the seminary's walls.[104] Nor was Bourdoise the only counterreformer of his generation to hold actors up as models for priestly performance.

Vincent de Paul, in a letter penned to one of his missionaries in 1638, pointed to changes in stage declamation in his attempt to convince the churchman to preach using a "common and familiar tone." "Would you believe, Sir," he writes of the efficacy of a natural voice, "that actors, having recognized this, have changed their way of speaking and no longer recite their verses with an elevated tone, as they used to, but with a medium voice and as if speaking familiarly?"[105] He concludes that preachers should do likewise.[106] Although often perceived by clergymen as rivals, the seventeenth century's best actors simultaneously represented a standard for excellence.

Bourdoise's spiritual biographies give few clues as to where he would have acquired his ideas about rehearsal. In comparison to terms like *bienséance* or *vraisemblance*, rehearsal received little attention in the seventeenth century's theater debates.[107] The register maintained by the orator of Molière's troupe, for example, contains only eighteen instances of words that refer to rehearsal—the term "repetition" recurs thirteen times, and the term "preparation" appears five times—in a manuscript that covers thirty years of the troupe's performance activity.[108] Nor did Bourdoise attend a Jesuit school where he might have performed plays as part of his education.[109] Rather, it seems likely that his affiliation with the lower legions of the legal profession, in addition to a three-month period spent as a lackey in Paris, would have acquainted Bourdoise with amateur theater performances and, by extension, the care with which actors prepared. Before the Wars of Religion, law clerks in France had a tradition of performing farces during civic rituals, such as royal entries and during Carnival.[110] Although many cities suppressed such performance after the wars, in Paris clerks who belonged to festive societies like the Basoche continued putting on plays into the 1580s.[111] Bourdoise's father, although not in Paris, belonged to this world. He worked as a lower magistrate, notary, and solicitor at the local court in the small town of Brou until his death, when Bourdoise was seven.[112] Bourdoise subsequently followed his father into the legal profession from 1596 to 1605, on his way to the priesthood, working as a clerk for the court solicitors in the towns of Brou and Illiers before moving to Paris.[113] Although the Basoche had stopped performing plays by the time Bourdoise reached Paris in the early 1600s, they owned one of the stage boxes at the Hôtel de Bourgogne and enjoyed the right until 1640 to parade from the Parlement de Paris to the theater during Carnival.[114] In Paris, Bourdoise also worked briefly as a lackey for a family in which the lady of the house loved to attend the theater.[115] His responsibilities sometimes required him to follow her to the Foire Saint-Germain or the Hôtel de Bourgogne and wait at the entrance. Bourdoise's fellow lackeys belonged to a demographic that loved attending shows from the theater pit.[116] Although the evidence allows for nothing more than speculation, Bourdoise's familiarity with clerks could have exposed him to stories of the plays that members of the legal profession had performed during his father's lifetime, while the appreciation his masters and fellow lackeys expressed for plays in Paris could have alerted Bourdoise to the power a well-rehearsed performance could exert over its audience.

Whatever the source of Bourdoise's attention to rehearsal, he grasped that a priest's ceremonial objectives required the same kind of learning necessary for stage playing. The priestly formation provided at the Seminary of Saint-Nicolas du Chardonnet reflected this awareness. Training activities characterized by a theatrical quality took place before a range of audiences. Although most practice sessions took place within the privacy of the seminary—like the rehearsals attended by the bishop of Geneva—the seminarians rehearsed eucharistic ceremonies publicly in the parish church once a week at five o'clock in the evening.[117] This weekly rehearsal, led by the *maître des cérémonies*—the priest responsible for ensuring the liturgy's smooth functioning—focused on the officers whose ceremonial responsibilities during Mass brought them into closest contact with the altar, namely, the celebrant, who consecrated the bread, the deacon and subdeacon, who read scripture and stood near the celebrant, and the acolytes, thurifers, and *cérémoniaires*, who held candles, carried incense, and led processions.[118] Periodically, the seminary also held a public rehearsal in which seminarians practiced general liturgical ceremonies, like how to help another priest put on his sacramental robes, how to walk in procession, or how to enter and exit the chancel.[119] Although the seminary's surviving rules do not specify the laity's involvement in such rehearsals, documents like the *Almanach spirituel* indicate a high probability that parishioners were present. Many of the rites and sacraments offered by the parish of Saint-Nicolas du Chardonnet, like the exposition of the Blessed Sacrament on Thursdays or the first Communion ceremony for children during Easter, took place at the five o'clock hour or shortly before it, making it likely that parishioners saw seminarians practice.[120] Men, women, and children from the parish would have been free to stop and watch, whether out of idle curiosity or pious interest.

Rehearsals at the church would have amplified the correlation between priestcraft and stagecraft implied by Bourdoise's maxim, underscoring simultaneously the churchman's responsibility to keep up a standard of achievement and

the degree to which in doing so he displayed his skill. The maître des cérémonies, whose objective was "to make everyone notice everything special" about the
ceremonies being rehearsed, conveyed the required standard of achievement.[121]
Feedback with instructions about how to improve followed each rehearsal, and
seminarians could not perform a ceremonial function until they had first rehearsed it in front of their superiors "and been judged capable."[122] The evaluations meted out by seminary instructors made the importance of conforming to
a standard explicit. Public rehearsals also figured liturgical action as a skill enacted before spectators. Seminary instructors formed an explicit audience, intent
on scrutinizing the seminarians' ceremonial abilities. As Carlson notes, the quality that "makes the performing arts performative" is that "these arts require the
physical presence of trained or skilled human beings whose demonstration of
their skill is the performance."[123] Even if parishioners were not always paying
close attention to rehearsals and were not authorized to judge clerical perfection,
their presence underscored the idea that ceremonial conduct involved a presentation of self in front of spectators. The artfulness of liturgical ceremonies thus
came to the fore through public rehearsal.

Despite the way the way rehearsals in the public space of the church constructed the clergyman as a performer who displayed his skills in keeping with a
standard, they largely avoided the implication that priests played roles in the way
that actors played parts. Private rehearsals, however, held in the seminary's *salle
des exercices*, or classroom, taught clergymen the sacraments using role-playing.
During these sessions, the distinctions between priest and *comédien*, prop and
ceremonial object, sacrament and play were more difficult to maintain. A mise-
en-scène created by the instructor transformed the classroom into a sacramental
scene in which seminarians represented the form and content of a sacrament
without actually accomplishing a sacramental action. The instructor's règlement
included a long list of objects needed for each sacramental rehearsal and outlined
his responsibility for gathering and preparing them before each exercise.[124] The
list for the baptism rehearsal blends theater and sacrament most thoroughly. La-
beled "Mémoire de ce qu'il faut preparer pour le sacrement de baptesme"
(Memo of that which it is necessary to prepare for the sacrament of baptism), its
title treats the rehearsal as a sacrament proper.[125] The list itself, however, mixes
props with ceremonial objects. A doll tops the list, which also includes "a
cushion to put under the infant's head."[126] Ceremonial objects follow. The list
calls for, among other things, two candles, an asperser, and a white stole.[127] Some
of these objects, though, would have probably been simulacra, like "the vessel of
holy oils" and the "book or Register of baptisms" included in the list.[128] Surely

seminarians did not practice baptism with consecrated oil from the sacristy, since to apply it to a doll would have bordered on idolatry. Likewise, it is unlikely that they practiced recording imaginary baptisms in the parish register. The list includes "a desk garnished with pens," which implies that seminarians did indeed practice writing the details of the playacted baptism, but probably in a book regularly used for rehearsals.[129]

The sacramental scene created for the rehearsal entailed not just props but also acting, in the sense of pretending to be a person one is not. To anoint a doll or write in the book that represented the baptismal register, seminarians had to step into an identity they did not yet possess, one that corresponded roughly to that of a rural curate or vicar.[130] The props listed for each exercise as well as the instructions given in the règlement regarding the distribution of parts thus suggest that seminary rehearsals did construct "priest" as a role to play. Although the règlement avoids explicitly theatrical language like *personnage*, or character, in some cases seminarians performed from a text that functioned like a script. When Jean d'Aranthon d'Alex, the bishop of Geneva, attended sacramental rehearsals at his diocesan seminary, for example, he often composed at least one half of a confession scene for the seminarians to perform. The author of his *Vie* writes, "He even took the time to give a confession in writing to he who played the penitent so as to discern in this way the mind and judgment of he who played the confessor."[131] By pairing a scripted performance with an improvised one, the bishop could better evaluate each player's pastoral capacities.

Further heightening the similarity between ceremonial rehearsal and playing a dramatic role, the seminarians selected for the honor of stepping into the identity of parish priest played the lead in a small cast. From among those not slotted to act as the priest, the instructor selected seminarians to represent the lay people who received the sacraments. These students played roles like godfather, godmother, sick person, or, as in the example above, penitent.[132] It does not take too much imagination to conjure up the potential for hilarity and irreverence that such playacting could invite. The règlement recognized that rehearsing the sacraments opened the door for comedy. It charged the instructor with choosing seminarians who were the least likely to have too much fun, stating he should designate "the most modest and serious" members of the group.[133] Anyone who fooled around by talking or laughing, he "warn[ed] gently and warmly but strongly to keep the prescribed order."[134] The behaviors chastised by the règlement imply that new seminarians readily treated ceremonial rehearsal like schoolboys or amateurs, playing and merry-making.

If seminarians took the actor's craft lightly when they first heard Bourdoise's maxim, rehearsal introduced them to the work required of performers. An instructor who succeeded in inspiring the seminarians in his charge to hold "in esteem and luster . . . the holy administration of the sacraments," as the règlement demanded, did so by teaching them to rehearse like professionals.[135] He directed rehearsals with diligence, ensuring the class could get through two sacramental scenes each time it met, he prevented interruptions, and he demanded precision.[136] The instructor's mandate declared, "He will make the exercise begin with the most decorum possible and will work to make sure every necessary detail in the enactment of each sacrament is observed exactly and entirely . . . right down to every sign of the cross ordered by the Ritual."[137] The inner dispositions required for good liturgical action received attention, too. Before rehearsing the ceremonies, seminarians had to name the spiritual states and devotional acts they were supposed to bring to and produce during each sacrament.[138] That is to say, although seminary rehearsals were representations and explicitly framed as artificial or as pretend, seminary rules treated their theatricality as capable of producing real effects. Seminary directors maintained that even ceremonial exercises, when conducted "exactly and religiously," "produce a very great piety in the heart of the faithful when they see them observed with honor and deference."[139] The seriousness with which seminary directors treated ceremonial rehearsal can therefore shed light on the serious attitude they adopted toward the theater. Laurent Thirouin has noted that "the enemies of the theater are those who believe the most in its power."[140] Rehearsals like those conducted at Saint-Nicolas du Chardonnet would have instilled an appreciation for the comédien's performance and alerted churchmen to stage playing's plenitude.

Seminary rehearsals also precipitated a convergence of priestly and theatrical styles of embodiment. The modest comportment that clergymen learned to master through rehearsal corresponded to the gestural conventions that, according to theater scholar Sabine Chaouche, early modern actors had to master in order to portray characters of high rank.[141] Like actors and orators, whose craft, in the words of a seventeenth-century rhetoric manual, required a "beautiful rhetoric of the body," early modern priests needed to attain what Chaouche calls "bodily eloquence."[142] To do so, they had to learn to régler—organize, regulate, control—their bodies. Seminary directors, like the theater theorists of the day, referred to this conventional physicality as bienséante, or "decorous," and worked hard to ensure that seminarians "maintain[ed] at all times" a correspondingly "respectful, modest and pious posture."[143] Similarly, François Hédelin (1604–1676), better known as the abbé d'Aubignac, author of a seventeenth-century treatise on theater practice, urged playwrights not to compose scenes that would cause their actors to "sin against decorum," or *la bienséance*.[144] Neither the young men who attended the Seminary of Saint-Nicolas du Chardonnet—many of whom came from poor families—nor the members of Paris's theater troupes belonged to social strata known for bodily decorum. Seminary-trained parish priests and tragic actors consequently converged in their status as royal subjects from bourgeois backgrounds who attained the marks of decorum through forms of labor, like rehearsal, not attributed to birth and family, and who did so to undertake a kind of work that involved public display in contexts the nobility deemed detrimental to rank.

In seventeenth-century France, the ideal of *l'honnête homme*, or the perfect gentleman, structured the standards by which worshippers and spectators judged whether priestly and theatrical comportment counted as bienséant or not. The honnête homme possessed a body that could please at court and that also signified virtue and dignity.[145] As Maurice Magendie has shown, the term "honnêteté" had two overlapping meanings, an aristocratic sense associated with worldly savoir-faire, and a bourgeois meaning associated with moral uprightness.[146] These two versions of the perfect gentleman did not perfectly coincide. Ecclesiastical proponents of a moral honnêteté in fact used the perfect gentleman's virtuous qualities as a weapon in their attack on aristocratic lifestyles, pitting the bourgeois ideal of l'honnête homme against its courtly counterpart. If, as Paul Bénichou argues, the tragic heroes staged by Pierre Corneille epitomized the heroic ideals that inspired the aristocratic honnête homme, the figure of the seminarian easily epitomized the perfect gentleman's moral aspect.[147] Nonetheless, these two versions of honnêteté shared, as André Lévêque points out, a number of *lieux communs*, "subjects about which all the theorists of the seventeenth-century [were] in agreement, regardless of their moral values," whether heroic or religious.[148] Standards for bodily decorum fell into this zone of agreement between the aristocratic honnête homme and the bourgeois perfect gentleman, between the Cornelian hero and the parish priest.

Bodily decorum demanded a combination of stillness and coded expression. Chaouche details the gestural conventions that composed decorous comportment. "The head must . . . at all times keep its natural position, which is to say straight" but "without being stiff."[149] In relation to the perfect gentleman's "naturally" upright head, a lowered head signaled humility, but a head held too high denoted pride, a head that lagged to the side lethargy, and an immobile head brutality.[150] As for the eyes, bienséance called for a gaze that achieved control without staring and without contorting the face. "Defaults of the eye, like sideways glances, fixed stares, or a gaze made too small by squinting, lascivious glances or unduly mobile eyes . . . confer upon the orator a ridiculous air, and make him the laughing stock of the public," writes Chaouche.[151] A gentleman did not twist his mouth or leave it half open, show his teeth, or lick, bite, or seal his lips.[152] Nor did he walk too fast, stomp or shake his feet, spread his legs, sway from side to side, gesticulate wildly with his hands, rub his face, spit, blow his nose, beat his chest, shrug his shoulders, clap or play with his hands, or slap his thighs.[153] In other words, he moderated his gestures, kept the inside of his body hidden—the interior of the mouth, sounds from the inner cavities—and limited the contact between parts of his body.

‘Seminary directors, as we have already seen, called this combination of moderated movement and coded expression "modesty." A manuscript entitled "Modesty Required of Churchmen" from the second half of the seventeenth century specified that clerical modesty consisted in precisely the kinds of gestures outlined by Chaouche: "outer composure, carriage, posture, gestures, eyes, gait, a grave rather than loose bearing, eyes that are wise and friendly, a way of walking that is neither affected nor hurried."[154] Priestly rehearsals transmitted modesty by teaching seminarians to suppress behaviors that would seem *malséants*—undignified and nondecorous—to observers. A règlement regarding "the modesty, respect, and reverence that one must observe during the divine office" instructed seminarians, "The first thing is when you are seated to be careful not to lean indecently, or cross your legs, or let your eyes wander here and there, nor put your hands in your pockets, but to observe a modest and honest composition, principally of the head and the eyes."[155] As the word "composition" reveals, maintaining a modest body in accordance with the norms for honnêteté and bienséance required artfulness. Like the courtier's manners or the actor's rendering of a prince, the clergyman's decorum demanded grace and could be destroyed by farcical humor. The règlement for the divine office warned seminarians "to take care not to stare fixedly at each other for fear of making each other laugh or some other levity."[156] By suppressing gestural habits associated with the peasant's life, with biological survival, and with the ludic or violent dimensions of human experience, seminary rehearsals crafted the foundations for a noble bearing. Through repetition, encouragement, and reprimand a seminarian learned to make no sound not required by ceremonies, keep his eyes—but not his head— "modestly lowered," place his feet side by side, ensure that his robe covered his knees when he sat and hung to his feet without any openings, hold his body straight, and carry his hat or breviary with both hands in front of his chest.[157] Seminary rehearsals thus endowed clergymen with a style of comportment fit for court, akin to the physical canvas out of which an actor crafted princes and kings.

## Conclusion: Gestural Continuity from Altar to Street

Modesty enrobed the body. It accomplished for a clergyman's gestural presence what the soutane accomplished for his flesh, covering him from head to toe so that no reflexive movement, no old habits that smacked of life in the village or on the farm might distract from or disrupt his clerical identity. Ritual theorist Ronald Grimes would describe modesty as ritualized behavior, the "repetitious bodily stylization that constitutes the baseline of quotidian human interaction" without being "culturally framed as ritual."[158] Seminarians, and by extension secular clergymen, were to enact modest gestures always and everywhere, not just during liturgical ceremonies. Modesty on its own was not set apart as a rite in the way the Eucharist was. Yet modest gestures provided the foundation for liturgical ceremonies by endowing churchmen with a demeanor appropriate for courtly settings. Prescriptions detailed the "proper way" to enact modesty and repetition inscribed modest gestures into the self and the community, while discourses about modesty elaborated its theological meaning by claiming that modesty originated with Jesus Christ, associating modesty with "sacredly held values" such as salvation and perfection, and attributing to modesty the "special power" to convert those who witnessed it.[159] According to Grimes's schema for ritual analysis, all these actions enhance the degree of ritualization of an activity.[160] Seminary training, by teaching clergymen to make modest gestures second nature, ritualized the everyday comportment of France's secular priests.

The ritualization of the secular clergy's everyday behavior accomplished a range of Counter-Reformation goals. As the gestural norms for modest comportment gained currency among secular clergymen, these norms, like wearing the soutane, helped to make the secular clergy visible as a professional group. Meanwhile, at the individual level, modesty made the boundaries of priestly performance more difficult to see by connecting clearly framed events, such as the administration of a sacrament, to the behaviors leading up to and following it. Gesturally, the ceremonies that were set apart as sacred blended into the modest comportment a priest was to observe at all times. This gestural blending, or continuity of gestural style in sacramental and non-sacramental settings, reinforced clerical authority by constructing a priest's daily habitual activities as liturgical. When a priest's manner of walking down the street, climbing the stairs, eating, and conversing seemed of a piece with his manner of sitting in the chancel or elevating the consecrated host, it became much more difficult to accuse him of hypocrisy or compare him to an actor. The perfect churchman's performance did not seem like a performance at all.

# CHAPTER 3

# Ceremonies

Modest priestly bodies like those that France's Counter-Reformation seminaries sought to foster served a larger purpose. Beyond making the secular clergy—or clergymen not in religious orders—visible as a professional group and creating gestural continuity between a priest's comportment at the altar and his pastoral responsibilities within the parish, the norms for bodily decorum taught in seminaries served to elevate the Mass by making it more beautiful, more kingly, and more reverent in its treatment of the consecrated Eucharist at its center. The metaphors used by seminary founders to explain the importance of liturgical ceremonies reveal the close correspondence between modest comportment and Counter-Reformation ideas about the Mass. In the same way that seminary manuals imagine modest gestures as a type of preaching, Jean-Jacques Olier urged students at the Seminary of Saint-Sulpice to think of the ceremonies of the Mass as "preaching for the eyes."[1] Ceremonies "hold the people in respect and reverence," Olier explained, and "are all the more effective when they are more perceptible."[2] His emphasis on the liturgy as something that the faithful should see and not just hear reflected a shift in Catholic worship away from the auditory toward the visual, as well as a call for priests to acquire a specialized set of bodily skills so that the clergy's collective action might "preach" during the sacraments. Whereas the metaphor of preaching for an individual clergyman's bodily comportment was meant to promote self-discipline and personal incorporation of clerical norms, Olier's analogy of liturgical ceremonies as preaching for the eyes pointed toward an additional skill that clergymen needed to master, the skill of coordinated action shared by multiple agents. Although he devotes most of his attention to the celebrant's gestures, by attributing agency to the ceremonies as a whole, Olier suggests that all the clergymen involved in Mass must contribute

together with equal skill to the liturgy so that Mass might "speak" effectively to
its witnesses.

The secular clergy's priestly identity, imagined through its relation to an ideal
of ecclesiastical perfection and expressed through modesty, found its fulfillment
in the performance of Mass. Seminary handbooks and pamphlets presented ceremonial competence as one of a priest's greatest responsibilities and one of the
chief ends of seminary training. Catholic reformers figured seminary training
as a "public treasure" whose value stemmed from its ability to equip churchmen
for liturgical excellence: "It regulates the churchman and prepares him for holy
orders," declared the dedicatory letter to a posthumous compilation of seminary
lessons by Claude de la Croix, "it teaches him to administer the sacraments with
reverence and it trains him to serve with dignity during the majestic ceremonies
of the church."[3] One of the pamphlets asserts that second only to a curate's duties to join himself to God through prayer and zealously seek God's glory in all
his work, a priest's obligation to conform to post-Tridentine liturgical standards
and conduct ceremonies on time and with precision ranked high among his responsibilities.[4] The pamphlet from 1657 entitled *Les Principaux devoirs d'un bon
curé* (The principal duties of a good parish priest) classified ceremonial duties as
central to a parish priest's obligations toward God, toward his parishioners, and
toward his physical church building. "He must have great devotion toward Our
Lord Jesus Christ in the holy Eucharist," the pamphlet instructs, before specifying a series of essential practices and standards for their completion.[5] In addition to ensuring that his parishioners provide a tabernacle or ciborium of precious
metal in which to preserve the consecrated Eucharist in the middle of the main
altar and an ever-burning candle to attend it, the good parish priest was supposed
to conduct the ceremonies of the Mass as flawlessly as possible: "He must administer the sacraments with dignity and great devotion, scrupulously carrying out
all the instructions and ceremonies contained in his diocese's handbook," directed the pamphlet. "He must say the divine office and celebrate the holy mass
with the greatest possible preparation, attention, and devotion, observing exactly
the instructions in his diocese's breviary and missal and the scheduled hours for
his prayers, as much as possible."[6] All of a seminary's efforts, from the regula-
tion of vestiary norms and bodily comportment to the training it offered in
prayer and doctrine, culminated in well-executed Masses.

Beauty alone did not define the well-executed Mass. In seventeenth-century
liturgical parlance, when conducted properly the ceremonies of the Mass generated *éclat*. Best translated as splendor or bedazzlement, éclat designated the
impression made by certain kinds of surprising, marvelous, or awe-inspiring

spectacles. Churchmen valued éclat—or, as I often call it in these pages, ceremonial splendor—because it gave material expression to the doctrine of divine presence, the theological idea that the eucharistic wafer becomes Christ's body upon consecration. Éclat's production, as French seminarians learned, was a central objective of liturgical ceremonies. According to the Council of Trent's decree on the sacrament of the Eucharist, issued in 1551, upon witnessing a consecrated host displayed in procession or in public places the church's adversaries should, "at the sight of so much splendor," either "pine away weakened and broken; or, touched with shame and confounded, at length repent."[7] Éclat, the decree implicitly proposed, forged a reliable link between seeing and believing.

Ceremonial splendor depended for its production on a combination of visibly striking material objects, such as candles and precious metals that would capture one's attention even if one did not understand their meaning, and on an enormous pedagogical effort on the part of the Catholic Church to train clergymen and lay people not only what to do but also how to interpret what they saw at Mass. In theoretical terms, éclat offers an example of the type of phenomenon Hal Foster identifies with visuality. Foster defines visuality as the "social fact" of seeing, which exists in a dynamic tension with vision, or "sight as a physical operation."[8] Whereas the "mechanism of sight" affords us "the datum of vision," Foster explains, visuality results from the "historical techniques" and "discursive determinations" that produce variations "among how we see, how we are able, allowed, or made to see, and how we see this seeing in the unseen therein."[9] Éclat thus arose conjointly from the ceremonial skill with which clergymen conducted the liturgy, the sensory input registered by early modern French eyes, and the interpretive frameworks Catholics learned from catechisms, sermons, devotional literature, sacramental participation, and life in a Catholic culture.

Éclat has significant ramifications for an analysis of priestly performance in early modern France, for it changes the boundaries of the agent carrying out the performance. In the context of the Mass, the celebrant—or priest who consecrated the Eucharist—constituted the nucleus of a corporate ritual agent composed of the entire congregation. Definitions given to the term "performance" in performance theory capture part of what a priest needed to do during Mass and account for some of the dynamics that liturgical enactment entailed but miss the overarching principals that gave coherence to liturgical action. As already demonstrated in Chapter 2, an individual clergyman's bodily discipline required him to master a type of patterned behavior and carry it out in accordance with a standard. These activities correspond to two of the definitional clusters Marvin Carlson delineates for the term "performance," that of performance as an action that entails repetition or doubling, hence involving a pattern, and performance as "the general success of [an] activity in light of some standard of achievement."[10] In seminary rehearsals and even more necessarily in the enactment of the Mass, a clergyman displayed his ceremonial skills, the display of skill corresponding to a third definitional cluster identified by Carlson. Priestly performance in its execution of éclat, however, departs from traditional definitions of performance at its margins. Whereas the act of framing or setting an activity apart from everyday life organizes most definitions of performance, éclat resulted from ceremonial overflow. Thanks to the constituent gestural repertoires on which it depended, such as modesty, a celebrant's ceremonial enactment had no hard boundary, no proscenium. In priestly performance the performer extended beyond the self. A priest, if he were to embody the ideal of the vray ecclésiastique, or true churchman, had to think and act as a node in an entity greater than himself. In the context of liturgical action, his movements gave rise to a ceremonial body that encompassed all the other bodies and objects whose movements were cued to those of the priest.

## The Theological Status of Ceremonies

Ceremonial action had an inherently social orientation and corporate structure such that a priest who conducted ceremonies did not act by himself or on his own behalf, even if he were alone. At the conceptual level, ceremonies occupied a central place in the larger concept of religion for seventeenth-century French speakers. The term "ceremonies" denoted repeated gestures like bowing and kneeling, actions that constituted religion's smallest but most essential building blocks. Antoine Furetière's *Dictionnaire universel* defined "Religion" as "cult of the true God, exterior ceremonies by means of which one testifies that one adores [God] with all one's heart."[11] Given the centrality of ceremonies to the concept of religion for early modern Catholics, an array of other terms that post-Enlightenment, post–French Revolution readers might no longer recognize as ceremonial in connotation would have been impossible to think, speak, or write without designating ceremonies. Terms for worship, like *culte*, designated the ensemble of orthodox bodily practices directed toward God. "Sacrament" referred to ceremonial actions by means of which God did something for, or extended grace to, humans. "Sacrifice" evoked actions done by humans for God. "Service" and "duty" in the context of religion expressed the idea that humans had an obligation to render ceremonies unto God. Even words that encompassed a strong spiritual or emotional aspect, like adoration, surrender, supplication, veneration, and respect, all retained a profoundly physical, ceremonial meaning. Religion and ceremonies were synonymous to such a degree that men and women who sought to talk and write about the work done by the mind, will, soul, spirit, or imagination during worship used the qualifier "interior" to designate such activities, differentiating *exercises intérieurs*, or "inner exercises," from the *exercises extérieurs*, or "outer exercises," that formed the substance of religious action. The emphasis that France's early modern seminaries placed on ceremonial training and skill reflected an understanding of "Religion"—often capitalized in seminary texts—as primarily a mode of action rather than a set of doctrines.

Protestant critiques of and challenges to Catholic worship infused seminary founders and directors with a sense of urgency in their task of equipping secular clergymen to skillfully conduct liturgical ceremonies.[12] Pamphlets against the Catholic Mass had long dismissed liturgical ceremonies as idolatrous and compared the priest's ornaments, vestments, and coded sacramental action to the role-playing, dancing, and stage antics of farcical actors.[13] For Catholics, these critiques of the Mass as satanically derived, idolatrous farce appeared "inherently seditious" and threatened the heart of the faith as well as the social order.[14] Liturgically, Protestant attacks on the Mass precipitated among Catholic reformers an effort to enhance the Mass's dignity and splendor and to ensure that the clergymen who enacted its ceremonies knew how to do so with skill. Ceremonial creativity and elaboration among Catholic reformers constituted a performance response to Protestant theologies. In contrast to Protestantism with its emphasis on faith and scripture, ceremonies not only defined and distinguished Catholic worship. They also constituted a polemical medium in their own right. During the sixteenth and seventeenth centuries, an array of new practices aimed at glorifying the sacrament of the Eucharist afforded Catholics a way to promote their central doctrines through ceremonies. Infused with an "apologetic logic," practices like Corpus Christi celebrations, the adoration of the consecrated host, or Blessed Sacrament, and the devotion of Forty Hours, in which churches organized three continuous days of adoration before the exposed Eucharist, provided a liturgical response to Protestant critiques of the Catholic faith.[15] In particular, Protestants rejected the doctrine of transubstantiation, the Catholic belief that during Mass "the Eucharistic bread and wine become the body and blood of Christ and are bread and wine no longer."[16] In rejecting Christ's real presence in the Eucharist, Protestant thinkers like Calvin and Zwingli mounted what were "ultimately frontal attacks on the traditional style of liturgical celebration as such."[17] These attacks demanded not only

a theological rebuttal but also a liturgical one. Alongside the spiritual suste-
nance that devout Catholics drew from liturgical ceremonies, ceremonial reform therefore also served polemical functions ranging from the evangelization
of heretics to the demonstration of Christ's presence.

Ceremonies thus enacted the post-Tridentine church's sacramental theology.
According to this theology, ceremonies were not a human creation but rather a
divine text expressed through the priest's human body.[18] Seminarians learned to
think of God as their author. The *Manuel des cérémonies romaines*, a liturgical
handbook by Vincent de Paul's Congregation of the Mission, figures ceremonies
as divinely created by opening with a letter addressed to "Our Lord Jesus Christ,
sovereign priest and author of the ceremonies."[19] Similarly, Mathieu Beuvelet advised clergymen at the Seminary of Saint-Nicolas du Chardonnet to undertake
each sacrament "adoring, in the moment, Our Lord as the Author of the sacrament that you are going to administer."[20] In designating ceremonies as divinely
created, both of these seminary texts expressed a theological principle commonly
found in the introductory chapter of seventeenth-century French diocesan Rituals, the liturgical handbooks issued by a bishop that contained instructions for
administering the seven sacraments. Like the Rituals of Bourges and Reims, diocesan handbooks declared it "a constant truth" that "the sacraments were instituted by Jesus Christ."[21] From this perspective, a priest who conducted
liturgical ceremonies engaged in an action that did not belong to him. His body
gave form to that which God had written.

Theologically, ceremonies facilitated salvation. In Beuvelet's words, ceremonies "accompany" the Christian "mysteries," or sacraments, which Beuvelet
considered "the most precious jewels" with which Christ endowed the Catholic
Church.[22] Sacraments mediated a Christian's relationship to the divine. Beuvelet writes, "There is nothing as important in the Church as the sacraments, which
contain the birth, the growth, the healing, the sanctification, the conservation,
and the perseverance of the Christian . . . and which have as their aim to unite
us to God and make us participants in the divine nature."[23] The esteem accorded
to ceremonies, as Beuvelet explained, derived from their antiquity, their meaning, and their function in relation to the sacraments. Ceremonies served "as the
extremely perfect visible marks and exterior acts of the religion we profess, and
the most proper and proportionate means to bring the people to an understanding of the adorable secrets hidden under these symbols," meaning the sacraments.[24] In more technical terms, the sacraments constituted "visible signs of
invisible grace," while ceremonies made up the matter—as opposed to the ver-
bal form—of the sacrament.[25] Thus, although ceremonies were not synonymous

with the sacraments, the church could not conduct the sacraments without ceremonies.

In addition to uniting humans to God, seminary founders and the bishops with whom they collaborated understood ceremonies as a means to maintain and make visible the hierarchical relations upon which the church's institutional structure, and the social order more broadly, depended. Olier, in his treatise on the Mass, wrote that "ceremonies are, in the Church, organs and instruments of respect."[26] Beuvelet agreed and taught in his *Instruction sur le manuel* (Guide to the diocesan Ritual) that priests must follow the prescribed ceremonies with precision "so that the dignity of our mysteries might be known and respected by the faithful who receive them, since there is nothing that renders our sacraments more noble and more worthy of veneration than our ceremonies when done well."[27] Ceremonies directed respect toward the sacraments. In doing so, ceremonies pointed worshippers toward God, who formed the primary object of the respect generated by ceremonies. Olier argued, "We see by experience the respect that these things [ceremonies] imprint in the minds of the poorest and most ignorant who . . . dispose themselves more readily to their duty and to the reverence they owe to God by means of these exterior and perceptible things."[28] Ceremonies secured God at the top of the hierarchy.

Ceremony's coded gestures, however, did more than incite parishioners to physically demonstrate their respect for the divine. The movements that manifested respect, such as genuflections, prostrations, and rules about when and where specific types of ritual participants could enter, exit, sit, stand, or hold certain objects, embedded those participants in a chain of interdependent authority descending from God all the way down to the newly baptized infant. Different segments of this interlocking chain came into view, depending on the sacrament or divine office celebrated. Catholic rites of passage at the beginning and end of life—baptism and extreme unction—displayed, for example, an individual's relation to the Christian community. Baptism situated children as protected by, and also subject to, the authority of their parents, godparents, and the church, while extreme unction prepared the believer to pass from the worldly order into the celestial realm, also conceived in hierarchical terms.[29] Similarly, ordination ushered a man into the clergy while simultaneously submitting him to his bishop, and confession reiterated an individual's "state" or place in the social order. A Catholic's participation in liturgical ceremonies manifested and regulated each individual's location in the social body.

A type of liturgical handbook called the Ceremonial reveals the vectors of respect created by ceremonies. Unlike the Missal or a diocesan Ritual, a

Ceremonial did not contain the words a clergyman should say during a sacrament or rite.[30] Nor did priests actually carry the Ceremonial during the sacraments, in the way they carried the Missal and the Ritual.[31] Rather, Ceremonials
were "designed as guides to the different liturgical actors" with the goal of "enabling the harmonious accomplishment of divine services."[32] Jean-Yves Hameline compares Ceremonials to stage directions and underscores their pedagogical
function.[33] In the parish of Saint-Nicolas du Chardonnet, home to the seminary
of the same name, the maître des cérémonies, or master of ceremonies, possessed a
manuscript of more than four hundred pages containing excerpts from the Parisian Ceremonial, translated into French.[34] Its table of contents displays the layers of authority manifested through ceremonies by listing the offices, or roles, of
the Mass in order of importance from those participants closest to the consecrated Eucharist to those farthest from it, an order likewise reflected in the progression of holy orders through which a clergyman passed as he moved up the
ranks from tonsured cleric to ordained priest. From the celebrant, who held the
eucharistic host in his hands, to the porter, who opened and closed the doors,
the Ceremonial specifies the movements they needed to enact in relation to
other ritual participants. Every movement required attention to one's own status in relation to the status of others. In reference to the chancel, for example,
the register advises, "Those who have a place in the high seats must be careful to
never pass in front of someone with a more honorable seat."[35] Dozens of other
ceremonial instructions for specific situations in which rank needed to be made
visible follow. After incensing the altar the celebrant had to extend his hand to
the deacon for a kiss, but only if the celebrant was the curate or a dignitary and
only in the context of a solemn Mass.[36] If a priest assisted the celebrant during
Mass, the deacon had to stand to the left of the priest and conduct his ceremonies after the *prêtre assistant,* signaling the priest's higher rank.[37] When the
curate or other high-ranking churchmen entered the chancel, the choir master
had to bow to him.[38] By manifesting social relationships, ceremonies inserted
individual ritual participants into a larger body.

   Given the status of ceremonies as a public good—a "treasure of the
Church"—a clergyman's liturgical action entailed more than just his own body.[39]
It entailed the process of making visible the social order as a representation of
Christ's body. Seminary directors consequently believed that liturgical mistakes
had grave consequences. Beuvelet warned, "All mistakes in this matter, whether
they are principally by ignorance or negligence, are never small, but all important."[40] Mistakes in matters of ceremony, Beuvelet continued, robbed Christ, their
founder, of that which he willed, showed contempt for the church's ordinances,

deprived the faithful of that which belonged to them, and rendered ministers guilty rather than bringing them grace.[41] Theologically, therefore, a priest's ceremonial performance extended beyond the boundaries of his individual self with his movements, in coordination with the movements of his fellow clergymen, manifesting the invisible grace contained in the sacraments as well as Christ's continued presence on earth through his church.

## Ceremonial Splendor

In the context of Counter-Reformation religious tensions, liturgical ceremonies served a crucial function in reinforcing the Catholic doctrine of transubstantiation, which held that the consecrated bread became Jesus Christ's body during the sacrament of the Eucharist. The Council of Trent asserted that "a conversion is made of the whole substance of the bread into the substance of the body of Christ" when the celebrant held the wafer and pronounced the words Jesus had spoken to his disciples while breaking bread with them at the Last Supper: "Take, and eat of it, all of you. For this is my body."[42] Based on the idea of Christ's presence in the eucharistic wafer, theological declarations attributed éclat to the consecrated host and identified this splendor as a cause for orthodox belief, as the Council of Trent did in its conviction, cited above, that anyone who saw the Eucharist would repent. An analysis of the way ceremonies helped generate the visual experience of éclat reveals how and why a priest's ceremonial enactment extended his boundaries as a performer and shows how éclat involved constantly deferring a ritual event's temporal and spatial borders to an unreachable horizon.

As a theological idea and as a ceremonial practice, éclat responded to a material challenge: the wafer known as the eucharistic host did not look very alive, nor did it look any different before and after being consecrated. Its material characteristics, or "accidental" qualities, remained the same. Theological treatises relied on rites and ceremonies to resolve the difference between the eucharistic wafer's visible characteristics and its desired visual impact, that is, between the sensory data offered to the human eye and what Catholics and non-Catholics alike were supposed to see when they witnessed the Blessed Sacrament. The Council of Trent's "Doctrine on the Sacrifice of the Mass" acknowledges in its discussion of liturgical ceremonies that "such is the nature of man, that, without external helps, he cannot easily be raised to the meditation of divine things."[43] Although the council does not state the matter explicitly, its arguments in favor of ceremonies account for the fact that a small, flat round of unleavened bread does not inspire much awe on its own. "Therefore has holy Mother Church instituted certain rites," the council explains, "to wit that certain things be pronounced in the mass in a low, and others in a louder, tone." The council continues, "She has likewise employed ceremonies, such as mystic benedictions, lights, incense, vestments, and many other things of this kind . . . whereby both the majesty of so great a sacrifice might be recommended, and the minds of the faithful be excited, by those visible signs of religion and piety, to the contemplation of those most sublime things which are hidden in this sacrifice."[44] Here, rather than emanating from the consecrated wafer, splendor arises from the performances that encircle it: the priest's bent knee, his raised hands, the modulation of his voice, his movement toward the altar, and the genuflecting worshippers who gaze upon the elevated host in adoration.[45] In the words of Olier, the "majestic Sacrifice of the altar" remained "hidden, without outwardly emanating any splendor from its person."[46] Rather, as Olier explained, Christ's divine presence entrusted the church with the responsibility of "enhancing its splendor and glory through the outer aspect of ceremonies."[47] Parishioners shared this responsibility. The Council of Trent mandated that Mass should not be celebrated "unless those who are present shall have first shown, by their decently composed outward appearance, that they are there not in body only, but also in mind and devout affection of heart."[48] Liturgical performance produced éclat, which in turn reinforced the doctrine of transubstantiation by endowing the small, round wafer with liveness.

In practice, éclat thus resulted from behaviors, such as genuflection, that treated the eucharistic wafer as if it were a person of high rank.[49] Modeled on courtly ceremonial, éclat entailed the idea that a person of noble extraction exuded authority in a way that even strangers could instantly recognize and that inspired spontaneous acts of reverence and self-abasement. One way that seventeenth-century France's reform-minded priests and seminary directors promoted such behavior was by emphasizing Jesus's royal epithets when teaching about the sacrament of the Eucharist and the ceremonies of the Mass. As Pierre de Bérulle explained in his *Discours de l'Eucharistie* (Discourse on the Eucharist), the first of Christ's attributes one should see in the Eucharist is "his presence on the earth as King and sovereign of his people."[50] Similarly, Olier compares the ceremonies of the Mass to those that encircle a king at his coronation. "If one prepares so many ceremonies for the crowning and the *Sacre* of Kings," he asks, "what must one not do to consecrate the Son of God, King of Kings and Lord of Lords?"[51] For Olier, the metaphor of a coronation explains why the Mass entails such actions as kneeling before the altar. Gestures like genuflection and open arms express the "profound amazement" that "obliges" the celebrant to "annihilate himself before the Divine Majesty" in the Eucharist.[52] Just as royal epithets such as "Divine Majesty" and "King of Kings" articulate the idea that the eucharistic wafer should be treated as a monarch, ceremonies such as kneeling produce splendor for that invisible monarch and convey its éclat to the laity.

Depictions of royal and divine authority provide a glimpse of how early moderns imagined éclat. They represent this kind of splendor as rays of light emanating outward from the person, place, or thing that possessed majesty, nobility, or honor. Louis XIV's well-known use of the sun as an emblem for his majesty offers a ready example. A *devise* or emblem engraved when Louis XIV declared war on Holland in 1672, for instance, bore the title "The King" and depicted a sun, followed by lines announcing his éclat (Figure 8).[53]

> In all the splendor (*éclat*) in which one wants me to appear
> Art cannot express with her most beautiful pens
> Either my strength or my rays.
> It belongs solely to me to make myself known.[54]

Of course, the association between rays of light and majestic splendor did not originate with Louis XIV. The emblem of the sun for kings has a legacy reaching back to the ancient world.[55] Likewise, the halo or nimbus, the symbol associated with royal sun cults, appears in artwork produced by a wide array of religious traditions from India to Rome from as early as the fourth century.[56] In Christian art after the fourteenth century, depictions of God in his kingly aspect as the Eternal Father frequently featured a "nimbus of rays diverging in a triangular direction."[57] Light rays, like sun rays, signaled a fusion of divinity and kingship.

Early modern Catholics drew on the same visual trope to represent God's presence in the Eucharist by picturing light shining forth from the consecrated bread. An engraving from the title page of a late seventeenth-century French translation of the Latin Mass, for example, used a visual device called a glory to designate Christ's majestic presence in the consecrated Eucharist (Figure 9). Like the halos that encircle the heads of saints and kings in Christian art, a glory surrounds a figure's entire body and signals its divinity.[58] In this case, the glory surrounds a monstrance, or vessel used for displaying the consecrated host when exposed for adoration at times other than the Mass. Rays of light burst from it on all sides, enveloping the monstrance in an elliptical halo and indicating that the Blessed Sacrament inside it contained the divine presence.

Figure 8. An emblem of Louis XIV entitled "The King Represented by a Sun," from *Devises à la Gloire du Roy: Sur ses conquestes dans la Hollande*; seventeenth century, G-F17ANO0001 © Médiathèque Simone Veil de Valenciennes.

Figure 9. The Blessed Sacrament exposed in a monstrance, from the title
page of *Missel romain selon le reglement du Concile de Trent, traduit en
françois*, engraving (Paris: Chez Jean de la Pierre, 1692), courtesy of the
Archives of Saint-Sulpice (Paris).

Obviously, Louis XIV did not actually emanate rays of light when he appeared in public. Nor did a visible halo radiate from the consecrated eucharistic
wafer when placed on display. The visual trope of rays of light designated a per-
ceptual ideal, that which French subjects were supposed to see, were taught to
see, and wanted to see when they saw the king or the holy host. Such images do
not depict what Foster calls the "datum of vision" but rather invite what David
Morgan calls a "sacred gaze," which he defines as the "particular configuration
of ideas, attitudes, and customs that informs a religious act of seeing as it occurs
within a given cultural and historical setting."[59] As Morgan's definition underlines by including "customs" in its list, visual experiences like éclat relied not only

on religious discourses but also on learned behaviors. Early modern images of divine glory in the Eucharist thus provide clues about the "practices of looking" that made seeing éclat possible.[60]

An anonymous painting entitled *Le Sacrifice de la messe* (The sacrifice of the Mass), which formerly adorned the Seminary of Saint-Sulpice's walls in Paris and now hangs in the entryway of La Solitude, the retirement home for Sulpician priests, suggests how ceremonial action shaped liturgical visuality in early modern France (Figure 10). According to Sulpician tradition, Olier commissioned the painting shortly before his death in 1657, although the conservationists who restored the painting in 2006 and 2007 estimated its creation date as closer to the late eighteenth or even the early nineteenth century.[61] Whether realized during Olier's lifetime or at a later date, the painting's portrayal of the Mass draws on the theology and liturgical practices of the Counter-Reformation.[62] The painting depicts the elevation, the ceremony in which the celebrant raised the eucharistic wafer over his head after its consecration so that the Catholic faithful could adore the divine presence it contained. Éclat emanates as light from the figures representing God at the top of the painting, a dove for the Holy Spirit and a bearded, gray-haired man for the Heavenly Father. A golden void occupies the middle of the painting, connecting the Father and Holy Spirit above to the uplifted host in the celebrant's hands, thereby denoting the consecrated wafer's identity as the third member of the Trinity: Jesus Christ, or the Son. Around the altar and on either side of the golden void, worshippers kneel. Those who genuflect at the altar's base represent the earthly church.[63] They gaze up at the consecrated host in the celebrant's hands. Above them kneels the heavenly church, composed of saints, martyrs, apostles, and angels, all of whom turn their eyes either toward the holy host or toward the rays of light that shine down from the Heavenly Father at the top of the painting.[64] Below the altar, a cutaway reveals souls in purgatory's flames, who constitute the suffering church.

Three clues regarding the ceremonial practices that shaped liturgical visuality emerge from the painting's configuration. First, *Le Sacrifice de la messe* depicts éclat as belonging to the realm of symbolic interpretation rather than vision's datum. It does so by dividing the scene into three horizontal layers. The middle layer depicts its content in a relatively literal way. The altar, for example, is dressed in a white cloth and bears four candles and a Missal. Worshippers carry prayer beads and prayer books, and an altar server even holds the priest's chasuble. Two symbolic layers representing Catholic realms of the afterlife—heaven and purgatory—frame the earthly altar top and bottom. The rays of light representing éclat, significantly, do not extend into the layer representing the celebration

Figure 10. *Le Sacrifice de la messe*, artist and date of creation unknown.
According to Sulpician tradition, Jean-Jacques Olier commissioned the
painting shortly before his death in 1657. It now hangs at La Solitude, the
retirement home for priests of the Society in Issy-les-Moulineaux, France.
Courtesy of the Society of Saint-Sulpice. Photo by Joy Palacios.

of Mass by the earthly church. Only the angels, saints, and martyrs feast their eyes directly upon the divine's splendor. Except for one nun to the right of the altar whose gaze seems to reach the heavens, the other earthly worshippers direct their eyes to the bare eucharistic wafer. They see the bread, not the light.

Yet, the worshippers' bodies offer a second clue about éclat's ceremonial basis. Even as the painting relegates éclat's visual trope—rays of light—to the heavens, *Le Sacrifice de la messe* creates a nimbus around the eucharistic host by arranging the Catholic faithful, both earthly and heavenly, in eight rings that radiate from the altar.[65] Their collective genuflections and adoring gazes form a sort of gestural glory around the Eucharist, framing the holy host. In art history and performance theory, framing has a special relationship to presence. The frame around a painting sets it apart for contemplation and places the artwork "in an exclusive state of presence" compared to the visible space around it.[66] In performance, too, presence erupts as such when we "[see] behavior through a deliberate frame."[67] Likewise, the social fact of seeing éclat depended on the physical involvement of worshippers in its production. The more actively they framed the altar with their bodies, the more likely they were to "see" the divine presence in the Eucharist.

Along with an awareness of presence, however, framing also introduces the possibility of artifice. Scholars from Richard Schechner to Bert States agree that one of the simplest ways to transform an everyday live action into a performance is to frame or highlight it.[68] At the same time, as Tracy C. Davis and Thomas Postlewait note in their study of theatricality, since antiquity the theater's opponents characterized performance as "illusory, deceptive, exaggerated, artificial, or affected."[69] Consequently, whenever the framing devices that generated presence during Mass drew too much attention to themselves, liturgical activity could slip down the slope into modes of performance, such as theater, associated with fakery and artificiality. The very mechanisms that framed the altar to produce éclat, whether material or gestural, therefore had the potential to discredit the divine presence, making whatever liveness a worshipper saw in the holy host vulnerable to being dismissed as an illusion, as empty theater.

*Le Sacrifice de la messe* offers a third clue about the practices of seeing essential to the production of liturgical éclat. The painting's edges as well as the viewer's position in relation to the image both suggest how liturgical practices simultaneously generated the visual experience of éclat through gestural framing and mitigated the possibility that framing devices, like genuflection, might signal artifice instead of presence. Each ring of worshippers fades into the distance and disappears beyond the scene's border, creating the impression that the glory formed by their bodies extends beyond the painting. The bowing bodies confound the frame they help create. Just as importantly, *Le Sacrifice de la messe* gives the viewer the ideal position from which to gaze at and adore the uplifted host, thereby positioning the viewer as a participant in the ceremonial actions depicted within the frame. A viewer who chooses to accept the painting's invitation extends éclat's representation beyond the canvas into his or her own body.

By exceeding the various frames that brought attention to and created a sense of divine presence for the Eucharist, ceremonial activity evoked eternity and counteracted the potential impression that the liturgical splendor of the Mass amounted to empty theatrics. Although the visual tropes for éclat implied a burst of light, a sudden and awe-inspiring presence, in Catholic teaching the consecrated wafer did not stop being Jesus's body when the celebrant lowered his hands after the elevation. Rather, the divine presence in the Eucharist simultaneously occupied the past, the present, and the future. As an engraving from a seventeenth-century devotional book shows (Figure 11), when the priest raised the consecrated bread above his head, devout Catholics trained themselves to see Jesus's Crucifixion as simultaneously present before their eyes in the uplifted host, as behind them in the historical past represented by the cross raised on Calvary, and as ahead of them in an eternal time to which believers aspired after death, represented by the cherubs who in the engraving flutter by the altar. The performance repertoire that made the divine presence manifest could not, therefore, rely on framing alone. Rather, it had to produce what performance theorist Rebecca Schneider calls an experience of "performance remains." Such performances evoke the "authentic" and the "real" by refusing to disappear.[70] At the Comédie-Française, no matter how enthralled the spectators had been by a performance, a play's artifice came into view when the actors ceased to declaim their lines and left the stage. The theatrical event's disappearance underscored its constructedness. By contrast, although often framed and staged, the incessant, public ceremonialization of Louis XIV's daily routine figured his kingship as an organic product of his personhood.

Often, a performance seems to linger because it "tangles or crosses temporal registers" such that "the past is given to lie ahead as well as behind."[71] Liturgical ceremonies not only framed the altar during Mass, their continuation beyond the event also achieved this temporal tangling. For example, whenever a parishioner's gestures recalled the Mass in an alternative context, like the genuflections Catholics enacted at home with morning or evening prayers, the performance repertoire of the Mass continued to operate even if the Mass as an event may have already ended that day. Liturgical ceremonies created the impression of tangled time by alternating back and forth between framing and overflow,

AD ELEVATIONEM HOSTIÆ.

Le Prestre fait l'eslcuation de l'Hostie.

Iesus-Christ esleué en Croix.

21

Figure 11. A devotional image of a priest performing the elevation while Jesus's Crucifixion recurs above and heaven watches, engraving in *Le Tableau de la croix representé dans les ceremonies de la Ste. messe* (Paris: Chez F. Mazot, 1651), courtesy of the Archives of Saint-Sulpice (Paris).

mingling bursts of intense presence with actions that prolonged that presence beyond the event's horizon. On the one hand, liturgical ceremonies created a sort of human halo around the altar, indicating the plenitude and majesty appropriate to God's person, while on the other hand these same ceremonies, when performed and repeated not only in the church but also outside it, caused the Mass to remain in worshippers' bodies as they passed from the sanctuary out into the city. Without both movements, ceremonies failed to produce splendor.

The secular clergyman's body, as an instrument in the liturgy's manifestation of both presence and permanence, bore responsibility for producing, for himself and for his parishioners, an experience of transubstantiation. Christ's visible glory in the Eucharist, as expressed through éclat, depended on the priest's ability to enact the ceremonies of the Mass correctly and gracefully in collaboration with his fellow clergymen. In a priest's capacity as ceremonial agent, the boundaries of his action and identity extended beyond himself to encompass the larger ritual body formed through the coordinated movements of the clergy and the Catholic faithful in worship.

## Ceremonial Patterns

Patterns of coordinated ceremonial action supported éclat's production. Identifiable in a wide range of liturgical ceremonies, the patterns themselves did not have names, perhaps because their shape—to borrow Dom Gregory Dix's term—drew from a broader repertoire of ritualized behaviors belonging to courtly culture, and thus not exclusively to the church. A performance analysis of the liturgical handbooks used in Paris's seminaries to teach clergymen how to conduct the ceremonies of the Mass between approximately 1640 and 1716 brings these ceremonial patterns into view.[72] These ceremonial sequences, which I call multiplicity, directionality, distribution, and synchronization, focused the attention of clergymen and worshippers on God as king. In doing so, ceremonial patterns acted as framing devices to convey the immediacy of God's presence by intensifying at least one marker of presence, whether place, time, or action.

Multiplicity framed the altar by outlining the borders of God's ecclesiastical court. In early modern France, a noble never appeared alone. Louis XIV's court at the palace of Versailles exemplified the principle of multiplicity. Versailles housed not just the king and his immediate family but also thousands of servants as well as members of France's aristocratic families, most of whom possessed both a room in the king's palace and a private family home in the city.[73] According to

Norbert Elias, by the mid-eighteenth century approximately ten thousand people inhabited the palace of Versailles.[74] Onstage princes, too, required an entourage. Jacques Scherer notes that the hero in seventeenth-century plays "must always be encircled by secondary characters. . . . He cannot go alone without offending the idea one forms of his power and dignity. He must have a 'suite,' all the more numerous the higher the rank he occupies."[75] Neither could the divine presence, conceived of in royal terms, make a solo appearance. Bienséance demanded that clerical bodies fill the chancel just as courtiers filled the antechambers that surrounded Louis XIV's room. To this end, seminary directors required seminarians to march in procession two by two to the parish church every Sunday for Mass, where those who did not participate directly in the liturgy's central ceremonies by performing an "office" like subdeacon or thurifer sat in seats that lined the outer edges of the chancel, called *stalles*.[76] Seminarians processed to the seminary chapel for private Masses in the same way, where the *règlement* for the Seminary of Saint-Sulpice makes it possible to infer that the stalles stretched along either side of the altar creating a frame three rows deep, which seminarians entered starting with the back row, making sure to always begin with the seats closest to the altar.[77] A worshipper who looked at the chancel from the nave would have seen an entourage of men with closely shaven heads and sacramental garments encircling the altar. Small parishes often had only one or two clergymen— when Bourdoise arrived in the parish of Saint-Nicolas du Chardonnet, only the parish priest and a vicar served its church.[78] But in parishes lucky enough to have a seminary or a large clerical population, dozens and even hundreds of clergymen sat in the chancel during Mass. The more clergymen in the chancel, the better. Multiple priestly bodies seated along the chancel walls constructed a clerical frame for God's presence, sent a strong ceremonial signal regarding his power, and magnified his splendor.

Directionality complemented multiplicity by making the human frame around the altar dynamic. It constituted the foundational ceremonial pattern and framing technique learned through the priestly rehearsals discussed in Chapter 2. In the same way that bienséance required an honnête homme to turn toward the person of greatest importance, seminarians learned to always turn toward objects in which the divine presence resided or with which divine presence was associated: toward the altar, toward the wafer, toward the chalice, toward the crucifix, and toward the Bible.[79] Directionality generated the impression of a majestic presence on the altar by marking the site of God's abiding. As Fanny Cosandey observes of ceremonial expressions of rank in early modern France's royal courts, "The centrality of the king was the absolute reference point for all spatial organization."[80] Like a responsive entourage upon a king's arrival, the clerical bodies that turned toward the altar focused all eyes on God as king. A type of ceremony called inclinations, which included bowing and kneeling, made directionality easy to teach, actualize, and modify. "We note three types of inclinations to observe during the divine office," explains a règlement from Saint-Nicolas du Chardonnet for comportment in the chancel. "The first is the profound inclination, which involves the body and the shoulders, otherwise known as humiliation.... The second is the medium inclination, which uses the shoulders and the head.... The third is the little inclination that is called a light inclination because it is done with the head only."[81] Genuflections entailed dropping onto either one or two knees and lowering the forehead ever so slightly.[82] These ceremonial sequences were so important that new seminarians received a one-on-one lesson in inclinations from a senior seminarian charged with the office of *introducteur*, or guide, who escorted the new student to the church to teach him "how to do the inclinations when entering the chancel or leaving it."[83] The painting supposedly commissioned by Olier and analyzed above, *Le Sacrifice de la messe,* depicts the power of directionality for producing the impression of full presence. All the bodies in the painting kneel toward the uplifted host, and the golden light that floods the painting's central panel seems to gather around the consecrated wafer as a result of their combined attention.

Whereas directionality framed a place, ceremonial distribution framed an action by giving different parts of the same action to different agents. In courtly ceremonial, the pattern of distribution expressed itself most vividly in the rites that governed a noble person's routine for getting ready for the day in the morning and getting ready for bed at night, or the *lever* and the *coucher*. Objects destined to adorn the king's body passed through many hands of progressively higher rank. When the king dressed, for example, a servant or valet brought the king's shirt, but handed it first to the dauphin, who then presented it to the king.[84] By the eighteenth century, Marie-Antoinette's shirt passed ceremonially through as many as four or five pairs of hands before she received it.[85] In a similar way, the ceremonies of the Mass distributed among multiple agents the actions that prepared the altar. When the celebrant arrived at the altar at the beginning of Mass, he incensed it, giving prayers to God in the form of fragrant smoke. The priest did not, however, carry the censer himself. The thurifer carried the censer and handed it first to the deacon, who handed it to the celebrant.[86] The fragrant smoke thus passed through three hands before reaching its majestic recipient. This distribution of a single task among multiple agents created the impression of a regal presence by showing its entourage at work.

Finally, synchronization came as close as possible to framing time by framing the Mass's primary ceremonial agent: the celebrant. Synchronization consisted in ceremonial sequences in which multiple clergymen simultaneously carried out physical actions for which one priest was identified, through framing, as the primary agent. The elevation at a solemn Mass offers the best example. In a solemn Mass, a celebrant had at least two clergymen assisting him—a deacon and a subdeacon—who stood at a slight diagonal behind him on either side. The placement of their bodies thus directed eyes toward the celebrant's agency. At the same time, the deacon and subdeacon mirrored the celebrant's gestures, amplifying his body. The handbook from the parish church of Saint-Nicolas du Chardonnet instructed the deacon to "remain standing to the right of the Celebrant, doing the inclinations, genuflections, and signs of the Cross like the Celebrant," both before and after the consecration.[87] Behind the deacon and subdeacon, all the other clergymen filling less important offices during the Mass also mirrored the celebrant. The handbook for the ceremonies of the Mass published by the priests from the Congregation of the Mission specified that "all the other inferior Ministers" who participated in a solemn Mass had to "conform to the Celebrant and the holy Ministers."[88] This meant doing the same ceremonies at the same time, even though the minor officers were not standing at the altar. When the celebrant made the sign of the cross, bowed toward the cross, inclined his head at the name of Jesus, or sat down, so did his fellow ministers.[89] By mirroring the celebrant's actions, synchronization framed the "now" of his gestures, making each gesture remarkable. Since the celebrant held the eucharistic wafer—and thus the divine presence—in his hands, synchronization also framed the "now" of God's body-as-bread, visually suggesting that the celebrant's exaggerated presence derived not from the ministers who mirrored him but rather from the power of the invisible king in the wafer. When deployed in concert, multiplicity, directionality, distribution, and synchronization transformed human bodies into a living and breathing ceremonial frame for the Eucharist. By visibly demarcating the altar, ceremonial framing evoked the visual experience of éclat.

Material transformations to church décor during the second half of the seventeenth century reinforced the framing function accomplished through ceremonial patterns, such as multiplicity, directionality, distribution, and synchronization. Steps that raised the altar, tabernacles that centered the altar, and sculptural pieces called *retables* that framed the altar all focused a worshipper's eyes back on the consecrated host, underlining the immediacy of the divine presence in the context of the liturgical event. Altar steps facilitated éclat's production by expressing God's high rank. As a seventeenth-century treatise on church design explains, "Altars must be raised . . . in the Church to the degree . . . that Jesus-Christ is [raised] above all the Church in dignity and in honor."[90] Raised altars also made liturgical ceremonies easier to see. The author of a guide to "everything curious and remarkable" in Paris complained in 1725 that the altar at the Church of Saint-Louis, which had three steps, was too low.[91] "To tell the truth, this Altar and all its accompaniments are not very well designed," the guide observed. "It is so low and so sunken that one can hardly discern the Priest when he performs the divine office."[92] Priests and parishioners at the Church of Saint-Sulpice must have felt similarly. Their new altar, completed in 1734, had seven steps, making it the sanctuary's visible focal point.[93]

The raised altars that gradually spread across France during the seventeenth and eighteenth centuries served not only to enhance the celebrant's visibility but also to display a receptacle for the consecrated Eucharist. Called a tabernacle and often fashioned to resemble a palatial temple, this receptacle redefined the sanctuary as God's abode.[94] In contrast to the bare altars of the medieval period that figured the altar as a site of sacrifice, the early modern period's tabernacle-adorned altars directed the worshipper's eyes toward a miniature palace in which God's presence was believed to reside.[95] Finally, the construction of a retable, or altar piece, generally accompanied the raising of an altar and the installation of a tabernacle. In its simplest form a retable was a painted or sculpted board that stood on the back edge of the altar's surface.[96] By the seventeenth century, a retable typically consisted of a central panel featuring a large, framed painting flanked on either side by columns or pillars.[97] Two side panels bearing sculptures frequently complemented the central panel, and a second level displaying an additional painting and sometimes topped by an attic often completed the ensemble.[98] A retable provided a dazzling frame for God's residence, providing a point of orientation for the liturgy's ceremonial patterns and drawing the worshipper's gaze along the church's longitudinal axis toward the high altar.

Although the production of éclat involved ceremonial and material framing to create the impression of God's immediate presence on the altar, ceremonial splendor ultimately had to overflow its frame to convey the eternal and all-encompassing nature of the divine presence. Good liturgical performance therefore required priests to conduct ceremonies in a manner that not only framed but also prolonged the sense of time, expanded the impression of space, and enlarged the horizon of action. In addition, good liturgical performance required priests to teach parishioners to participate in the liturgy's extension by repeating—or in Schechner's terms, "restoring"—behaviors both inside and

outside the church that were key to the main sacramental event.[99] A Mass celebrated with éclat thus figured the altar as a node in an expansive ceremonial web
rather than a théâtre that designated, by the second half of the seventeenth
century, an increasingly self-contained dramatic world to which spectators were
privy without being participants. To work, ceremonial splendor had to create continuity between the chancel and the nave and absorb the secular realm into its
folds. A brief excavation of the ceremonial overflow that extended from the altar to the church's exterior will reveal the logic that organized the liturgical
repertoire.

The liturgy's extension had its seeds in the ceremonial patterns that framed
the altar to create a burst of "now" associated with the divine presence. So as to
also produce the sense of tangled time required to convey eternity, ceremonial
framing had a fragile quality. Each ceremonial framing device contained the potential to overflow the boundaries it set. If a framing device intensified one
marker of presence—place, time, or action—it inevitably did so by confound-
ing another. Directionality, for example, framed the altar as the place, the privileged site, of God's presence, but simultaneously prolonged the temporality
associated with that presence. Directionality amplified time by causing the
ceremonial action to remain in the temporality of salutation. Between people,
the moment of greeting establishes and acknowledges presence. During the Mass,
inclinations continually reiterated the temporality of salutation every time an entrance, exit, vestment, word, or object signaled the place of God's presence.
Clergymen bowed deeply toward the main altar every time they approached it
wearing a cope—or sacramental cloak—in order to sing or to incense objects.[100]
Each time a clergyman entered or exited the chancel for any other reason, a medium bow renewed the initial burst of presence experienced through greeting.
The rules for ceremonial conduct at Saint-Nicolas du Chardonnet's altar told
seminarians, "When entering or exiting the Chancel, or when passing through
the middle, you turn toward the altar and you devoutly do a medium inclination . . . if the Blessed Sacrament is exposed visually, you genuflect."[101] For example, members of the chorus bowed their heads and shoulders toward the altar
before and after announcing a psalm, before and after being sprinkled with holy
water, and before and after beginning a procession around the inside of the
church.[102] In similar fashion, clergymen did a small inclination, or light bowing
of the head, each time they said the name of a person closely associated with the
divine presence in the Eucharist, like Jesus, Mary, or the saint to whom the Mass
was dedicated.[103] Directionality consequently not only located the place occupied
by a noble presence but also reiterated and prolonged the instant of encounter in

which a noble presence dazzled those who met it. It framed a person or place but stretched time.

Ceremonial distribution, too, framed one aspect of presence while simultaneously expanding another. By framing an action—like the passing of a shirt or the gift of incense—ceremonial distribution created, at the same time, the impression of amplified space. Each additional agent who handled an object destined for the altar augmented the amount of space required for the ceremony in question. When the ceremonial distribution took a processional form, as it did for the blessing of holy water, the amplification of space extended the action across multiple parts of the church, joining, for example, the altar and the sacristy. After blessing the water in the sacristy, the celebrant processed to the altar between his deacon and subdeacon, preceded by the acolytes, bearing candles, and the thurifer, who carried the liturgical bucket and baton for sprinkling holy water, called the aspersorium and aspergillum.[104] Once at the altar, an additional minister, responsible for the holy water, presented the aspergillum to the deacon, who then passed it to the celebrant, who proceeded to sprinkle holy water on the altar, himself, and the assembly.[105] Symbolically, the altar's space therefore expanded in proportion to the frame created through ceremonial distribution. At the same time, by parsing an action into multiple, similar sequences and extending the moments of contact between the celebrant and his ministers, distribution made the area around the altar seem bigger by slowing down the ceremonies such that the spaces associated with worship required more time to traverse. Ceremonial distribution, even as it allocated focused attention on a specific action, simultaneously created the impression of liturgical space as expansive.

Likewise, synchronization, which framed time by framing the "now" of the elevation, also enlarged the Mass' horizon of action by expanding the subject boundaries of the celebrant. All the clergymen who mirrored the celebrant's actions merged, ceremonially, with his sacramental body, enlarging him. The ministers standing closest to the celebrant during the elevation made this merger visible through physical contact at critical moments. For example, when the celebrant lifted the consecrated host, touch literalized the expansion of his bodily boundaries. Kneeling to his left and right, the deacon and subdeacon each grasped the lower edge of the celebrant's sacramental robe and raised it as he raised the wafer.[106] Synchronization did more than just expand the celebrant's body. It functioned like a gestural echo, triggering a series of ceremonial resonances that pointed toward the celebrant's raised hands without replicating them. First, the celebrant's upward gesture rippled outward into light. As he raised his hands, two torchbearers entered, genuflected, and placed themselves on either side of the altar, echoing the elevation by intensifying the light around it. On a solemn feast day, there were as many as four or six torchbearers.[107] Behind the celebrant, the elevation rippled not only into the bodies of the deacon and subdeacon but also unfurled into the body of the thurifer, who fell to his knees behind the subdeacon, put incense in his censer, "and incens[ed] continuously while the holy host and chalice were raised."[108] Smoke turned to sound as the thurifer's incense prompted the *cérémoniaire*, or master of ceremonies, to ring a hand bell announcing the transformation of bread into God's body.[109] Sound turned to silence as a hush swept across the chancel in honor of the divine presence the celebrant finally placed on the altar in the form of a wafer.[110] This ripple effect created the visual impression that the objects believed to harbor God's presence pulsed with vitality. Synchronization thus created the gestural equivalent of rays of light emanating from the eucharistic bread outward from the consecrated host toward the far reaches of the chancel.

The gestural echo that rippled through the chancel amplifying each of the celebrant's gestures overflowed into the nave, absorbing the laity into the celebrant's extended subject boundary. This ceremonial overflow did not occur spontaneously. In the same way that seminarians had to learn how and when to restore ceremonial behaviors to generate éclat, the laity, too, had to learn how to participate in liturgical ceremonies. At both the Seminary of Saint-Nicolas du Chardonnet and the Seminary of Saint-Sulpice, Bourdoise and Olier trained parishioners by employing seminarians to run frequent catechism classes— courses that covered basic Catholic doctrine and practice—and to enforce ceremonial norms among worshippers during Mass. The catechism at Saint-Nicolas du Chardonnet, for example, taught children how to kneel in front of the Blessed Sacrament upon entering the church, how to make the sign of the cross in unison with the deacon when he read the Gospel, how to kneel during the Antiphony of the Virgin, and how to kneel during the *sanctus* that preceded the elevation.[111] The laity learned to extend even the smallest gestural echoes, like the one created when all the clergymen in the chancel bowed their heads when saying a holy name. The manual published for the seminarians who taught the catechism included these requirements of them: "When pronouncing the Blessed names of Jesus and Mary they do a reverence if standing, and if seated . . . they do only a bowing of the head."[112] Pamphlets published in the parish about how to attend Mass reminded adults to kneel as soon as the celebrant reached the base of the altar, and a clergyman charged with the office of doorkeeper circled the nave four or five times during Mass to model modesty, wake sleepers, quiet the noisy, and make sure the laity participated as they were supposed to in the ceremonies of the Mass.[113] This litany of bows during the Mass insistently oriented all bodies toward the same point, intensifying the altar's place as the site of God's presence, but also expanded the Mass's horizon of action to include the bodies of all the worshippers in attendance. Synchronized inclinations absorbed the laity into the one great clerical body that simultaneous actions produced.

The ceremonial overflow that accompanied ceremonial framing kinesthetically erased any distinction between visual foreground and hidden background that the altar's spectacular display inadvertently produced. The bowing bodies during Mass figured the sanctuary as a backless space, an infinitely extendable space that simulated the infinite space-time generated by God's heavenly throne. Inclinations transformed the sanctuary into a backless space by absorbing all the prepositional relations possible between a body and the altar—*à, autour, sous, sur, vers, dans, derrière* (to, around, under, on, toward, in, behind)—into a frontal relation. In the same way that a courtier appears *before* not behind a king, and a king appears *before* not behind his people, inclinations converted even the dustiest, most obstructed corners of old church buildings into part of the altar's *devant*, its front. As a result, proximity mattered more than visibility, and the most sought-after seats in which to attend Mass were not necessarily those that provided the best view.[114] Since all corners of the church participated in the altar's devant, seats close to the altar trumped seats far from the altar even if the closer seats offered no view at all. As the church wardens' register for the parish of Saint-Sulpice reveals, nobles who could afford to build side chapels around the edge of the church attended Sunday Mass from these private enclaves, some of which were actually behind the altar.[115] The less wealthy but nonetheless well-off parishioners sat in rented benches around the perimeter of the chancel, again flanking the back and sides of the altar, where the high backs of the clergy's stalles blocked their view of the ceremonies.[116] The poor complained that they had no place to sit at all.[117] Inclinations, a gesture performed *before* a majestic presence, consequently placed all these bodies in a relation of devant, extending the altar's front to all parts of the church building through their bowed limbs.

The priest's task of incensing the altar demonstrates the inclination's usefulness for generating a space of pure devant. Since the altar corresponded to God's throne, it was imperative that the altar not have a back. Illusions have a front and a back, infinities do not. Incense helped render the altar backless by wrapping it in a cloud of aromatic smoke, but because the priest must pass around and behind the altar with at least his hand to apply the incense, liturgical handbooks insisted on the inclinations with extra urgency. The *Manuel des cérémonies romaines* describes in detail each movement required during the incensing, emphasizing the repeated inclinations with the word "derechef," or "once again." As soon as the celebrant received the censer from the deacon, he offered a profound inclination to the cross, which sits on top of the altar. The text then begins to highlight further inclinations as the priest incenses the more hidden parts of the altar. First for the right side of the altar and then for the left, the manual repeats, "then having *once more* done an inclination or genuflection, he incenses in three strokes of equal distance the top of the altar toward the back part."[118] The ceremonial for the parish of Saint-Nicolas du Chardonnet specifies that the priest incensed not just the back part of the altar's surface but the whole back side of the altar during this process.[119] While incense erased the altar's back, inclinations iterated and reiterated its devant.

Thanks to inclinations, the devant of the altar could extend beyond the chancel and nave into the streets, reaching as far as a worshipper's trained body could go. The catechism manual used by seminarians at Saint-Nicolas du Chardonnet instructed them to teach the parish's children that they had to, "in passing before Churches, Crosses or Images of Saints, or before Priests or Monks, offer them reverence."[120] The *Manuel des cérémonies romaines* gave similar instructions to clergymen, training them to offer a profound inclination whenever they passed a high altar, to genuflect whenever they encounter a priest carrying the Blessed Sacrament, and to offer a medium inclination to any prelate on their path.[121] Similarly, a tract outlining "la journée chrétienne," or "the Christian day," informed adults that it was "necessary to kneel before a devout Image" every morning and night, in addition to offering reverence to the Blessed Sacrament if one encountered it being carried through the city.[122] By extending the altar's front along the extremities of the worshipper's mobile body, inclinations naturalized ceremonies, incorporating the production of liturgical éclat into the practices of everyday life. So long as worshippers anywhere in the world were bowing, the Mass overflowed its frame and absorbed the surrounding world.

## Conclusion: The Priest's Body as Ceremonial Node

Rather than an independent agent displaying his skills or stepping into a role, a priest engaged in liturgical action is better conceived as a node in a larger ceremonial body. His individual, physical body coordinated and connected the bodies that surrounded him so that their collective action represented Christ's presence as king in the eucharistic wafer. Theological discourses expressed the priest's nodal function by attributing to him numerous roles simultaneously, which conveyed the idea that the priest did not play a part but rather served as the physical anchor for the suite of metaphors that made Christ's presence thinkable. Beuvelet advised priests to reflect on these metaphors before administering a sacrament, imagining Christ "in one of the particular states" that had a close rapport with the ceremonial action at hand: "For a baptism, adore him in the Jordan; on your way to hear confession, [adore him] as he who made himself sin for men and as their doctor; when administering the Eucharist, [adore him] as sovereign priest and victim all at once; when applying the holy oil in extreme unction, [adore him] as the virtue of the Eternal Father and the strength of Christians; when celebrating a marriage, as the Church's bridegroom."[123] The implication was that the priest's body collected and conveyed all these metaphors simultaneously—doctor, priest, victim, virtue, strength, and bridegroom—even though in a given sacrament one metaphor might prevail over the others. In his function as a node, the priest served as a connecting point for these many metaphors.

Through ceremonies, the priest's body made the full range of metaphors for Christ available all at once and facilitated the Catholic faithful's participation in those metaphors. By echoing the priest's movements and partaking in ceremonial patterns of multiplicity, directionality, distribution, and synchronization, clergymen and lay people gave form to the larger ceremonial body for which the priest served as node. His responsibility as node was to render Christ's presence and Christ's grace perceptible in the sacraments, which in turn hinged on an extensive clerical and disciplinary apparatus aimed at producing the visual experience of éclat, or ceremonial splendor. This apparatus entailed the vestiary norms and trained gestures examined in Chapters 1 and 2, as well as catechistic and missionary efforts in which seminaries engaged to train laypeople how to act and think as Catholics. For ceremonial splendor, this meant that éclat combined doing and seeing. To see éclat at Mass, one needed both to bend and bow in concert with one's fellow faithful and to expect to see Christ's radiant presence. For a priest, éclat meant that his liturgical action required more than his own body. A vray ecclésiastique needed a well-trained clergy and parish in order to conduct Mass with ceremonial splendor. Whether he was the celebrant or a lowly clergyman in the chancel stalles, the ideal liturgical performance of a priest required the individual to recede into the ceremonial patterns that generated éclat.

CHAPTER 4

# Publics

The ceremonial body for which the priest's physical presence served as an organizing node during liturgical ceremonies made the priest public, open to all. All Catholics, at least in theory, participated in this public body mobilized on Christ's behalf by the priest through coordinated ceremonial action. Not only was the priest's quality as a public person wrapped up in the production and maintenance of éclat, or ceremonial splendor, in the context of the sacraments, especially the Eucharist, as discussed in the previous chapter; as an integral component of ecclesiastical selfhood, éclat reinforced the performative structure of priestly identity. By rendering the priest public, ceremonial splendor turned the secular clergyman's identity outward, where the Catholic faithful bore a degree of responsibility for helping to produce it and where the laity, whether authorized to or not, could judge, criticize, and even mock or deride the priests who performed before them. This public layer of priestly identity made all the more urgent the less visible features of priestly performance analyzed in the previous three chapters, such as rehearsal, self-examination, and submission to the hierarchical cycle of evaluation by ecclesiastical superiors. Without the constant, hard-to-see work of training the clerical self to ceaselessly wear the proper robes, enact the correct gestures, adopt the right attitude, and coordinate ceremonially with others, neither priestly identity nor liturgical éclat could be attained. A priest's public quality, however, raised the stakes. In his capacity as a public figure, a priest risked discrediting himself and the larger institution he represented and maintained. Mistakes, whether ceremonial or personal, could rupture éclat or, worse, plunge the priest into public sin, aligning him with figures such as actors.

In many respects, priests and actors occupied opposite ends of the cultural spectrum in early modern French thought. Priests were not supposed to attend plays, and actors could not become priests.[1] Yet the quality of being public joined them. Seminary founders, like Jean-Jacques Olier of the Seminary of Saint-Sulpice, emphasized the parish priest's status as a *personne publique,* or "public person." Olier wrote that "being public persons," priests were "chosen . . . to render unto God by their religion the duties of the entire world" and were "charged by their condition to enclose in their prayers all religion and to have, in themselves, as much as all mankind together."[2] A priest's status as a public person arose from his responsibility for the church's pastoral and liturgical tasks, or what early modern clergymen called "exterior" functions like ceremonies, sacraments, and preaching. In a treatise on the priesthood based on Olier's teachings and published in 1676, its probable author, Louis Tronson, defined priests in terms of their publicness at the altar.[3] "Ecclesiastics are those who publicly perform these outer functions," such as the Mass, wrote Tronson, "and who are established by God to render unto Him these public duties on behalf of and in the name of all the faithful."[4] A priest, most especially a secular priest who served as curate to a parish, belonged to the category of personne publique because he carried out his duties for others, for a public. Churchmen considered actors public because they believed stage players brought harm to others, inciting them to sin, and because actors conducted their functions before an audience, or publicly. The theater's most extreme critics rejected actors as "public poisoners who spread their venom by the eyes and ears."[5] Both priests and actors were public because they conducted their professional activities in full view of others and because their activities were thought to entail moral consequences for those who witnessed them.

Public personhood entailed theological and practical risks for clerical authority in seventeenth-century France, as evidenced by the way ecclesiastical discourses used the concept of publicness to police the boundary between those who could and could not participate in the Catholic Church's liturgical ceremonies. Diocesan Rituals—the liturgical handbooks, issued by a bishop for his diocese, that contained instructions for conducting the sacraments and sacramentals for which a parish priest was responsible—designated those sinners whom a priest should exclude from the church's sacraments as "public sinners." The department of the Holy See that oversaw the liturgy was known as the Sacred Congregation of Rites.[6] In 1614 it issued a Roman Ritual, designed to serve as a template to which bishops could refer when developing a Ritual for their own diocese.[7] Among those to whom Communion should be refused on the basis of public sin, the Roman Ritual listed the excommunicated, those under interdict, prostitutes, those living together without being married, usurers, magicians, and sorcerers.[8] French bishops sometimes added to this list of public sinners in their own Rituals. Most notably for a study concerned with performance, after 1649 actors increasingly found themselves categorized as public sinners by diocesan Rituals. According to Jean Dubu's analysis of 127 diocesan Rituals published in France between 1600 and 1713, twenty-six of the Rituals listed actors as public sinners.[9] The wrong kind of publicness could result in ceremonial exclusion.

A priest who performed his duties poorly could slip from one end of the spectrum to the other, from public personhood as a source of authority to the position of public sinner excluded from sacramental participation. In his Ritual of 1673, for example, Nicolas Pavillon, the bishop of Alet, placed poorly performing parish priests on a list of people to whom confessors should refuse absolution. "Who are the people to whom one must defer or refuse absolution for being engaged in the next occasions of sin, until they have removed themselves from these occasions?" asked Pavillon.[10] Parish priests topped the list of public persons who should be treated as public sinners: "This also includes certain public persons, such as curates, judges, doctors, apothecaries, and surgeons, who are not capable of their responsibilities and of their jobs, with the result that they are exposed to a constant danger of making mistakes and significant injustices and who are consequently on the verge of sin."[11] Pavillon's Ritual, known for its rigorism and accused of Jansenism, constitutes an extreme example. Pavillon nonetheless belonged to the French Counter-Reformation and helped further the seminary movement. By bringing together public personhood and public sin and linking them to skill, his Ritual highlights a clergyman's positive publicness as a mutable quality. Ordination did not automatically ensure that a priest's publicness differentiated him from sinners. Rather, a priest had to construct himself as a public person and remain vigilant against situations that might elicit resemblances between his own activities and activities associated with negative forms of publicness.

To some degree, the construction of a secular clergyman as public person depended on his own actions. He needed to wear his soutane and tonsure, comport himself with modesty, and master liturgical ceremonies so that he could conduct them without mistakes. As demonstrated in Chapter 3, however, the production of éclat, or ceremonial splendor, through liturgical action required not only the priest's own skill but also the skillful participation of his clergy and laity. The importance of ceremonial coordination to a priest's daily liturgical tasks meant that he needed to manage the people in relation to whom he occupied the status of public person. He needed to do his utmost to ensure that they knew how to form the type of public required by éclat, while at the same time continually moderating his interactions with lay Catholics so that his own particularity remained subordinated to his clerical function. Situations in which a clergyman might come into view as a private person exposed to a critical gaze belonging to individuals outside the hierarchically organized and institutionally legitimized channels of clerical evaluation posed a challenge to the construction and maintenance of public personhood. Similarly, interactions could erode public personhood in situations in which a clergyman's behavior could potentially foster social bonds that privileged his private body over the ceremonial body his physical presence instantiated in liturgical contexts. Consequently, a vray ecclésiastique regulated his contact with others so that when, where, who, and how they saw him supported, as much as possible, the construction of his clerical identity as a public person. Furthermore, he understood that the public personhood he constructed belonged not just to him but to all secular priests. Damage to any one priest's public personhood did damage to the shared professional identity and social function of the secular clergy.

## Professionalization and Publicity

As the foundation of seminaries improved the secular clergy's liturgical and pastoral skills, their professional stature and reputation increased, too. Bishops and seminary directors engaged in the Counter-Reformation, like Pavillon and Olier, depicted secular priests, especially curates, as public persons in part to assert the secular clergy's religious life and function as equal to that of regular priests. Their use of the term "public" differs significantly from its post-Enlightenment connotations, where the "public" refers to the voluntary gathering of people to "deliberate on common concerns, evaluate competing proposals for change, and eventually arrive at a *public opinion*."[12] Early modern public personhood corresponded more closely to the phenomenon Jürgen Habermas calls "publicity" in the brief section of *The Structural Transformation of the Public Sphere* devoted to pre-Enlightenment conceptions of the public. As I use it here, "publicity" encapsulates the positive forms of seeing and being seen that secular clergymen needed to foster in order to avoid disrepute.

Since the 1980s, when Habermas's work became available in English, scholarship has treated the quality of being public as a positive trait enjoyed only by people of rank under the ancien régime. Norbert Elias's *Court Society* and a series of monographs on France's early modern state ceremonies, also published in the 1980s, reinforced the relationship between the quality of being public and rank.[13] This publicity, as Habermas calls it, identified a person's authority with his or her physical body, but in a way that attributed that authority to a source beyond the person's control, such as God or birth. Habermas describes the publicness specific to early modern people of rank as an "aura of feudal authority."[14] "This *publicness* (or *publicity*) *of representation*," writes Habermas, "was something like a status attribute . . . inseparable from the lord's concrete existence, that, as an 'aura,' surrounded and endowed his authority."[15] Priests like Pavillon and Olier would have called this aura éclat, or "radiance," seeing in it the splendor associated with majesty.[16]

Unlike the public sphere that, according to Habermas's model, emerged through and facilitated critical discussion among private people about matters of general concern, publicity resided in and emanated from a person of rank's bodily presence. Habermas's favorite example is the manorial lord, who had to represent his status as lord publicly. Habermas writes, "He displayed himself, presented himself as an embodiment of some sort of 'higher' power."[17] A prince, too, represented his lordship "not for but 'before' the people," just as the nobleman "was authority inasmuch as he made it present. He displayed it, embodied it in his cultivated personality."[18] Other socially desirable characteristics, especially those thought to correlate with rank, like virtue, operated according to the same principle. "Virtue must be embodied," writes Habermas, "it had to be capable of public representation."[19] Publicity therefore consisted, at least in part, in the physical embodiment of abstract possessions, like social status or virtue. This embodiment gave positive publicness, or "publicity," an intrinsic quality.

The publicness associated with rank entailed an elastic subject boundary. All the props required in the public representation of lordship adhered to the noble "I," even though the nobleman could not be reduced to the sum of such props. Habermas notes that, in staging publicity, supports included such elements as "insignia (badges and arms), dress (clothing and coiffure), demeanor (form of greeting and poise) and rhetoric (form of address and formal discourse in general)," all of which were "wedded" to the lord as "personal attributes."[20] Habermas offers a useful term for these props, calling them "surroundings." People often made up the "surroundings," right along with objects. For example, Habermas observes that "the relationship of the laity to the priesthood illustrates how the 'surroundings' were part and parcel of the publicity of representation (from which they were nevertheless excluded)."[21] Habermas does not dwell on the relationship between props and aura, but his work suggests that the aura of authority associated with social rank resided in the "surroundings" that amplified the subject boundary of an appropriately public person; the more dense and populous the surroundings, the greater the aura of authority.

Seventeenth-century French dictionaries, however, paint a less glorious picture of publicness than Habermas does. As even a quick comparison of the way Antoine Furetière and his contemporary César-Pierre Richelet defined the term "public" suggests, early moderns, at least in France, considered publicness a largely negative attribute rather than a lordly one. Early moderns applied the adjective "public" in three basic scenarios: in cases of exposure, in instances of common ownership or general accessibility, and in relation to types of authority grounded in writing and legislation rather than rank.[22] The *Dictionnaire françois* published by Richelet in 1680 defined the adjectival form of "public" in two ways, the first of which pertains to exposure and the second of which pertains to general accessibility:

> Public, adj. Known, manifest. [His crime is public and people can talk about it. The thing is not yet public, but it will be soon.]
> Public, adj. Prostituted to the whole world. Of bad life. The word public in this sense is said of girls and women. [In law the servants in cabarets are considered public.][23]

For Richelet, an act done "publicly" joined these two meanings, making something known or manifest to the whole world indiscriminately. For example, his definition for the adverbial form of "public" reads: "Publicly, adv. In Public. In view of the world."[24] Furetière likewise links publicness to prostitution, along with the notion that things "known and manifested to everyone" were bad.[25] This common thread between Richelet and Furetière implies that exposure and accessibility constituted the core qualities of publicness. As their examples demonstrate—crimes, prostitution, public penance—for Richelet and Furetière the publicness acquired through exposure and accessibility had strongly criminal connotations.

Furetière's definition of the adjective "public" differs from Richelet's by adding several positive examples, namely, merchants, preachers, and lawyers. These positive examples suggest that in special cases the potentially criminal aspects of exposure and accessibility could translate into legitimacy and authority when channeled through the proper forms and functions. The use of "public" in relation to women provides an interesting example. Furetière observes that although in most cases the term "public" is "injurious" to a woman and "signifies that she prostitutes herself to all comers," he notes that in the eyes of the Palace of Justice a woman who owns a shop (*une Marchande*) is legitimately "public" so long as she "maintains an open boutique and is obliged to do so by the things that she sells."[26] The form of the open shop, as opposed to the privacy of a brothel, le-gitimized the female merchant's exposure, just as the function of selling goods classified as "commerce" by the Palace of Justice authorized her accessibility. Similarly, although Furetière acknowledges that appearing before an audience entails a risk—"It takes boldness to appear in public"—he does not attribute criminality to those who practice professions requiring oratory: "Lawyers speak in public. Preachers preach in public. This President has given a public audi-ence," he writes.[27] Reading between the lines, two factors legitimized these forms of publicness. First and most important, their exposure arose from a rec-ognized function, such as presenting a legal case, and was legitimized by the medium of delivery, such as a pulpit. Second, skillful display also seemed to le-gitimize these forms of positive publicness. For example, speech legitimized by a pulpit could still incite ridicule. For preachers, the conversion of negative pub-licness into authority also depended on the proficiency of their sermon delivery; not just on the pulpit but also on their performance in the pulpit.

Those who listened to and evaluated a preacher helped determine the posi-tive or negative valence of his publicness. In its substantive form, the term "pub-lic" in the seventeenth century was beginning to acquire the connotation of judgment. More than anything, early moderns considered the theater audience a "public" because it possessed the capacity to critique a play and its performers.[28] As Hélène Merlin-Kajman points out in her analysis of the seventeenth-century usage of the term "public," a slippery relation characterized the meaning of "pub-lic" as an adjective and the instances in which it referred, however vaguely, to a collective.[29] This slipperiness appears most clearly in Furetière's 1690 example of the author "who gives his works to the *public*," a phrase that seems to evoke at once a group of potential readers, akin to an audience, but still relies on the idea of publicness as a quality resulting from exposure.[30] By the early eighteenth century, however, a firm conceptual link associated the notion of the "public" as a substantive with the activity of judgment. Under the entry for "public" in the 1702 edition of Furetière's *Dictionnaire universel*, his editors added multiple ci-tations that figure the public, in its substantive form, as a judge. "However dis-paraged the public might be," reads the first, "there is not a more incorruptible judge and sooner or later it renders justice."[31] "If your work is good," reads an-other, "the public will render it justice."[32] A third example states, "The public is an inexorable judge that should be handled better than it is."[33] Although the clear association between the public as a collective and judgment does not enter Fu-retière's dictionary until the turn of the eighteenth century, the literary exam-ples that develop this idea derive from seventeenth-century authors. In them, as

Merlin shows, the figure of the "public" emerges as a "fictive person referring to the totality of virtual readers and spectators of a literary work."[34] A public person's visibility and exposure opened him or her to the public's critique.

By the second half of the seventeenth century, professionalization made secular clergymen both more visible and more available in relation to their lay flocks than they had been at the end of the sixteenth century. Visibility and availability followed from the Catholic Counter-Reformation's promotion of an ecclesiastical ideal in which the *parfait ecclésiastique*, or "perfect churchman," as one seventeenth-century handbook called him, operated as a "mirror and a light in which the people must look at themselves."[35] As discussed in Chapter 1, strictly enforced rules for clerical robes in the seventeenth century made secular clergymen much easier to identify at a glance than they had been in the Middle Ages.[36] As secular clergymen grew more visible, their public status grew as well. Residency requirements further enhanced their public quality by increasing the secular clergyman's availability to the laity. Absenteeism had always been prohibited, but the Council of Trent had renewed old penalties and introduced new ones, insisting, "It is not lawful for anyone who holds a benefice requiring personal residence to absent himself, save for a just cause approved by the bishop, who even then shall, for the cure of souls, substitute a vicar in his stead."[37] Under renewed pressure to live in the parishes and dioceses where they possessed an ecclesiastical office or benefice, secular clergymen became more available to the laypeople in their spiritual care.[38] Aware of being watched and wanting to reinforce their status as models, secular clergymen who pursued their own perfection sought to be seen. Living where he worked, the perfect churchman made himself available to walk in processions, conduct sacraments, and deliver last rites to his flock at all times of the day and night. Visible and available, the perfect churchman was thus public, and, if all went well, public in a positive way.

This increased publicness, however, brought risks as well as advantages. Although the robes worn by the perfect churchman served as a key mechanism for advancing the secular clergy's professionalization, they also inspired anxiety about the difference between true and false priests, a concern Molière leveraged in crafting the first version of his *Tartuffe*. Likewise, although a priest who resided in his parish or diocese had more opportunities to serve as a model to his flock, the lay people with whom he interacted simultaneously had more occasions to evaluate his pastoral and sacramental skills. Whereas evaluation within the authorized, hierarchical channels represented by ecclesiastical rank and reinforced by France's new seminaries was central to priestly training in the post-Tridentine period, lay evaluation of clerical action fell outside these legitimized

boundaries. Judgment outside official channels had the potential to erode public personhood by focusing attention on a clergyman's individual characteristics—
his particularity—rather than on the ecclesiastical office he embodied. At the
same time, judgment removed the person engaged in the act of evaluation from
participation in the surroundings, or extended subject boundary, of the public
person, thereby rupturing éclat's production.

Seminary-trained clergymen were aware of how judgment conducted outside the authorized channels could reduce a priest to a private person while simultaneously converting a worshipper into a spectator, or someone who was
more engaged in watching ceremonies than in participating in them. Within the
seminary milieu, clergymen treated their own misplaced judgment as a sin and
sometimes confessed among themselves to indulging in aesthetic criticism of the
way other priests celebrated Mass. A small manuscript conserved at the Archives
of the Society of Saint-Sulpice in Paris, entitled "Dix conferences aux confesseurs"
(Ten conferences for confessors), contains such a confession. Unlike most surviving seminary documents, which indicate what priests *should* do rather than
describing what they did do, this manuscript's anonymous author speaks can-
didly in the first person about the feelings and challenges he has faced in the
course of pursuing priestly perfection. He admits both to critiquing his own performance and the performance of others.

The author's self-critiques reveal how the discernment associated with aesthetic judgment highlighted a priest's particularity. "I was ashamed of not performing well," he admits, confessing that during Mass he used to not wear his
glasses, so as to look better, even though, paradoxically, by trying to improve
his personal appearance he made more mistakes, since he could not see.[39] After
confiding that he "discovered later that others had felt this same temptation,"
the author recounts how he worried excessively about what worshippers thought
of him.[40] Even when he conducted Mass for nuns at a nearby convent, in which
case a screen or cloister separated the altar from the women so that they could
not see him, the potential evaluations of worshippers obsessed him: "I have
often found myself tempted to have beautiful ornaments and to say the mass at
the best decorated altars, even when I was before the screen of the nuns. O my
Lord, how many times have I had the temptation to go back over my voice, over
my gestures, over what I did in some particular ceremony, imagining that these
girls would see me, which wasn't true, and I was not ashamed to not be attentive to
you."[41] In these examples, aesthetic self-evaluation places individual characteristics and actions in the foreground—the author's glasses, gestures, and voice—
which in turn diminishes the liturgy's religious efficacy.

If self-criticism spiritually interrupted the author's own performance of the Mass, his evaluation of other priests, he confesses, sometimes brought his liturgical participation to a halt. The manuscript's author recounts how his critique of his fellow priests on occasion compelled him to chase them down after Mass to tell them everything they did wrong. Referring to himself in the first-person plural to suggest that others have sinned in the same way, he recalls: "One fault is the contempt in which we hold the practice of others, and this here, O My Lord, is great … never are we at the mass except with distraction, looking with condemnation at he who says the mass, and scorning him. Even just the temptation causes chagrin. Sometimes it goes without reason so far as to the audacity to go into the sacristy to accuse he who said the mass in a way we did not like. O My God, I have failed formerly in this."[42] The author presents aesthetic judgment as a source of both personal failure and liturgical interruption. When caught up in judging the performance of other clergymen, he does not participate as he should and instead becomes "undevout and unreligious."[43] Rather than his focusing on the divine majesty in the transubstantiated host, his eyes roam, and he concentrates on "the way others do things."[44]

Although the author does not explicitly categorize his misdirected attention as spectatorship, his narrative aligns evaluation and taste with distraction. Evaluation and taste belong to the types of judgments made by the "public" in Furetière's 1702 examples and lead the clergyman to behave more like a member of a theater audience than like an extension of the celebrant's ceremonial body. The anonymous author of the "Dix conferences aux confesseurs" admits that when he, like some of his fellow priests, found the Mass lacking, he sometimes chose to not go at all: "Other times we absent ourselves from the Divine Office because they do it badly … I preferred to go elsewhere and waste my time," he continues, now addressing God, "whereas Your intention is that we go praise you inwardly as one should even more willingly in places where you are poorly honored by the outer forms of worship."[45] In this clergyman's example, judgment gave rise to personal choice over religious duty and institutional obligation: he preferred to do something else rather than attend a Mass he deemed poorly conducted. Whether worshippers judged a priest's work to be artificial, spectacular, or unsatisfactory, clergymen agreed that criticism outside the authorized channels had the potential to void liturgical ceremonies. Aesthetic criticism could cause ceremonies to devolve into distraction or make entertainments more appealing than the Mass. By directing a witness's attention in ways not conducive to the production of éclat, not subject to hierarchical channels of evaluation, and likely to prioritize the clergyman's particularity on the one hand and the parishioner's preferences on the other, judgment posed a challenge to the production of public personhood.


## Managing the Public

Given public personhood's reliance on an entire community for its construction, an important part of a vray ecclésiastique's work entailed managing the public. In other words, a priest had to structure interactions with lay participants in ways that supported publicity, minimized exposing a priest's particularity, and mitigated lay judgment. Clergymen were not always eager to manage the public. Doing so did not necessarily make them personally well-liked, more comfortable, or better positioned financially, since the benefits of public personhood accrued first and foremost to the priesthood as an institution. The task of imposing discipline on the laity in an effort to promote liturgical éclat often entailed, for example, standing up to parishioners who had wealth or political power. Repeated reminders in seminary rules and ecclesiastical pamphlets about a curate's duty to treat rich and poor alike in the confessional and at the altar, refusing the sacraments to unrepentant sinners regardless of their rank, suggests how difficult it was in practice for a clergyman to manage his parishioners in accordance with the ideal of the perfect churchman. Despite and perhaps because of the difficulty clergymen faced in coordinating and responding to lay behaviors, we find ecclesiastical guidelines, edicts, and advice insisting all the more that clergymen train and regulate when, where, and how the Catholic faithful should receive the sacraments and socialize with their priests.

Seminary-trained clergymen learned to use the catechism to regulate lay behavior. With roots in the forms of instruction given to new Christians during the early church, the catechism afforded the Counter-Reformation Catholic Church an essential tool. Used relatively rarely during the medieval period, the form was revived and modified by Protestants, "producing printed texts designed to be not only read and internalized but also memorized and recited," thereby "combin[ing] both the written and oral aspects of religious education."[46] Soon after Luther and Calvin produced their own Protestant catechisms in 1529 and 1541, Catholic bishops began to follow suit, although Catholic catechisms largely addressed clerical audiences until Robert Bellarmine published a catechism in 1597 designed so that children could memorize it.[47] In the mid-seventeenth century, during the same period in which bishops began to found seminaries for their dioceses, they also began to issue their own catechisms, modeled on sixteenth-century catechisms like Bellarmine's. According to Karen Carter, between 1650 and 1700, French bishops published at least fifty-seven different catechisms.[48] As Carter shows, these diocesan catechisms of the seventeenth century "emphasized behavior rather than doctrine," both through recitation and "by teaching proper religious behavior in both word and deed during catechism classes."[49] Among other behavioral skills, children learned "to sit still in church, pray, respect the church and its priests, give a proper confession, take communion, and obey those in authority over them."[50] These "societal expectations and behaviors," Carter observes, "could last a lifetime, even if children eventually forgot the exact words of the catechism itself."[51] For the liturgical production of ceremonial splendor and the public personhood that shared éclat's logic, the behavior learned by young Catholics through catechism classes inclined them to participate in what Habermas would call the "surroundings" of the priest and ultimately of the divine presence in the consecrated Eucharist. Catechism taught Catholic bodies to participate in the gestures that conveyed God's majesty in the sacraments.

Seminaries such as Saint-Nicolas du Chardonnet and Saint-Sulpice in Paris blended clerical reform and lay reform by entrusting their seminarians with the task of running the parish catechism.[52] At Saint-Nicolas du Chardonnet, the catechistic methods were held in such high regard by the curate that he asked the seminary to publish a handbook for use in the parish and to enable other parishes to follow the seminarians' example. The resulting *Reglemens et matieres des catechismes qui se font en la paroisse de S. Nicolas du Chardonnet* (Rules and content of the catechisms practiced in the parish of Saint-Nicolas du Chardonnet), published in 1668, gives a thorough representation of the way clergymen in the parish trained parishioners in matters of religious practice. Seminarians learned to conduct the catechism on Friday afternoons at three o'clock by presenting a thirty-minute catechism lesson to children from the parish school, or *petite école*, brought to the church for that purpose by the schoolmaster.[53] As the seminary rules specified, this Friday lesson "was more for the practice and instruction of the churchmen of the seminary than for the instruction of the children."[54] Seminarians put their training to use on Sundays after vespers, when five of them were selected by the parish priest and supervised by the seminary's prefect and subprefects of the catechism to lead forty-five-minute catechism sessions.[55] These seminarians gathered the parish's children in the church and divided them into five classes of different levels.[56] As children mastered the doctrinal content and behavioral requirements of one level, they advanced to the next.

In terms of comportment, catechism classes taught children a simplified version of the modesty that seminarians learned in their own training. Lay Catholics did not wear the soutane, but the catechist enforced modest dress among his
pupils, "mak[ing] sure that the clothes of the children did not have any worldli-
ness, superfluities, or nakedness," so as to "gently warn them" against such forms
of dress if necessary.[57] Children who stood out to the catechists as "the most modest" received praise and even small prizes in the form of pious images of Christian symbols such as the Trinity or the Last Judgment, with the goal of "motivating
the children and keeping them in modesty."[58] As at the seminary, where modest
dress and ceremonial rehearsal had an equalizing effect among clergymen
from diverse backgrounds, catechism classes, too, at least in theory, treated
children from all types of families with the same rank-blind forms of respect.
Catechists were not to use pet names or titles when addressing children but
rather to call them by their given names. The rules advised: "One will not use
any of these terms, neither 'my son,' nor 'my daughter,' and even less Monsieur
or Mademoiselle, but one will call them simply by their proper name or sur-
name."[59] Seminarians were to "not hold the rich in higher regard than the poor,
but to love them all equally."[60] This equal treatment had a theological foundation.
Mathieu Beuvelet, author of many handbooks for the Seminary of Saint-Nicolas
du Chardonnet, reminded seminarians, when conducting the catechism, to re-
call "the esteem that God accords to souls, and in particular to those of the
poorest and most abject of the children that you will teach, saying in your heart,
'O Jesus my Lord! That you loved this soul when you shed your precious blood
for it."[61] In much the way it did among clergymen at the seminary, the practice
of modesty during catechism taught children to hold social rank slightly at bay
in religious settings.

Modesty's equalizing force served the production of public personhood by
positioning the divine hierarchy, as understood by Catholic doctrine, above the
social hierarchy, orienting ceremonial signs of respect toward Christian symbols
and the clergymen who administered them. Catechists frequently reminded
children to say quietly to themselves the prayer that the catechism instructor said
aloud, to make the sign of the cross at the beginning of the catechism class, to
bow whenever saying the names of Jesus and Mary, to attend Mass daily, "how
to listen to [Mass], and with how much modesty they should attend," how to do
a reverence when entering a church, and how to kneel before the consecrated Eucharist.[62] All these behaviors contributed to the ceremonial patterns discussed
in Chapter 3 that produced éclat, or splendor, for the divine presence by figuring the consecrated host as monarch attended by an entourage.

Catechism training likewise supported the construction of the priest as public person—and thus as a privileged vehicle for liturgical éclat—by teaching lay Catholics to keep their distance from clergymen, to treat them with the same types of ceremonial respect directed toward religious symbols, and to avoid looking at them too closely. The catechist was to "never permit that the children touch his hands, nor his soutane, nor his surplice, nor look at him fixedly, especially the girls."[63] If children came too close or looked at him too intently, the catechist was to "to correct them harshly, showing them a face that was rather severe, and something other than gentle."[64] The catechist was to likewise keep his distance from the children, in particular the girls, "never looking at them except in passing and only as much as necessity requires, and not talking together with them informally."[65] Distance insulated the clergyman's particularity from exposure, ensuring that children learned to see the catechist, and by extension all clergymen, as belonging to a type and that this type carried more importance than the specific features of an individual clergyman's body or personality. From the children's perspective, catechism would lead them to associate the clergyman's soutane-covered body with churches, crosses, and saints, since the catechist reminded the children regularly that they should, "when passing in front of churches, crosses, or images of the saints, or in front of priests or monks, bow to them."[66] If a child needed to speak with a clergyman, he or she learned to "speak with respect and humility, always replying when questioned [by the priest], 'Yes, my Father,' or 'Yes, sir, no sir.'"[67] In fact, catechism trained lay Catholics to think of interactions with clergymen as highly structured. Children learned to enter and exit the church for catechism "without sound and with modesty" and to remain silent and seated unless called upon.[68] By associating clergymen with religious symbols, ensuring a degree of social distance between clergymen and laity, and by training lay children to perceive clergymen as those who asked the questions and possessed the answers, catechism methods obscured a churchman's individual qualities and mitigated lay inclinations to judge or evaluate priests.

As Catholics emerged from childhood into adulthood, rules and guidelines continued to mediate lay interactions with priests. Some of these rules restricted lay behavior, others restricted clerical behavior, and all had theological justifications. Cumulatively, though, their social effect in terms of clerical identity was to set the priest apart, protecting him from lay evaluation and reducing the chance that he might appear before parishioners as more man than priest. First among these rules was the requirement that lay Catholics attend Mass in their own parish and not elsewhere. Beuvelet asserted the primacy of the parish Mass by defining it as "a legitimate assembly of Christians, which customarily takes place on certain days in a public church destined for that function under the direction of a hierarchical pastor."[69] This "triumph of the parish," as Joseph Bergin calls it, "was portrayed at the time as a return to a putative status quo ante."[70] Indeed, handbooks like Beuvelet's cite ecclesiastical canons and constitutions dating back to the first century to demonstrate the Catholic's obligation to attend Mass in his or her own parish.[71] In Bergin's words, however, "there was a large degree of innovation at work behind this rhetoric of returning to the proper order of things."[72] Medieval prescriptions may have directed Catholics to stay in their parishes, but lack of local resources, the ravages of war, and competition from religious orders meant that such rules "had remained a dead letter."[73] Clerical residency, in conjunction with local efforts to restore, expand, and decorate parish churches, helped "put the parish at the centre of normal religious life."[74] Although the parish's "triumph" remained imperfect, the requirement that Catholics attend their local parish church reinforced the secular clergy's professional stature.

In practical terms, the emphasis on parish attendance supported public personhood by reducing competition between clergymen, whether between nearby parishes, between parishes and neighboring monasteries, or between local clergymen and those traveling through a region. Whether or not the parish clergy enacted ceremonies and undertook their pastoral duties with skill, seminary handbooks and diocesan Rituals required Catholics to attend the parish Mass. Beuvelet clearly specifies that the parish church constitutes a "public church" in order to "distinguish parishes (which are called mother churches, baptismal churches, matrices, cathedrals, basilicas, older and more venerable, etc.) from the churches of the religious orders, which are only called chapels, oratories, or monasteries," adding that "regulars have never had permission to build churches to receive the general population or parishioners, but only for their own use."[75] The message to parishioners was that the reception of sacraments from any church other than the parish church would be invalid.

Similarly, bishops, in collaboration with seminaries, prohibited clergymen from conducting the sacraments outside their diocese of origin without written permission. For example, Louis Antoine de Noailles (1651–1729), archbishop of Paris, issued an ordinance in 1697 "bann[ing] under pain of suspension any priests who are not from our Diocese and who do not hold an ecclesiastical title or post approved by Us, to say the mass, nor to do any of the functions of their order without having obtained written permission from Us, or from our vicar generals, or from the directors of the Seminary of Saint-Nicolas du Chardonnet, whom We have commissioned to examine them [the traveling clergymen]."[76] By limiting the movement from place to place of parishioners, on the one hand, and of clergy on the other, such regulations aimed to restrict what would now be called church hopping or church shopping on the part of the faithful and freelance pastors on the part of churchmen. Lay judgment of local clergymen does not figure explicitly in such regulations. Handbooks, ordinances, and canons cite tradition, legitimacy, and spiritual well-being as reasons for enjoining parishioners to receive sacraments from their home parish. Likewise, the reasons given for restricting rove clerics focus on their lax behavior. Nonetheless, by reducing points of comparison and eliminating parishioner choice, such regulations also reduced the likelihood that Catholics would evaluate their clergy.

Rhetorically, theological explanations of the parish's role as the legitimate source for sacraments and sacramentals fostered public personhood by figuring the parish, rather than its clergy, as the main character or agent, and as a character intimately linked to the parishioner's own body. Beuvelet cited the "services that we receive from the parish in health and sickness" as one of the key reasons the church obliged Catholics to receive sacraments in their parish.[77] He expressed these services as a generative process akin to birth and death. Beuvelet positions the parish clergy as part of a biological process by using the metaphor of the church as mother—a tradition dating from the first centuries of Christianity.[78] He writes:

> It is in the parish that we are conceived in grace, that we take a new birth, that we are made children of God and regenerated at the baptismal font. It is there that we are elevated as in the arms of our Mother in the spirit of Christianity by the means of teaching and preaching. It is there that we receive the meal of the holy Eucharist and that we must take our rest after death. It is there that we are lifted from our sins by the sacrament of penitence and that we are fortified against relapses. It is there that we are obliged to receive the viaticum before making that great voyage from this life to the next. It is there that, as from an arsenal, we receive the weapon of extreme unction to battle at the end of our life against our invisible enemies. It is there that we find these visible angels whom, after having received us into the family of Jesus Christ, deliver us into eternity.[79]

Here, the clergy, to whom Beuvelet does not explicitly refer, figure metaphorically as the voice of the mother church, transmitting her teachings, and as the visible angels who, like surrogate mothers, birth (*enfantent*) Christians from the worldly to the heavenly realm. Imagined as interwoven with the parishioner's body, the parish clergy were neither private individuals nor sufficiently distant from the Catholic faithful for the laity to watch and judge.

The metaphorical alignment of clergymen with motherhood went hand in hand with rules that drastically restricted interactions between clergymen and women. Clergymen, especially priests, were to avoid any situation in which they were alone with a girl or woman.[80] They could live with their own mother, sister, or aunt as long as the clergyman had a room of his own and the female relative's "conduct was without reproach, and also edifying."[81] Clergymen were nonetheless encouraged to live instead in an ecclesiastical community, in a college, or in a house shared with other clergymen "where there [were] no girls or women."[82] According to the archbishop of Paris, a priest could not have a female domestic unless she was at least fifty years old, and at the Seminary of Saint-Nicolas du Chardonnet they decided in 1664 to not even hire women to wash the dishes.[83] In situations in which priestly obligations called for direct interactions with a woman, rules regarding dress and gesture imposed distance. When women received Communion, they were to lower their head coverings, and when they made confession they were to wear a veil over their faces, restricting eye contact.[84] For their part, clergymen who heard women's confessions were to avoid "long conversations with them, even under the pretext of piety," and to ensure that confessions were never heard "in secluded places or darkened chapels" but rather "in places exposed to the view of everyone."[85] A clergyman striving toward ecclesiastical perfection might rarely see or speak with a woman outside the words and actions absolutely necessary to administer the sacraments.

Episcopal and seminary rules treat contact with women as a source of potential sin. Part of this sin's danger arose from the way the feelings, sensations, and actions associated with romantic and erotic attachment would activate a clergyman's particularity at the expense of his public personhood. Beuvelet notes that priests who confess or converse with "persons of this sex," meaning women, have often "started with the spirit and finished miserably with the flesh."[86] Understood in its literal sense as skin and body, flesh refers to that which the soutane covers and modesty enfolds so as to construct the clergyman as a human vessel capable of generating éclat for the consecrated Eucharist. In the way the apostle Paul used the idea of flesh to denote the dynamics of temptation and salvation, it refers to all that is counter to ecclesiastical perfection and by extension, for an author like Beuvelet, all that erodes public personhood.[87]

Regulations on contact with women belong to the much more extensive set of guidelines that regulated human interaction of all kinds, across all genders, sexes, and social ranks, for seminary-trained clergymen. In much the way confession with women needed to take place in full view of others while simultaneously imposing physical distance between priest and penitent, seminary rules required clergymen to always appear in public in groups of at least two, to take their daily recreation in groups of at least three, and to avoid repeatedly socializing with the same clergymen during breaks.[88] Seminarians could not enter each other's rooms without permission from the superior and were to keep a degree of distance between each other at all times, except when greeting each other before or after a long journey.[89] The rules at the Seminary of Saint-Sulpice, for example, specified that "so as to maintain ecclesiastical gravity and modesty, one must abstain from touching each other even playfully."[90] Such regulations aimed at suppressing intimate friendships that, if they flourished, could damage the larger structures that sustained priestly professionalization, such as rules and hierarchical channels of feedback and evaluation. "It is necessary to avoid with care from contracting these individual friendships," state the rules at the Seminary of Saint-Sulpice, "which are only founded on natural inclination and not on charity and the desire for perfection, and for which the least bad consequences are dissipation, the waste of time, contempt for others, the infraction of rules, and mistrust of those who guide us."[91] Intimacy with women and friendships based on mutual inclination or attraction both threatened to erode a clergyman's publicness, his maintenance of an identity that did not belong to himself and whose construction involved the participation of others through ceremonial actions that all could see.

Efforts to manage lay behavior supported the priest's publicity by fostering modes of interaction conducive to the ceremonial cooperation that generated éclat. While ceremonial cooperation protected priests from the laity's evaluative gazes by absorbing everyone into a single liturgical agent, an archival strategy also insulated priests against the negative publicness that could result from the increased access parishioners had to their clergymen because of post-Tridentine reforms. This archival strategy consisted in multiplying the number of records a parish priest needed to keep and standardizing those records to increase their authority. The use of writing differentiated a priest's visibility from forms of exposure associated with negative publicness in at least two ways. First, record keeping placed the clergyman in the position of authorized observer rather than observed. Seminary instructions and liturgical handbooks instructed priests to keep three types of parish registers, in which they recorded the name, date, and details of each baptism, marriage, and burial in the parish.[92] A handful of these registers survive from the fifteenth and sixteenth centuries, in the seventeenth century their careful maintenance became widespread, and by the eighteenth century nearly every parish possessed "the almost complete series" of parish registers.[93] The preponderance and standardized form of parish registers by the end of the eighteenth century attest to the rise of the parish priest as archivist. In addition to registers, seminary handbooks also taught priests how to prepare and keep *testaments*, or wills, for sick and dying parishioners.[94] Lastly, seventeenth-century parish priests learned to keep a *Registre de l'estat des ames*, or Register of the State of Souls, in which they noted moral and religious information about each parishioner. All these documents afforded priests the opportunity to take up their pens in the context of administering the sacraments. With a pen in hand, a priest removed himself from the vulnerable position of being watched and evaluated and established himself instead as the participant authorized to evaluate others.

Second, record keeping further insulated a priest from forms of visibility that had negative connotations by subordinating a clergyman's personal presence to his ecclesiastical office. A robe-wearing, document-carrying parish priest was not a private man. He was the parish's memory in the flesh. Parish registers, Registers of the State of Souls, and wills secured the legal and spiritual identities of each person whose name a priest inscribed upon their pages. As Pierre Goubert and Daniel Roche explain in their overview of early modern French parish life, an infant's "act of baptism would constitute the only legal foundation for his existence: whoever was not baptized did not exist, even civilly."[95] Priestly archival writing constituted a parish community's primary governmental record. Without it, parishioners could not, without great difficulty, construct for themselves appropriate forms of publicness. Likewise, the Register of the State of Souls made the parish priest arbiter of other people's publicness. A pamphlet on how to be a good priest instructed churchmen not only to keep track of who was and was not a Christian and who had or had not confessed and received Easter Communion, but also to continually evaluate and make notes about his parishioner's lives. Every six months, the parish priest was to "go over in his mind each family to see how they behave, and if he there finds any disorder, to seek a way to remedy it."[96] The pamphlet warned priests to keep a special eye out for people who could be classified as public sinners while they were preparing the register: "He must particularly watch out for those who lead a bad and scandalous life, and try to convert them to God: And if they are public sinners, or manifestly in the near occasion of sin, [he must] refuse them the usage and administration of the Sacraments, of which they are unworthy."[97] The archival documents that supplemented a parish priest's interactions with his parishioners therefore insulated his own public appearances from scrutiny by positioning him as the party who passed judgment on which "public" activities qualified as sin.

## Conclusion: A Performance Definition of Public Personhood and Public Sin

Priests who relied on the categories "public sinner" and "public person" to advance clerical reform provided few definitions for these terms. The way seminary training and liturgical manuals taught secular priests to understand their bodily boundaries and manage their interactions with lay Catholics does, however, make it possible to venture a performance definition for these categories. In performance terms, a public person can be defined as an individual man or woman who is exposed to public view and made available for public consumption by the obligations of rank or office, but whose individual presence or particularity remained obscured by some combination of splendor and function. The category of public sinner, by contrast, encompassed people whose work involved exposure and availability, but whose activities were not legitimized by either ceremonial cooperation or archival insulation. When applied to actors by priests, the designation "public" thus meant the equivalent of "particular and exposed," whereas when priests applied the term "public" to themselves it meant "shrouded in an aura of authority." A clergyman, although highly visible in his distinctive robes and constantly on display when conducting his liturgical functions, was rarely given to view. A web of gestural codes, social norms, hierarchically organized relationships, and theological discourses shrouded his body and influenced how, when, and what lay Catholics saw when they looked at a priest. Ideally, when a clergyman stood before them at the altar or beside them at the deathbed, laypersons saw not an individual but the manifestation of a type. The man who embodied this type remained invisible. His positive publicness depended on his abnegation of self in favor of an entity constructed through ceremonies and writing in collaboration with the entire Catholic community and reiterated daily through banal acts like eating, drinking, teaching, learning, praying, birthing, and dying.

At the same time, the priest's quality as public person made him vulnerable. His own mistakes could thrust him from positive publicness to public sin. Likewise, failure to manage his relations with parishioners could disrupt a clergyman's efforts to construct and maintain his identity as public person. If a priest and his fellow secular clergymen did not train their parishioners to treat priests as they would a religious symbol, or if secular clergymen did not leverage their archival responsibilities to establish themselves as those who watched rather than as those evaluated, the secular priest's positive publicness could erode. Even when secular clergymen approached ecclesiastical perfection, conducting ceremonies with grace and skill and fostering a well-trained laity, the collaborative effort that was required to continually generate positive publicness made priestly identity susceptible to interruptions. Other public figures, like actors, whose activities competed with the church's ceremonies posed a threat both to liturgical éclat and to the secular clergyman's public personhood. A secular clergyman's public personhood, by turning his identity outward and involving the public in its construction, made the priest vulnerable to rivals even when those rivals, like actors, seemed at first glance to make no comment on religious affairs and to by and large respect Catholic practice. It is to the rivalry between church and theater that we now turn.

# CHAPTER 5

# Rivals

Without parishioner collaboration, secular clergymen could not generate the ceremonial splendor that manifested Christ's presence in the consecrated Eucharist or sustain the public personhood required by their priestly office. The liturgy's need to overflow the chancel, in combination with the Counter-Reformation priest's extended subject boundaries, led clergymen to perceive a wide range of parishioner behavior as competition to the Mass. Among the activities that clergymen considered threats to liturgical éclat in the seventeenth century, the theater ranked high. According to an ordinance issued by the archbishop of Paris in 1697, plays topped the list of spectacles that clergymen were to avoid "upon pain of ecclesiastical suspension," along with balls, operas, gatherings for games or gambling, and "other profane spectacles," all of which the archbishop deemed "entirely opposed to the holiness that the profession and work of clerics demands of them" because of the "tumult, conversations, and representations" characteristic of such events.[1] As such proscriptions conveyed, the places and activities prohibited to priests constituted rivals to the ideal of the vray ecclésiastique and the post-Tridentine values he represented.

Churchmen had not always perceived the theater as antithetical to the Catholic Church's liturgical and pastoral goals. From as early as the ninth century, Catholic authorities in France had either deployed theatrical representations in the context of worship or tolerated them as a mode of religious engagement. Latin liturgical plays, vernacular mystery plays, and other "historico-religious" dramas performed by amateurs nourished the faith, whether through the ceremonial embodiment of biblical characters and narratives during Mass or by providing a way to celebrate the feast day of a patron saint, honor a special guest, or commemorate a liturgical event like Corpus Christi.[2] Priests and civic authorities

alike held the performers of these religious dramas in high regard and participated themselves as actors.[3] Attitudes toward religious theater began to change
in the mid-sixteenth century, however, as evidenced by the Parlement de Paris's
decision to outlaw the performance of mystery plays in 1548.[4] The rift between
the church and the theater in France continued to widen over the next century
as the cultural transformations wrought by the Wars of Religion (1562–1598),
combined with the professionalization of actors and the Counter-Reformation's
emphasis on the liturgy's splendor, put the status and meaning of theatrical representation in question. By the 1640s, parish priests in Paris began to alienate actors from liturgical participation by refusing to administer sacraments to stage
players.

Stories and anecdotes about the way secular clergymen treated actors in sacramental situations during the second half of the seventeenth and beginning of
the eighteenth centuries demonstrate how Counter-Reformation priests navi-
gated rivalries at the parish level with individuals, like actors, whose work fostered community structures that churchmen considered detrimental to liturgical
bonds.[5] Rivalries between priests and actors show how clergymen used ceremonies to create a cycle of sacramental exclusion and reabsorption of figures who
posed a threat to éclat, thereby reinforcing the Catholic Church's perceived cultural dominance during periods in which churchmen suspected that the liturgical repertoire was in fact losing ground to alternative models for organizing social
interactions in urban space. As the history of interactions between priests and
actors in the parish of Saint-Sulpice between 1641 and 1730 shows, seminary-
trained priests used the threat of non-burial and the application of sacramental
exclusion as a last resort when they felt their professional gains were in jeopardy
or their cultural hold was slipping. In such instances, parish priests seized the
opportunity to assert the importance of the church's ceremonies by temporarily
excluding actors from the sacraments before reintegrating them into the liturgical community. Meanwhile, the last rites—especially the processions that accompanied the viaticum—afforded priests a symbolic victory over the theater by
ceremonially deconstructing an actor's identity and absorbing his or her home
and body into the sacramental network that linked parish spaces to the altar.
During the second half of the seventeenth century, a clerical self-conception in
which a priest's presence extended beyond himself to include his fellow clergymen and parishioners made sacramental reabsorption all the more important. In
contrast, a decline in clerical efforts to liturgically reabsorb actors into the liturgical community in the early eighteenth century suggests not only the theater's rise

as a culturally privileged form in France but also a shift in priestly identity away from éclat toward governance.

## The Sacramental Exclusion of Actors

Theater historians have emphasized sacramental exclusion as central to most of the available anecdotes about interactions between priests and actors in early modern France. These sacramental refusals demonstrate the lived effects, for theater practitioners, of the surge in what Jonas Barish has called antitheatrical prejudice in seventeenth-century France.[6] Alongside the professionalization of the theater, which produced the likes of Pierre Corneille, Jean Racine, and Molière, ecclesiastical statements, policies, and prohibitions against the stage and its players also intensified. The Catholic Church did not seek a ban on the performance of plays. France's more conservative bishops, however, declared actors public sinners, and similarly minded parish priests denied them the sacraments of marriage, the Eucharist, and the viaticum, as well as accompanying rites like Christian burial, unless they renounced the stage.[7] The Ritual of Paris, for example, listed actors as public sinners in 1654, explicitly denying them Communion.[8] Denied sacramental inclusion, they then experienced ritual exclusion. As a popular seminary handbook based on thirty-eight Rituals from dioceses throughout France and surrounding countries explained, public sinners were deprived of Christian burial "out of reverence due to holy sites and the immunity and sanctity of the Church, which does not allow in its enclosure any but those presumed to have died with a living faith."[9] Although burial was not a sacrament, a person outside the eucharistic community could not, according to ecclesiastical authorities, enjoy "community of the grave."[10]

Prescriptions do not always translate into actions, making the exact scale of the sacramental and ritual exclusion of actors difficult to determine. Given the destruction of Paris's early modern parish registers during the Commune fires of 1871, sources like Auguste Jal's *Dictionnaire critique de biographie et d'histoire* offer a way to establish a partial repertoire of actors whose parish priests threatened to withhold the sacraments or burial. Parish records for the provinces did not suffer the same fate, but seventeenth-century France's non-Parisian theaters remain understudied. Consequently, a systematic history of seventeenth-century troupes and theaters outside the capital would need to precede an attempt to catalogue the refusal of sacraments to actors outside Paris.[11] Nonetheless, between

1649 and 1713, nineteen French dioceses plus Quebec issued Rituals that explicitly excluded stage players from some combination of Communion and the last
rites.[12] Whether or not parish priests consistently abided by such Rituals, the
specter of sacramental exclusion and the accompanying menace of being denied
a Christian burial shaped the way early modern French Catholics perceived the
theater.

Rarely does the historical record provide enough information to recount in
exhaustive detail all the words and gestures exchanged between a given actor and
his or her parish clergy on the occasion of a disagreement regarding the sacraments. Cumulatively, however, actors' fragmented stories sketch a composite picture of the way liturgical and theatrical repertoires collided when stage players
sought to participate in or receive the Catholic Church's sacraments and ceremonies. Although memorable partly for the way it deviates from the norm,
the story of Adrienne Lecouvreur's liturgical woes gives a face to the composite figure of the actor this chapter explores. On 30 March 1730, Lecouvreur
(1692–1730), an actor from the Comédie-Française, died at her home amid ru-
mors of poisoning.[13] Her friends and admirers considered her the most accomplished female actor of her day; her acting was, according to the author of a
pamphlet published the year of her death, one of the four wonders of Paris.[14]
Lecouvreur lived in a house situated on the rue des Marais-Saint-Germain in
the parish of Saint-Sulpice, where Racine had died, giving it a theatrical past
almost as big as her reputation.[15] While Lecouvreur's talent earned her the fame
she enjoyed during her lifetime, she owes to the parish priest of Saint-Sulpice
part of the fascination she exerts over historians and theater lovers.

Saint-Sulpice's curate refused to grant Lecouvreur a Christian burial. A
seminary-trained clergyman and former seminary director named Jean-Baptiste
Languet de Gergy (1675–1750), he did so on the grounds that she had not renounced her profession before dying and had therefore not received the sacraments.[16] Excluded from Christian burial, her body, "accompanied by a squadron
of watchmen," was carried secretly at midnight "like a packet" to the Seine by
two porters, who dug a hasty grave in a construction site near what is now the
Quai d'Orsay and dumped her body "in a vague plot of land or on the banks of
the river."[17] Her precise resting place remains a mystery, and the circumstances
of her interment have long provoked outrage. Legend has it that she died in Voltaire's arms and that the *philosophe* then penned a poem in protest, vowing to
treat her "sad tomb" as a shrine.[18] More than 150 years later, George Monval
decried her treatment as an "event unmatched in theatre history!"[19] Indeed,
Lecouvreur's fate was extreme. Clergymen considered the denial of Christian

burial the church's "greatest punishment."[20] The exceptionally unceremonious handling of Lecouvreur's corpse, which in a ceremonially conscious culture smacked of cruelty, heightened the drama with which Lecouvreur's legacy would thereafter be ripe.

In its severity, Lecouvreur's story reinforced the specter of sacramental exclusion. Absolute sacramental and ritual exclusion of the kind suffered by Lecouvreur was, however, more an exception than the rule.[21] Even Molière, whose curate famously denied him a Christian burial when his sudden death did not leave him enough time to renounce his profession and receive the sacraments, eventually obtained a spot in sacred ground and an interment at 9 P.M. after his widow appealed to the archbishop of Paris and Louis XIV.[22] In the other known cases for which some documentary trace exists, the actor renounced the stage—or, as in Molière's case, the family avowed his intention to do so—and then the church reclaimed the actor's body through ceremonial action. Nor were sacramental refusals reserved for actors, as demonstrated by a 1666 handbook outlining various cases in which priests should withhold sacraments from all kinds of people, ranging from gentlemen to churchmen, if the visibility of their wrongdoing rendered their sin public.[23] "According to the doctrine of the holy Fathers and all the theologians since Saint Thomas," the handbook states, "one is obliged to refuse the sacraments to public sinners." A public sinner, it clarifies, is "someone who perseveres in a mortal sin that is manifest, either due to the obviousness of the action or because it was confessed publicly or because the accusation was made by ecclesiastical or secular courts."[24] Formal lists given by Rituals included prostitutes, usurers, and heretics, but all kinds of people could fall into public sin. Regardless of such injunctions, parish priests clearly had trouble turning parishioners away from the sacraments and denying rites like burial, hence the need for handbooks to remind priests of this duty and hence the surprise of figures such as Voltaire when the church withheld its ceremonies from Lecouvreur.

Thus, when compared to the other anecdotal and archival fragments that recount stories of actors who struggled to obtain Catholic rites and sacraments upon death, Lecouvreur's story stands out in that her parish priest followed through on the threat of sacramental refusal, withholding even the smallest Catholic ceremonies. He did not resort to the mainstays of the liturgical repertoire, like processions and nighttime funerals, that had been, for much of the previous century, among the church's preferred ways of signaling the theater's moral inferiority. The unusual ceremonial inertia in response to Lecouvreur's death reveals that the so-called sacramental refusals that constituted the Catholic Church's primary mode of redress against the stage's perceived iniquities are best considered not as exclusions but rather as the preface to sacramental reabsorption. The threat of non-burial prompted most actors to publicly repent, enabling them to receive the viaticum, extreme unction, and burial, at which point the church reabsorbed them into the liturgical community.

## Priests and Actors in the Parish of Saint-Sulpice

The parish of Saint-Sulpice provides an ideal case study for the sacramental exclusion and reabsorption of actors under the ancien régime. Gaston Maugras observed in his 1887 study of the legal status of French actors that most spats between priests and actors in late seventeenth-century Paris occurred within its jurisdiction.[25] Curiously, the parish has nonetheless received little attention in scholarship examining early modern debates about the theater. Its story, however, can provide a useful point of comparison for future studies on other French parishes. The parish of Saint-Sulpice exhibited a pronounced version of the tensions that characterized the relationship between the Catholic Church and theaters in France during the second half of the seventeenth and early eighteenth centuries. Within its borders, priests and actors pursued their vocations in close proximity, occasionally tussling over space. The parish housed more or less side by side the parish church, a monastery, and a seasonal fair called the Foire Saint-Germain, where, from at least the mid-sixteenth century, acrobats, tightrope dancers, and marionette players performed each year for a period of approximately three months between early February and Palm Sunday.[26] A parishioner or a priest needed merely to cross the rue des Aveugles to reach the fairgrounds—which occupied the lot directly across the street from the Church of Saint-Sulpice—and partake of, or take offense at, its entertainments. Thrust together as neighbors, it was only a matter of time before priests and performers in the parish began to clash over the proper ways to use the local environs.

The confluence of priests and performers further intensified in 1642, when the parish welcomed Jean-Jacques Olier as its new curate. A disciple of the great Catholic reformer Pierre de Bérulle, who advocated for an elevated view of the priesthood, Olier wanted to provide adequate training to secular priests, meaning those who did not belong to religious orders and therefore lived, so to speak, in the world.[27] He had founded a seminary the previous year, which he brought with him to his new parish, installing it first in his presbytery and then in a house on the rue Guisarde, which was attached to the presbytery by a garden.[28] In addition to the Seminary of Saint-Sulpice, Olier founded two other ecclesiastical organisms in his parish, a community of priests who dedicated themselves to assisting Olier with his pastoral duties, and a selective group of twelve priests who helped Olier run the seminary. The first, called the Communauté des Prêtres de la Paroisse Saint-Sulpice, boasted more than fifty members by 1645, and between sixty and eighty during the second half of the seventeenth century.[29] The second, called the Compagnie des Prêtres de Saint-Sulpice, devoted themselves to developing the seminary and training young churchmen. Although Olier established their number in honor of Jesus's apostles, twelve core members proved insufficient. He soon expanded the Compagnie to include seventy-two associated members.[30] Priests, priests-in-training, and seasonal performers thus all frequented the streets that surrounded the church.

An influx of professional actors during the century's last three decades increased yet again the frequency with which priests and performers crossed paths in the parish. In 1673, Molière's former troupe, displaced after his death from their theater at the Palais-Royal, near the Louvre, moved into an old *jeu de paume*, or indoor tennis court, in the parish.[31] Called La Bouteille, its precise location is not known. The renovated tennis court became known as the Théâtre Guénégaud, however, and was probably situated near where the rue Guénégaud intersects the rue Mazarine, only a few blocks from the Church of Saint-Sulpice.[32] In 1680, by Louis XIV's command, the actors from the Hôtel de Bourgogne, Paris's oldest theater, joined those at the Théâtre Guénégaud to form the Comédie-Française, making the parish of Saint-Sulpice Paris's theatrical epicenter.[33] After a two-year absence from the parish, the Comédie-Française returned in 1689 and moved into a building even closer to the Church of Saint-Sulpice, another former jeu de paume, L'Étoile, on the rue des Fossés Saint-Germain-des-Prés, just two hundred meters from their previous theater hall.[34]

The close quarters in which priests and actors worked in Saint-Sulpice did from time to time give rise to collaboration in sacramental settings, in particular upon the occasion of a birth. For the sake of a baby, priests allowed actors to serve as godparents. Parish registers in these cases did not mention the godparent's theatrical profession and cited instead alternate identifications, such as "bourgeois de Paris" and, most famously in the case of Molière, "tapissier valet de chambre ordinaire du Roy."[35] Nonetheless, when the recipient of a sacrament was an actor rather than a child or third party, priests took a much firmer stance. An actor's sacramental desires provided an opportunity for churchmen to negotiate with performers who, when on stage, created competition for religious services and challenged ecclesiastical authority by attracting parishioners to an activity the church deemed a potential prompt to sin.

This tendency toward competition rather than collaboration between priests and actors comes through clearly in documents surviving from the parish of Saint-Sulpice. By 1692, its priests had an international reputation for refusing sacraments to actors. When the orator from Molière's troupe, Charles Varlet (1635–1692), Sieur de La Grange, died on 1 March of that year, the rumor spread all the way to Holland that the curate at Saint-Sulpice had refused to bury him. The *Mercure galant* described and corrected the rumor, reporting that Varlet had actually lived and died in the parish of Saint-André des Arcs, "where he was buried at the hour of noon in the presence of over a thousand people."[36] While inaccurate regarding the details surrounding Varlet's death, the Dutch rumor resonated because a story concerning sacramental conflicts between priests and actors at Saint-Sulpice had a certain verisimilitude. Starting with an encounter between a performer from the Foire Saint-Germain and one of Olier's clergymen in the late 1640s, a string of sacramental negotiations between Sulpician priests and actors punctuated the parish's history right up to the French Revolution.[37]

A complete list of sacramental refusals and stage renunciations remains a historian's dream. Nonetheless, among the actors in the parish of Saint-Sulpice known to have grappled one way or another with the sacramental consequences of their profession upon death, those following the creation of the Comédie-Française and preceding the non-burial of Adrienne Lecouvreur begin with an actor named Brécourt (b. 1638), who died in 1685 after formally renouncing the stage in the presence of witnesses.[38] In 1686, an actor known as Rosimond—born Claude Larose (c. 1640)—died suddenly in the parish without having time to renounce his profession and was buried "without clergy, without light and without any prayers in a part of the cemetery of Saint-Sulpice where they put infants who die without baptism."[39] Two years later, his fellow actor Jean-François Juvénon (1650–1688), Sieur de La Thuillerie, had enough time before he died to renounce his profession and thus received a proper burial.[40] In 1693, Jean-Baptiste Siret Raisin (b. 1656), known as "the little Molière," fell ill, as chroniclers tell it, after a large meal and a bath and then renounced his profession in front of a notary before receiving Christian burial.[41] Maurice Vondrebeck (b. 1649?), a German fairgrounds performer renowned for his tightrope act, died in 1694 and received burial from the priests of Saint-Sulpice, presumably after renouncing his profession.[42] And finally, four years later, the famous Marie Desmares (b. 1641), known as La Champmeslé and remembered as the actor "that Racine formed," became sick and died on 15 May 1698 after having confessed and renounced her profession to the curate of Saint-Sulpice, who granted her burial in the parish cemetery.[43] Her husband, Charles Chevillet, Sieur de Champmeslé, by contrast, died suddenly in 1701 without having had time to renounce the stage and was buried in his home garden.[44]

As one could surmise from even this brief overview, the frequency with which priests withheld the viaticum and extreme unction until an actor renounced the stage and was subsequently reabsorbed in the sacramental community ebbed and flowed in relation to circumstances that brought priests and actors into close contact in the parish of Saint-Sulpice. Such negotiations surged after 1680, when the number of professional actors in the parish doubled with the creation of the Comédie-Française.[45] A history internal to the Society and Seminary of Saint-Sulpice also influenced the rhythm of sacramental refusals. As discussed in the introductory chapter, during the period in which sacramental refusals punctuated the theater's history—roughly between 1640 and 1730—the secular priests responsible for sacraments at the parish level were forging a new professional identity through seminary education. Seminaries, first founded in the late 1630s and early 1640s, taught secular clergymen how to conduct ceremonies, teach, preach, administer sacraments, and, as analyzed in previous chapters, comport themselves like vrays ecclésiastiques, or in keeping with post-Tridentine expectations for true priests.[46] The years just before and after 1680 marked a turning point for the priests of Saint-Sulpice, as the seminary and the compagnie that ran it transitioned from a period of early experimentation and expansion to a period of institutionalization. Olier's immediate successors had passed away shortly before 1680, entrusting the seminary and the parish church to a third generation of leaders entirely trained within what had become the Sulpician method, and this third generation committed itself to formalizing and enforcing the rules and techniques developed by their predecessors.[47] Whereas the first generation of Sulpician priests approached wayward parishioners in a spirit of improvisation, by 1680 the third generation considered it their duty to protect and reinforce the authority and reputation established by Olier and maintained by his successors.

## Spatial Confrontations and Priestly Extension

The physical proximity of priests and actors in the parish of Saint-Sulpice increased the likelihood of sacramental encounters between the two groups. Close contact alone, however, does not explain ecclesiastical action against actors. If churchmen and actors had used space in the same way, perhaps their interactions would have remained largely harmonious. Instead, theater troupes and seminary-trained priests approached parish space with often incompatible paradigms. More specifically, confrontations between churchmen and performers arose to an important degree from the way seminary-trained priests conceived of their identity in spatial terms. This spatial understanding of priestly selfhood, shared by churchmen affiliated with seminary training across France and therefore not restricted to the parish of Saint-Sulpice, disposed priests to see performers as rivals.

The notion of *étendu*, or extension, best captures the spatial conception of priestly identity that prompted churchmen, like the third generation of Sulpicians, to consider the sacramental reabsorption of actors a priority. Étendu envisioned the priest's person as extending potentially to infinity—or at least as far as God's kingdom on earth—and certainly to the edges of the territory under his jurisdiction.[48] In seminary manuals, the term occurs with the greatest frequency to describe the interconnectedness of ecclesiastics. According to a treatise on priestly vocation owned by Olier's successor, Louis Tronson, and incorporated into the *Traité des saints ordres* attributed to Saint-Sulpice's founder, the lower clergy in a parish constituted an extension of the parish priest. "The deacon who sings the Gospel for the priest, the subdeacon who reads the prophecies and the epistles, the acolytes who carry the candles in front of the Gospel," explains the handbook, "all these are extensions of the priest, and like the multiplication of his person. By them he is all at once in different places."[49] Likewise, a parish priest participated in the étendu of his bishop, and so on up the hierarchy all the way to Christ, in whose extension all churchmen participated. "Priests are the extensions of Jesus Christ," the *Traité* assured its readers.[50] A priest consequently had a corporate identity expressed not only through his own body but also through the bodies of his subordinate clergy.

In the same way that a parish priest's clergy contributed to his person and extended his presence, his flock, too, constituted part of his ecclesiastical identity. Theologically, a priest covered or stood in for his congregation before God, absorbing them into the church's metaphorical body. His long, black ecclesiastical garment, the soutane, represented the way a priest's identity extended beyond himself to include those in his charge. As the Tronson-owned treatise on priestly vocation explains, "The apostles and priests are the successors of his [Christ's] Spirit for honoring and glorifying God in the place of the world, and for this reason the soutane is so ample, representing the roundness and extension of the earth."[51] The "world" or "earth" encompassed by the soutane represented, in practice, the parish or diocese in which a priest had cure of souls. Seminary literature expressed the priest's responsibilities toward his flock in metaphors like motherhood and nourishment that conveyed the idea that an intimate, physical connection of dependence and provision tied parishioners to their priest. An educational tract entitled *Les Principaux devoirs d'un bon curé,* for example, instructed parish priests "to have a mother's heart toward all [his parishioners]."[52] A priest was not, consequently, conceived by Catholic reformers and seminary founders as an autonomous individual. Rather, the notion of étendu attributed to churchmen a nested identity. On the one hand, a priest gave form to his bishop's extension, or étendu, who in turn partook of the pope's and of Christ's. Meanwhile, the priest expressed this étendu in his relationship with his parishioners, to whom he distributed Christ's grace and for whom he interceded at the altar, rendering a parish priest's personhood difficult to distinguish from his cure. According to seminary literature, a good bishop produced good priests, and a good priest produced good parishioners.[53] At the parish level, then, the behavior of parishioners revealed, and thus helped constitute, a priest's ecclesiastical personhood, with the result that the presence of brothels, theaters, and bars all reflected poorly on a priest.

A priest's nested identity had profound implications for his activity within a parish, translating into spatial practices that sought to position the parish church as the nucleus of an ever-widening circle of order. Theatrical activity in a parish disrupted this order, frustrating priestly efforts to live up to the ideals associated with étendu. In relation to parishioner behavior, étendu imposed on priests a responsibility to know as much as possible about the people living in his jurisdiction. Étendu consequently required surveillance, and surveillance meant physically visiting every home and establishment in the parish. As *Les Principaux devoirs d'un bon curé* explains, the good parish priest "must in due course visit with skill each family in his parish and converse discretely with its individuals so that, knowing with more certainty all that happens, he can with prudence and opportunely resolve problems, both general and particular."[54] In the course of these visits, the parish priest was to record the name, address, age, social status and profession of each parishioner, with a note indicating whether he or she had received Communion and been confirmed.[55] By walking the parish's streets and visiting each house, churchmen whose vocation prohibited them from attending plays had the opportunity to come to know local performers by name, as well as to discover any ways in which their offstage lives failed to conform to church doctrine.

Despite the persistent idea in early modern antitheatrical literature that actors led dissolute lives, confrontations between priests and stage players in the parish of Saint Sulpice did not arise from the immoral behavior of stage players, at least as far as parish histories, surviving excerpts from parish registers, and *mé-moires* composed by the parish's priests indicate. Rather, evidence suggests that tensions between the church and the theater derived from the way a Counter-Reformation conception of priestly étendu led Sulpicians to seek control over the church building and the streets surrounding it. In the same way a priest's person extended beyond himself to include others, so the church building encompassed the area around it. Sounds and ceremonies, like church bells and processions, linked the altar—conceived as God's throne—to urban space outside the church's walls, expressing God's glory. According to Olier, bells transmitted the "joy of the Mysteries" celebrated at the altar and "supplement[ed]" the priest, "exciting the people to their duty" toward God.[56] Likewise ceremonies, such as the priest's gestures at Mass and the processions that accompanied the Blessed Sacrament, caused Christ's Spirit to "rain down upon" the people, spilling out from the altar to contiguous spaces.[57] At the same time, in much the way the good priest was expected to fortify himself against secular influences like fashion and plays, the parish church building was, ideally, impermeable to worldly activities and uses, an architectural nucleus from which God's glory emanated untarnished.[58] A good parish priest carefully regulated the uses, entrances, and exits of his church, taking "great care for the cleanliness and maintenance of his church, and ensuring that it [was] well shut and closed on all sides."[59] A well-maintained and strictly regulated church building expressed all at once the sanctity of Christ's presence on the altar and his outward radiation through sacraments and services.[60]

In order to put étendu into practice, priests faced a significant cultural task, which involved retraining parishioners accustomed to using church facilities for a variety of purposes to see the church building as a space restricted to religious uses. Edicts and episcopal instructions that aimed at regulating the way parishioners used church buildings record, in their attempts at prohibition, the degree to which parishioners treated church buildings as an extension of other public spaces, passing in and out of them continually and, by their actions, insisting on the church's permeable character. Lay people grazed their flocks, set up markets, hosted festivals, and even put on shows in the church's cemetery. Episcopal instructions required priests to make sure the cemetery had a "door that locked with a key," that its land not be "worked or sown" or used as a barn for beating grain, and, most interestingly for the question of theater conflicts, that "no one conduct fairs, markets, dances, manufacturing, or plays in it," all of which implied that well into the seventeenth century these practices were common in

French parishes.[61] People also promenaded in the church's interior, stashed wood and other precious resources in niches, and converted the church into a granary in winter.[62] They had their local priest announce properties for sale and for rent from the pulpit, buried their family members inside the church regardless of saintliness, collected alms in the nave, made confession in the passageways, and hurried in and out to participate in confraternity events.[63] Rather than a static site for unitary action, a parish church served as a hub for polyvalent, heterogeneous, simultaneous activities. This polyvalence challenged étendu's realization.

In the parish of Saint-Sulpice, a practical consideration further frustrated the clergy's desire to limit the church building's permeability. After Olier assumed the office of parish priest in 1641, he almost immediately launched a rebuilding campaign.[64] What better way to affirm the parish church's status as God's throne room than to make it anew in a size that conveyed its importance and according to a floor plan oriented around the high altar? The construction, however, proceeded slowly and left the priests of Saint-Sulpice with a dislocated, disjointed, partial building for almost ninety years. According to the parish churchwarden's register, in 1645 the architect, Christophe Gamard, traced the foundations for a new chancel in what was at the time the church's cemetery.[65] Not until 1673, the year that Molière's former troupe settled into the neighborhood, was the new chancel sufficiently complete to allow demolition of the old. After tearing down the old chancel, the churchwardens had the old nave temporarily connected to the new chancel. Unexpectedly, this temporary hybrid proved quite permanent because the church ran out of funds in 1678, the year a clergyman named Claude Bottu de La Barmondière (1631–1694) became the parish priest.[66] It was on Barmondière's watch that the priests at Saint-Sulpice began to refuse sacraments to actors with greater frequency, beginning with his insistence in 1685 that the actor known as Brécourt renounce the stage in order to receive burial.[67] Construction on the church did not start again until 1718, the new nave did not go up until 1723, and the new high altar was not consecrated until 1734.[68] During the intervening years, Saint-Sulpice's priests and parishioners made do with a tiny nave appended awkwardly to a large chancel, and for at least part of that time the floors differed in height.[69] During the period in which sacramental refusals to actors increased, Saint-Sulpice's church building quite literally defied distinctions between inside and outside, open and closed, new and old, chancel and cemetery, structural integrity and structural dissolution. A stymied construction campaign prolonged the church's permeability. Its disjointed structure did little to support the priestly identity that the clergy of Saint-Sulpice wanted to

instantiate, symbolizing instead their still-precarious professional progress and
their failure to fully realize Christ's extension, or étendu, on earth.


## Processions and the Provisional Expression of Étendu

In the absence of a building that expressed étendu in light and stone, the priests
of Saint-Sulpice vigilantly sought out and protected ceremonial practices that asserted priestly extension through the more provisional medium of gesture. Processions served this purpose particularly well, enabling priests to simultaneously
mitigate the church's porous boundaries by coordinating comings and goings and
to realize étendu extemporaneously, as it were, in areas like streets and squares
that seem to a twenty-first-century observer like non-church spaces but that
priests considered essential to God's glory. From an ecclesiastical perspective, the
church could not mark the liturgical calendar properly without processions.[70]
They preceded parish Masses, marked feast days, and accompanied the consecrated Eucharist whenever priests carried it to the sick or dying. In terms of
étendu, religious processions proved an extremely effective way of demonstrating, on the one hand, a priest's connection to his flock, and on the other the role
of the church building as a nucleus from which God's glory emanated. The Ritual of Alet, for example, articulated the way a procession enacted a priest's
nested identity. "Why in the procession do the faithful go and return together,
and in the company of their pastor?" the Ritual asks. "To teach us that a Christian must live and die in the faith and communion of the Church, and under
the direction of his pastor," it replies, underlining the interdependence of priest
and parishioner.[71] More important, a procession required a reverent response
from its witnesses, thereby expressing the altar's extension to all the spaces
through which a procession moved. Protocol required those who saw an ecclesiastical procession pass by with a consecrated wafer to genuflect in adoration. A
devotional pamphlet urged Catholics to "put yourself on your knees and say, 'I
adore you, my Lord Jesus-Christ,'" whenever they encountered the Blessed Sacrament in procession.[72] Priests did not leave spectator behavior to chance. Seminary handbooks instructed them to "make those who are in the street kneel" as
a procession passed.[73] By enforcing ceremonial participation, churchmen temporarily engulfed the spaces through which they walked with a performance of
étendu. To interrupt, impede, or ignore a procession consequently constituted a
direct attack—whether the perpetrator intended it so or not—on the authority
implied by priestly extension. Under such conditions, stage performers posed

a special menace to ecclesiastical étendu because theater crowds impeded processions.

During the decade prior to Barmondière's decision in 1685 to demand a renunciation from Brécourt before burying him, the priests at Saint-Sulpice believed that theatrical enterprises were encroaching upon their ceremonial territory. Performers from the Foire Saint-Germain posed the initial threat to parish processions. According to Simon de Doncourt (1714–1782), one of the earliest historians of the parish, in 1678 a group of entertainers took up residence during the fair on the rue des Quatre-Vents, a street behind the church.[74] Doncourt describes them as "marionette puppeteers, tightrope dancers, and other wandering entertainers."[75] The troupe was probably headed by Charles Allard and his pupil Vondrebeck, and it consisted of twenty-four entertainers who "had earned admiration first for their dances and acrobatics, their Italian postures, their tricks, their vaulting, and their dangerous balancing acts."[76] At some point before the festival season of 1678, Allard and Vondrebeck's troupe had started to "frame their exercises in little scenes with dialogue, which served as introduction and commentary for their acrobatics and dancing."[77] Their entertainments also made use of theatrical costumes. Jal's *Dictionnaire* notes that Allard dressed as Scaramouche and that his brother played Arlequin.[78] Prohibited by the fair's regulations from setting up their performance equipment inside the fairgrounds, where only merchants could erect stalls, the entertainers in question conducted their performances on temporary stages along the street. According to Doncourt, "this street was the one in the entire suburb where the very great Blessed Sacrament passed the most often when carried to the sick."[79] In other words, to the priests of Saint-Sulpice the rue des Quatre-Vents had great importance for the expression of étendu because they processed along it numerous times each week when administering the sacraments to parishioners who were not able to physically come to the church.

The troupe's encroachments on priestly étendu called for a defense. Barmondière had assumed the office of parish priest in November of the same year the seasonal performers moved into the rue des Quatre-Vents. His predecessors would have handled such a situation by trying to outcompete worldly diversions through liturgical splendor, fighting spectacle with spectacle. In some instances, contests over parish space pitted a priest against an entertainer in one-to-one ceremonial sparring. Joseph Grandet (1646–1724), a seminarian at Saint-Sulpice from 1671 to 1673, recounts an anecdote in which Olier sees a street performer "entertaining the masses" in a public square. In response, Olier launched his own solo performance and "began to preach from the other side of the street" until he had gained "more auditors than the clown who, finally, seeing that he had been abandoned, came to listen to him like the others and converted."[80] The anecdote, although unverifiable, but must have resonated with the second generation of Sulpicians who suddenly found themselves neighbors not only of street performers like the one in the anecdote but also of some of Paris's best professional actors.

When Barmondière confronted the entertainers on the rue des Quatre-Vents, however, unlike his predecessor he did not mount a direct ceremonial campaign. The Church of Saint-Sulpice had maintained a dense liturgical calendar ever since Olier's tenure. An additional increase in the number of services would not have resulted in a significant victory against the performers. Moreover, stalled progress on the church building's renovation limited the production of ceremonial splendor, reducing still further the appeal of a liturgical offensive against theatrical entertainments. Instead, when entertainers attempted to settle in the streets around the church in 1678, the priests of Saint-Sulpice initially attempted to shore up étendu with legal force, turning to the police and the king, who had weapons and laws on their side. At first, these external alliances seemed to guarantee conditions more amenable to processions. Barmondière filed a complaint with the lieutenant of police, Gabriel Nicolas de La Reynie (1625–1709), who granted the curate's request to prohibit the performers from living on the rue des Quatre-Vents and to fine any property owner who rented to them five hundred *livres* and imprisonment.[81] The marionette players, tightrope walkers, and other performers were thus forced to move. Barmondière continued to pursue them each time the performers attempted to live and work in the network of streets surrounding the church and fairgrounds, obtaining La Reynie's help to chase them from the rue des Cordeliers the following winter.[82] By working with the police, the priests of Saint-Sulpice succeeded in protecting, temporarily, their ceremonial territory.

This apparent victory for Barmondière and his collaborators, however, ended up aggravating the encroachment of theatrical activity on spaces that the priests considered ancillary to the church and its sacramental activities. In approximately 1683, the seasonal performers whom Barmondière had chased from the rue des Quatre-Vents and the rue des Cordeliers at last obtained permission to conduct their entertainments within the fairground, sharing space with the merchant stalls. To the clergy's great surprise, this change in fact undermined the victory that the priests of Saint-Sulpice thought they had won. The market and the church's cemetery shared a wall. Once inside the *foire*, the entertainers built their temporary stage against this wall, so that the cemetery wall served to support their makeshift theater space. Doncourt writes with indignation, "How could it be that there are spectators in a place separated from the cemetery by only the slightest partition?"[83] The new stage revealed the permeability of the church building, making a mockery of the priests' aspiration to possess the kind of closed church conducive to priestly extension.

Ten years later, when the actors from the Comédie-Française opened their new theater at L'Étoile—the remodeled tennis court near the church—they, too, occupied space along the processional path. In a complaint submitted to Louis XIV, Barmondière beseeched the king to prevent the actors from settling in the parish of Saint-Sulpice, protesting vigorously that their presence would interfere with the parish's Corpus Christi procession and processions for the sick and dead.[84] Barmondière considered the situation so dire that he even tried to buy L'Etoile from the actors, offering them five thousand livres of his own money, a price that Doncourt claims exceeded the land's value.[85] Neither Barmondière's request to the king nor his attempt to purchase the land obtained the desired results. The actors from the Comédie-Française continued building their new theater. Barmondière's strategic alliances and financial resources failed him, and Saint-Sulpice's priests found their processional practices deeply compromised.

The resulting theater crowds presented a double challenge to priestly authority. First, the traffic created before and after a play made the act of procession difficult. Priests had to fight their way through bodies and vehicles, which did not help them carry themselves with dignity. As Doncourt lamented, "Is it not scandalous that we cannot carry the Holy Viaticum to the sick without the greatest difficulty due to the multitude of vehicles that encircle the Church and occupy the streets where we need to pass?"[86] Second, people hurrying to the theater or waiting outside its doors did not form a particularly responsive gathering of witnesses for a procession. The failure to bow and pray in response to processions might be one reason priests described spectators as "disordered," as a "mass of faithless people, crooks and other villains, who gather together and cause great chaos."[87] No amount of devotional fervor demonstrated by the actors could outweigh the disruption their theater posed to processions. According to Gaston Maugras, for the first decade or more of the troupe's tenure at L'Etoile they in fact donated a monstrance and other ornaments, including an expensive silver gift valued at three thousand francs, for an altar erected in front of the theater along the Blessed Sacrament's path.[88] Yet, regardless of the actors' attempts at processional participation, their theater significantly wounded the priests' expression of étendu along the rue des Fossés-Saint-Germain.

Unappeased, the Sulpicians renounced their procession pathway. Doncourt writes, "Since that time, we no longer put the monstrance or conduct the Corpus Christi procession, nor any other, in that street."[89] He continues: "We also do things in such a way so as to never pass by there [the Comédie-Française] when carrying the Blessed Sacrament or Extreme Unction to the sick, nor when we do funeral processions and burials, unless the sick or deceased person lives on that street, in which case we go to the house of the sick or deceased by the shortest possible route, and we do not cross the street, but retrace our steps and return the way we came."[90] The local authority and spatial extension created by the priests of Saint-Sulpice along the rue des Fossés-Saint-Germain through annual processions and processions for the dead receded from around the Comédie-Française's building. The horizon of their priestly étendu shrank. In the ceremonial vacuum left when they abandoned their once-prized processional route, France's premier theater hall suddenly enjoyed the type of radiating enclosure that the priests coveted for their own building. Meanwhile, the clergy, its foes, scuttled back and forth in the theater's shadow.

## Stage Renunciations and Sacramental Reabsorption

In a period when priestly aspirations regarding the realization of étendu had received a series of harsh blows in the parish of Saint-Sulpice, an actor's illness and death presented a valuable opportunity to recruit key components of theatrical representation for the production of priestly extension. Three sacraments, received as close as possible to a person's last days, prepared a Catholic for death: penance, the viaticum—or last Communion—and extreme unction. These rites, as Barmondière would have administered them to Brécourt in 1685, show how a priest could turn an actor's malady into a processional take-back of lost ceremonial territory by demanding that an actor renounce the stage to receive the sacraments.

Although no documents—such as anecdotes or eyewitness accounts—that describe the interactions between Brécourt and Barmondière survive aside from the renunciation text, we see in seminary pamphlets and handbooks from the mid-seventeenth century outlines of the sequence of events that a curate would have tried to follow. The sacraments making up the last rites entailed at least four processions, a procession from the church to the person's house to administer the viaticum and extreme unction, followed by a procession from the house back to the church, and then, after the person's death, a procession from the church to the house to gather the body, followed by a procession from the house to back to the church. If a sick person lived long enough to receive Communion more than once before dying, each Communion multiplied the number of processions by two. These processions reabsorbed an invalid into the liturgical community. In doing so, the processions transformed the penitent's body and abode from self-contained sites into permeable nodes in the network of ceremonial pathways that composed the clergy's étendu and sustained the church's local authority. When analyzed from a performance perspective, in cases in which the penitent happened to be an actor the process of administering the sacraments before death achieved a twofold victory over the theater by recruiting the actor's body into the production of étendu and reorganizing key elements of theatrical play—namely, spectators, spectacles, and stages—in a way that served priestly extension.

First, when the sick person was an actor, the crowd that gathered to march in procession with the parish priest to an invalid's home to administer the last rites represented the church's ability to wrest spectators away from the theater and organize them into a liturgical body headed by the cross and oriented around the Blessed Sacrament. Before undertaking a viaticum procession, a priest tried to assemble as many participants as possible. Matthieu Beuvelet's much-used seminary handbook, *Instruction sur le manuel* (Guide to the diocesan Ritual), taught curates to designate a regular time for taking Holy Communion to the sick—preferably right after Mass, when more people were likely to join the procession—told curates to encourage family members to invite friends and neighbors, and specified that curates should summon people by tolling the church bells.[91] Given the importance that priests placed on planning and publicizing processions in advance, the assembly that gathered to carry the viaticum to an actor would likely attract admiring theatergoers, as well as family, friends, and neighbors, many of whom would be theater professionals themselves.[92] A procession consequently provided an opportunity to transform theater spectators into liturgical participants actively engaged in the expression of étendu.

Second, as the procession participants gathered into a sick person's house to witness the reception of the sacraments, the priest displaced the actor as the one to watch, replacing theatrical spectacle with liturgical ceremony. During the last rites, the priest had all the interesting lines, asked all the questions, and coordinated all the action. It was in this context that a curate demanded that an actor, as a "public sinner," renounce the theater. After asking those in attendance to briefly withdraw out of earshot while the priest heard the invalid's confession—which had the advantage, when dealing with actors, of preventing them from retaking center stage through a touching performance of contrition—the priest required the actor to make a public apology for his or her stagecraft before receiving absolution.[93] Without absolution, the actor could not receive the last rites or burial. With his friends, family, and, quite possibly, theatergoers watching, the actor thus ushered himself offstage, as Brécourt did, renouncing his profession. Religious performance replaced stage playing.

Finally, viaticum processions enabled priests to turn an actor's home into a proxy for the church building, symbolically replacing the stage with an altar. This temporary transmutation reversed the church's own permeability: whereas actors had turned the cemetery into a theater, here priests converted the actor's home into a chapel. To welcome the procession, the invalid's family had to remove any "dishonest paintings" and hang white sheets on all the walls.[94] The invalid, too, had to be draped in white. Beuvelet made these stipulations: "[That] the bed of the sick person be entirely covered with white linens so that nothing dirty appears, that there be a white napkin in front of him, and another around his neck that covers him entirely in the front."[95] These preparations absorbed the sick person's body into the liturgical setting, whitewashing, like the walls, his or her presence as a character with agency in the ensuing encounter. For an actor, this blotting out of his or her body achieved a sort of erasure. Near the invalid and positioned to be "in the sick person's view," the family placed a table dressed as an altar. Covered in a white tablecloth, it featured the objects necessary for liturgical spectacle: "a crucifix in the middle, two candelabra on either side with white candles, a stoup with an asperser to its right, [and] behind the cross a painting, or white linen, where one can attach bouquets."[96] By extending the church's territory into the interior space of an actor's house, a priest compensated for the territorial losses imposed, from an ecclesiastical perspective, upon the church by the theater. By setting up an altar-like surface in an actor's room, a priest symbolically converted theatrical space into a scene for the expression of étendu. The broad outlines of a viaticum procession—people proceeding through the street, rearranging furniture, hanging sheets, and making public apologies—thus transformed an invalid's home and person into ceremonial sites and objects linked to the Eucharist and constitutive of the curate's priestly extension.

Similarly, the details of administering the sacrament divided the sick person's body into a range of ceremonially linked zones by isolating each body part for liturgical action. For an actor, this ceremonial appropriation of the body symbolically short-circuited its ability to mimetically transmit the passions. Seventeenth-century actors, playwrights, and audiences understood acting in rhetorical terms.[97] The actor's vocal and gestural repertoire derived from the same sources as that of the orator or preacher: from the techniques associated with the fifth step for composing a discourse, *actio*.[98] In accordance with rhetorical principles, an actor therefore structured his or her performance by means of a series of more or less coded gestures intended to convey the meaning of a dramatic poem.[99] Certain parts of the body bore the greatest responsibility for conveying the rank and moral identity of each character and transmitting the passions, in particular the head, eyes, arms, hands, and legs.[100] The ceremonies of the viaticum and extreme unction carried special resonance when administered to stage players because the rites focused on these body parts.

As the penitent received Communion, first the head, then the hands, then the eyes, then the tongue had to remain still. The body parts, or zones, could not interact with one another unless in doing so they assumed the form of a ceremonial object. "Being ready to receive the holy Host," wrote Beuvelet of the good communicant, "you must keep your body straight and still, without tilting the head, either before or after receiving the holy Host."[101] The communicant could not touch one hand to the other unless they were "folded in a cross, one inside the other."[102] The eyes had to stay arrested, gazing intently at the floor and then directly at the wafer.[103] Finally the tongue—for an actor the vehicle of declamation—had to reveal itself and remain extended until the priest had deposited the wafer and withdrawn his hand.[104] These moments of stillness in the administration of the viaticum isolated the body parts essential to seventeenth-century *actio*. In the case of an actor, the obligation to submit each expressive organ to ceremonial action liturgically neutralized the physical extremities by means of which a stage player created an onstage character and conveyed the passions.

The sacrament of extreme unction, which supplemented a sick person's last confession, then reconnected the communicant's ceremonially activated body parts by associating them with sacramental objects that in turn linked the invalid to the priest, the beyond, and the extended church community; in other words, to the widest horizons of priestly extension. When administered to an actor, extreme unction conquered theatrical spectacle with ceremony by replacing a person's private body with a liturgical body, a body that could engage in symbolic action but not, given its global, networked character, imitate a specific person the way an actor played a role. A series of liquids, crosses, and prayers, deployed in waves, progressively unified the assembly of believers into one liturgical agent and exteriorized the inner work the invalid could no longer do. After aspersing both the sick person and the assembly with holy water flung in the shape of a cross—a gesture that figured them as one—the priest covered the sick person's body with objects that externalized the work of penance, placing a hair-cloth shaped like a cross on the patient's head and drawing a cross on his or her chest with ashes.[105] The priest then proceeded to anoint each of seven zones on the sick person's body: the eyes, ears, nostrils, mouth, chest, back of the hands, and tops of the feet.[106] The holy oil signaled on the body's outside the work that the Holy Spirit would do on the inside. Meanwhile, the people's prayers further activated the action operated by the oil, thereby merging their voices with the penitent's body. In Beuvelet's words, "In the sacrament of extreme unction one receives grace in proportion to the prayers said."[107] Although the sick person's soul would have to face the hour of death alone, liturgically the sacrament distributed his or her body and human agency among these other participants, who bore the responsibility of interceding with God on the invalid's behalf as he or she passed to the next life. Interpreted through a performance lens, extreme unction, when administered to an actor, therefore reclaimed the body parts formerly dedicated to transmitting the passions on stage and redirected them to prayer. At the same time, the sacrament incorporated the player's body into the priest's extended presence, or étendu, thereby giving expression to Christ's body, the church.

## Conclusion: Competing Performance Regimes

Like Adrienne Lecouvreur's charismatic stage performances, the ceremonies that sacramentally reabsorbed most actors into the liturgical community upon death were ephemeral. That is to say, ceremonies ceased to exist as soon as completed. In the same way that frontispieces and the published version of a play do not fully capture a given performance, the documents that make it possible to reconstruct, to some extent, a viaticum procession or extreme unction prayer are not in themselves ceremonies, only the record of them. The tendency to disappear defines performance, and also makes the study of it challenging.[108] Performances, such as liturgical ceremonies conducted on streets and in private homes, that do not announce themselves as performances to the same degree as do plays are consequently easy to overlook. A methodological imbalance has therefore quietly characterized scholarship on France's early modern theater debates: while the theater has been viewed as a producer of both texts and performances, the church has been treated as primarily a discursive entity. When reconstituted and contextualized, the liturgical ceremonies granted to, conducted around, and, on occasion, withheld from stage players in the seventeenth and early eighteenth centuries provide an important reminder that debates about the theater's moral status had a significant spatial dimension. Parties advocating for and against the theater used what could be called performance repertoires to work out answers to difficult problems like "Are plays sinful?" and "Does the theater strengthen society or undermine the social order?"[109]

The Saint-Sulpice case study demonstrates that when dealing with cultural transformations that come to a head as artistic polemics, such quarrels entail not just a confrontation of ideas but also negotiations among performance regimes. By performance regime, I mean the way a group—whether a small community or a big institution—uses elements like spectacle, spectatorship, setting, role-playing, and participation to conduct its affairs, represent itself to others, and promote internal cohesion.[110] Although some scholars, like Paul Friedland, argue that during the long seventeenth century the church, the king, and the theater all shared the same "theory and practice of representation," the spatial negotiations between priests and actors at the parish level suggest otherwise.[111] The theater provoked a moral debate in part because its professionalization reorganized the way early modern people understood and experienced the relationship between space, power, and authority. Residents of the parish of Saint-Sulpice sensed this reorganization most acutely in spatial disputes about the way in which plays and worship overflowed church and theater buildings.[112] For churchmen influenced by Counter-Reformation seminary training, developments in theatergoers' behavior before and after attending plays directly challenged the post-Tridentine ideal of the priesthood as represented by the concept of étendu. Consequently, access to and control over city streets, the timing and movement of people, and the responsiveness of passersby when clergy processed with the Blessed Sacrament all precipitated tension between priests and actors. Meanwhile actors—especially those from the professional troupes—did not have a great need to control the sounds and crowds that emanated from or gathered around their theater. These emanations certainly enhanced the excitement of attending a play, but the nature of the spectacle that drew people to the Comédie-Française would not have been diminished if the theater had soundproof walls or an entryway large enough so that everyone could wait inside before the show. For priests, by contrast, the sounds and movements that emanated from the church building constituted a crucial extension of the liturgical action conducted at the altar. To block, impede, or ignore bell ringing and processions was equivalent, from an ecclesiastical perspective, to interrupting Mass, impeding the priest's representation of Christ on earth, and insulting God's divine presence in the Blessed Sacrament; all weighty moral wrongs. When confronted by such perceived offences, an actor's death afforded clergymen an opportunity to temporarily regain the upper hand in spatial contests with the theater by incorporating a performer, his or her home, and potentially a number of theatergoers as well into the priestly extension that expressed étendu.

One might ask, in conclusion, why Languet de Gergy did not want to reabsorb Lecouvreur into the liturgical community, ceremonially reclaim her house, or even conduct the humblest of funeral rites. Why did he forgo the chance to use gesture and movement to contest the theater's growing cultural importance by recruiting one of its stars into the church's ceremonial network? A man who left very few written documents among his legacy, Languet de Gergy did not reveal his intentions in ink.[113] Nonetheless, in the genealogy of the vray ecclésiastique, Languet de Gergy marks a turning point. On the one hand, he enjoyed the full professional legitimacy his predecessors had wanted for the true churchman. Olier, Bourdoise, and their fellow mid-seventeenth-century Catholic reformers would have recognized in him an exemplary seminarian, able to resist pressure to bend the rules. From this perspective, Languet de Gergy had the resolve to scandalize the likes of Voltaire because he enjoyed the full authority crafted for secular clergymen during the previous ninety years since the foundation of Paris's *grands séminaires* in the 1640s. Thanks to institutions such as the Seminaries of Saint-Sulpice and Saint-Nicolas du Chardonnet, by the early eighteenth century the secular clergy enjoyed the prestige that accrued to a professional group that had achieved visibility as a recognizable type. Material supports further enhanced Languet de Gergy's performance of authority. Whereas Olier and Barmondière had faced architectural limitations when producing éclat because incomplete church renovations left the building disjointed, Languet de Gergy benefited from a church building constructed to post-Tridentine norms for ceremonial splendor. Its completion, one could argue, began to give clearer material expression to God's glory, thereby relieving some of the burden for étendu's production from outward-focused spatial practices like viaticum processions. In 1718, Languet de Gergy had renewed construction on the parish church.[114] In 1723, he had initiated the completion of the nave by leading the construction workers in a procession around the church's circumference.[115] When Lecouvreur died in 1730 the nave was still not quite complete—according to Doncourt the church was not "sufficiently closed" so as to be rededicated as a new building until 1745.[116] But the building had already begun to lose its permeable character. As the ideal of the vray ecclésiastique reached a crescendo, the absorption of stage rivals grew less important. Secure in their professional

identity, early eighteenth-century secular clergymen did not need to distinguish themselves from, and then liturgically reintegrate, actors.

On the other hand, even as Languet de Gergy embodied the performance
of authority imagined by mid-seventeenth-century Catholic reformers who had
promoted the ideal of the vray ecclésiastique, his complete refusal of last rites to
Lecouvreur also signaled a shift in the performance of priestly identity that would
gradually reduce the importance of ceremonies once the secular clergy's professional status was attained. In one sign of this shift, ceremonies turned in-
ward. Processional practices oriented toward the church building rather than
its surroundings took on greater importance as Languet de Gergy directed his
ceremonial energies toward furthering the church's construction, marking each
new phase of the project with an elaborate ceremony.[117] Secular clergymen also
sought new, less embodied forms of social legitimation. Unlike the seminary
curriculum of the seventeenth century with its emphasis on the priest's ceremonial skill, by the early eighteenth century, seminaries began to remake themselves as "veritable places for the teaching of philosophy and theology" and
to vie with universities for academic recognition.[118] Whereas seventeenth-
century Catholic reformers sought to distinguish the secular clergy through
liturgical expertise, eighteenth-century seminary directors began to focus on
more abstract forms of legitimization, such as credentials, which would make
actors less important as rivals or models for priestly performance.[119]

Liturgical paradigms for conceptualizing the priest's relation to his fellow
clergymen and his flock also gave way to more abstract notions. A close reading
of Sulpician seminary manuals suggests that by the early eighteenth century the
interconnectedness of bishop, parish priest, and parish, articulated through
concepts like étendu, had begun to recede into the background of clerical self-
understanding. The mystical element that had infused mid seventeenth-century
treatises on the priesthood's importance gave way toward the end of the century
to metaphors for governance, even though it was still present in notions of the
clergy as a "corps," or body.[120] A treatise from 1692, for example, on "the essence,
dignity and sanctity of the clergy" attributed to Charles de Lantages (1616–1694),
the Sulpician in charge of the seminary in Puy, repeatedly refers to the bishop's
authority as that of a governor's. Rather than participating in their bishop's étendu
as an extension of his ecclesiastical person, the priests in a diocese "receive[d] their
deputation" to "help" the bishop "instruct, govern and sanctify the Christian
people."[121] Instead of emphasizing the qualities that unified the bishop, priests,
the lower clergy, and the faithful, Lantages's text foregrounds the priesthood's

hierarchical nature, distinguishing "inferior ministers" from the "superiors" to whom they were "subordinated."[122] Seventeenth-century texts had certainly shared this hierarchical vision of the priesthood. Yet, Olier and his immediate successors had spiritualized each person's place in this hierarchy in a way that underscored a churchman's interdependence with his parish. As concepts like étendu faded from the pre-Enlightenment religious imaginary, a more atomized understanding of priestly identity began to emerge. Whereas a priest seeking to continually reestablish a ceremonial connection with his parish in order to realize Christ's extension on earth had a strong motivation to ultimately administer the sacraments to dying actors, a priest-as-governor did not, because his conformity to the priestly ideal of his time hinged less on spatial markers for relationship and more on effective administration. The shift from étendu to governance made the liturgical reabsorption of wayward parishioners like Lecouvreur less urgent. In some ways, then, Lecouvreur's ceremonial exclusion signaled the end of the seventeenth century's ceremonially constructed vray ecclésiastique.

# Conclusion

## Ceremonial Specialization and the Divergence
## of Performance Repertoires

Two young seminarians dressed in the long, black robes worn by Catholic clergymen scurried through a darkening Parisian side street in the parish of Saint-Sulpice. In the distance, where the building they approached faced the rue des Fossés-Saint-Germain-des-Prés, laughter, shouts, and horse hooves clamored as a crowd of theatergoers gathered in front of the Comédie-Française for the five o'clock performance. Furtively, the seminarians glanced from side to side before slipping into one of the theater's side doors, which opened into a narrow hallway. Above and around them, muffled by the corridor's walls, the footsteps of the other theatergoers gently vibrated as the seminarians followed the hallway toward the rounded theater boxes called *baignoires* that bordered the orchestra pit and from which spectators could watch a play unseen. Here, safely in their seats, the seminarians settled in to watch Molière's *Tartuffe*, the play that had catalyzed French debates about hypocrisy, religious devotion, and clerical identity since its debut in 1664.

I have imagined this scene based on a detail from the memoirs of the famous eighteenth-century actor François-Joseph Talma (1763–1826). Curious about the old theater hall where the Comédie-Française performed from 1689 to 1770, Talma went to visit it. His guide showed him the site of the old parterre and stage, transformed into a courtyard and warehouse, and lastly directed Talma's attention toward "a small corridor with its opening in the neighboring street and corresponding to the *baignoires*."[1] The guide told him, "It is by this corridor that the priests of Saint-Sulpice who wanted, without being seen, to watch *Tartuffe* and *Mahomet*, made their entry and their exit."[2] Whether the guide recounted a rumor or a fact, the story of Sulpician priests secretly watching *Tartuffe* in the late seventeenth and early eighteenth centuries offers a counterpoint to the *Miroir des prêtres* (Mirror of priests) with which our story of priestly performance opened. Here, rather than examining themselves against the behavioral norms and standards of the vray ecclésiastique—or post-Tridentine ideal of the "true churchman"—as they would do during their seminary lessons, these clergymen secretly watching *Tartuffe* presumably saw a reflection of their professional type refracted through the stage's parodic mirror.

The Tartuffe they saw would not be wearing the dark robe and small collar the character wore in the first production in 1664, which had signaled to a seventeenth-century audience Tartuffe's clerical associations by leveraging the investiture paradigm for clerical dress that seminaries had helped promote between the 1640s and 1660s. Rather, as Molière attested, in the revised versions of the play he had "disguised the character under the trappings of a man of the world" by giving him the opposite of clerical dress: "a small hat, long hair, a big collar, a sword, and lace all over his clothes."[3] Nonetheless, from an ecclesiastical perspective, in the absence of a ritual defrocking, once a priest always a priest. By changing Tartuffe's clothes without changing the performance repertoires from which Molière had constructed Tartuffe, Molière could not entirely dissociate Tartuffe from the clergy. A priestly pamphlet from the mid-seventeenth century entitled *Des Clercs desguisez, ou de l'habit clerical, selon les Saints Canons* (Of disguised clergymen, or of clerical dress according to the Holy Canons) might as well have been about Tartuffe. It declared: "Those churchmen who, against the order of the Church and the authority of the Holy Canons, nourish their hair and appear ordinarily without their tonsure . . . and those who almost always wear a short robe, would merit with justice the shameful name of 'Degraded.'"[4] Such disguised priests, as evidenced by the pamphlet's exasperation, remain priests, hence the author writes that they "would merit" the name "Degraded" rather than that they are degraded. Instead, these priests disguised in worldly clothes, "these Messieurs," writes the author, "say everywhere that they can do their hair and dress according to the fashion of the times and that, being engaged to haunt high society and to meet with precious company, they would be inconvenienced in such situations to appear as good churchmen and that, if they did, others would take them for *dévots* and for reformers."[5] Tartuffe's embodied practices, regardless of his clothes, would have reflected the ancien régime's seminary-trained secular clergy. The persistently clerical connotations of Tartuffe's character even when disguised as a courtier demonstrate why performance analysis must inform the study of antitheatrical sentiment.

Throughout this book, I have highlighted the performance practices of France's seventeenth-century secular churchmen, the type of churchmen who served as curates in French parishes, who administered sacraments to the Catholic laity, who by the second half of the century were increasingly trained in seminaries, and who, when faced with sick or dying actors, were likely to refuse to accord them the last rites or burial unless the actor renounced the stage. Although crucial to the history of antitheatrical sentiment in France and direct agents in the relationship between the church and the theater, these priests have received little scholarly attention in research on what, in French studies, is called *la querelle de la moralité du théâtre*, or early modern polemics about the theater's moral standing. Their story and the performance dynamics integral to the creation of priestly identity during the French Counter-Reformation reveal historically specific roots of antitheatrical sentiment that an intellectual history alone cannot uncover.

The intellectual trends that might have influenced parish priests who spurned actors are well known. Arguments against the theater changed little between the early seventeenth century and the Revolution, blending elements inherited from the church fathers, ecclesiastical councils, and Roman law. France's theatrical entertainments, so the basic argument went, descended directly from ancient Roman spectacles steeped in paganism and idolatry, which made spectators and actors alike guilty of breaking their baptismal promise to flee the devil.[6] Moreover, although it was not technically true, many early modern priests believed actors to be excommunicated, citing council decisions from Arles (452) and Constantinople (692), among others.[7] A second line of argument complemented the traditional reliance on the church fathers. Best represented by Pierre Nicole and Bossuet, it maintained that even though French plays bore little resemblance to the violent entertainments condemned by Tertullian, Chrysostom, and Augustine, their apparent moral purity in fact made plays all the more dangerous by enabling depictions of love to incite the passions in unsuspecting theatergoers.[8] The theater's most extreme critics consequently denounced stage players as much for their skill as for any link to paganism, rejecting them as "public poisoners who spread their venom by the eyes and ears."[9] Well-made plays composed and performed in keeping with bienséance and vraisemblance proved as dangerous for the soul and for the church as bawdy farces.

Despite many thorough studies of the content, rhetorical structure, legal foundations, and political implications of French discourses against the theater, the underlying forces that would prompt individual clergymen to put antitheatrical sentiment into practice against actors have remained elusive.[10] Each time scholars have examined ecclesiastical action against actors in search of a predictive pattern, they have been disappointed. As Ferdinando Taviana puts it, "That which we know are nothing but episodes (condemnations of actors, interruption of plays, demolitions of theatres, prohibitions against women players, etc.), anecdotes ... that do not manage to form a coherent whole."[11] This difficulty derives in part from a lack of research on the relationship between ecclesiastical attitudes toward actors and changes in religious practice. Consequently, although a rich body of scholarship details the meaning making accomplished by liturgical, civic, and royal ceremonies in early modern France, scholarship on French antitheatricalism has largely overlooked the way the ceremonial aspects of priestly activity may have constituted a coherent response to the theater's growing cultural influence.[12] All parish priests engaged in ceremonies, ceremonial concerns shaped their aspirations and anxieties, ceremonies mediated their responses to wayward parishioners, and those priests who did read theological tracts or intervene in doctrinal disputes eventually had to translate their intellectual positions into ceremonial actions.

By focusing on the way priests learned to conduct ceremonies and on how those ceremonies structured their modes of embodiment, their professional self-presentation, their public status, and their relationship to rivals, my intention in this book has been to show that antitheatrical sentiment in early modern France has a performance history. This history constitutes an important strand in the larger story of the transformations that reshaped priestly identity and liturgical practice during the French Counter-Reformation of the seventeenth and early eighteenth centuries. Within the broader context of religious change in early modern France, antitheatrical sentiment's performance history has at least three dimensions: social, ceremonial, and generic. In terms of social transformations, antitheatrical sentiment intensified during the second half of the seventeenth century in conjunction with the simultaneous professionalization of both secular priests and actors. Whereas in the 1630s noble families like that of Jean-Jacques Olier viewed the office of parish priest as demeaning and stage players had to insist that they were not *bateleurs* or *farceurs*, by the early 1700s an extensive body of ecclesiastical literature positioned the parish priest as the ideal churchman, and actors at the Comédie-Française enjoyed the king's royal patronage and a name that linked them to the emerging nation-state's identity. The parallel efforts of secular priests and actors to establish themselves as professionals bred tension between the two groups.

One reason simultaneous professionalization fostered competition between secular priests and actors concerned the visible and, in early modern terms, public nature of both pastoral and theatrical work. Given the negative connotations associated with visibility when not tempered by ceremonies or writing, secular priests and actors alike needed to differentiate their accessibility to the gaze of parishioners and spectators from forms of exposure classified as sin. In order to legitimize their crafts, both groups had needed to use a range of strategies. Secular priests and actors alike had struggled, during the second half of the seventeenth century, to reshape the discourses that defined their professions. Secular priests legitimized their office by positioning their task as more difficult than that of regular priests. Actors legitimized their craft by differentiating their artistic production as comédiens from the popular spectacles offered by traveling troupes. Likewise, both groups strengthened the institutions that granted legitimacy to their work, secular priests by establishing seminaries that provided specialized training, and actors by attaching their troupes to fixed theater buildings and securing royal patrons. For both secular priests and actors, however, the greatest source of social legitimacy and cultural authority derived from the way the members of each group standardized and controlled their performances so as to designate priestcraft and stagecraft as highly skilled, vocationally specific activities. For priests in particular, for whom the accusation of artifice could unravel their religious authority, professionalization entailed policing the boundaries between their own specialized performances and those of other groups, such as actors. In the context of parallel professionalization, antitheatrical discourses and ecclesiastical action against actors served to protect the social gains made by the secular clergy.

The ceremonial dimension of antitheatrical sentiment's performance history follows from the professionalization of secular priests. As this book's examination of the performative structure of priestly identity has shown, religious statements against plays, actors, and the stage in early modern France constituted but one expression among many of the cultural tensions that induced churchmen to simultaneously look to the theater as a model for the renewal of Catholic priestcraft and dispute the theater's place in public life. Although French priests did deploy discursive arguments against the theater, incorporating them into sermons and reiterating them in pamphlets on how to be a priest, they also used the church's specialized modes of religious performance in the form of liturgical ceremonies and sacraments to refute the premises of theatrical performance, exert control over actors, and promote liturgical practice as the kingdom's dominant representational paradigm. In other words, priests used ceremonies to influence the modes of seeing and being seen deployed in public settings such as the church, the theater, and the court during the second half of the seventeenth century.

As the secular clergy gained ceremonial expertise over the course of the seventeenth century, the French Counter-Reformation's liturgical vibrancy also grew. The Mass was already, in John Bossy's words, a "social institution" during the medieval period, which would have shaped the way parishioners interpreted other cultural activities.[13] Its greater visibility and standardization after the Council of Trent meant that for most men and women in seventeenth-century France, liturgical performance provided the paradigm for viewing and interpreting spectacles. Although surviving documents make it impossible to ascertain the precise number of Masses celebrated versus plays performed in a city like Paris for a given year in the reign of Louis XIV, they do allow for a rough comparison. Paris had fifty-two parishes by 1789, each of which offered a High Mass (*grande messe*) at the main altar of its parish church on Sundays and feast days.[14] Numerous chapels, convents, and monasteries did the same. In addition, each church or chapel scheduled a wide array of other Masses, prayer services, and public devotions throughout the week. A guide to liturgical and devotional events in and around Paris published annually for most of the years between 1647 and approximately 1775, entitled *L'Almanach spirituel*, shows how a devout Catholic could attend Mass or public prayer every day of the year.[15] In 1667, for example, a Catholic could hear the Divine Office twenty-four hours a day, 365 days a year by going from church to church around the city.[16] Without even considering the Masses celebrated each day for the dead or for rotating feast days, on Mondays the devout could attend a Solemn Mass at Saint-Eustache or a Mass of Saint Roch in the churches of Saint Barthelemy and Saint Leu Saint Gilles, on Wednesdays they could visit the exposition of the Blessed Sacrament in the parish of Saint-André-des-Arts, on Thursdays they could attend a Solemn Mass of the Blessed Sacrament "in most parishes," on Fridays they could attend a High Mass at Saint Sauveur or a Solemn Mass of the Blessed Sacrament at Saint Gervais, and on Saturdays they could attend a High Mass of the Holy Virgin in "many parishes and monasteries" or a Solemn Mass in the chapel of the reformed Premonstrez in the faubourg Saint-Germain.[17] Religious spectacles dominated the cultural scene in early modern Paris.

By contrast, even in 1660, the year in which Paris boasted the most theatrical choice during the seventeenth century with six acting troupes, an avid theatergoer would not have been able attend a play every day of the year.[18] Before 1680, troupes performed an average of two or three times a week in the public theaters, typically on Friday, Sunday, and Tuesday.[19] If the king summoned a troupe to give a private performance at court, though, performances scheduled for the public stage were often canceled for lack of players.[20] After the merger of Paris's three main troupes in 1680, the newly formed Comédie-Française performed every day of the week during the theatrical season.[21] During the same period, the Italian troupe also performed every day but Friday.[22] Periods of rest punctuated the year. Theaters closed during Advent, Lent, and Holy Week, as well as during periods of mourning in honor of the death of important members of the royal family or the nobility.[23] These theatrical closures for religious observance corresponded to periods in which churches offered a greater number of liturgical spectacles than usual, such as the processions from church to church, Masses in music, first Communion ceremonies, adorations of the cross and of the Blessed Sacrament characteristic of early modern Easter festivities.[24] Thus, although the theater's cultural status and influence grew as the seventeenth century progressed, liturgical performance outpaced and overwhelmed theatrical performance in terms of frequency, accessibility, and sheer number of attendees.

The logic, expectations, and practices common to the liturgical repertoire informed the way audiences responded to plays and the types of arguments the theater's critics adopted in their attacks on plays and playgoing. France's antitheatricalists evaluated plays through the lens of Masses, describing theatrical performance in liturgical terms. A mid-seventeenth-century sermon against marionettes and plays provides just one example.[25] Conserved in a small, handwritten notebook of sermons against entertainments that were likely pronounced in the Parisian parish of Saint-Sulpice during Lent, the sermon begins by equating the seventeenth-century's plays and farces to the Roman spectacles against which Cyprian railed in the third century, and then chastises parishioners for attending them.[26] "You have made a game and a pastime out of what was formerly an act of idolatry," declares the sermon, "and after having renounced idols, you still make exceptions for this extravagant and libertine cult that remains prohibited to you."[27] The term "culte" referred to physical acts of worship, to ceremonies. Theatergoers chose diabolical ceremonies over saintly ones, the preacher protested. Plays amounted to a perverse liturgy.

The liturgy's dominance in seventeenth-century France's representational culture points to the generic dimension of antitheatrical sentiment's performance history and poses a methodological challenge to the metaphor most commonly used by scholars to interpret early modern ceremonial. Researchers regularly analyze the spectacular features of royal and liturgical ceremonies as a form of theater. Pierre Mélèse begins his study of the seventeenth-century theater with the assertion that "the pomp of the century of Louis XIV depends, itself, on the art of *mise-en-scène*, and the Sun King is the first among all actors, the most frequently in representation."[28] Jean-Marie Apostolidès associates the early modern theater with religious ceremony, analyzes the liturgy as theater, and then locates both under the category of ritual in order to conclude that the Mass and the theater share a parallel political function, that of sacrifice.[29] Frédérique Leferme-Falguières describes courtly ceremonial as a "permanent theater," and Ralph Giesey calls it a "theater" that "follows the King."[30] Most recently, Philippe Martin uses the theater metaphor to structure his historical overview of the Mass, entitling his book *Le Théâtre divin* (The divine theater).[31] Theater metaphors permeate contemporary scholarship on early modern ceremonial.[32]

The theater metaphor certainly offers interpretive advantages. It makes early modern ceremonies intelligible to twenty-first-century readers by shedding light on the complex game of seeing and being seen that was integral to ceremonial domination and the production of royal majesty. Its incumbent distinction between actors and spectators makes the theater metaphor useful for dissecting the roles occupied by ceremonial's various agents. Lucien Bély thus conceives of court ceremonies as a "political spectacle" in which "each gesture and decorative detail needed to be seen and understood" by the nobles and royal subjects who served as the king's spectators.[33] The actor-spectator framework also helps explain the blend of physical proximity and social distance generated in ceremonial situations. On the one hand, the higher a person's rank in early modern France, the more he or she lived a life surrounded by others. The more important the noble, the larger the number of ladies or gentlemen in waiting, pages, lackeys, servants, and other individuals in his or her service. Norbert Elias observes, "Great lords and ladies needed an army of domestics," and indicates that by 1744 the palace of Versailles, according to at least one report, had a population of ten thousand people.[34] In the midst of this physical proximity, the king had to "introduce the necessary distance with his courtiers."[35] Ceremonial activities achieved this goal by visually and mentally marking the distances that "separated . . . the members of the society from each other."[36] The metaphor of the theater spectator who passively watches actors on an elevated stage from the cramped pit or box conveys the separation and passivity that these ceremonies presumably imposed on their witnesses in the course of marking social distances.[37]

Despite its rewards, the theater metaphor poses a range of interpretive problems. The chief disadvantage is that the theater metaphor obscures the aspects of early modern ceremonies that people could enact, feel, or imagine but not technically see in an objective sense. Worshippers in churches, people in crowds, and even playgoers with lateral views of the stage could not always see very much or very well, such that the notion of a spectator does not adequately represent their experiences. An interpretive frame that encompasses touch and sound in addition to sight would expand our understanding of the way ceremonies functioned. Although a theater metaphor has the potential to signal these other sensory registers, it usually does not. Second, because the theater metaphor often comes coupled with anachronistic assumptions about spectator passivity, it neutralizes the agency of ceremonial and theatrical participants. Despite research by scholars like Barbara Mittman and Jeffrey Ravel demonstrating that early modern spectators were neither distant nor passive in relation to onstage action, as a metaphor the theater nonetheless stands in for a dynamic in which the watcher has less power than the doer.[38] Third, by sweeping all ceremonial activities under the sign of theater, it becomes more difficult to discern the variety of performance logics that operated in early modern representational cultures. I am most interested in the logics that organized liturgical and theatrical obligations, but it is quite possible that other regular activities under the ancien régime, like gambling, masques, and the promenade, would also benefit from fewer theatrical metaphors. Seeing and being seen were important to all these activities, but the interplay of sight, sound, and touch, as well as the use of space and time, differed significantly from activity to activity. It would be worthwhile to ascertain these nuanced differences. Finally, the theater metaphor is arguably an important reason that scholars have had difficulty articulating why early modern conflicts between the church and the theater occurred in the first place. If everything was already theatrical, what could possibly be at stake in the performance of plays? What could be dangerous about actors?

Without minimizing the importance of seeing and being seen, performance as an analytical lens offers an interpretive mode that does not inevitably lead back to the theater. Performance decenters the eyes to consider the entire body's contribution to meaning making. Richard Schechner's definition of performance as "showing doing," for example, encompasses the notion of spectacle while at the same time avoiding the passive connotations associated with spectatorship.[39] A performer may be "showing doing," but that does not mean that the person watching is not doing something too. For Schechner, performance consists of "strips of behavior"—whether the sequence of movements that compose a ceremony or the series of actions that identify an onstage character—that "can be rearranged or reconstructed."[40] This focus on repeatable behaviors expands the points of comparison possible between two activities defined as performance, like Masses and plays.

A focus on strips of behavior brings to light an otherwise hidden gestural layer within antitheatrical discourses, which in turn points toward new answers regarding early modern conflicts between the church and the theater. Jacques-Bénigne Bossuet's treatise against the theater provides just one example of how arguments against the theater mobilized a liturgical logic rooted in ceremonial gestures. Bossuet, the bishop of Meaux and a frequent preacher at Louis XIV's court, cast the dangers of theatrical identification in religious language by comparing the spectator's interest in onstage characters to worship: "Thus, the poet's sole intention, the entire aim of his work, is that they [the spectators] are, like his hero, captivated by beautiful people, that they serve them [the characters] like gods; in a word, that they sacrifice everything to [the characters]."[41] By equating theater spectatorship to worship, Bossuet advanced the argument that the experience of watching a play interfered with a Catholic believer's religious obligations. He did not go so far as to assert that play watching amounted to idolatry, although many of his fellow churchmen did.[42] Nor did Bossuet choose to issue an episcopal letter. The stated purpose of his *Maximes et réflexions sur la comédie* (Maxims and reflections on plays) was to counteract a short tract in favor of the theater that had circulated widely among Paris's educated, playgoing public earlier in 1694. This theater apology, attributed to a monk named Francesco Caffaro (1650?–1720), "made itself read by its brevity."[43] In response, Bossuet offered his own readable text as an antidote in the form of "short reflections filled with great religious principles."[44] Rhetorically, the language of worship appealed to readers by evoking the hotly debated theological problems posed by images and icons while simultaneously drawing on metaphors familiar to them from love poetry.

Bossuet's reliance on the metaphor of worship, however, was more than a rhetorical embellishment. In a liturgical context, the verbs on which the metaphor hinged—*servir* (to serve), *sacrifier* (to sacrifice)—referenced specific bodily practices that constituted a recognizable set of behaviors associated with attending Mass but also applicable in other domains. As Olier explained in the introduction to his *Explication des cérémonies de la grande messe de paroisse* (Explanation of the ceremonies of the high parish Mass), "God wants to be served and honored," to which end he instituted liturgical ceremonies.[45] The gestures conveying service and sacrifice included movements for marking the Christian's body, like the sign of the cross or the application of holy water, as well as physical actions that transmitted God's glory through the worshipper's limbs, like genuflections, inclinations, and prostrations. According to Olier, for example, the genuflections and adorations conducted by a priest at the foot of the altar during Mass expressed "the profound astonishment that obliges him to humiliate and annihilate himself before the divine Majesty."[46] Bossuet's own catechism taught the children in his parish that God created them to "know, love and *serve* him," taught them how to assist the clergy, or "serve at the mass," and taught them that in presenting the bread and wine before the altar during the Eucharist a priest offered a sacrifice.[47] Clergymen and laypeople alike in early modern France understood that serving a divinity required a well-trained body. Bossuet's argument against the theater therefore accused playgoers of misdirecting their liturgical actions.

This misdirection was more than metaphorical. Catholic prayer required the same gestures associated with the verbs "servir" and "sacrifier." In teaching children to pray, Bossuet's catechism taught them first and foremost the sign of the cross and gave careful instructions about how to bow when passing in front of the altar.[48] Theatrical captivation disrupted the concentration necessary for such spiritual exercises. "Amid all these commotions in which all the pleasure of plays consists," writes Bossuet in his *Maximes*, "who can lift his heart to God, who does not fear, in these foolish joys and foolish sorrows, to extinguish in himself the spirit of prayer, and interrupt this exercise, which, according to the word of Jesus Christ, must be perpetual for a Christian?"[49] Liturgical ceremonies required continuous application, which theatrical entertainment rendered impossible. The comparison Bossuet draws between the captivated spectator and the devout worshipper therefore points to a conflict between the Mass and the theater rooted as much in gestural practices—in the timing and application of recognizable strips of behavior—as in theology and philosophy.

Antitheatrical sentiment, in other words, had a generic dimension that arose from divergences between the performance repertoires out of which stage plays and Masses were composed. By this, I mean that spectacles in France's parish churches and public theaters deployed many similar elements, ranging from elevated performance spaces to candles to courtly gestures, but the spectacles organized these elements according to distinctive, and at times incompatible, logics. In his *Maximes*, Bossuet wrestles with this generic dimension by tracing what I call the performatic tensions between liturgical and theatrical participation. Diana Taylor invented the term "performatic" to solve a semantic problem in performance studies. She recognized that she could not, without provoking confusion, use the term "performativity" to talk about the way embodied practices create or transfer cultural knowledge and social norms. Although performativity would seem to refer to the various physical qualities or effects of performance, theorists adopted the notion of performativity from linguistic philosophers. As a result of this heritage, performativity refers primarily to the capacity of discursive practices like speech acts or the normative uses of language to produce real effects in the embodied realm, rather than the reverse. Taylor therefore coined the term "performatic" "to denote the adjectival form of the nondiscursive realm of performance."[50] Thus, discourses are performative, whereas performances are performatic.

By highlighting the capacity of embodied practices to do things in an Austinian sense, Taylor's term offers a complement, and sometimes an antidote, to the theater metaphor traditionally used to interpret early modern ceremonies. According to J. L. Austin, a performative speech act transforms the identity of the speaker by defining or redefining social bonds.[51] His classic example is the statement "I do" in marriage.[52] Taylor's term makes the same phenomenon thinkable for bodily actions. A performatic gesture, like performative speech, instantiates or reiterates a social relation. A bow presents the simplest example, instantiating or reiterating a difference in status.[53] The bowed heads and moving hands evoked by Bossuet through the verbs "servir" and "sacrifier" had a performatic function by creating and sustaining ecclesiastical authority.

By extension, it then becomes possible to theorize performatic formations that operate in the realm of gesture according to the principles described by Michel Foucault at the level of discourse, what he calls discursive formations.[54] Foucault draws his favorite examples of discursive formations from law and medicine. Discursive formations consist of statements among which one can identify regular patterns of dispersion, for example "an order, correlations, positions and functions, [and] transformations."[55] The patterns of dispersion that make up a discursive formation give rise to a "field of strategic possibilities," which in turn "permit the activation of incompatible themes, or . . . the establishment of the same theme in different groups of statement[s]."[56] In other words, discursive formations enjoy coherence thanks to the rules that guide not the content of statements but their organization and relation to other statements. At the same time, discursive formations tolerate a high degree of heterogeneity by setting the parameters for the kinds of statements that *can* be said and for their possible meanings, rather than dictating which statements will or must be said. A statement made up of the exact same words might therefore appear in more than one discursive formation but with quite different effects, not because the statement's content has changed but because the logic connecting it to other statements differs from one discursive formation to another. The physical behaviors associated with the theater and the Mass, even when they share common gestures like the bow, follow distinct patterns of dispersion. They constitute performatic formations.

Other terms that evoke the idea that performance genres organize bodies, objects, and spaces according to distinctive patterns of dispersion include the notion of repertoire and the concept of performance regimes, both of which I have used throughout this book.[57] Whether we opt for one term or the other, the important point is that the inner logic organizing theatrical activity—by which I mean both performing on stage and watching a performance from within an audience—unraveled the ceremonial glue that provided sociocultural coherence to a society organized around rank. Secular priests, who had both a religious and a professional investment in the liturgical repertoire's smooth operation, felt particularly threatened by the theater and by those who performed in it. Their own social advancement in relation to the regular clergy on the one hand and their authority over their parishes on the other depended on ceremonies conducted well and without interruption. The verbs that trouble Bossuet revolved around notions of movement. Something about the theater experience moved— rearranged, misaligned, disrupted—the organization of bodies and objects in space and time that was crucial for producing ceremonial splendor. If the ceremonies of the Mass elaborated a performatic formation, theatrical activity—even when embedded within the ceremonial framework at court—very often presented a performatic interruption.

As a performatic formation, the Catholic liturgy of the French Counter-Reformation—or at least the idealized version of it prescribed by France's early modern seminaries and constitutive of the secular clergy's professional identity— linked participants together in what can be thought of as supplemental relations. Olier chose the term "supplement" to describe a priest's liturgical function. In a text prepared for publication by Louis Tronson and attributed to Olier, the founder of Saint-Sulpice wrote: "The priest serves merely as *supplement* to the host, which cannot offer itself in a perceptible way."[58] While supplementing the eucharistic wafer, the priest simultaneously supplemented the laity's agential lack. Olier wrote in his *Mémoires*, "The priest is to supplement the religion and respect of all the people, mute to God's praise and insensitive to their duty. For this reason, the priest or pastor must consider himself as containing in himself alone all the religion of his People."[59] The divine presence could not express itself, the host could not offer itself, and the worshippers could not hear the call, perceive their duties, or fulfill their obligations. The priest's body, by carrying out the ceremonies of the Mass, completed and connected these other parties, people, and objects in the moment of sacrifice.

The supplemental relations that connected priests to other parties, people, and objects operated in multiple directions, making the limits of a clergyman's personhood hard to identify. Objects supplemented priest. "The bells are the supplement for the word and the voice," wrote Tronson.[60] Priests supplemented other priests. Olier believed that priests devoted strictly to liturgical ceremonies, like abbots, monks, and cathedral canons, supplemented clergymen who were devoted to pastoral care.[61] The first group, whose "principal functions are to praise [G]od assiduously through a magnificent service . . . with grand ceremonies," could not simultaneously attend to the needs of the laity, whereas the second group applied itself to the needs of the laity and consequently could not satisfy their ceremonial duties with the same assiduity as the monks.[62] Thus, priests supplemented each other. And the laity participated in this supplementary logic too. Although ecclesiastical texts rarely admit the degree to which laypersons supplemented priestly action, the lone missionary, cut off from the usual supplemental network, occasionally recognized this dynamic. For example, Jacques Gravier, a Jesuit missionary in New France, wrote to his superior of the Kasaskia converts who attended his chapel, "[They] are of great assistance to the missionary, and do more than I—or rather they do all, and I do nothing, or almost nothing."[63] Through supplements and supplementation, the liturgical repertoire managed the flow of agency in a highly stratified society. Supplemental relations transferred agency among liturgical participants without completely depleting any of them. An ongoing process of agential delegation and accumulation created and maintained the supplemental relations at the heart of the liturgical repertoire, weaving priests, host, worshippers, and divine presence together into an interconnected entity.

In the process of agential transfers accomplished by the liturgical repertoire, the perfect churchman, as imagined by seminary directors, functioned as a receptacle, a site of agential accumulation. As suggested by the title of a small tract written by an archdeacon from the church of Chartres named Nicolas Janvier and published at a press near the Seminary of Saint-Nicolas du Chardonnet, the liturgical repertoire deposited in the priest a surplus of the "power, right, and duty" to act. Janvier's tract, entitled *Des Prestres et curéz: De leur institution, puissance, droicts & devoirs en l'Eglise* (Of priests and curates: Of their institution, power, rights, and duties in the church), described priests as "the channel by which the divine Graces flow into the Faithful."[64] Seventeenth-century texts about priests and the priesthood also figured the priest as a container. Matthieu Beuvelet, liturgist at the seminary of Saint-Nicolas du Chardonnet, compared the priest to the Virgin Mary's womb. The Holy Spirit entered her womb to conceive Jesus, and the Holy Spirit entered the priest at his ordination to enable him to produce Jesus's body and blood at the altar: "Consider the connections between the Priest's functions and the office of Mother of God: If she has conceived the Verb incarnate in her chaste entrails, it is this same Verb that the Priest produces at the altar by the words of the consecration. . . . But notice principally the connection between these two excellent dignities in the following . . . that just as, to produce and form the Body of the Son of God in the belly of the sacred Virgin, the Holy Spirit was given to her, the same Holy Spirit is given to the Priest in the ordination."[65] This surplus of agency did not, however, constitute a self-generated feature of a priest's presence in the world, nor did it derive from his particularity. To the contrary, the agency that accumulated in priests inhabited them.

The mystically inclined, like Olier, experienced this habitation as a physical sensation. In his memoirs for 30 July 1644, Olier describes a sudden awareness of being inhabited while saying a Mass to the Holy Spirit on the feast day of Saint Anne: "And at the same time it pleased the goodness of GOD to say to me: I want you to take the place of the holy Spirit over these children; and at the same *feeling myself filled with the holy Spirit from my feet to my head*, I felt that as I turned toward them to say 'Dominus vobiscum,' I had a certain substance in me capable of feeding them, *as if from me it went out over them*."[66] Olier's acute awareness of himself as a receptacle or channel for an agency not his own corresponded to a moment in the Mass in which he actively transferred spiritual agency to others. The celebrant said the Latin phrase "Dominus vobiscum," which means "The Lord be with you," many times during a standard Mass, turning in each instance toward the worshippers, spreading his hands as he would in a benediction, and then joining his hands in front of his chest. In a Low Mass, for example, the celebrant said "Dominus vobiscum" at the beginning of the *Oraisons*, or prayers, before the Gospel reading, before the Offertory, at the conclusion of Communion, and twice during the end of the Mass.[67] Olier does not specify during exactly which utterance he felt the Holy Spirit pass through his body. It seems likely, though, that this habitation occurred during the Mass's opening prayers because in his *Explications des cérémonies de la grand'messe de paroisse*, Olier describes the *Dominus vobiscum* with the same vocabulary of an ambient agency that passes through and fills bodies. Olier writes, "The priest opens his hands when he says *Dominus vobiscum* because he wants the Holy Spirit . . . to be dilated and spread over all in plenitude."[68] The *Dominus vobiscum* foregrounded the basic similarity between ecclesiastical and lay bodies in the liturgical system. Both functioned as receptacles and passageways for an agency that always had a foreign and public character, an agency that belonged to everyone a little and to no one completely.

Within the ebb and flow of agential delegations and accumulations intrinsic to the liturgical repertoire, the priest constituted a supplemental fold. As other bodies and beings were folded into his, the agency that accumulated in the priest acquired a monstrous quality, associating him with the image preferred by anti-theater writers to disparage playgoers in the theater pit, the many-headed monster. In a chapter on the grandeur of priestly obligations, Tronson wrote: "The Priest is a prodigy of grace, and if the word monster could be taken in a good sense, one could say he is a monster of saintliness. For in nature one calls a monster that which has a hundred heads, a hundred feet, or a hundred eyes: And the Priest by grace is someone with a hundred hearts; and he must have even more than that, because he must have millions of [hearts], he must have as many of them as there are reasonable creatures living on the earth."[69] The image of the monster foregrounds the way the liturgical repertoire distributed agency unevenly, endowing some bodies and objects with a surplus of agency.

Not only did the liturgical repertoire distribute agency unevenly, it also embedded lower-status functions or dispersions within higher-status functions or dispersions. In the manuscript from which Tronson drew his inspiration for the monster image, the author attributed the priest's monstrosity to what he called the priest's extension, his enfolding into one body all the lower clerical orders that composed the church: "A Priest is a Magnificent thing; and the extension of his spirit has no bounds, it entails, in their totality, all the inferior orders that represent in part something of what he is and what he must be in the Church."[70] Thus, although the progression from layperson to cleric to priest involved climbing a rigid hierarchy, participants in this hierarchy are best imagined not as scaling a staircase but rather as adding layers to their extension, like nested Russian dolls.

In some respects, liturgy accomplished through ceremonial patterns what seventeenth-century theater—especially tragedy—achieved through the representation of passion. Apologists located theater's capacity for moral good in its "overflow of the passions," arguing, as Georges de Scudéry did, that "in dramatic poems, well-represented passions, having first seized the poet, pass from him to the actor who recites, and from the actor to the people who listen," thereby using pleasure to guide the audience toward virtue.[71] Passions created a linkage, or *enchaînement*, between the parties involved in theatrical representation. Racine mastered this *enchaînement* through characters steeped in "majestic sadness."[72] These characters, Nicholas Paige argues, "acted as a host for the viewer's identification by having passions they could share—quite literally"—with the audience.[73] Jacques Scherer goes so far as to identify Racinian tragedy, and all theater, as

ceremonial, precisely for its ability to accomplish a "mysterious action" by producing in the audience real feelings by fictional means.[74] As Paul Friedland
observes, the seventeenth-century theory that the actor's real feelings generated real passions in the audience had an incarnational structure: "By lending
their bodies to the words of the author and giving flesh to the spirit of the character, actors performed a profane version of Christ's Incarnation."[75] In its emotional
effects, early modern theater produced bonds that resembled the supplemental accumulation Olier attributed to the liturgy.

Yet, in its organization of space, time, bodies, and objects, seventeenth-
century French theater worked quite differently from Counter-Reformation
Masses. In contrast to the supplemental relations that defined the liturgy as a performatic formation, what René Bray has called "the law of concentration" began
to structure theatrical practice in the seventeenth century as theater apologists,
playwrights, and their patrons acquired a taste for plays that observed the unity
of action, time, and place.[76] Rather than the ceremonial overflow and agential
extension that was so important to the liturgical production of éclat, plays fostered a kind of seeing that Sabine Chaouche characterizes as "visual pockets."[77]
One relatively late example points to the need for more research on the early modern theater's capacity to unravel ceremony by condensing, slicing, or repackag-
ing its supplemental relations as an emotional effect.

The great tragic actor Michel Baron (1653–1729) elicited emotional responses
from the audience by breaking majesty's ceremonial norms onstage in a way that
literalized splendor's performatic operations, its visuality. Baron had begun his
stage career in the seventeenth century under Molière and retired in 1691, but
he returned to the Comédie-Française in 1720.[78] He had an acting style his contemporaries, like Elena Balletti of the Comédie-Italienne, described as "true and
natural," an effect he achieved in some cases by representing the effects of ceremonial relations rather than enacting ceremonial structures.[79] For example, according to Balletti, when Baron played the leading role in *Horace*, he took Curiace
"by the arm and brought it repeatedly to his chest and heart *to render sensible
the magnitude of his feelings*."[80] This gesture bothered Balletti. She maintained
that as a hero Horace should embody the "grandeur of action and the elevation
of birth" of a "nature that is worthy of majesty."[81] A nature worthy of majesty
would not have used touch in such a direct or abundant way to make its greatness felt. Balletti objected: "In such a case this represents to me the truth and
nature not of a hero, but of a citizen, a merchant or a simple foot soldier. . . . I
think that a hero could say the same thing with the same force when he finds
himself more than six feet away from the person to whom he speaks, by adapting

his gaze and his tone of voice."[82] As Balletti's critique of Baron's acting choices suggests, she recognized that splendor resulted not from visible effects but from visual impression, that although éclat entailed a certain kind of intimacy it also required distance. A spatial margin should encircle a person of high rank, who should nonetheless be able to achieve a sense of connection without bridging this gap. Baron broke this rule and literalized the visceral contact implicit in an encounter with éclat. Rather than deploying multiplicity, directionality, or synchronization to construct Horace's greatness as a visual phenomenon, Baron reduced it to a visible representation. Although he made no reference to the Eucharist, his stage playing thus eroded the fabric of ceremonial splendor on which liturgical éclat and priestly identity relied.

An action or representation that extracted an object, person, gesture, or place from the interlocking and embedded network of supplemental relations that gave the early modern French liturgy its dynamism was akin to cutting a branch from a tree, rendering a living being a dead, or at least different, thing. A modern analogy would be the display of a ritual artifact in a museum where that object's former ties to the production of cultural meaning can no longer operate as they did in its native context. The early modern theater, with its capacity to pull material from a wide range of sources and build it into a self-contained dramatic world, could therefore do precisely such an extraction. By isolating a handful of liturgical elements, the theater could erode the liturgical repertoire's inner logic by redeploying these elements as part of a theatrical representation in which agential delegations and accumulations no longer operated, and instead these liturgical elements were given to view in a demystified or resignified way. Conversely, priests could use liturgical performance to reappropriate bodies and objects that the theater had extracted from the church's system of supplemental relations, such as the corpse of an actor and the insufficiently devout body of a playgoer, endowing them anew with the shared agency that characterized the liturgical repertoire. Antitheatrical sentiment's performance history thus encompasses not only those actions and behaviors explicitly directed against the stage and its players but also the broad spectrum of performance activities that oriented the eyes, arms, legs, movements, thoughts, and feelings of early modern French Catholics toward the altar, as the site of ceremonial splendor and the nexus of a performatic formation premised on agential transfer and communal identity.

# NOTES

The following abbreviations are used in the notes.

AN    Archives nationales de France
BN    Bibliothèque nationale de France
BSG  Bibliothèque Sainte-Geneviève
SS    Archives des prêtres de la Compagnie de Saint-Sulpice (Paris)

## INTRODUCTION

1. "Mais comme pour descrouvrir les taches de vostre visage vous regardez volo[n]tiers les Miroirs qui vous sont presentez, & ne manquez pas tout aussitost de vous essuyer soigneusement: Regardez celuy-cy qui est presenté à vostre ame": *Miroir des prestres et autres ecclesiastiques* (Paris: Pierre Trichard, 1659), 3–4.

2. "Si vous n'aviés perdu le sens, vous ne voudriez pas faire publiquement les fonctions de vos ordres, avec des taches au visage qui vous rendissent difforme aux yeux des assistans; Vous estes sans doute bien plus temeraires & insensez, si vous en souffrez en vostre ame qui vous rendent criminel, ou tant soit peu desagreable aux yeux de Dieu": *Miroir des prestres*, 3.

3. The genre of the priestly mirror draws on the much older genre of the prince's mirror, which dates from the twelfth century in Europe but for which models exist from ancient Egypt and Mesopotamia, as well as from classical Greece. See Roberts Michael and Christine F. Salazar, "Prince's Mirror," in *Brill's New Pauly*, 2006, http://dx.doi.org.ezproxy.lib.ucalgary.ca/10.1163/1574-9347 _bnp_e415580; for a brief discussion of this heritage, see Elin Diamond, *Unmaking Mimesis: Essays on Feminism and Theater* (London: Routledge, 1997), i–ii.

4. "Miroir, se dit figurément en Morale, de ce qui nous represente quelque chose, ou qui la met comme devant nos yeux": Antoine Furetière, "Miroir," in *Dictionnaire universel* (La Haye: Arnout et Renier Leers, 1690).

5. "Le Prestre est un miroir & une lumiere en laquelle les peuples doivent se mirer, pour connoistre en la voyant les tenebres dans lesquelles ils cheminent, & pour rentrer en eux mesmes, disans: Pourquoy ne suis-je pas aussi bon que ce Prestre?": Jean Avila, *Discours aux prestres contenant une doctrine fort necessaire à tous ceux lesquels estans élevez à cette haute dignité desirent que Dieu leur soit propice au dernier jugement*, 3rd ed. (Paris: Pierre Trichard, 1658), 12–13.

6. Richard Schechner, *Performance Studies: An Introduction* (London: Routledge, 2002), 28.

7. "La discipline Ecclesiastique": Claude de la Croix, *Le Parfaict ecclesiastique ou diverses instructions sur toutes les fonctions clericales* (Paris: Pierre de Bresche, 1666), áiiij.

8. "Les parfaits Modeles que les Ecclesiastiques doivent imiter; les Livres vivans, qu'il leur faut étudier," "le parfait Ecclesiastique": Croix, áiij, áiijv.

9. W. B. Worthen, "Drama, Performativity, and Performance," *PMLA* 113, no. 5 (1998): 1097.

10. Studies on priestly masculinity in early modern France are needed, on the model of Jennifer Thibodeaux's work on celibacy and masculinity from the eleventh through the fourteenth centuries. See Jennifer D. Thibodeaux, *The Manly Priest: Clerical Celibacy, Masculinity, and Reform in England and Normandy, 1066–1300*, The Middle Ages Series (Philadelphia: University of Pennsylvania Press, 2015). Other studies of medieval clerical masculinity include Lynda Coon, *Dark Age Bodies: Gender and Monastic Practice in the Early Medieval West* (Philadelphia: University of Pennsylvania Press, 2010); and P. H. Cullum and Katherine J. Lewis, eds., *Religious Men and Masculine Identity in the Middle Ages*, Gender in the Middle Ages (Rochester, NY: Boydell Press, 2013).

11. Judith Butler, *Gender Trouble: Feminism and the Subversion of Identity* (New York: Routledge, 1990), 173.

12. Butler, *Gender Trouble*, 173.

13. Butler, *Gender Trouble*, 173, emphasis in original.

14. Fumaroli, for example, focused attention on Italy's Charles Borromeo, who served as a model for reform-minded secular priests in France. See Marc Fumaroli, "La Querelle de la moralité du théâtre avant Nicole et Bossuet," *Revue d'histoire littéraire de la France* 70, nos. 5-6 (1970): 1009–10; Gaston Maugras points out the sizable role the priests of the parish of Saint-Sulpice played in conflicts with actors. See Gaston Maugras, *Les Comédiens hors la loi*, 2nd ed. (Paris: Calmann Lévy, 1887), 136–37. In scholarship on Molière, priests associated with the Society of the Blessed Sacrament receive attention, especially as potential avatars for Tartuffe. See, for example, Francis Baumal, *Tartuffe et ses avatars "de Montufar à Dom Juan": Histoire des relations de Molière avec la Cabale des Dévots* (Paris: Emile Nourry, 1925), xiv–xvii, 1–40.

15. For the quarrel's main arguments, see Moses Barras, *The Stage Controversy in France from Corneille to Rousseau* (New York: Institute of French Studies, 1933); Marc Fumaroli, "La Querelle de la moralité du théâtre au XVIIe siècle," *Bulletin de la Société française de philosophie* 84, no. 3 (1990): 65–97; Simone de Reyff, *L'Église et le théâtre: L'Exemple de la France au XVIIe siècle* (Paris: Cerf, 1998). For a comparative approach, see Jonas Barish, *The Antitheatrical Prejudice* (Berkeley: University of California Press, 1981). For rhetorical analysis, see Marc Fumaroli, "Sacerdos sive rhetor, orator sive histrio: Rhétorique, théologie, et 'moralité du théâtre' en France de Corneille à Molière," in *Héros et orateurs: Rhétorique et dramaturgie cornéliennes* (Geneva: Librairie Droz, 1990), 449–92; Laurent Thirouin, *L'Aveuglement salutaire: Le Requisitoire contre le théâtre dans la France classique* (Paris: Champion, 1997); Sylviane Léoni, *Le Poison et le remède: Théâtre, morale et rhétorique en France et en Italie, 1694–1758* (Oxford: Voltaire Foundation, 1998). For the debate's legal aspects, see Maugras, *Les Comédiens hors la loi*; Jean Dubu, "Le Rituel romain et les rituels des diocèses de France au XVIIe siècle," in *Les Églises chrétiennes et le théâtre (1550–1850)*, by Jean Dubu (Grenoble: Presses Universitaires de Grenoble, 1997), 71–94. For antitheatricalism's political import, see Déborah Blocker, *Instituter un "art": Politiques du théâtre dans la France du premier XVIIe siècle* (Paris: Honoré Champion, 2009), esp. 279–364.

16. H. Outram Evennett, *The Spirit of the Counter-Reformation: The Birkbeck Lectures on Ecclesiastical History Given in the University of Cambridge in May 1951*, edited by John Bossy (Cambridge: Cambridge University Press, 1968), 20.

17. "Une renaissance religieuse admirable;" "où la sainteté abonde": Léon Aubineau, *Notices littéraires sur le dix-septième siècle* (Paris: Gaume Frères et J. Duprey, 1859), 27.

18. Bruno Latour, *We Have Never Been Modern*, trans. Catherine Porter (Cambridge, MA: Harvard University Press, 1993), 10–12.

19. "'Réaction ecclésiastique' contre le théâtre": Fumaroli, "La Querelle de la moralité du théâtre avant Nicole et Bossuet," 1008.

20. This rough definition of performance draws on Marvin Carlson, *Performance: A Critical Introduction* (New York, 2004), esp. 1–5. See also Robert A. Schneider, *The Ceremonial City: Toulouse Observed, 1738–1780* (Princeton, NJ: Princeton University Press, 1995), 8–12.

21. For a pioneering study on preaching in early modern France, see Isabelle Brian, *Prêcher à Paris sous l'Ancien Régime: XVIIe–XVIIIe siècles* (Paris: Classiques Garnier, 2014). For an analysis of the sermonic discourse of one of the century's best-known preachers, see Anne Régent-Susini, *Bossuet et la rhétorique de l'autorité* (Paris: Honoré Champion, 2011).

22. "Matériellement, elle est un ensemble de maisons groupées autour d'une église et d'un cimetière": René Taveneaux, *Le Catholicisme dans la France classique, 1610–1715: Première partie*, vol. 1, Regards sur l'histoire: Histoire moderne (Paris: Société d'Éditions d'Enseignement Supérieur, 1980), 43.

23. Bruno Restif, *La Révolution des paroisses: Culture paroissiale et réforme catholique en Haute-Bretagne aux XVIe et XVIIe siècles* (Rennes: Presses Universitaires de Rennes, 2006), chap. 1, pars. 12–18; Joseph Bergin, *Church, Society and Religious Change in France, 1580–1730* (New Haven: Yale University Press, 2009), 29.

24. Bergin, *Church, Society and Religious Change in France*, 29–30, 208–9, 216–18; Taveneaux, *Le Catholicisme dans la France classique* (1980), 1:43.

25. Croix, *Le Parfaict ecclesiastique*, 71–88.

26. "Ce Religieux a quitté son Monastere, & vit seculierement dans le monde": Antoine Furetière, "Seculierement," in *Dictionnaire universel* (La Haye: Arnout et Renier Leers, 1690), Gallica.

27. Arthur Vermeersch, "Religious Life," in *The Catholic Encyclopedia* (New York: Robert Appleton, 1911), http://www.newadvent.org/cathen/12748b.htm; Antoine Furetière, "Regulier, ere," in *Dictionnaire universel* (La Haye: Arnout et Renier Leers, 1690), Gallica; Antoine Furetière, "Religieux, euse," in *Dictionnaire universel* (La Haye: Arnout et Renier Leers, 1690), Gallica.

28. "Cure, n.1," in *OED Online* (Oxford University Press, June 2020), https://www-oed-com.ezproxy.lib.ucalgary.ca/view/Entry/46000?rskey=PJZ9NQ&result=1&isAdvanced=false; Antoine Furetière, "Curé," in *Dictionnaire universel* (La Haye: Arnout et Renier Leers, 1690), Gallica; William Fanning, "Cure of Souls," in *The Catholic Encyclopedia* (New York: Robert Appleton, 1908), http://www.newadvent.org/cathen/04572a.htm.

29. "Prestre pourveu d'une Cure": Furetière, "Curé."

30. Fanning, "Cure of Souls."

31. Nicole Lemaître, "Le Prêtre mis à part ou le triomphe d'une idéologie sacerdotale au XVIe siècle," *Revue d'histoire de l'Église de France* 85, no. 215 (1999): 276, https://doi.org/10.3406/rhef.1999.1371.

32. "Inversent la hiérarchie pasteur/homme de la messe," "oriente la fonction du prêtre vers le sacrement des sacrements, l'Eucharistie": Lemaître, "Le Prêtre," 279.

33. Lemaître, "Le Prêtre," 285.

34. For a brief account in English of the state of France's secular clergy in the early days of Catholic reform, see Henry Phillips, *The Theatre and Its Critics in Seventeenth-Century France* (Oxford: Oxford University Press, 1980), 9–11.

35. As a reference point, unskilled building laborers in Paris earned 6.65 grams of silver per day between 1600 and 1620 and 6.19 grams of silver per day between 1680 and 1700. See Jan L. Van Zanden, "Wages and the Standard of Living in Europe, 1500–1800," *European Review of Economic*

*History* 3, no. 2 (1999): 181; Robin Briggs, *Early Modern France: 1560–1715* (Oxford: Oxford University Press, 1977), 174; Taveneaux, *Le Catholicisme dans la France classique* (1980), 1:129–30.

36. Jeanne Ferté, *La Vie religieuse dans les campagnes parisiennes (1622–1695)* (Paris: Librarie Philosophique J. Vrin, 1962), 145–46; Antoine Degert, *Histoire des séminaires français jusqu'à la Révolution* (Paris: Gabriel Beauchesne, 1912), 8.

37. Ferté, *La Vie religieuse dans les campagnes parisiennes*, 146.

38. "Oh! si vous aviez vu . . . la diversité des cérémonies de la messe, il y a quarante ans, elles vous auraient fait honte; il me semble qu'il n'y avait rien de plus laid au monde, que les diverses manières dont on la célébrait": Vincent de Paul, *Correspondance, Entretiens, Documents: Entretiens aux missionnaires, tome 2*, edited by Pierre Coste, vol. 12 (Paris: Librairie Lecoffre, 1924), 258.

39. "Qu'il n'entendait rien en l'administration des sacrements," cited by H. Roure, "Le clergé du sud-est de la France au XVIIe siècle," *Revue d'histoire de l'Église de France* 37, no. 130 (1951): 169, https://doi.org/10.3406/rhef.1951.3115.

40. "L'estat Ecclesiastique estoit extrémement décheu": Croix, *Le Parfaict ecclesiastique*, áij. De la Croix attributes the previous century's ecclesiastical decline to the chaos of the Wars of Religion, a view that was not shared by Protestant critics.

41. "Le modèle du bon prêtre ne correspond désormais plus seulement à un idéal, mais également, dans un nombre non négligeable de cas, à une réalité": Restif, *La Révolution des paroisses*, chap. 4, par. 53.

42. Robert N. Swanson, "Apostolic Successors: Priests and Priesthood, Bishops, and Episcopacy in Medieval Western Europe," in *A Companion to Priesthood and Holy Orders in the Middle Ages*, edited by Greg Peters and C. Colt Anderson, vol. 62, Brill's Companions to the Christian Tradition (Leiden: Brill, 2016), 8–9.

43. "Le prêtre est un médiateur, mis à part pour le ministère de l'eucharistie et du pardon": Lemaître, "Le Prêtre," 285.

44. On the ritual separation of priests through ordination, see Swanson, "Apostolic Successors: Priests and Priesthood, Bishops, and Episcopacy in Medieval Western Europe," 7–20.

45. Bernard Chédozeau, *Chœur clos, chœur ouvert: De l'église médiévale à l'église tridentine (France, XVIIe–XVIIIe siècle)* (Paris: Les Éditions du Cerf, 1998), 15, 21, 41.

46. "Une nouvelle église, l'église tridentine": Chédozeau, *Chœur clos, chœur ouvert*, 42, emphasis in original.

47. Joy Palacios, "Actors, Christian Burial, and Space in Early Modern Paris," *Past and Present* 232, no. 1 (August 2016): 146–47, https://doi.org/10.1093/pastj/gtw010.

48. "Le concile de Trente et surtout l'École française de spiritualité sauront au contraire mettre en scène le nouveau prêtre, le faire valoir aux yeux des fidèles": Lemaître, "Le Prêtre," 288.

49. Philippe Martin, *Le Théâtre divin: Une histoire de la messe, XVIe–XXe siècle* (Paris: CNRS Éditions, 2010). For the medieval period, Bossy sets aside the theater metaphor as inadequate. See John Bossy and Marie-Solange Wane-Touzeau, "Essai de sociographie de la messe, 1200–1700," *Annales: Economies, sociétés, civilisations* 36, no. 1 (1981): 46, https://doi.org/10.3406/ahess.1981.282715.

50. "Ils prenoient quatre sols de salaire par teste de tous les François; et il y avoit tel concours, que les quatre meilleurs prédicateurs de Paris n'en avoient pas tous ensemble autant quand ils preschoient": Pierre de L'Estoile, *Mémoires-Journaux de Pierre de L'Estoile (tome premier): Journal de Henri III, 1574–1580*, edited by G. Brunet et al., vol. 1 (Paris: Libraire des Bibliophiles, 1875), 151.

51. "Les ruses et les mensonges de l'histrion à la sincérité de l'orateur sacré": Léoni, *Le Poison et le remède*, 80.

52. "SEIGNEUR, quelques-uns d'entre vos Ministres . . . negligent presque entierement ce saint Exercice des Ceremonies; ils n'en sçavent plus les Loix ny la methode; & s'ils en pratiquent encore quelque chose, c'est avec si peu d'ordre & avec tant d'irreverence, que les Peuple . . . perdent le respect qu'ils devroient avoir pour les choses saintes; en sorte que l'honneur de vos Eglises & la sainteté des divins Offices, n'est à plusieurs qu'une occasion de babil, & un rendez-vous de divertissement": *Manuel des cérémonies romaines, tiré des livres romains les plus authentiques, & des ecrivains les plus intelligens en cette matiere, par quelques-uns des prêtres de la Congrégation de L.M.* (Lyon: Benoist Bailly, 1679), iir–iiiv.

53. See, for example, Jacques Benigne Bossuet, "Maximes et réflexions sur la comédie," in *L'Eglise et le théâtre: Maximes et réflexions sur la comédie précédés d'une introduction historique et accompagnées de documents contemporains et de notes critiques*, edited by Charles Urbain and Eugene Levesque (Paris: Bernard Grasset, 1930), 225–26.

54. "D'éloigner de son esprit toute idée de divertissement": "Reglement général du Séminaire de S. Sulpice" (1682), fol. 113v, MS Fr. 11760, BN.

55. "N'est pas un divertissement innocent": Armand de Bourbon Conti, prince de, *Traité de la comédie et des spectacles, selon la tradition de l'Église, tirée des conciles & des saints père* (Paris: Louys Billaine, 1666), 9.

56. According to Claude Barthe, Olier composed his treatise on the ceremonies of the Mass based on the notes from these conferences: see "Introduction," in *L'Esprit des cérémonies de la messe: Explication des cérémonies de la grand'messe de paroisse selon l'usage romain* ([Perpignan:] Tempora, 2009), 8.

57. Regarding the refusal of sacraments to an actor, see Jean du Ferrier, "'Memoires [ecclésiastiques] de feu Mr [Jean] du Ferrier'" (n.d.), fols. 195–97, MS 1480, BSG; cited by Étienne-Michel Faillon, *Vie de M. Olier, fondateur du séminaire de Saint-Sulpice*, 4th ed., vol. 2 (Paris: Poussielgue frères, 1873), 373–74.

58. For a detailed table, see Jean Dubu, *Les Églises chrétiennes et le théâtre (1550–1850)* (Grenoble: Presses Universitaires de Grenoble, 1997), 86–93.

59. "Si vous estes capable de vostre charge," "Si vous souffrez vostre Eglise plus sale que vostre chambre," "Si vous celebrez la saincte Messe, ayant passé quasi tout le jour precedent, à boire & manger sans necessité": *Miroir des prestres*, 5, 9, 10.

60. "Ce Miroir est donc pour faire voir quelques points où beaucoup d'Ecclesiastiques (qui n'ont pas l'esprit de leur profession, ou qui n'ont pas eu le bonheur d'estre instruits en des Seminaires) ne font pas ordinairement reflexion": *Miroir des prestres*, 4.

61. "Vous en faire instruire au plustost en quelque Seminaire, ou à quelques autres personnes de mesme profession, capables de vous faire connoistre vos obligations, & de vous en instruire par pratiques": *Miroir des prestres*, 6.

62. In its relation to Catholic reform, France was exceptional because it never officially received the Council of Trent into law. See Victor Martin, *Le Gallicanism et la réforme catholique: Essai historique sur l'introduction en France des décrets du Concile de Trente (1563–1615)* (Geneva: Slatkine Reprints, 1975), xi. France's speed in founding Tridentine seminaries, however, was similar to the timeline elsewhere, as in Italy. See Kathleen M. Comerford, "Italian Tridentine Diocesan Seminaries: A Historiographical Study," *Sixteenth Century Journal* 29, no. 4 (1998): 999–1022.

63. Bergin, *Church, Society and Religious Change in France*, 200.

64. Bergin, *Church, Society and Religious Change in France*, 200.

65. Bergin, *Church, Society and Religious Change in France*, 202.

66. For a brief introduction to these four seminaries and the stories of their foundation, see Ferté, *La Vie religieuse dans les campagnes parisiennes*, 146–52. Debate exists about which seminary opened first. On paper, Bérulle's establishment precedes the others. He created the French Oratory with the goal of reforming the clergy in 1611 and received the Abbey of Saint-Magloire from the bishop of Paris in 1620 for that purpose, but he did not welcome its first students until 1642. See Degert, *Histoire des séminaires français* (1912), 133–36, 166. Although Bourdoise's seminary did not receive its letters patent from the archbishop until 1644, he established his priestly community in the parish of Saint-Nicolas du Chardonnet in 1612 and had already trained more than five hundred clergymen by 1644. See P. Schœnher, *Histoire du Séminaire de Saint-Nicolas du Chardonnet, 1612–1908, d'après des documents inédits*, vol. 1, Quelques pages de L'histoire religieuse du diocèse de Paris (Paris: Société Saint Augustin, 1909), 40, 123.

67. On the Roman catechism, see Karen E. Carter, *Creating Catholics: Catechism and Primary Education in Early Modern France* (Notre Dame, IN: University of Notre Dame Press, 2011), 29. On the Roman Missal and its influence in French liturgical handbooks, see C. Davy-Rigaux, B. Dompnier, and D.-O. Hurel, eds., *Les Cérémoniaux catholiques en France à l'époque moderne: Une Littérature de codification des rites liturgiques*, Église, liturgie et société dans l'Europe moderne (Turnhout, Belgium: Brepols, 2009), 25. On the Roman Ritual, see Annik Aussedat-Minvielle, "Histoire et contenu des rituels diocésains et romains imprimés en France de 1476 à 1800: Inventaire descriptif des rituels des provinces de Paris, Reims et Rouen" (doctoral dissertation completed under the direction of Jean Delumeau, Paris, France, Université de Paris I, Panthéon-Sorbonne, 1987), 21.

68. See Herbert Thurston, "Missal," in *The Catholic Encyclopedia* (New York: Robert Appleton, 1911), http://www.newadvent.org/cathen/10354c.htm; Aussedat-Minvielle, "Histoire et contenu des rituels," 21.

69. Thurston, "Missal"; René Taveneaux, *Le Catholicisme dans la France classique, 1610–1715: Deuxieme partie*, vol. 2, Regards sur l'histoire: Histoire moderne (Paris: Société d'Éditions d'Enseignement Supérieur, 1980), 136. Taveneaux incorrectly cites the Missal's publication date as 1568.

70. For a full history of the council's fate in France, see Martin, *Le Gallicanism et la réforme catholique.*

71. This position came to be called "Gallicanism" at the beginning of the twentieth century. Thomas I. Crimando summarizes this position in an accessible way in "Two French Views of the Council of Trent," *The Sixteenth Century Journal: The Journal of Early Modern Studies* 19, no. 2 (1988): 169–70.

72. Briggs, *Early Modern France*, 167–68; Taveneaux, *Le Catholicisme dans la France classique* (1980), 2:21.

73. Briggs, *Early Modern France*, 174.

74. Taveneaux, *Le Catholicisme dans la France classique* (1980), 2:136–37.

75. Taveneaux, *Le Catholicisme dans la France classique* (1980), 2:136.

76. On the diffusion of liturgical and ecclesiastical publications in the seventeenth century, see Roger Chartier and Lydia G. Cochrane, "Urban Reading Practices, 1660–1780," in *The Cultural Uses of Print in Early Modern France* (Princeton, NJ: Princeton University Press, 1987), 191. See also Henri-Jean Martin, *Livre, pouvoirs et société à Paris au XVIIe siècle, 1598–1701*, vol. 2, HathiTrust (Geneva: Librairie Droz, 1969), 617–25.

77. See chapter 18 of the twenty-third session, entitled "Method of Establishing Seminaries for Clerics, and of Educating the Same Therein," in *The Council of Trent: The Canons and*

*Decrees of the Sacred and Oecumenical Council of Trent*, edited by J. Waterworth, translated by J. Waterworth, Hanover Historical Texts Projects (London: Dolman, 1848), 187–92, http://history .hanover.edu/texts/trent.html.

78. For a full discussion of this decree, see "La Question des séminaires aux Concile de Trente," in Antoine Degert, *Histoire des séminaires français jusqu'à la révolution*, vol. 1 (Paris: Gabriel Beauchesne, 1912), 1–29.

79. Degert, *Histoire des séminaires français*, 1:23.

80. "Elle avait posé des principes et esquissé des plans": Degert, *Histoire des séminaires français*, 1:28.

81. Dominique Julia, "L'Éducation des ecclésiastiques en France aux XVIIe et XVIIIe siècles," in *Problèmes d'histoire de l'éducation: Actes des séminaires organisés par l'École française de Rome et l'Università di Roma—La Sapienza (janvier–mai 1985)*, Collection de l'École française de Rome 104 (Rome: École française de Rome, 1988), 143.

82. On the first attempts to found seminaries in France after the Council of Trent, see chapters 3 and 4 in Degert, *Histoire des séminaires français* (1912), 1:41–100.

83. Degert, *Histoire des séminaires français*, 1:174–75; Paul Broutin, *La Réforme pastorale en France au XVIIe siècle: Recherches sur la tradition pastorale après le Concile de Trente*, vol. 2, Bibliothèque de théologie, série II: Théologie morale (Tournai, Belgium: Desclée, 1956), 227. The average age of entry at the Seminary of Saint-Sulpice during the second half of the seventeenth century was twenty-four-and-a-half. See Gwénola Hervouët, "Le Séminaire de Saint-Sulpice, 1642–1700: Étude sociologique et religieuse." (Mémoire de maîtrise sous la direction de M. le Professeur Bely, Paris, Université de Paris IV—Sorbonne, 1999), 15–16.

84. "Quoique la chose semble raisonable. . . . Oh! que cela a de fâcheuses suites," in a letter dated 13 May 1644: Vincent de Paul, *Correspondance, Entretiens, Documents: Correspondance (janvier 1640–juillet 1646)*, edited by Pierre Coste, vol. 2 (Paris: Librairie Lecoffre. J. Gabalda, 1921), 460.

85. "Non pour les apprendre les sciences, mais l'usage d'icelles," in a letter dated 15 September 1641: Vincent de Paul, *Correspondance, Entretiens, Documents*, 2:188.

86. "Seminary, n.1," in *OED Online*, March 2012, http://www.oed.com/view/Entry/175684; Pierre Bourdieu, *Outline of a Theory of Practice*, translated by Richard Nice (Cambridge: Cambridge University Press, 1977), 72.

87. "Le Seminaire est un lieu destiné pour y donner les semences, & les premices de l'Esprit Ecclesiastique à tous les sujets d'un Clergé": Jean-Jacques Olier, "Projet de l'establissement d'un séminaire dans un diocèse, où il est traité premierement de l'estat & de la disposition des sujets, secondement de l'esprit de tous leurs exercices, par un prestre du clergé" (printed document with handwritten notes and rough draft manuscript by Olier; Paris: Jacques Langlois, 1651), 5, Ms. 20, SS. Olier's treatise was republished in "Projet pour l'établissement d'un séminaire dans un diocese," in *Vie de M. Olier, fondateur du séminaire de Saint-Sulpice*, by Étienne-Michel Faillon, 4th ed., 3 vols., vol. 3 (Paris: Poussielgue frères, 1873), 551–614.

88. "[Lieux] où tant d'habiles hommes travaillent avec un soin incroyable à former des Ouvriers dignes de servir à l'Autel," see "l'Epistre" in the preliminary pages of Croix, *Le Parfaict ecclesiastique*, non-number page.

89. "Défunt le bon M. Bourdoise a été le premier à qui Dieu a inspiré de faire un séminaire pour y apprendre toutes les rubriques," conference from 5 August 1659: Vincent de Paul, *Correspondance, Entretiens, Documents* (1924), 12:289. See also Antoine Degert, *Histoire des séminaires français jusqu'à la révolution*, vol. 2 (Paris: Gabriel Beauchesne, 1912), 128.

90. Degert, *Histoire des séminaires français* (1912), 2:128.

91. "Avant lui, on ne savait ce que c'était; il n'y avait pas de lieu particulier où on les enseignât; un homme, après sa théologie, après sa philosophie, après de moindres études, après un peu de latin, s'en allait dans une cure, y administrait les sacrements à sa mode": Vincent de Paul, *Correspondance, Entretiens, Documents* (1924), 12:289. See also Degert, *Histoire des séminaires français* (1912), 2:127–28.

92. Bergin, *Church, Society and Religious Change in France*, 197.

93. Julia, "L'Éducation des ecclésiastiques en France aux XVIIe et XVIIIe siècles," 143–46.

94. Julia, "L'Éducation des ecclésiastiques en France aux XVIIe et XVIIIe siècles,"149.

95. Patrick Collinson, *The Religion of Protestants: The Church in English Society, 1559–1625* (Oxford: Clarendon Press, 1982), 97. For the English clergy, see also Rosemary O'Day, *The English Clergy: The Emergence and Consolidation of a Profession, 1558–1642* (Leicester: Leicester University Press, 1979). For a comparative discussion, see Luise Schorn-Schütte, "Priest, Preacher, Pastor: Research on Clerical Office in Early Modern Europe," *Central European History* 33, no. 1 (2000): 1–39.

96. Wietse de Boer, "Professionalization and Clerical Identity: Notes on the Early Modern Catholic Priest," *Nederlands Archief voor Kerkgeschiedenis / Dutch Review of Church History* 85, no. 1 (2005): 372.

97. "Ceux qui ne jugent que selon la surface des choses, disent que jamais les Peuples, & le Clergé ne furent meilleurs; mais ceux qui penetrent plus avant, pleurent de voir les uns & les autres si eloignez de leur perfection, & desesperent de les y voir jamais, tant il y a encore à faire & à attendre": Adrien Bourdoise, *L'Idée d'un bon ecclésiastique ou les sentences chrétiennes et cléricales de Messire Adrien Bourdoise, d'heureuse mémoire, prestre de la Communauté de Saint Nicolas du Chardonnet* (Paris: Jacques de Laize de Bresche, 1684), 7–8.

98. Henri Bremond, *Histoire littéraire du sentiment religieux en France depuis la fin des guerres de religion jusqu'à nos jours*, vol. 3 (Paris: Librairie Bloud et Gay, 1923), 3–4. For a nuanced evaluation of Bérulle's influence, see Yves Krumenacker, *L'École française de spiritualité: Des Mystiques, des fondateurs, des courants et leurs interprètes* (Paris: Les Éditions du Cerf, 1998). For a selection of Bérulle's writings in English, see William M. Thompson, ed., *Bérulle and the French School: Selected Writings*, translated by Lowell M. Glendon (New York: Paulist Press, 1989), 105–90.

99. Keith Beaumont, "Pierre de Bérulle (1575–1629) and the Renewal of Catholic Spiritual Life in France," *International Journal for the Study of the Christian Church* 17, no. 2 (2017): 82, 87, https://doi.org/10.1080/1474225X.2017.1351085. As Beaumont argues, Bérulle's theology contributed to seventeenth-century France's dynamic lay spirituality as well.

100. Beaumont, "Pierre de Bérulle, " 79.

101. Degert, *Histoire des séminaires français* (1912), 1:146–49; Gérard Carroll, *Un Portrait du prêtre: Les Retraites de 10 jours pour les ordinands*, vol. 1 (Paris: Pierre Téqui, 2004), 54. The seven orders are generally understood to be doorkeeper, reader, exorcist, acolyte, subdeacon, deacon, and priest. See Hubert Ahaus, "Holy Orders," in *The Catholic Encyclopedia* (New York: Robert Appleton, 1911), http://www.newadvent.org/cathen/11279a.htm.

102. "N'admettre personne aux Ordres qui n'eust la science requise & les autres marques d'une veritable Vocation . . . travaillant envers ceux que l'on voudroit admettre, à les rendre capable de leurs obligations, & à leur faire prendre l'Esprit Ecclesiastique": Louys Abelly, *La Vie du venerable serviteur de Dieu Vincent de Paul, institueur et premier superieur general de la Congregation de la Mission*, 2nd ed., vol. 1 (Paris: Florentin Lambert, 1668), 167.

103. Degert, *Histoire des séminaires français* (1912), 1:149.

104. Abelly, *La Vie du venerable serviteur de Dieu Vincent de Paul*, 1:169, 171; Degert, *Histoire des séminaires français* (1912), 1:150–54.

105. Abelly, *La Vie du venerable serviteur de Dieu Vincent de Paul*, 1:171; Robert Maloney, "Préface," in Gérard Carroll, *Un Portrait du prêtre: Les Retraites de 10 jours pour les ordinands*, vol. 1 (Paris: Pierre Téqui, 2004), 13.

106. Maloney, "Préface," 14; Degert, *Histoire des séminaires français* (1912), 1:155–56.

107. Degert, *Histoire des séminaires français* (1912), 1:154; Carroll, *Un Portrait du prêtre*, 1:24.

108. Carroll, *Un Portrait du prêtre*, 1:57–58; Degert, *Histoire des séminaires français* (1912), 1:156–57, 179–80.

109. Carroll, *Un Portrait du prêtre*, 1:58.

110. Degert, *Histoire des séminaires français* (1912), 1:174; Degert, *Histoire des séminaires français*, 1912, 2:6.

111. Degert, *Histoire des séminaires français* (1912), 2:6–7.

112. "Notre grande réforme sacerdotale touchait presque à son terme": Henri Bremond, *Histoire littéraire du sentiment religieux en France depuis la fin des guerres de religion jusqu'à nos jours*, vol. 1 (Paris: Bloud et Gay, 1916), xvi.

113. In 1698, Louis XIV issued a declaration urging bishops who had not already done so to establish a diocesan seminary, adding momentum to the expansion of seminary institutions. See Degert, *Histoire des séminaires français* (1912), 1:348.

114. Julia, "L'Éducation des ecclésiastiques en France aux XVIIe et XVIIIe siècles," 157; Degert, *Histoire des séminaires français* (1912), 2:18.

115. "Reglement général du Séminaire de S. Sulpice"; "Règlement général du Séminaire de Saint-Sulpice" (Paris, 1710), Ms. 1342, SS.

116. "Barbes sales de Saint-Sulpice": Louis de Rouvroy, duc de Saint-Simon, *Mémoires*, vol. 1, Les Grands écrivains de la France (Paris: Hachette, 1951), 170; "les supérieurs de séminaires;" "une mer d'occupations frivoles, illusoires, pénibles, toujours trompeuses... qui aboutissaient d'ordinaire à des riens": Louis de Rouvroy, duc de Saint-Simon, *Mémoires*, vol. 2, Les Grands écrivains de la France (Paris: Hachette, 1951), 177.

117. Degert, *Histoire des séminaires français* (1912), 1:147–54.

118. Degert, *Histoire des séminaires français* (1912), 1:175. For an example of the Seminary of Saint-Nicolas du Chardonnet's efforts to raise money to support the scholarship, see *Abrégé du petit livre de la bourse cléricale*, 1654. This pamphlet, conserved at the BnF under call number RP-311, lacks a publication date but is estimated to have been published circa 1654.

119. Degert, *Histoire des séminaires français* (1912), 1:190; Ferté, *La Vie religieuse dans les campagnes parisiennes*, 156.

120. Julia, "L'Éducation des ecclésiastiques en France aux XVIIe et XVIIIe siècles," 160–65; Hervouët, "Le Séminaire de Saint-Sulpice, 1642–1700," 18. Later, these "petits" seminaries would evolve into preparatory schools that provided the college-style training required to enter the main seminary. See Anthony Viéban, "Ecclesiastical Seminary," in *The Catholic Encyclopedia* (New York: Robert Appleton, 1912), http://www.newadvent.org/cathen/13694a.htm.

121. Julia, "L'Éducation des ecclésiastiques en France aux XVIIe et XVIIIe siècles," 163; Ferté, *La Vie religieuse dans les campagnes parisiennes*, 155–56.

122. "La véritable école nationale de formation des futurs évêques": Julia, "L'Éducation des ecclésiastiques en France aux XVIIe et XVIIIe siècles," 163.

123. Louis Bertrand, "L'Episcopat Sulpicien: Catalogue biographique des évêques de France élevés du séminaire de Saint-Sulpice aux XVIIe et XVIIIe siècles," *Bulletin trimestriel des anciens élèves de Saint-Sulpice*, no. 38 (August 1905): 428.

124. Dubu, for example, treats the bishop's creation of a diocesan ritual as an individual and uncontested act of authority rather than a form of authorship arising from interclerical relations

at the diocesan level and involving collaboration. See Dubu, *Les Églises chrétiennes et le théâtre (1550–1850)*, 71–85.

125. Max Weber, "The Three Types of Legitimate Rule," translated by Hans Gerth, *Berkeley Publications in Society and Institutions* 4, no. 1 (1958): 1.

126. Bruce Lincoln, *Authority: Construction and Corrosion* (Chicago: University of Chicago Press, 1994), 11.

127. Laura Feldt, "Reframing Authority: The Role of Media and Materiality," *Postscripts: The Journal of Sacred Texts, Cultural Histories, and Contemporary Contexts* 8, no. 3 (2018): 187, https://doi.org/10.1558/post.33710.

128. Lincoln, *Authority: Construction and Corrosion*, 11.

129. Emile Durkheim, *The Elementary Forms of Religious Life*, translated by Karen E. Fields (New York: Free Press, 1995), 44.

130. Douglas A. Marshall, "The Ritual Production of Belonging and Belief," in *Understanding Religious Ritual: Theoretical Approaches and Innovations*, edited by John P. Hoffmann, Routledge Advances in Sociology (London: Routledge, 2012), 35.

131. David Román, *Acts of Intervention: Performance, Gay Culture, and AIDS* (Bloomington: Indiana University Press, 1998), xvii. Although Román's discussion focuses specifically on theatrical production, Marvin Carlson uses Román's idea to help explain performance as patterned behavior more broadly. See *Performance: A Critical Introduction*, 2nd ed. (New York: Routledge, 2004), 4.

132. Judith Butler, *Undoing Gender* (London: Routledge, 2004), 1.

133. For a good example of this kind of reading of theatrical sources, see Virginia Scott, *Women on the Stage in Early Modern France: 1540–1750* (Cambridge: Cambridge University Press, 2010), 108. Through close reading, Scott identifies "specifics about what the playwright [Corneille] assumes the actress to be capable of representing," thereby taking an important step toward filling a gap in scholarship on acting techniques on the early modern stage, for which little is known about norms for female performers.

134. For a brief account of liturgical practices promoted by both Gallican and Jansenist reformers, see Isabelle Brian, "Catholic Liturgies of the Eucharist in the Time of Reform," in *A Companion to the Eucharist in the Reformation*, edited by Lee Palmer Wandel (Leiden: Brill, 2014), 200. On Saint-Vallier's use of the sacrament of penance, see Guy Plante, *Le Rigorisme au XVIIe siècle: Mgr de Saint-Vallier et le sacrement de pénitence (1685–1727)* (Gembloux, Belgium: Éditions J. Duculot, Gembloux, 1970).

135. Henry Phillips, *Church and Culture in Seventeenth-Century France* (Cambridge: Cambridge University Press, 1997), 16, 191; Anthony D. Wright, *The Divisions of French Catholicism, 1629–1645: "The Parting of Ways"* (London: Routledge, 2016), 12, 21–22, 25, 55, 158.

136. At least one student from the seminary of Saint-Nicolas du Chardonnet—a young priest named Lancelot—left Bourdoise's circle in 1638 to join the Jansenists at their monastery, where he became an influential teacher alongside Pierre Nicole. See Schœnher, *Histoire du Séminaire de Saint-Nicolas du Chardonnet*, 1:132; Pavillon collaborated with Vincent de Paul, Olier, and François Perrochel to compose manuals for the ordination retreats in the 1630s. See Carroll, *Un Portrait du prêtre*, 1:14–15. From my perspective, these transfers and collaborations demonstrate a shared liturgical repertoire and mutual interest in clerical discipline, shared interests that could persist alongside doctrinal differences.

137. Wright, *The Divisions of French Catholicism*, 157.

138. "Moins intéressé par les idées elles-mêmes que par leur application, spontanément tourné vers la pastorale, les oeuvres, la morale ou les règles de vie": Taveneaux, *Le Catholicisme dans la France classique* (1980), 2:302.

139. This is not to say that liturgical practices were identical everywhere. As Wright shows, Gallican tendencies led some bishops to include local rites even in their Roman missals, and as I discuss in Chapter 5, some bishops excluded actors while others did not. In my view, however, these small variations did not fundamentally alter the post-Tridentine liturgy's internal logic and may in fact derive from it. See Wright, *The Divisions of French Catholicism*, 70–71.

140. In his now-canonical study, Jonas Barish argues that in France antitheatrical sentiment "streamed outward from the dynamic center of French moralism, the Jansenism of Port-Royal." See Barish, *The Antitheatrical Prejudice*, 192; Henry Phillips provides a more nuanced analysis, concentrating the Jansenist influence in the years from 1660 to 1680. See *The Theatre and Its Critics in Seventeenth-Century France*, 15.

## CHAPTER 1

1. Gérard Ferreyrolles, *Molière: Tartuffe*, Études littéraires (Paris: Presses Universitaires de la France, 1987), 5; Georges Couton, "Notice sur *Le Tartuffe ou l'Imposteur*," in Molière, *Oeuvres complètes*, edited by Georges Couton, vol. 1 (Paris: Éditions Gallimard, 1971), 839.

2. "Supprimer et déchirer, étouffer et brûler," "ruiner la Religion catholique, en blâmant et jouant sa plus religieuse et sainte pratique, qui est la conduite et direction des âmes et des familles par de sages guides et conducteurs pieux": Pierre Roullé, "Le Roi glorieux au monde ou Louis XIV le plus glorieux de tous les rois du monde," in Molière, *Oeuvres complètes*, edited by Georges Couton, vol. 1 (Paris: Éditions Gallimard, 1971), 1143–44; Roullé presents his demand that Molière burn his play as a decision already made by the king, but Molière's own letters to Louis XIV inform us that the king's pronouncements were not so harsh. See Molière, "Premier placet présenté au roi sur la comédie du 'Tartuffe,'" in *Oeuvres complètes*, edited by Georges Couton, vol. 1 (Paris: Éditions Gallimard, 1971), 890.

3. Couton, "Notice sur *Le Tartuffe ou l'Imposteur*," 838, 844. Private readings and private performances were allowed. See Gustave Larroumet, "Molière et Louis XIV," *Revue des Deux Mondes (1829–1971)* 77, no. 1 (1886): 75.

4. W. D. Howarth, *Molière: A Playwright and His Audience* (Cambridge: Cambridge University Press, 1982), 305, 308–9.

5. Couton, "Notice sur *Le Tartuffe ou l'Imposteur*," 836.

6. "Grand chapeau, cheveux courts, petit collet, pas d'épée, habit sans dentelles": Couton, "Notice sur *Le Tartuffe ou l'Imposteur*," 835, 891. Couton arrives at this costume description for the début performance by reversing the description Molière gives in his second Placet au Roi, where the playwright laments that even after he changed the title character's name to Panulphe in 1667 and modified the costume so that it consisted of a small hat, long hair, large collar, a sword, and lace all over the clothes, France's devout population continued to attack the play.

7. Roullé's letter against Molière's play demonstrates this chain of signification, linking the representation of a priest-like character to an attack on the church, religion, and the reverence due to the sacraments. See Roullé, "Le Roi glorieux," 1143–44.

8. "L'usage des collets dans la Communauté de St. Nicolas a esté des le commencement de son establissement de les porter modestes et tout simples quant a la façon": "Coûtumier ou registre des usages plus ordinaires de la Communauté et du Séminaire de St. Nicolas du Chardonnet par ordre alphabetique" (n.d.), fol. 66v, MM 476, AN. This entry in the *coutumier* cites a pamphlet from 1658 and a community decision from 1671.

9. "Livre dans lequel sont escrits tous les Reglemens de chaque office, et Exercice du Seminaire desquels le prestre doit avoir une parfaite connoissance" (n.d.), fol. 248r, AN MM 475.

10. "En ce sens on appelle Petit collet, un homme qui s'est mis dans la reforme, dans la devotion, parce que les gens d'Eglise portent par modestie de petits collets, tandis que les gens du monde en portent de grands ornés de points & de dentelles": Antoine Furetière, "Collet," in *Dictionnaire universel* (La Haye: Arnout et Renier Leers, 1690).

11. "Et quelquefois il se dit en mauvaise part des hypocrites qui affectent des manieresmodestes, & sur tout de porter un petit collet": Furetière, "Collet."

12. "Entretien du reglement des ecclesiastiques quant a l'exterieur" (1657), 121r–23, MS Fr. 14428, BN.

13. Adrien Bourdoise, *Le Désireux de parvenir salutairement à l'estat ecclesiastique, se faisant instruire des propres moyens d'y arriver. Premiere partie. Contenant la preparation requise pour recevoir la tonsure, ou clericature; et les devoirs clericaux de ceux qui sont tonsurez* (Paris: Pierre Menier et Jean Mestais, 1623), 64–67. The tonsure candidate arrived for the ceremony with a circle already shaved at the crown of the head, but the bishop symbolically cut the candidate's hair in five places during the ceremony.

14. "Avoir les cheveux courts & esgaux": *Abrégé de la tonsure* (Paris: Pierre Trichard, n.d.), 2. This pamphlet is conserved at the BN (D-49744) as part of a bound collection of tracts on ecclesiastical discipline. Based on the other pamphlets in the volume, it was probably printed sometime between 1663 and 1672.

15. Victor Turner, "Betwixt and Between: The Liminal Period in *Rites de Passage*," in *The Forest of Symbols: Aspects of Ndembu Ritual* (Ithaca, NY: Cornell University Press, 1967), 93–99; "Resolutions arrestees a Paris par messeigneurs les evesques, et quelques supérieurs de séminaires, avec Monsieur, mil six cens cinquante sept" (Paris, 1657), fol. 127, Ms. Fr. 14428, BN.

16. "Par laquelle cérémonie nous est signifié, qu'il faut déposer toutes pensées & convoitises superfluës, comme sont celles des choses temporelles, des richesses, des honneurs, des délices, & choses semblable": Bourdoise, *Le Désireux*, 32.

17. "Il est commendé aux prestres de ne pas raser leurs cheveux, ni aussi de ne pas nour[r]ir leur chevelure, mais seulement de les tondre a une certaine mesure pour leur apprendre qu'ils ne doivent pas s'appliquer totalement au soin des choses extérieures, ni aussi les quitter entièrement, mais s'appliquer avec médiocrité . . . et autant que la pure nécessité, la charité, ou l'obéissance le demande": "Coûtumier ou registre des usages plus ordinaires de la Communauté et du Séminaire de St. Nicolas du Chardonnet," fols. 63v–64r.

18. "Nous ordonnons aussi que tous Prestres faisans residence en ce Diocese . . . seront toûjours vestus de soutane longue, honneste, & decente": Francisci de Harlay, *Synodicon ecclesiae parisiensis* (Paris: Apud. Franciscum Muguet Regis et illustrissimi Archiepiscopi Parisiensis Typographum, 1674), 395–96.

19. "D'estoffe et façon simple": "Entretien du reglement des ecclesiastiques quant a l'exterieur," fols. 121r–23v; "Coûtumier ou registre des usages plus ordinaires de la Communauté et du Séminaire de St. Nicolas du Chardonnet," fol. 339v.

20. Maureen C. Miller, *Power and the Holy in the Age of the Investiture Conflict: A Brief History with Documents*, Bedford Series in History and Culture (New York: Palgrave Macmillan, 2005), 43–44; Louis Trichet, *Le Costume du clergé: Ses origines et son évolution en France d'après les règlements de l'église* (Paris: Les Éditions du Cerf, 1986), 130–33.

21. Miller, *Power and the Holy in the Age of the Investiture Conflict*, 44.

22. "On connoist chaque chose par son extérieur; on connoist la diversité & distinction des espèces des arbres à leurs fleurs, feüilles & fruits. Un Pommier n'emprunte jamais les feüilles d'un

Poirier, chaque arbre garde la forme de son espèce, selon que Dieu luy a donné; il n'y a que les Ec-clésiastiques, qui ne se contentans pas de leur extérieur, & méprisans l'habit que l'Eglise leur a donné & ordonné, se déguisent en prenant des habits de toutes les façons & couleurs qu'il leur plaist": Adrien Bourdoise, *L'Idée d'un bon ecclésiastique ou les sentences chrétiennes et cléricales de Messire Adrien Bourdoise, d'heureuse mémoire, prestre de la Communauté de Saint Nicolas du Char-donnet* (Paris: Jacques de Laize de Bresche, 1684), 37.

23. Maureen C. Miller, *Clothing the Clergy: Virtue and Power in Medieval Europe, c. 800–1200* (Ithaca, NY: Cornell University Press, 2014), 13.

24. Alejandra Concha Sahli, "The Meaning of the Habit: Religious Orders, Dress and Iden-tity, 1215–1650" (Ph.D. dissertation, University College London, 2017).

25. Concha Sahli, "The Meaning of the Habit," 11.

26. See especially *Briefve histoire de l'institution des ordres religieux, avec les figures de leurs habits, gravées sur le cuivre par Odoart Fialetti, Bolognois* (Paris: Adrien Menier, 1658); and Adrien Schoonebeek, *Histoire des ordres religieux de l'un & de l'autre sexe; ou l'on voit le temps de leur fon-dation, la vie abrégé, de leurs fondateurs, & les figures de leurs habits*, 2nd ed. (Amsterdam: A. Schoonebeek, 1695). A second edition of Schoonebeek's volume appeared in 1700.

27. Schoonebeek, *Histoire des ordres religieux de l'un & de l'autre sexe*, LXXIII, LXXXIV, XCVIII, XCCII.

28. "Ils sont vêtus en Prêtres séculiers, sans autre changement": Schoonebeek, *Histoire des ordres religieux de l'un & de l'autre sexe*, XIV.

29. "Un Ecclésiastique qui auroit eu peine à porter les cheveux courts, la Couronne, une Sou-tane, une ceinture de laine & le reste des habits modestes, n'en a aucune chose estrange; se ren-dant Capucin, d'estre habillé d'une façon, selon le monde, toute contraire & ridicule, tant en la matière qu'en la forme: D'où vient cela? Sinon que n'ayant jamais connû la dignité de son estat Cleri-cal, il ne l'a jamais aimé, & ainsi il n'est pas merveille s'il a méprisé tout ce qui estoit de son de-voir": Bourdoise, *L'Idée d'un bon ecclésiastique*, 36–37.

30. Trichet, *Le Costume*, 60–61.

31. Joseph Bergin, *Church, Society and Religious Change in France, 1580–1730* (New Haven: Yale University Press, 2009), 64.

32. Bergin, *Church, Society and Religious Change in France*, 64.

33. Bergin, *Church, Society and Religious Change in France*, 64.

34. See, for example, Bourdoise, *L'Idée d'un bon ecclésiastique*, 21; See also René Taveneaux, *Le Catholicisme dans la France classique, 1610–1715: Première partie*, vol. 1, Regards sur l'histoire: Histoire moderne (Paris: Société d'Éditions d'Enseignement Supérieur, 1980), 138.

35. *The Council of Trent: The Canons and Decrees of the Sacred and Oecumenical Council of Trent*, edited and translated by J. Waterworth, 172, Hanover Historical Texts Projects (London: Dolman, 1848), http://history.hanover.edu/texts/trent.html.

36. For more on the early modern idea of clothing as a mark in the context of literal marks on the skin, see Katherine Dauge-Roth, *Signing the Body: Marks on Skin in Early Modern France* (London: Routledge, 2020), 1–18, 37–38.

37. "La soutane est l'habit de la religion de J.C. par lequel nous faisons profession exterieure-ment de nous revestir interieurement de la religion de Jesus envers son pere": "'Marques de voca-tion à l'estat ecclesiastique'" (n.d.), fols. 1, 9, MS 163, SS.

38. "Investiture," in *OED Online* (Oxford University Press, 2019), https://www-oed-com .ezproxy.lib.ucalgary.ca/view/Entry/99050?redirectedFrom=investiture.

39. Robert W. Ackerman, "The Knighting Ceremonies in the Middle English Romances," *Speculum* 19, no. 3 (1944): 289.

40. *Robes and Honor: The Medieval World of Investiture*, edited by Steward Gordon, 1 The New Middle Ages (New York: Palgrave Macmillan, 2001), 1; Abigail Brundin, "On the Convent Threshold: Poetry for New Nuns in Early Modern Italy," *Renaissance Quarterly* 65, no. 4 (2012): 1127; Frédérique Lachaud, "Liveries of Robes in England, c. 1200–c. 1330," *English Historical Review* 111, no. 441 (1996): 279.

41. Ann Rosalind Jones and Peter Stallybrass, *Renaissance Clothing and the Materials of Memory*, Cambridge Studies in Renaissance Literature and Culture (Cambridge: Cambridge University Press, 2000), 2.

42. Jones and Stallybrass, *Renaissance Clothing and the Materials of Memory*, 2.

43. On the French context see Daniel Roche, *The Culture of Clothing: Dress and Fashion in the "Ancien Régime,"* translated by Jean Birrel (Cambridge: Cambridge University Press, 1994), although he does not discuss the theater. On the French context, see also Louise Godard de Donville, *Signification de la mode sous Louis XIII* (Aix-en-Provence: EDISUD, 1978). On the English context see especially Jones and Stallybrass, *Renaissance Clothing and the Materials of Memory*; *Clothing Culture, 1350–1650*, edited by Catherine Richardson (Hampshire, England: Ashgate, 2004); Peter Hyland, *Disguise on the Early Modern English Stage* (Burlington, VT: Ashgate, 2011); Robert I. Lublin, *Costuming the Shakespearean Stage: Visual Codes of Representation in Early Modern Theatre and Culture* (Burlington, VT: Ashgate, 2011).

44. Jürgen Habermas, *The Structural Transformation of the Public Sphere: An Inquiry into the Category of Bourgeois Society* (Cambridge, MA: MIT Press, 1989), 7, emphasis in the original.

45. Habermas, *The Structural Transformation of the Public Sphere*, 8.

46. Jones and Stallybrass, *Renaissance Clothing and the Materials of Memory*, 5, 11.

47. François Hédelin d'Aubignac abbé, *La Pratique du théâtre*, edited by Hélène Baby (Paris: Honoré Champion, 2011), 66–69; Samuel Chappuzeau, *Le Théâtre françois par Samuel Chappuzeau, accompagné d'une préface et de notes*, edited by Georges Monval (Paris: Jules Bonnassies, 1875), 110–12.

48. Diana de Marly, *Costume on the Stage: 1600–1940* (London: B. T. Batsford, 1982), 19–20.

49. Louis Trichet, *La Tonsure: Vie et mort d'une pratique ecclésiastique* (Paris: Les Éditions du Cerf, 1990), 9, 63, 97.

50. Bergin, *Church, Society and Religious Change in France*, 64.

51. Claude de la Croix, *Le Parfaict ecclesiastique ou diverses instructions sur toutes les fonctions clericales* (Paris: Pierre de Bresche, 1666), 76, 621–25; Jean-Jacques Olier, "Projet de l'establissement d'un séminaire dans un diocèse, où il est traité premierement de l'estat & de la disposition des sujets, secondement de l'esprit de tous leurs exercices, par un prestre du clergé" (Printed document with handwritten notes and rough draft manuscript by Olier; Paris: Jacques Langlois, 1651), 35, Ms. 20, SS.

52. "Ancien Pontifical": Bourdoise, *Le Désireux*, 46.

53. "Je n'ay jamais veu de Clercs en nostre Paroisse, qui eusse[n]t le surpelis sur le bras": Bourdoise, *Le Désireux,* 60.

54. Trichet, *Le Costume*, 130–33.

55. "Environne tout leur corps, et qui ne laisse rien voir d'eux que sous un habit de mort": Gilles Chaillot, Paul Cochois, and Irénée Noye, eds., *Traité des Saints Ordres (1676), compare aux écrits authentiques de Jean-Jacques Olier (†1657)* (Paris: Procure de la Compagnie de Saint-Sulpice, 1984), 77.

56. "On portera toujours la soutane et la ceinture et l'on aura les cheveux courts et modestes, et la tonsure bien marquée, et l'on ne se presentera pas même à sa porte en robe de

chambre et sans chapeau ou bonnet quarré": "Reglement général du Séminaire de S. Sulpice" (1682), fol. 123v, MS Fr. 11760, BN.

57. For a helpful overview of the reformers' complaints, see G. R. Evans, *The I. B. Tauris History of Monasticism: The Western Tradition* (London: I. B. Tauris, 2016), 175–77.

58. Taveneaux, *Le Catholicisme dans la France classique*, 1:57–58.

59. Concha Sahli, "The Meaning of the Habit," 286.

60. Olier, "Projet de l'establissement d'un séminaire," iij.

61. "Le S. Clergé est proprement ce corps puissant que Dieu a establi dans l'Eglise pour tenir teste au siecle, " "Ainsi cét Ordre magnifique du Saint Clergé . . . a sur soy l'esprit universel de la Religion de JESUS-CHRIST": Olier, "Projet de l'establissement d'un séminaire," iij, 6. In my translation, I added the clarification "vices of" based on the next phrase, which reads "& s'opposer . . . a ses vices" (and oppose itself . . . to its vices).

62. Olier, "Projet de l'establissement d'un séminaire," 41.

63. "Celles-là n'attaquaient que la piété and la religion, dont ils se soucient fort peu; mais celle-ci les attaque et les joue eux-mêmes, et c'est ce qu'ils ne peuvent souffrir": Molière, "Second placet présenté au roi dans son camp devant la ville de Lille en Flandre," in *Oeuvres complètes*, edited by Georges Couton, vol. 1 (Paris: Éditions Gallimard, 1971), 892.

64. Francis Baumal, *Tartuffe et ses avatars "de Montufar à Dom Juan": Histoire des relations de Molière avec la Cabale des Dévots* (Paris: Emile Nourry, 1925), 1.

65. "Tout livre mettant en scène des personnages réels ou faisant allusion à des personnages réels sous des noms supposés ou altérés": Fernand Dujon, *Les Livres à clefs: Études de bibliographie critique et analytique pour servir à l'histoire littéraire*, vol. 1 (Paris: Édouard Rouveyre, 1888), v.

66. Baumal, *Tartuffe et ses avatars*, 1.

67. In Henry Phillip's words, "The Compagnie's aim was in many ways to police the sacred in the social space," see *Church and Culture in Seventeenth-Century France* (Cambridge: Cambridge University Press, 1997), 21; For the most complete account of the Compagnie du Saint-Sacrement, see Raoul Allier, *La Cabale des dévots, 1627–1666* (Paris: Librairie Armand Colin, 1902).

68. Emanuel S. Chill, "Tartuffe, Religion, and Courtly Culture," *French Historical Studies* 3, no. 2 (1963): 167. Several of these characters are rather obscure. The Marquis de La Mothe-Fénelon was the uncle of François Fénelon, mentioned by Auguste Jal in *Dictionnaire critique de biographie et d'histoire, errata et supplément pour tous les dictionnaires historiques d'après des documents authentiques inédits* (Paris: Henri Plon, 1876), 572. According to the site *Amorial Charentais*, Antoine de Salignac had a nephew named François Pons, without indication that he was an abbot. "De Salignac de La Mothe-Fénelon," *Armorial Charentais* (blog), accessed May 11, 2021, http://jm .ouvrard.pagesperso-orange.fr/armor/fami/s/salignac_fenelon.htm. Baumal also lists the Marquis de Fénelon, the Count d'Albon, and the Count of Brancas without providing further information about their identities. See Baumal, *Tartuffe et ses avatars*, 200.

69. Baumal, *Tartuffe et ses avatars*, 2–8.

70. Chill, "Tartuffe, Religion, and Courtly Culture," 168.

71. Chill, "Tartuffe, Religion, and Courtly Culture," 167, 169.

72. Chill, "Tartuffe, Religion, and Courtly Culture," 169–70.

73. Bruno Latour, *We Have Never Been Modern*, translated by Catherine Porter (Cambridge, MA: Harvard University Press, 1993), 10.

74. Latour, *We Have Never Been Modern* 10–11, 13–48.

75. Latour, *We Have Never Been Modern* 22–24.

76. "Estre Prestre & homme, est chose quasi incompatible": Bourdoise, *L'Idée d'un bon ec-clésiastique*, 66; Latour, *We Have Never Been Modern*, 10–11.

77. "L'ordre de JÉSUS Christ": Chaillot, Cochois, and Noye, *Traité des Saints Ordres*, 304.

78. Ordination requirements deemed stage playing a "default of reputation" that rendered a person unable to receive holy orders. See "Entretiens des ordinands sur les matieres de devotion (Tome I)" (n.d.), fol. 17r, Ms. 157, SS. This manuscript, the first of two volumes and tiny enough to fit into a small hand, contains ten "entretiens," or lessons, on the devotional practices required by priests. It was probably composed between 1634 and 1657; "des Joüeurs, des Baladins, des Chasseurs": *Des Clercs desguisez, ou de l'habit clerical, selon les saints canons* (Paris: Pierre Trichard, n.d.). This pamphlet, conserved in a bound collection of similar tracts (BN, D-49744), probably dates from the 1650s, based on the date of the latest royal ordinance cited in the collection.

79. "Esprit Ecclesiastique": Olier, "Projet de l'establissement d'un séminaire," 5.

80. La Comédie-Française, *Registre de La Grange (1658–1685), précédé d'une notice bi-ographique*, Archives de la Comédie-Française (Paris: J. Claye, 1876), 65; Couton, "Notice sur *Le Tartuffe ou l'Imposteur*," 834–35.

81. "Un succès très vif et très durable": Couton, "Notice sur *Le Tartuffe ou l'Imposteur*," 834–47.

82. Molière, *Tartuffe: A Verse Translation*, edited by Constance Congdon and Virginia Scott, translated by Constance Congdon (New York: W. W. Norton, 2009), 31; "Laurent, serrez ma haire avec ma discipline, / Et priez que toujours le Ciel vous illumine": Molière, "Le Tartuffe ou l'imposteur," in *Oeuvres complètes*, edited by Georges Couton, vol. 1 (Paris: Éditions Gallimard, 1971), 938.

83. G. C. Alston, "Hairshirt," in *The Catholic Encyclopedia* (New York: Robert Appleton, 1910), http://www.newadvent.org/cathen/07113b.htm.

84. Hannah G. McClain, "Corporal Penance in Belief and Practice: Medieval Monastic Precedents and Their Reception by the New and Reformed Religious Orders of the Sixteenth Century," *Footnotes: A Journal of History* 2 (2018): 183.

85. "Si no[us] avons chastié nostre chair, et puni specialement les membres qui ont servi au peché": "Recueil de la conduite d'un ecclesiastique pour vivre conformement a la saincteté de vie qu'il doit mener, reduit en examens composé et digeré par un tres scavant et pieux ecclesiastique d'une illustre communauté de Paris" (Seminary of Saint-Sulpice, Paris, n.d.), fol. 143, 906, SS. This manuscript, attributed to Tronson, likely dates from sometime during his tenure as superior of the Society of Saint-Sulpice between 1676 and 1700.

86. On the diminished role of corporal penance, see McClain, "Corporal Penance in Belief and Practice," 177–78.

87. "'Marques de vocation à l'estat ecclesiastique,'" 9v–10r; "Règlement général du Séminaire de Saint-Sulpice" (Paris, 1710), 224v–25, Ms. 1342, SS; *Des Clercs desguisez*, 4.

88. See, for example, "Reglement général du Séminaire de S. Sulpice"; and "Règlement général (SS Ms. 1342)."

89. "Livre dans lequel sont escrits tous les Reglemens de chaque office," 37r.

90. "Reglement de vie pour l'avenir": Pasté, *Abrégé du reglement du seminaire paroissial de S. Nicolas du Chardonnet, pour l'usage des seminaristes* (Paris: Pierre Trichard, 1672), 18.

91. "Des libertins, des Heretiques, des Athées, des joüeurs, des yvrognes, des blasphemateurs, des femmes, des filles": Pasté, *Abrégé du reglement du seminaire paroissial de S. Nicolas du Chardonnet*, 22–23.

92. For a comparison between the tabernacle where the consecrated Eucharist was stored and the king's chamber, see Étienne-Michel Faillon, *Vie de M. Olier, fondateur du séminaire de Saint-*

*Sulpice*, 4th ed., vol. 2 (Paris: Poussielgue frères, 1873), 375–77. For an example of the metaphor of a clergyman as servant to a great lord, see Jean-Jacques Olier, *Lettres de M. Olier, fondateur du séminaire de Saint-Sulpice, nouvelle édition revue sur les autographes, considérablement augmenté, accompagné de notes biographiques et précédée d'un abrégé de la vie de M. Olier* (Paris: Libraire Victor Lecoffre, 1885), 222–23.

93. "O Que Dieu seroit bien honoré dans nos Eglises, si on s'y comportoit en sa presence, comme on se comporte dans la maison des Grands, ou en leur presence": Bourdoise, *L'Idée d'un bon ecclésiastique*, 77.

94. "En entrant dans le clergé, on vous a déclaré que vous entriez dans sa maison [de Dieu] pour lui rendre service, étant dorénavant comme un de ses domestiques, qui doivent assister continuellement auprès de sa personne," letter 101, "A un jeun clerc" (9 June 1643), in Jean-Jacques Olier, *Lettres de M. Olier, curé de la paroisse et fondateur du Séminaire de Saint-Sulpice*, edited by Eugene Levesque (Paris: J. de Gigord, 1935), 222–23. The "entry" to which Olier refers is a ceremony called the Tonsure, when a man received his clerical robes and had the crown of his head shaved. The Tonsure did not constitute an ordination, but it made the tonsured man into a cleric. Churchmen thought of the Tonsure as the doorway to the priesthood. For a history of the practice, see Trichet, *La Tonsure*.

95. James F. Gaines, *Social Structures in Molière's Theater* (Columbus: Ohio State University Press, 1984), 129.

96. Gaines, *Social Structures in Molière's Theater*, 129.

97. "Mon frère, vous seriez charmé de le connaître, / . . . / Ha! si vous aviez vu comme j'en fis rencontre, / vous auriez pris pour lui l'amitié que je montre. / Chaque jour à l'église il venait, d'un air doux, / Tout vis-à-vis de moi se mettre à deux genoux. / Il attirait les yeux de l'assemblée entière / Par l'ardeur dont au Ciel il poussait sa prière; / Il faisait des soupirs, de grands élancements, / Et baisait humblement la terre à tous moments": Molière, "Le Tartuffe" (1971), 906–7.

98. For an interesting analysis of genuflection in Tartuffe, see Jacques Scherer, *Structures de Tartuffe*, 2nd ed. (Paris: Société d'Éditions d'Enseignement Supérieur, 1974), 229–31.

99. *Manuel des cérémonies romaines, tiré des livres romains les plus authentiques, & des ecrivains les plus intelligens en cette matiere, par quelques-uns des prêtres de la Congrégation de L.M.* (Lyon: Benoist Bailly, 1679), 10–11.

100. "Et lorsque je sortais, il me devançait vite, / Pour m'aller à la porte offrir de l'eau bénite": Molière, "Le Tartuffe" (1971), 907.

101. "De vrays Prestres & Pasteurs": Olier, "Projet de l'establissement d'un séminaire," 3; Bourdoise, *L'Idée d'un bon ecclésiastique*, 76.

102. "Un Predicateur mourroit de confusion, s'il avoit fait une faute notable en un Sermon: Si un Orateur en haranguant devant un Prince, un Comedien de mesme sur un Theâtre; à cet effet les uns & les autres estudient, se preparent, & repetent une infinité de fois, &c. afin d'agréer, & reüssir à leur plaisir, & honneur. Et (ce qui est déplorable) on ne se soucie point dans les divins Offices qui se recitent devant & en la presence de la divine Majesté, de faire cent fautes, faute de preparation. Y a-il de la Foy parmy les Ecclesiastiques": Bourdoise, *L'Idée d'un bon ecclésiastique*, 32. I consider this passage and Bourdoise's connection to the theater more closely in Chapter 2.

103. "Livre dans lequel sont escrits tous les Reglemens de chaque office," fols. 114v–116r, 104r–104v.

104. "Un cousin pour mettre sous la teste de l'Enfant": "Livre dans lequel sont escrits tous les Reglemens de chaque office," fol. 106r.

105. "Livre dans lequel sont escrits tous les Reglemens de chaque office," fol. 105r.

106. Antoine Degert, *Histoire des séminaires français jusqu'à la révolution*, vol. 2 (Paris: Gabriel Beauchesne, 1912), 140–43.

107. "Il devoit faire voir ce que le devot fait en secret, aussi bien que l'hypocrite": P.-L. Jacob, ed., *Observations sur le Festin de Pierre par de Rochemont et réponses aux observations, réimpressions textuelles ees éditions originelles de Paris, 1665* (Geneva: J. Gay et fils, 1869), 10; I have used the English translation given by Chill, "Tartuffe, Religion, and Courtly Culture," 156.

108. Chill, "Tartuffe, Religion, and Courtly Culture," 171, 173–74.

109. Chill, "Tartuffe, Religion, and Courtly Culture," 174.

110. Molière, "Le Tartuffe" (1971), 946.

111. Chill, "Tartuffe, Religion, and Courtly Culture," 176.

112. See, for example, Pierre Nicole, *Traité de la comédie, et autres pièces d'un procès du théâtre*, edited by Laurent Thirouin (Paris: Honoré Champion, 1998), 62–64.

113. "Il n'y a quasi point en ce siecle d'Ecclesiastique, si spirituel, & tel qu'il soit, dont la vie, l'habit, & les employs soient conformes aux Regles & Canons de l'Eglise": Bourdoise, *L'Idée d'un bon ecclésiastique*, 20.

114. "Mr. Bourdoise faisoit beaucoup parler de luy, à cause que son zele avoit trop d'ardeur, & n'avoit pas toûjours assez de prudence": Philibert Descourveaux, *La Vie de Monsieur Bourdoise, premier prestre de la Communauté de S. Nicolas du Chardonnet* (Paris: François Fournier, 1714), 113.

CHAPTER 2

1. According to Joseph Bergin, thirty-six seminaries were established in France between 1642 and 1660, fifty-six between 1660 and 1682, and twenty-five between 1683 and 1720. See *Church, Society and Religious Change in France, 1580–1730* (New Haven: Yale University Press, 2009), 200.

2. "La forme qu'ils doivent observer en leur exterieur, pour se conformer entierement à l'esprit de l'Eglise, marqué dedans les Sacrez Conciles": Matthieu Beuvelet, *Conduites pour les exercices principaux qui se font dans les séminaires ecclesiastiques, dressées en faveur des clercs demeurans dans le Seminaire de S. Nicolas du Chardonnet* (Lyon: Hierosne de la Garde, 1660), 17. On Beuvelet, see Joseph Grandet, *Les Saints prêtres français du XVIIe siècle, ouvrage publié pour la première fois, d'après le manuscrit original*, edited by G. Letourneau, vol. 2 (Angers: Germain et G. Grassin; A. Roger et F. Chernoviz, 1897), 254–56.

3. Beuvelet, *Conduites*, 3.

4. *Miroir des prestres et autres ecclesiastiques* (Paris: Pierre Trichard, 1659), 9, 10, 14, 20, 26–27.

5. "O la belle predication que de paroistre en modestie devant les peuples": "Recueil de la conduite d'un ecclesiastique pour vivre conformement a la saincteté de vie qu'il doit mener, reduit en examens composé et digeré par un tres scavant et pieux ecclesiastique d'une illustre communauté de Paris" (Seminary of Saint-Sulpice, Paris, n.d.), fol. 204, 906, SS. On Tronson, see Louis Bertrand, *Bibliothèque sulpicienne ou histoire littéraire de la Compagnie de Saint-Sulpice*, vol. 1 (Paris: Alphonse Picard et Fils, 1900), 123–55. See also Pierre Boisard, *La Compagnie de Saint Sulpice: Trois siècles d'histoire*, vol. 1 (Paris: La Compagnie de Saint Sulpice, 1959), 49–55.

6. "C'est ce qu'on aspelle predication muette": "Conférences épiscopales" (late seventeenth century), fol. 118r, Ms. Fr. 14428, BN.

7. "Les Exercices de l'Oraison mentale, les Conferences de pieté, Theologie morale, Catechisme Romain, de la pratique des Sacremens, des Catechismes, des Ceremonies, du Plein-Cha[n]t, &c": Beuvelet, *Conduites*, aiijv; Jean-Jacques Olier lists the main subjects taught in seminaries as

"des Ceremonies, du Chant, de l'administration des Sacremens, & de la maniere de bien cate-
chiser & précher" (ceremonies, singing, the administration of the sacraments, and how to preach
and teach the catechism well). See "Projet de l'establissement d'un séminaire dans un diocèse, où
il est traité premierement de l'estat & de la disposition des sujets, secondement de l'esprit de tous
leurs exercices, par un prestre du clergé" (Printed document with handwritten notes and rough
draft manuscript by Olier; Paris: Jacques Langlois, 1651), 31, Ms. 20, SS.

8. "De grands progrez dans la perfection": Louis Tronson, "Entretiens" (Paris, n.d.), fol. 1r,
Ms. 50, SS.

9. "S[ain]tes inentions et des dispositions xtiennes": Tronson, "Entretiens," fol. 16r.

10. "L'interieur est a la verité ce qu'il y a de principal, c'en est l'ame et la vie de sorte que sans
cela, quelque belle apparence et quelqu'éclat qu'elles ayent au dehors, elles sont mortes, elles sont
infructueuses, et sans merite devant Dieu; comme nous avons dit cependant il est necessaire ab-
solument de regler aussy l'exterieur . . . car . . . quoy que l'exterieur ne soit que le corps de l'action
il sert pourtant a l'action tant de mesme que le corps sert a l'ame. . . . Il est impossible que l'exterieur
soit deregle, et que l'interieur n'en souffre pas": Tronson, "Entretiens," fols. 18v–19r.

11. "Enfin la charité mesme de n[ot]re prochain nous y oblige, car nous le devons edifier, nous
sommes obligez de luy donner exemple, or nous ne le scaurions faire que par l'exterieur": Tronson,
"Entretiens," fol. 19r.

12. "O la Belle chose que la modestie, elle attire par sa seule voix tous les coeurs a son Imitation": "Recueil de la conduite d'un ecclesiastique," fol. 197.

13. "Adorable et aymable tout ensemble aux yeux des Anges et des hommes": "Recueil de la
conduite d'un ecclesiastique," fol. 196.

14. "Adorons N. S. J. C. le vray modelle de la modestie qui a esté si remarquable et si char-
mante en luy": "Recueil de la conduite d'un ecclesiastique," fol. 194.

15. "Avons no[us] tellem[ent] suivi la reigle de la modestie que donne S. Augustin qu'il ny ay
rien eu dans tout nostre exterieur qui n'ay edifié n[ot]re prochain et qui n'aye este conforme a la
saintete de n[ot]re estat": "Recueil de la conduite d'un ecclesiastique," fol. 195.

16. "L'esprit universel de la Religion de JESUS-CHRIST": Olier, "Projet de l'establissement d'un
séminaire," 6.

17. "Puisque l'Eglise ne peut subsister sans ces Ministres essentiels": Olier, "Projet de
l'establissement d'un séminaire," 6–7.

18. "Les Reguliers pretendent que leur état est plus parfait que celui des Seculier": Antoine
Furetière, "Seculier, iere," in *Dictionnaire universel* (La Haye: Arnoud et Reinier Leers, 1701).

19. "Que le Prestre, lequel estant hors de l'Autel desirera marcher bien co[m]posé, & avec la
gravité & la modestie convenable à sa dignité, se souvienne de la grandeur en laquelle il a este
mis, & co[m]bien l'affaire qu'il a traité à l'Autel est grande & importante": Jean Avila, *Discours
aux prestres contenant une doctrine fort necessaire à tous ceux lesquels estans élevez à cette haute
dignité desirent que Dieu leur soit propice au dernier jugement*, 3rd ed. (Paris: Pierre Trichard,
1658), 7; Juan de Ávila's pedagogical philosophy influenced the Council of Trent's decree on the
establishment of seminaries. See David Coleman, "Moral Formation and Social Control in the
Catholic Reformation: The Case of San Juan de Avila," *Sixteenth Century Journal: The Journal of
Early Modern Studies* 26, no. 1 (1995): 27–29.

20. "L'innocence de la saincteté de la vie," "Rapporter là [par des meditations] toutes les actions qu'on fait comme autant de moyens & de dispositions pour bien celebrer la Messe, ainsi que
Nostre Seigneur rapportoit toute sa vie au Sacrifice qu'il devoit offrir en la Croix": Beuvelet, *Conduites*, 68, 69.

21. "Ne faites jamais aucune action qu'elle ne soit accompagnée de modestie": Tronson, "Entretiens," fol. 19r.

22. "Recueil de la conduite d'un ecclesiastique," fols. 194–210.

23. "La modestie est une vertu qui compose selon la biensance et l'honnestete Chrestienne to[us] les mouvemens exterieurs, le parler, le marcher, les regards, la posture, les gestes, le maintient du corps et g[e]n[er]allem[ent] tout nostre exterieur": "Recueil de la conduite d'un ecclesiastique," fol. 195.

24. "La modestie fait que l'on tient d'ordinaire la teste droite, sans le lever trop haut, sans la pencher d'un costé ny d'autre, et sans la tourner legerement et a toutes occasions": "Recueil de la conduite d'un ecclesiastique," fol. 196.

25. "L'on tienne ordinairement les yeux baissez, qu'on ne les remue point avec trop de promptitude": "Recueil de la conduite d'un ecclesiastique," fol. 196.

26. "Que le regard soit doux et benign et non point affreux et rebutant": "Recueil de la conduite d'un ecclesiastique," fol. 196.

27. "Elle porte a avoir le front serein, les levres ny trop ouvertes, ny trop serrées . . . sans qu'il y paroist rien de constraint, de sever, et de melancholique": "Recueil de la conduite d'un ecclesiastique," fol. 196.

28. "La modestie fait tenir le corps dans une posture bienseante": "Recueil de la conduite d'un ecclesiastique," fol. 197.

29. "Elle empesche de se courber par trop et aussy de se redresser avec trop d'effort": "Recueil de la conduite d'un ecclesiastique," fols. 197–98.

30. "Elle ne souffre point qu'on change de posture a tout moment ou que l'on s'appuye tantost sur un pied tantost sur un autre": "Recueil de la conduite d'un ecclesiastique," fol. 198.

31. "Elle empeche qu'on estende les bras et les jambes avec une trop gr[a]nde dissolution": "Recueil de la conduite d'un ecclesiastique," fol. 198.

32. "Recueil de la conduite d'un ecclesiastique," fols. 200–201.

33. "Elle souffrira plustot . . . qu'on la soubçonne mesme de paresse que de faire paroistre la moindre legereté dans ses demarches": "Recueil de la conduite d'un ecclesiastique," fols. 200–201.

34. "Mon Dieu je recognois que je nay point fait attension a la pluspart de ces reigles fasses moy la grace de les observer doresnavant": "Recueil de la conduite d'un ecclesiastique," fol. 197.

35. "Modestie universelle des vestments, & l'usage mediocre que l'on fera de toutes les choses necessaires à la vie," "fonder ces sujets dans la mortification de tous les appetits naturels, & les faire aspirer à une mort parfaite de tout le monde": Olier, "Projet de l'establissement d'un séminaire," 37, 38.

36. "Obvier à l'inconvenient qui se trouve dans le genre de vie qu'il faut instituer pour satisfaire à l'inégalité des personnes, & à la diversité des conditions qui pourront composer le Seminaire": Olier, "Projet de l'establissement d'un séminaire," 37. I have changed the order of the sentence slightly in my English translation for easier reading.

37. "Les accoustumer à des aises si contraires aux travaux & incommoditez de la campagne," "lasser & rebuter les personnes de condition": Olier, "Projet de l'establissement d'un séminaire," 37.

38. "Se flatter dans leur sensualité," "retrancher . . . le superflu de leur condition": Jean-Jacques Olier, "Projet de l'establissement d'un séminaire," 37, Ms. 20, SS.

39. "Evite les grimaces affectées, les mines contrefaites et tous ce qui ressent quelque artifice": "Recueil de la conduite d'un ecclesiastique," fol. 196.

40. "Estudiant tellement ses pas qu'on y remarque quelque artifice" : "Recueil de la conduite d'un ecclesiastique," fol. 201.

41. Marvin Carlson, *Performance: A Critical Introduction*, 2nd ed. (New York: Routledge, 2004), 1–2.

42. Carlson, *Performance: A Critical Introduction*, 2–5.

43. Richard Schechner, *Between Theater and Anthropology* (Philadelphia: University of Pennsylvania Press, 1985), 35, 37; Carlson, *Performance: A Critical Introduction*, 3–4.

44. Schechner, *Between Theater and Anthropology*, 37.

45. Schechner, *Between Theater and Anthropology*, 36.

46. Schechner, *Between Theater and Anthropology*, 37.

47. Carlson, *Performance: A Critical Introduction*, 4.

48. Carlson, *Performance: A Critical Introduction*, 4.

49. Jansenist reformers also relied on models under the rubric "science of saints." See Daniella Kostroun, *Feminism, Absolutism, and Jansenism: Louis XIV and the Port Royal Nuns* (Cambridge: Cambridge University Press, 2011), 37–38, 60–64.

50. Pasté, *Abrégé du reglement du seminaire paroissial de S. Nicolas du Chardonnet, pour l'usage des seminaristes* (Paris: Pierre Trichard, 1672), 32. The règlement refers to Pierre Fourier as the "P[ère] de Mataincour," or the Father of Mattaincourt.

51. "Livre dans lequel sont escrits tous les Reglemens de chaque office, et Exercice du Seminaire desquels le Prestre doit avoir une parfaite connoissance" (n.d.), fols. 202r–205r, AN MM 475; "Reglement général du Séminaire de S. Sulpice" (1682), 110v–11, MS Fr. 11760, BN.

52. "Plus pratiques, morales, et devotes que doctrinales": "Livre dans lequel sont escrits tous les Reglemens de chaque office," fol. 66r.

53. "Livre dans lequel sont escrits tous les Reglemens de chaque office," fol. 66v.

54. "Parceque la plus part de tous ceux qui entrent dans le seminaire sont personnes fort seiches et steriles pour le desir de leur perfection . . . et tres peu exercez dans la pratique des vertus chrestiennes, c'est pourquoy ils doivent souvent estre excités, eschaufés, instruits et nourris de ces choses par des lectures frequentes": "Livre dans lequel sont escrits tous les Reglemens de chaque office," fol. 66r.

55. "Interroger quelqu'un de la compagnie quel sentiment il a conçeu sur la lecture qu'on a fait": "Livre dans lequel sont escrits tous les Reglemens de chaque office," fol. 66v.

56. Nicolas Janvier, *Des Prestres et curez: De leur institution, puissance, droicts & devoirs en l'Eglise* (Paris: Pierre Trichard, n.d.), 2. This pamphlet was published sometime between 1634 and 1694, the dates of Trichard's activity as printer.

57. "Il nous a mis sous la conduite d'un Evesque qui doit estre plein de zele pour nous exciter à la perfection que nous devons avoir," "or il [S. Pierre] donne advis au Clergé qu'il leur [aux evêques] soit hú[m]ble & obeïssant": Avila, *Discours aux prestres*, 19–20.

58. On Claude de la Croix, see Grandet, *Les Saints prêtres français du XVIIe siècle*, 2:257–60.

59. "A qui peut-il donc mieux appartenir, qu'à vous, Messeigneurs, qui imprimés aux Prestres le caractère du Sacerdoce; qui reglés toutes les actions de leur vie . . . ?": Claude de la Croix, *Le Parfaict ecclesiastique ou diverses instructions sur toutes les fonctions clericales* (Paris: Pierre de Bresche, 1666), á iij. The printer, Pierre de Bresche, wrote the dedicatory letter.

60. "Le Prelat, qui est le Saint Espoux de son Eglise, & qui doit fournir à ses besoins, ne peut pas estre present à tout son Diocese, pour instruire & officier, pour offrir & administrer en personne, tous les biens necessaires au salut de ses peuple": Olier, "Projet de l'establissement d'un séminaire," 1.

61. "Plusieurs bouches & plusieurs mains, plusieurs membres & plusieurs ministres": Olier, "Projet de l'establissement d'un séminaire," 1.

62. "Le vray & unique superieur du Seminaire, est Monseigneur l'Evesque, " "dirigent la maison dans la main de Monseigneur l'Evesque": Olier, "Projet de l'establissement d'un séminaire," 7, 11.

63. "Le bien considerer, afin que prenant plaisir à le bien pratiquer, ils attirent sur eux la Benediction du Ciel, en se soumettant parfaitement à l'ordre de leurs Directeurs": Pasté, *Abrégé du reglement de S. Nicolas du Chardonnet (1672)*, á.

64. "Reglement général du Séminaire de S. Sulpice," fols. 122r, 126r.

65. "Il donne aussi quelques avis sur les manquemens, & sur les defauts qu'on a pû remarquer durant la Semaine": Pasté, *Abrégé du reglement de S. Nicolas du Chardonnet (1672)*, 7.

66. "Luy rendre compte . . . de l'employ de son temps, & de la fidelité au present Reglement": Pasté, *Abrégé du reglement de S. Nicolas du Chardonnet (1672)*, 16.

67. "Reglement général du Séminaire de S. Sulpice," fols. 104r, 127r; Pasté, *Abrégé du reglement de S. Nicolas du Chardonnet (1672)*, 9–10; "Livre dans lequel sont escrits tous les Reglemens de chaque office," 32r.

68. "Livre dans lequel sont escrits tous les Reglemens de chaque office," fol. 32r.

69. "Estre toujours prest de les aider en toutes rencontres, lorsqu'il s'agit de leur avancement spirituel": "Livre dans lequel sont escrits tous les Reglemens de chaque office," fol. 33r.

70. "Leur imposer souvent la fidelité aux regles du seminaire jusqu'aux moindres": "Livre dans lequel sont escrits tous les Reglemens de chaque office," fol. 37r.

71. "Recevoir ses avis comme de la part de Dieu, communiquer avec luy de temps en temps pour luy rendre compte de la fidelité en nos resolutions, & luy decouvrir avec simplicité nos peines & nos tentations": Pasté, *Abrégé du reglement de S. Nicolas du Chardonnet (1672)*, 10.

72. "Les supporter fraternellement dans leurs manquemens, & les en relever s'il est possible avec douceur": Pasté, *Abrégé du reglement de S. Nicolas du Chardonnet (1672)*, 17.

73. "Par conseil, instruction, ou autrement, autant que les regles le permettent": Pasté, *Abrégé du reglement de S. Nicolas du Chardonnet (1672)*, 17.

74. "Si les manquemens sont notables, & contre l'edification publique, & le bon ordre de la Maison, en donner avis au Prefet pour y remedier": Pasté, *Abrégé du reglement de S. Nicolas du Chardonnet (1672)*, 17.

75. "Se rendre tres-fidele pour l'interieur & pour l'exterieur à tous les avis, & à toutes les Regles marquées cy-dessus en veüe de Dieu seul": Pasté, *Abrégé du reglement de S. Nicolas du Chardonnet (1672)*, 18.

76. "À genoux et attentivement": "Reglement général du Séminaire de S. Sulpice," fol. 110r. At the Seminary of Saint-Sulpice, the examen particulier followed immediately after a reading from the New Testament. At Saint-Nicolas du Chardonnet, the examen particulier followed the recitation of Tierce and Sexte. See Pasté, *Abrégé du reglement de S. Nicolas du Chardonnet (1672)*, 2.

77. "Sur quelque vertu, quelque vice ou quelque imperfection, afin de nous faire connoître les principales fautes qu'on peut commettre sur cette matiere, cette connoissance nous étant nécessaire pour nous faire éviter ces fautes, nous faciliter la pratique de la vertu, et nous élever à la perfection chrétienne et ecclésiastique": "Reglement général du Séminaire de S. Sulpice," fol. 110r.

78. "Reglement général du Séminaire de S. Sulpice," fol. 110r; Beuvelet indicates that one should only target one vice or virtue at a time, dividing it into smaller pieces so as to better master it. See Beuvelet, *Conduites*, 37.

79. "Il faut outre cela que chacun s'attache pendant un temps bien plus considérable comme d'un mois ou de deux à s'examiner sur un défaut ou une pratique de vertu particuliere, dans le temps qui lui sera marqué pour cela par son Directeur": "Reglement général du Séminaire de S. Sulpice," fol. 110r.

80. At the Seminary of Saint-Sulpice, this concluding examen was called the "examen de conscience." At the Seminary of Saint-Nicolas du Chardonnet, it was called the "examen de la journée." See "Reglement général du Séminaire de S. Sulpice," fol. 114v; Pasté, *Abrégé du reglement de S. Nicolas du Chardonnet (1672),* 3. See also Beuvelet, *Conduites,* 33.

81. "Regardez par la Foy la divine Majesté en vous même, connoissant, destestant, jugeant, condamnant, punissant vos pechés jusques au moindre": Beuvelet, *Conduites,* 185.

82. "Ceux qui auroient manqué à quelque point du Reglement pendant le jour et qui ne s'en seroient pas encore excusés auprés de M. le Supérieur ou de celui qui tient sa place, doivent le faire aprés la priere avant de sortir de la Salle": "Reglement général du Séminaire de S. Sulpice," fol. 115r.

83. "Edifient beaucoup les Peuples": Pasté, *Abrégé du reglement de S. Nicolas du Chardonnet (1672),* 10.

84. "Admirons le grand S. François marchant avec une telle modestie qu[e] ... to[u]s ses pas estoient autant de secretes predications, et l'eclat de cette vertu qui paroissoit dans cette demarche estoit si surprenant ... qu'il gaignoit ainsy le monde à J.C.": "Recueil de la conduite d'un ecclesiastique," fol. 200.

85. "L'ignorance & le peché," "gemissent incessamment," "de vrays Prestres & Pasteurs": Olier, "Projet de l'establissement d'un séminaire," 3.

86. "Envers ses paroissiens": *Les Principaux devoirs d'un bon curé* (Paris: Pierre Trichard, 1657), 12.

87. "Avoir un coeur de mere envers tous, pour supporter patiemment les peines & difficultez qu'il trouvera à les eslever à la perfection de la vie Chrestienne": *Les Principaux devoirs d'un bon curé,* 12.

88. "Comme bon Pasteur il doit nourrir son troupeau": *Les Principaux devoirs d'un bon curé,* 13.

89. Beuvelet, *Conduites,* 243.

90. "Une docilité d'esprit en chacun d'eux, pour se rendre plus susceptible des enseignemens & advis qu'il aura à leur donner de la part de Dieu, lequel ils doivent regarder en sa personne": Beuvelet, *Conduites,* 243–44.

91. "Fait des representations," "pour donner des spectacles": Antoine Furetière, "Théâtre," in *Dictionnaire universel* (La Haye: Arnout et Renier Leers, 1690). }

92. "Se dit figurément en Morale.... Les Princes doivent prendre garde à leurs actions, parce qu'ils sont sur un grand théâtre, qu'ils sont bien observez." Furetière, "Théâtre."

93. "Entretiens des ordinands sur les matieres de devotion (Tome I)" (n.d.), fol. 17r, Ms. 157, SS; Jean Dubu, *Les Églises chrétiennes et le théâtre (1550–1850)* (Grenoble: Presses Universitaires de Grenoble, 1997), 88.

94. Schechner, *Between Theater and Anthropology,* 37.

95. Carlson, *Performance: A Critical Introduction,* 4.

96. "Il se faisoit un plaisir de voir ses Seminaristes, l'un faire le Penitent, & l'autre le Confesseur, pour juger de la capacité de l'un & de l'autre, pour la conduite & pour la direction des ames": *Éclaircissemens sur la vie de Messire Jean d'Aranthon d'Alex, évêque, et prince de Genève, avec de nouvelles preuves incontestables de la vérité de son zèle contre le jansénisme & le quiétisme* (Chambery: Jean Gorrin, 1699), 107–8.

97. "C'est la coûtume dans les Seminaires": *Éclaircissemens sur la vie de Messire Jean d'Aranthon d'Alex,* 107.

98. "Un Predicateur mourroit de confusion, s'il avoit fait une faute notable en un Sermon: Si un Orateur en haranguant devant un Prince, un Comedien de mesme sur un Theâtre; à cet effet les uns & les autres estudient, se preparent, & repetent une infinité de fois, &c. afin d'agréer, & reüssir à leur plaisir, & honneur. Et (ce qui est déplorable) on ne se soucie point dans les divins

Offices qui se recitent devant & en la presence de la divine Majesté, de faire cent fautes, faute de preparation. Y a-il de la Foy parmy les Ecclesiastiques": Adrien Bourdoise, *L'Idée d'un bon ecclésiastique ou les sentences chrétiennes et cléricales de Messire Adrien Bourdoise, d'heureuse mémoire, prestre de la Communauté de Saint Nicolas du Chardonnet* (Paris: Jacques de Laize de Bresche, 1684), 32. The "leur" in the quote is ambiguous. Based on the context, I take it to refer to the pleasure and honor of the nobles before whom the orator or actor performs, but it could also refer to the pleasure felt and honor received by the performer.

99. "La pluspart des jeunes Predicateurs"; "se taire": Bourdoise, *L'Idée d'un bon ecclésiastique*, 30–31.

100. "Eloquent, qui sçait bien la Rhétorique, & qui la met en pratique": Antoine Furetière, "Orateur," in *Dictionnaire universel* (La Haye: Arnout et Renier Leers, 1690).}

101. "Le principal point de l'orateur, c'est de sçavoir exciter les passions."

102. "Ainsi la Comédie, par sa nature même, est une école et un exercice de vice, puisque c'est un art où il faut nécessairement exciter en soi-même des passions vicieuses": Pierre Nicole, *Traité de la comédie, et autres pièces d'un procès du théâtre*, edited by Laurent Thirouin (Paris: Honoré Champion, 1998), 38. See also Jacques Benigne Bossuet, "Maximes et réflexions sur la comédie," in *L'Eglise et le théâtre: Maximes et réflexions sur la comédie précédés d'une introduction historique et accompagnées de documents contemporains et de notes critiques*, edited by Charles Urbain and Eugene Levesque (Paris: Bernard Grasset, 1930), 174–77.

103. "Coûtumier ou registre des usages plus ordinaires de la Communauté et du Séminaire de St. Nicolas du Chardonnet par ordre Alphabetique" (n.d.), fols. 191r, 192v, MM 476, AN.

104. The Bibliothèque nationale de France has editions from 1660, 1661, 1664, 1672, and 1833.

105. "Croiriez-vous, Monsieur, que les comédiens, ayant reconnu cela, ont changé leur manière de parler, et ne récitent plus leurs vers avec un ton élevé, comme ils faisaient autrefois; mais ils le font avec une voix médiocre, et comme parlant familièrement": Vincent de Paul, *Lettres de S. Vincent de Paul, fondateur des Prêtres de la Mission et des Filles de la Charité*, vol. 1 (Paris: Librairie de D. Dumoulin, 1882), 67.

106. Vincent de Paul, *Lettres*, 1:68.

107. John Golder, "Molière and the Circumstances of Late Seventeenth-Century Rehearsal Practice," *Theatre Research International* 33, no. 3 (2008): 250, 251, https://doi.org/10.1017/S0307883308003957.

108. Golder, "Molière and the Circumstances of Late Seventeenth-Century Rehearsal Practice," 251.

109. On Bourdoise's piecemeal education, see P. Schœnher, *Histoire du Séminaire de Saint-Nicolas du Chardonnet, 1612–1908, d'après des documents inédits*, vol. 1, Quelques pages de L'histoire religieuse du diocèse de Paris (Paris: Société Saint Augustin, 1909), 11–29. For a very brief synopsis of Jesuit theater in France, see Hélène Baby and Alain Viala, "Le XVIIe siècle ou l'institution du théâtre," in *Le Théâtre en France des origines à nos jours*, edited by Alain Viala (Paris: Presses Universitaires de France, 1997), 157–58. For a longer study, see William H. McCabe, S.J., *An Introduction to the Jesuit Theater: A Posthumous Work*, edited by Louis J. Oldani, S.J. (St. Louis, MO: Institute of Jesuit Sources, 1983). For a study of Jesuit theater practice in relation to Jesuit antitheater discourses, see Ruth Olaizola Sanchez, "Les Jésuites au théâtre dans l'Espagne du siècle d'or: Théories et pratiques, 1588–1689" (dissertation, Paris, l'École des Hautes Études en Sciences Sociales, under the direction of Yves Hersant, 2005).

110. Sara Beam, *Laughing Matters: Farce and the Making of Absolutism in France* (Ithaca, NY: Cornell University Press, 2007), 180–92.

111. Beam, *Laughing Matters*, 196.

112. Schœnher, *Histoire du Séminaire de Saint-Nicolas du Chardonnet*, 1:11–12.

113. Philibert Descourveaux, *La Vie de Monsieur Bourdoise, premier prestre de la Communauté de S. Nicolas du Chardonnet* (Paris: François Fournier, 1714), 10, 21–24. Schœnher implies that Bourdoise also worked briefly as a clerk for solicitors in Paris, although the source for his claim is unclear; see *Histoire du Séminaire de Saint-Nicolas du Chardonnet*, 1:12, 18.

114. Beam, *Laughing Matters*, 197.

115. Descourveaux, *La Vie de Monsieur Bourdoise*, 22.

116. Beam, *Laughing Matters*, 150.

117. See the folios entitled "Reglement de la pratique des ceremonies de l'eglise pour tous les ordres mineurs et majeurs ou sacrez et autres fonctions ecclesiastiques" in "Livre dans lequel sont escrits tous les Reglemens de chaque office," fols. 114v–116r.

118. "Livre dans lequel sont escrits tous les Reglemens de chaque office," fol. 114v. The office of maître des cérémonies seems to date from the fifteenth century. In Rome, the role may have originally entailed the responsibility for teaching ceremonies to ordinands. By the early modern period, the pope's maîtres des cérémonies managed all ceremonial events, both liturgical and courtly. See G. Constant, "Les Maîtres de cérémonies du XVIe siècle: Leurs *Diaires*," *Mélanges d'archéologie et d'histoire* 23 (1903): 161–229, https://doi.org/10.3406/mefr.1903.6295. At Saint-Nicholas du Chardonnet, the maître des cérémonies had a pedagogical function in relation to seminarians and coordinated all the parish church's liturgical activities.

119. "Livre dans lequel sont escrits tous les Reglemens de chaque office," fols. 114r–114v.

120. See, for example, Martial du Mans, *Almanach spirituel, de l'an 1651, pour la ville et Fauxbourgs de Paris: Où sont marquées les festes, confrairies, indulgences pleniere, predications, assemblées, et conferences de pieté, qu'il y aura chaque jour de cette année dans les eglises, paroisses et monasteres de Paris, a l'usage des personnes devotes, par le P. Martial du Mans, religieux penitent* (Paris: Georges Josse, 1651), 353v, 360r.

121. "Pour faire remarquer a tous ce quil y a de particulier": "Livre dans lequel sont escrits tous les Reglemens de chaque office," fol. 115r.

122. "Jugés capables": "Livre dans lequel sont escrits tous les Reglemens de chaque office," fols. 26r, 117r.

123. Carlson, *Performance: A Critical Introduction*, 3.

124. "Il verra et examinera si toutes les choses necessaires pour l'administra[t]on du Sacrement qu'on doit exercer sont entieremet et Exactement preparées dans la chambre des exercices": "Livre dans lequel sont escrits tous les Reglemens de chaque office," fol. 105r.

125. "Livre dans lequel sont escrits tous les Reglemens de chaque office," fol. 106r.

126. "1. La poupée," "14. Un coussin pour mettre sous la teste de l'Enfant": "Livre dans lequel sont escrits tous les Reglemens de chaque office," fol. 106r.

127. "6. Un cierge ou deux," "8. Un aspersoir," "9. Une estolle blanche": "Livre dans lequel sont escrits tous les Reglemens de chaque office," 106r.

128. "4. Le vaisseau des s[ai]ntes huiles," "13. Un livre ou Registre des baptesmes": "Livre dans lequel sont escrits tous les Reglemens de chaque office," 106r.

129. "12. Une escritoire garnie de plumes": "Livre dans lequel sont escrits tous les Reglemens de chaque office," 106r.

130. The règlement explicitly presents sacramental training as a corrective to the "neglected" and "dishonored" administration of the sacraments by curates and vicars in the countryside; see "Livre dans lequel sont escrits tous les Reglemens de chaque office," fol. 104v.

131. "Il prenoit même la peine de donner une Confession par écrit à celui qui faisoit le Pénitent pour discerner par là l'esprit & le jugement de celui qui faisoit le Confesseur": *Éclaircissemens sur la vie de Messire Jean d'Aranthon d'Alex*, 108.

132. "Livre dans lequel sont escrits tous les Reglemens de chaque office," fol. 105r.

133. "Il nommera quelqu'un de la compagnie des plus modestes et serieux pour remplir les offices necessaires de chaque Sacrment ex. g. parain, marain, malade, Ex": "Livre dans lequel sont escrits tous les Reglemens de chaque office," fol. 105r.

134. "Il ne suffrira pas non plus qu'on s'amuse a causer et rire, sil y en avait quelqu'un il les advertira doucement et charitablement, mais fortement de garder lordre prescrit": "Livre dans lequel sont escrits tous les Reglemens de chaque office," fol. 105r.

135. "Mettre en estime et en lustre ... cette exacte et sainte administration des sacremens": "Livre dans lequel sont escrits tous les Reglemens de chaque office," fol. 104v.

136. "Livre dans lequel sont escrits tous les Reglemens de chaque office," fol. 105r.

137. "Il fera commencer l'exercice avec le plus de bienseance quil sera possible et tachera de faire observer exactement et entierement toutes les choses dans la pratique de chaque sacrement qui sont necessaires ... jusques a un signe de croix ordonne dans le Rituel": "Livre dans lequel sont escrits tous les Reglemens de chaque office," fol. 105r.

138. "Livre dans lequel sont escrits tous les Reglemens de chaque office," fol. 105r.

139. "Exactement et religieusement," "produisent une tres grande pieté dans le cœur des fidels quand ils les voyent observer avec honneur et avec deference": "Livre dans lequel sont escrits tous les Reglemens de chaque office," fol. 104r.

140. "Les ennemis du théâtre sont ceux qui croient le plus en son pouvoir": Laurent Thirouin, *L'Aveuglement salutaire: Le Requisitoire contre le théâtre dans la France classique* (Paris: Champion, 1997), 20.

141. Sabine Chaouche, *L'Art du comédien: Déclamation et jeu scénique en France à L'âge classique (1629–1680)* (Paris: Honoré Champion Editeur, 2001), 27–28.

142. "Belle Rhétorique du corps": René Bary, *La Rhétorique française* (Amsterdam: J. de Ravenstein, 1679), 102. Quoted in Sabine Chaouche's discussion of "l'éloquence du corps"; see Chaouche, *L'Art du comédien*, 17.

143. "Qu'ils s'estudient a garder tousjours une posture bien seante, respectueuse modeste et pieuse": "Livre dans lequel sont escrits tous les Reglemens de chaque office," fol. 117v.

144. "Pécher contre la bien-séance": Hédelin François d'Aubignac l'abbé, *La Pratique du theatre, oeuvre tres-necessaire a tous ceux qui veulent s'appliquer a la composition des poëmes dramatiques, qui pour profession de les reciter en publique, ou qui prennent plaisir d'en voir les representations* (Paris: Antoine de Sommaville, 1657), 363.

145. For an example of the perfect gentleman's courtly aspect, see Nicolas Faret, *L'Honnête homme, ou l'art de plaire à la cour,* edited by Maurice Magendie (Geneva: Slatkine Reprints, 1970). For an example of his moral aspect, see Armand l'abbé de Gérard, *Le Caractere de l'honneste-homme morale: Dédié au Roy par M. l'abbé de Gérard* (Paris: Chez Amable Auroy ruë Saint Jacques, attenant la Fontaine, S. Severin, 1688).

146. Maurice Magendie, *La Politesse mondaine et les théories de l'honnêteté, en France, au XVIIe siècle, de 1600 à 1660,* vol. 1 (Paris: Librairie Félix Alcan, 1926), 466–73.

147. See especially chapter 1, "Le Héros cornélien," and chapter 4, "La Démolition du héros" in Paul Bénichou, *Morales du grand siècle* (Paris: Gallimard, 1984), 15–67, 128–48.

148. "De sujets sur lesquels tous les théoriciens du dix-septième siècle sont d'accord, quelles que soient leurs valeurs morales": André Lévêque, "'L'Honnête homme' et 'l'homme de bien' au XVII siècle," *PMLA* 72, no. 4 (1957): 622.

149. "La tête doit ainsi garder à tout instant une position naturelle, c'est-à-dire être droite," "sans être raide": Chaouche, *L'Art du comédien*, 35, 40.

150. Chaouche, *L'Art du comédien*, 35–36.

151. "Les défauts de l'oeil, tels que les regards de travers, les regards fixes, trop petits à cause d'une trop forte compression des paupières, leur lascivité ou leur excès de mobilité . . . confèrent à l'orateur un air ridicule, et en font la risée du public": Chaouche, *L'Art du comédien*, 44.

152. Chaouche, *L'Art du comédien*, 49.

153. Chaouche, *L'Art du comédien*, 50–51, 58, 75–76, 78.

154. "En la contenance exterieure, port, maintien, gestes, yeux, marcher, port grave et non leger, maintien gracieux et serieux, gestes modestes, yeux sages et affables, marcher non affeté ny precipité": "Conférences épiscopales," fol. 117v. These folios, entitled "De la Modestie requise aux Ecclesiastiques," are bound with a manuscript entitled "Resolutions arrestées a Paris par messeigneurs les Evesques, et quelques superieurs de seminaires avec Monsieur, mil six cens cinquante sept" (fols. 121r–131v). The folios on modesty do not indicate their year of creation, but I date them as late seventeenth century based on the surrounding folios.

155. "La 1ere chose est quand on est assis de prendre garde de ne se point appuyer indecemment, ny croiser les jambes, ny avoir la veue egarée ça et la, ny les mains dans les pochettes, mais observer une composition modeste et honneste principalement de la teste et des yeux": "Livre dans lequel sont escrits tous les Reglemens de chaque office," fol. 160r.

156. "Prendre garde de ne pas se regarder fixement les uns les autres, de crainte de s'exciter a rire, ou a quelque autre legereté": "Livre dans lequel sont escrits tous les Reglemens de chaque office," fol. 160r.

157. "Avoir la veue modestement baissée": "Livre dans lequel sont escrits tous les Reglemens de chaque office," fol. 160r.

158. Ronald L. Grimes, *The Craft of Ritual Studies* (New York: Oxford University Press, 2014), 193.

159. The qualities I list are drawn from Grimes's table of twelve actions that increase the rituality of an activity. See *The Craft of Ritual Studies*, 194.

160. Grimes, *The Craft of Ritual Studies*, 193–95.

CHAPTER 3

1. "Des predications par les yeux": Jean-Jacques Olier, *Explication des cérémonies de la grande messe de paroisse* (Paris: Jacques Langlois, 1656), 7.

2. "Tiennent les peuples dan[s] le respect & da[n]s la reverence"; "sont d'autant plus efficaces, qu'elles sont plus sensibles: Olier, Olier, *Explication*, 7.

3. "Tresor public"; "Il regle l'Ecclesiastique & le prepare aux Ordres sacrés: Il instruit à conferer les Sacrements avec reverence: Il le forme pour servir dignement aux Cérémonies augustes de l'Eglise": Claude de la Croix, *Le Parfaict ecclesiastique ou diverses instructions sur toutes les fonctions clericales* (Paris: Pierre de Bresche, 1666), áijr–áiijv.

4. *Les Principaux devoirs d'un bon curé* (Paris: Pierre Trichard, 1657), 3–4. This pamphlet is republished as chapter 9 in Croix, *Le Parfaict ecclesiastique*, 71–81.

5. "Il doit avoir une grande devotion envers Nostre Seigneur JESUS-CHRIST, en la sainte Eucharistie": *Les Principaux devoirs d'un bon curé*, 4.

6. "Il doit adminstrer dignement les Sacremens, & y avoir une grande devotion: practiquant religieusement toutes les rubriques & ceremonies contenuës au Manuel de son Diocese; " "Il doit

dire son Office divin, & celebrer la sainte Messe avec la plus grande preparation, attention & devotion quy luy sera possible: observant exactement les rubriques du Breviaire & du Missel de son Diocese, & les heures reglées pour l'Office, autant que faire se pourra": *Les Principaux devoirs d'un bon curé*, 5.

7. *The Council of Trent: The Canons and Decrees of the Sacred and Oecumenical Council of Trent*, edited and translated by J. Waterworth, Hanover Historical Texts Projects (London: Dolman, 1848), 79, http://history.hanover.edu/texts/trent.html. For a late seventeenth-century French translation of the Council of Trent that uses the term éclat, see L'abbé Chanut, trans., *Le Saint Concile de Trente oecumenique et general, celebré sous Paul III, Jule III et Pie IV, souverains pontifes, nouvellement traduit* (Paris: Sebastien Mabre-Cramoisy, 1674), 121.

8. Hal Foster, "Preface," in *Vision and Visuality*, edited by Hal Foster, Dia Art Foundation, Discussion in Contemporary Culture 2 (Seattle, WA: Bay Press, 1988), ix.

9. Foster, "Preface," ix.

10. Marvin Carlson, *Performance: A Critical Introduction*, 2nd ed. (New York: Routledge, 2004), 3–4.

11. "Culte du vray Dieu, ceremonies exterieures par lesquelles on témoigne qu'on l'adore dans son coeur": Antoine Furetière, "Religion," in *Dictionnaire universel* (La Haye: Arnout et Renier Leers, 1690). For an explanation of the term "ceremonies," see also C. Davy-Rigaux, B. Dompnier, and D.-O. Hurel, eds., *Les Cérémoniaux catholiques en France à l'époque moderne: Une Littérature de codification des rites liturgiques*, Église, liturgie et société dans l'Europe moderne (Turnhout, Belgium: Brepols, 2009), 22.

12. Pamphlets against the Mass disseminated Protestant ideas in the sixteenth century and portrayed the Catholic Mass as a form of idolatry or magic derived from Satan. See Christopher Elwood, *The Body Broken: The Calvinist Doctrine of the Eucharist and the Symbolization of Power in Sixteenth-Century France* (New York: Oxford University Press, 1999), 77–112.

13. Pierre Viret, *Les Cauteles, canon et ceremonies de la messe* (Lyon: Pour Claude Ravot, 1564), 8, 33, 62, 67–68.

14. Elwood, *The Body Broken*, 111–12.

15. "Une pensée apolégitique": René Taveneaux, *Le Catholicisme dans la France classique, 1610–1715: Deuxieme partie*, vol. 2, Regards sur l'histoire: Histoire moderne (Paris: Société d'Éditions d'Enseignement Supérieur, 1980), 373. See also Isabelle Brian, "Catholic Liturgies of the Eucharist in the Time of Reform," in *A Companion to the Eucharist in the Reformation*, edited by Lee Palmer Wandel (Leiden: Brill, 2014), 197–98.

16. Raymond Moloney, *The Eucharist*, Problems in Theology (Collegeville, MN: Liturgical Press, 1995), 54.

17. Johannes H. Emminghaus, *The Eucharist: Essence, Form, Celebration*, translated by Linda M. Maloney (Collegeville, MN: Liturgical Press, 1997), 83.

18. By emphasizing God as the creator of liturgical ceremonies, Counter-Reformation Catholics protected the liturgy from charges of idolatry. On idolatry, see Ellen McClure, *The Logic of Idolatry in Seventeenth-Century French Literature*, Gallica (Cambridge: D. S. Brewer, 2020), 7–14.

19. "À Notre Seigneur Jesus-Christ souverain prestre et auteur des ceremonies": *Manuel des cérémonies romaines, tiré des livres romains les plus authentiques, et des ecrivains les plus intelligens en cette matiere, par quelques-uns des prêtres de la Congrégation de L.M.* (Lyon: Benoist Bailly, 1679), áijr.

20. "Adorant pour lors Nostre Seigneur, comme Auteur du Sacrement, qu'on va administrer": Matthieu Beuvelet, *Instruction sur le manuel par forme de demandes et réponses familieres pour servir à ceux qui dans les séminaires se préparent à l'administration des Sacremens, où se*

*voyent recüeillies les choses les plus remarquables qui se trouvent dans la pluspart des Manuels quis sont en usage dans l'Eglise, et la resolution de plusieurs difficultez de pratique,* 4th ed., vol. 1 (Paris: Georges Josse, 1659), 8.

21. "Une verité constante": Anne de Levy de Vantadour, *Rituel de Bourges, fait par feu Monseigneur l'Illustrissime et reverendissime messire Anne de Levy de Vantadour, patriarche, archevêque de Bourges, primat des aquitaines: Publié par Illustrissime et reverendissime Monseigneur, Messire Jean de Montpezat de Carbon, patriarche, archevêque de Bourges, primat des Aquitaines,* vol. 1 (Bourges: Jean Toubeau, 1666), 1. "Les Sacremens ont été instituez par JESUS-CHRIST": Charles Maurice le Tellier, *Rituel de la province de Reims, renouvellé et augmenté par Monseigneur l'Illustrissime et reverendissime Messire Charles Maurice le Tellier, archevêque, duc de Reims, premier pair de France, etc. Et publié dans son diocèze par son autorité* (Paris: Frederic Leonard, 1677), 1.

22. The full quote reads, "C'est d'avoir un tres-grand sentiment des Mysteres que l'on traitte, & des Ceremonies qui les accompagnent"; "les plus precieux joyaux": Beuvelet, *Instruction sur le manuel,* 1:5, ávv.

23. "Il n'y a rien de si grand dans l'Eglise que les Sacremens, lesquels contiennent la naissance, l'accroissement, la guerison, la nourriture, la sanctification, la conservation, & la perseverance du Chrestien . . . & qui ont pour fin de nous unir à Dieu, & nous faire participants de la nature divine": Beuvelet, *Instruction sur le manuel,* 1:5.

24. "Comme des marques visibles & des actes exterieurs tres-parfaits de la Religion que nous professons, & des moyens les plus propres & les plus proportionnés pour faire venir le peuple en connoissance des secrets adorables cachés sous ces Symboles": Beuvelet, *Instruction sur le manuel,* 1:6.

25. "Signes visibles de la grace invisible": Vantadour, *Rituel de Bourges,* 1:ár.

26. "Les Ceremonies sont en l'Eglise des organes & des instrumens du respect": Olier, *Explication,* 7.

27. "Afin que la dignité de nos Mysteres soit connuë & respectée par les fideles qui les reçoivent, n'y ayant rien qui rende nos Sacremens plus augustes & plus dignes de veneration, que nos Ceremonies bien-faites": Beuvelet, *Instruction sur le manuel,* 1:15.

28. "Nous voyons par experience le respect que ces choses impriment dans l'esprit des plus pauvres & des plus ignorans, qui . . . se disposent plus facïlement à leur devoir, & à la reverence qu'ils doivent à Dieu, par le moyen de ces choses exterieures et sensibles": Olier, *Explication,* 6–7.

29. For the foundational study on rites of passage, see Arnold van Gennep, *The Rites of Passage,* translated by Monika B. Vizedom and Gabrielle L. Caffee (Chicago: University of Chicago Press, 1960), 10–25. For a thorough analysis of rites of passage in early modern Europe, see Edward Muir, *Ritual in Early Modern Europe,* 2nd ed. (Cambridge: Cambridge University Press, 2005), 21–61.

30. Davy-Rigaux, Dompnier, and Hurel, *Les Cérémoniaux catholiques en France à l'époque moderne,* 77.

31. Davy-Rigaux, Dompnier, and Hurel, *Les Cérémoniaux catholiques en France à l'époque moderne,* 77.

32. "Conçus comme des guides pour les différents acteurs du culte, ils doivent permettre l'accomplissement harmonieux du service divin": Davy-Rigaux, Dompnier, and Hurel, *Les Cérémoniaux catholiques en France à l'époque moderne,* 77.

33. Jean-Yves Hameline, "Introduction," in *Les Cérémoniaux catholiques en France à l'époque moderne: Une littérature de codification des rites liturgiques,* edited by Cécile Davy-Rigaux,

Bernard Dompnier, and Daniel-Odon Hurel, *Église, liturgie et société dans l'Europe moderne* (Turnhout, Belgium: Brepols, 2009), 32.

34. "Registre dans lequel sont contenus les reglemens des officiers de l'Autel et du Choeur selon l'usage de Paris et de cette paroisse de St. N.D.C." (n.d.), MM 492, AN. The manuscript does not bear a date, but it includes only excerpts from Jean-François de Gondi, archbishop of Paris from 1622 to 1654, which leads me to date it as mid-seventeenth century. Three published Ceremonials are known for Paris during the seventeenth and early eighteenth centuries, dated 1656, 1662, and 1703. See Davy-Rigaux, Dompnier, and Hurel, *Les Cérémoniaux catholiques en France à l'époque moderne*, 547–48.

35. "Ceux qui ont rang dans les hautes chaires doivent observer qu'il ne faut jamais passer devant celuy qui est a une place plus honorable": "Registre dans lequel sont contenus les reglemens des officiers de l'Autel," fol. 1v.

36. "Registre dans lequel sont contenus les reglemens des officiers de l'Autel," fol. 24v.

37. "Registre dans lequel sont contenus les reglemens des officiers de l'Autel," fols. 54r–55r.

38. "Registre dans lequel sont contenus les reglemens des officiers de l'Autel," fol. 96r.

39. "Les thresors de l'Eglise": Beuvelet, *Instruction sur le manuel*, 1:ávv.

40. "Parce que toutes les fautes en cette matiere, si principalement elles se font par ignorance ou par negligence, ne sont jamais petites, mais toutes importantes": Beuvelet, *Instruction sur le manuel*, 1:15.

41. Beuvelet, *Instruction sur le manuel*, 1:15.

42. Waterworth, *The Council of Trent*, 78; "Prenez, & mangez-en tous. CAR CECI EST MON CORPS": *Missel Romain selon le reglement du Concile de Trent, traduit en françois* (Cologne: Jean de la Pierre, 1692), 19–20. In seventeenth-century France, the Mass was still said in Latin. By the second half of the century, however, a Parisian could buy a French translation of the Roman Missal, like the one I have cited here. Capital letters indicated the moment in which the transubstantiation occurred.

43. Waterworth, *The Council of Trent*, 156.

44. Waterworth, *The Council of Trent*, 156.

45. For a helpful summary of the Catholic doctrine of transubstantiation in the seventeenth century and an interesting analysis of transubstantiation in semiotic and performative terms, see Frédéric Cousinié, *Le Saint des saints: Maîtres-autels et retables parisiens du XVIIe siècle* (Aix-en-Provence: Publications de l'Université de Provence, 2006), 19–21.

46. "Cachez sans repandre a l'Exterieur aucun Eclat de sa persone": Jean-Jacques Olier, "Autographes de M. Olier, fondateur du Séminaire de St. Sulpice: Divers écrits, tome I" (n.d.), fol. 79, Ms. 14, SS.

47. "Laisse a l'Eglise a rehausser par . . . l'Exterieur de ces Ceremonies son Eclat et sa gloire": Olier, "Autographes de M. Olier, fondateur du Séminaire de St. Sulpice: Divers écrits, tome I," fol. 79.

48. Waterworth, *The Council of Trent*, 161. Seventeenth-century tracts reiterate this decree. See Pierre Le Gendre, *Declaration des papes, des conciles, des cardinaux, et des docteurs; touchant l'obligation d'entendre la messe paroissiale châcun en sa paroisse* (Paris: Guillaume Sassier, 1651), 16.

49. On the mutual reinforcement of liturgical and courtly ceremonial repertoires, see Fanny Cosandey, *Le Rang: Préséances et hiérarchies dans la France d'ancien régime*, Kindle Edition (Paris: Éditions Gallimard, 2016), chap. 5.

50. "Sa Presence au milieu de la Terre, comme Roy & souverain de son peuple": Pierre de Bérulle, *Les Oeuvres de l'eminentissime et reverendissime Pierre Cardinal de Bérulle, instituteur et premier superieur de la Congregation de l'Oratoire de Jesus-Christ Nostre Seigneur, augmentées de*

*divers opuscuples de controverse & de pieté, avec plusieurs lettres,* edited by François Bourgoing (Paris: Antoine Estienne, 1644), 705.

51. "Si l'on prepare tant de ceremonies pour le Couronnement & le Sacre des Roys, que ne faut-il pas pour consacrer le Fils de DIEU, Roy des Roys & Seigneur des Seigneurs?": Olier, *Explication,* 2.

52. "Le profond estonnement qui l'oblige à s'abîmer & à s'aneantir devant la Majesté Divine": Olier, *Explication,* 2.

53. For Louis XIV's use of art and representation to promote his authority during the Dutch War, see Peter Burke, *The Fabrication of Louis XIV* (New Haven: Yale University Press, 1992), 75–83.

54. "Le Roy"; "Dans tout l'éclat ou l'on me veut paroistre / L'art ne peut exprimer par ses plus beaux crayons, / Ny ma force ny mes rayons, / Il n'appartient qu'a moy de me faire connoistre": "Devises a la Gloire du Roy sur ses conquestes dans la Hollande" (1672), Salles des estampes M92731, BN.

55. Louis Hautecoeur, *Louis XIV: Roi-Soleil* (Paris: Librairie Plon, 1953), 31–38.

56. E. H. Ramsden, "The Halo: A Further Enquiry into Its Origin," *Burlington Magazine for Connoisseurs* 78, no. 457 (1941): 123–31.

57. "The Glory, Nimbus, and Aureola," *Art Amateur* 5, no. 1 (1881): 9.

58. "The Glory, Nimbus, and Aureola," 9.

59. Foster, "Preface," ix; David Morgan, *Sacred Gaze: Religious Visual Culture in Theory and Practice* (Berkeley: University of California Press, 2005), 3, http://troy.lib.sfu.ca/record =b4586481~S1a.

60. Marita Sturken and Lisa Cartwright, *Practices of Looking: An Introduction to Visual Culture* (Oxford: Oxford University Press, 2001), 10.

61. For an engraving of the painting and an explanation of its symbolic significance, see Étienne-Michel Faillon, *Vie de M. Olier, fondateur du séminaire de Saint-Sulpice,* 4th ed., vol. 3 (Paris: Poussielgue frères, 1873), 142, 176–78. The claim that Olier commissioned "La Messe" is based on a passage from the Vie written by his successor, M. de Bretonvilliers, which describes a painting whose themes correspond to those of "La Messe." The passage, which does not give the painting a name or designate the artist, suggests that Olier saw it in a dream or vision before commissioning it. See Alexandre le Ragois de Bretonvilliers, "Vie de M. Olier par M. de Bretonvilliers, tome II" (Vie manuscrite, n.d.), fol. 263, Ms. 109, SS. The restoration report does not indicate how the conservationists who carried out the repairs arrived at the conclusion that the painting was created in the late eighteenth or early nineteenth century. See Geneviève Guttin and Gisèle Caumont, "Rapport de restauration de la couche picturale 'Le Sacrifice de la messe': Maison de retraite des prêtres de Saint Sulpice 'La Solitude'-Issy-les-Moulineaux" (Conseil Général, Hauts-de-Seine, 2007).

62. The strong similarities between the composition and content of *Le Sacrifice de la messe* and other depictions of the Mass from the seventeenth and early eighteenth centuries can be evaluated thanks to two works that reproduce engravings side by side. See Philippe Martin, *Le Théâtre divin: Une Histoire de la messe, XVIe–XXe siècle* (Paris: CNRS Éditions, 2010), 175–76. See also Davy-Rigaux, Dompnier, and Hurel, *Les Cérémoniaux catholiques en France à l'époque moderne,* 267–81. Similarities between the celebrant and altar in *Le Sacrifice de la messe* and the frontispiece of the following early eighteenth-century manual are particularly strong. See Pierre Le Brun, *Explication literale, historique et dogmatique des prieres et des ceremonies de la messe, suivant les anciens auteurs, et les monuments de la plupart des eglises, avec des dissertations et des notes sur les endroits difficiles, et sur l'origine des rites* (Paris: Florentin Delaulne, 1716).

63. Faillon, *Vie de M. Olier*, 3:178.

64. Faillon, *Vie de M. Olier*, 3:178.

65. Where I only count eight rings, Faillon identifies nine angelic hierarchies grouped into three orders. See Faillon, *Vie de M. Olier*, 3:176.

66. "En état de présence exclusive": Louis Marin, "Le Cadre de la représentation et quelques-unes de ses figures," in *De la représentation*, edited by Daniel Arasse et al. (Paris: Gallimard Le Seuil, 1994), 347.

67. Bert O. States, "Performance as Metaphor," *Theatre Journal* 48, no. 1 (1996): 16.

68. Richard Schechner, *Performance Studies: An Introduction* (London: Routledge, 2002), 2; States, "Performance as Metaphor," 19.

69. Thomas Postlewait and Tracy C. Davis, "Theatricality: An Introduction," in *Theatricality*, edited by Thomas Postlewait and Tracy C. Davis (Cambridge: Cambridge University Press, 2003), 4.

70. Rebecca Schneider, *Performing Remains: Art and War in Times of Theatrical Reenactment* (New York: Routledge, 2011), 12. For the classic essay on performance's disappearance, see Peggy Phelan, "The Ontology of Performance: Representation Without Reproduction," in *Unmarked: The Politics of Performance* (London: Routledge, 1993), 146–66.

71. Schneider, *Performing Remains*, 21.

72. As I explain in the book's Introduction, Paris's most influential Counter-Reformation seminaries were all founded in the early 1640s. See Jeanne Ferté, *La Vie religieuse dans les campagnes parisiennes (1622–1695)* (Paris: Librarie Philosophique J. Vrin, 1962), 148, 151. The publication of Pierre Le Brun's liturgical handbook in 1716 offers a convenient endpoint for the period analyzed here. See Le Brun, *Explication literale, historique et dogmatique des prieres et des ceremonies de la messe*.

73. Norbert Elias, *The Court Society*, translated by Edmund Jephcott (New York: Pantheon Books, 1983), 80.

74. Elias, *The Court Society*, 80.

75. "Le héros en effet doit toujours être entouré de personnages secondaires.... Il ne saurait aller seul sans heurter l'idée qu'on se fait de sa puissance et de sa dignité. Il lui faut une 'suite,' d'autant plus nombreuses qu'il occupe un rang plus élevé": Jacques Scherer, *La Dramaturgie classique en France* (Paris: Librairie Nizet, 1959), 40.

76. "Reglement général du Séminaire de S. Sulpice" (1682), fol. 117v, MS Fr. 11760, BN. For images of chancel stalls, see Elaine C. Block, "Liturgical and Anti-Liturgical Iconography on Medieval Choir Stalls," in *Objects, Images, and the Word: Art in Service of the Liturgy*, edited by Colum Hourihane, Index of Christian Art 4 (Princeton, NJ: Princeton University Press, 2003), 161–79.

77. "Reglement général du Séminaire de S. Sulpice," fol. 118r.

78. Philibert Descourveaux, *La Vie de Monsieur Bourdoise, premier prestre de la Communauté de S. Nicolas du Chardonnet* (Paris: Francois Fournier, 1714), 68.

79. Maurice Magendie, *La Politesse mondaine et les théories de l'honnêteté, en France, au XVIIe siècle, de 1600 à 1660*, vol. 1 (Paris: Librairie Félix Alcan, 1926), 162.

80. "La centralité du roi est un absolu auquel se réfère toute l'organisation spatiale": Cosandey, *Le Rang*, chap. 5.

81. "Nous remarquons trois sortes d'Inclinations a observer a l'office divin. La premiere c'est l'Inclination profonde qui est du corps et des Espaules que l'on appelle autrement humiliation.... La seconde est l'Inclination mediocre qui est des Espaules et de la teste.... La troisiéme C'est la petite inclination qui est appellée une Inclination legere parce qu'elle ne se fait que de la teste seulement": "Registre dans lequel sont contenus les reglemens des officiers de l'Autel," fols. 10r–11r.

82. Regarding the nuances of genuflection, see the "Avertissement" at the beginning of *Manuel des cérémonies romaines*, non-numbered page.

83. "La maniere de faire les Inclinations en entrant au choeur et en sortant": "Livre dans lequel sont escrits tous les Reglemens de chaque office, et Exercice du Seminaire desquels le Prestre doit avoir une parfaite connoissance" (n.d.), fol. 239r, AN MM 475.

84. Henri Brocher, *À la cour de Louis XIV: Le Rang et l'étiquette sous l'ancien régime* (Paris: Librairie Félix Alcan, 1934), 43.

85. Brocher, *À la cour de Louis XIV*, 207.

86. Olier, *Explication*, 220–21; "Registre dans lequel sont contenus les reglemens des officiers de l'Autel," fols. 111r–112v.

87. "Durant tout le temps du Canon devant et apres la consecration il ne rend aucun service au Celebrant proche le livre, mais au lieu de ce service il demeure debout a la droite du Celebrant, faisant les inclinations, les genuflexions, et les signes de Croix comme le Celebrant": "Registre dans lequel sont contenus les reglemens des officiers de l'Autel," fol. 54v.

88. "Tous les autres Ministres inferieures . . . doivent . . . se conformer au Celebrá[n]t & aux Ministres sacrez": *Manuel des cérémonies romaines*, 228.

89. *Manuel des cérémonies romaines*, 228–29.

90. "Les Autels doivent être élevés . . . autant élevés dans l'Église . . . que Jésus-Christ l'est au dessus de toute l'Eglise en dignité & en honneur": Jean-Baptiste Thiers, *Dissertations ecclésiastiques, sur les principaux autels des églises, les jubés des églises, la clôture du chœur des églises* (Paris: Antoine Dezallier, 1688), 77.

91. For a full description of the church, including an excerpt from an inventory from 1791 that indicates the number of stairs leading to the altar, see Cousinié, *Le Saint des saints*, 214–19.

92. "A dire le vrai, cet Autel & tous ses accompagnemens ne sont pas d'une invention fort heureuse. Il est si bas & si enfoncé, qu'on a de la peine à discerner le Prêtre quand il fait l'office divin": Germain Brice, *Nouvelle description de la ville de Paris et de tout ce qu'elle continent de curieux et de plus remarquable*, 8th ed., vol. 2 (Paris: Julien Michel Gandouin, 1725), 173.

93. Henri François Simon de Doncourt, *Remarques historiques, sur l'église et la paroisse de S. Sulpice, tirées du premier volume des instructions & prieres à l'usage de ladite paroisse*, vol. 1 (Paris: Nicolas Crapart, 1773), 12. According to Jules Corblet, diocesan Rituals began prescribing three steps for altars as early as the fifteenth century, and Charles Borromeo called for five steps. See *Histoire dogmatique, liturgique et archéologique du sacrement de l'eucharistie*, vol. 2 (Paris: Société Générale de Librairie Catholique, 1886), 74.

94. Bernard Chédozeau, *Chœur clos, chœur ouvert: De l'église médiévale à l'église tridentine (France, XVIIe–XVIIIe siècle)* (Paris: Les Éditions du Cerf, 1998), 46, 215–16.

95. On medieval altars, see Chédozeau, *Chœur clos, chœur ouvert*, 29.

96. Its name in French derives from the Latin description of its position on the altar, retro for behind and tabula for table. See Corblet, *Histoire dogmatique, liturgique et archéologique du sacrement de l'eucharistie*, 2:123.

97. On the development of altar pieces from the tenth to seventeenth centuries, see Corblet, *Histoire dogmatique, liturgique et archéologique du sacrement de l'eucharistie*, 2:123–25.

98. Cousinié, *Le Saint des saints*, 77.

99. Schechner defines restored behaviors as "strips of behavior" that "can be rearranged or reconstructed," like "organized sequences of events, scripted actions, known texts, [and] scored movements." Ceremonies provide a good example of restored behavior. See Richard Schechner, *Between Theater and Anthropology* (Philadelphia: University of Pennsylvania Press, 1985), 35–36.

100. "Registre dans lequel sont contenus les reglemens des officiers de l'Autel," fol. 10r.

101. "En entrant ou en sortant du Choeur, ou en passant par le milieu on se tourne vers l'autel, et l'on fait devotement inclination mediocre, si le St. Sacrement estoit exposé en evidence, l'on fait genuflection": "Registre dans lequel sont contenus les reglemens des officiers de l'Autel," fol. 1v.

102. "Registre dans lequel sont contenus les reglemens des officiers de l'Autel," fol. 10v.

103. "Registre dans lequel sont contenus les reglemens des officiers de l'Autel," fol. 11v.

104. *Manuel des cérémonies romaines*, 430–31.

105. *Manuel des cérémonies romaines*, 432–33.

106. "Registre dans lequel sont contenus les reglemens des officiers de l'Autel," fols. 51r, 76v.

107. "Registre dans lequel sont contenus les reglemens des officiers de l'Autel," fol. 107r; *Manuel des cérémonies romaines*, 271–72.

108. "Il encense sans interruption pendant qu'on esleve la s[ain]te hostie et le calice": "Registre dans lequel sont contenus les reglemens des officiers de l'Autel," fol. 114v.

109. *Manuel des cérémonies romaines*, 274.

110. *Manuel des cérémonies romaines*, 274.

111. *Reglemens et matieres des catechismes qui se font en la paroisse de S. Nicolas du Chardonnet, dressez par l'ordre de Monsieur le Curé dudit lieu pour servir à ceux qui sont employez de sa part à faire le catechisme dans son eglise et autres* (Paris: Gabriel Targa, 1668), 35, 53, 55, 118.

112. "Que prononçans les Saints Noms de JESUS & MARIE, s'ils sont debout, ils fassent la reverence, s'ils sont assis ils . . . fassent seulement une inclination de la teste": *Reglemens et matieres des catechismes qui se font en la paroisse de S. Nicolas du Chardonnet*, 34.

113. *Instruction familiere pour bien entendre la Sainte Messe* (Paris: Pierre Trichard, n.d.), 2. This pamphlet is one of fifty-nine tracts about ecclesiastical discipline that were each published separately and then bound in a single volume (BN D-49744). The pamphlets do not bear a date but were published between 1634 and 1694, the years of Pierre Trichard's activity as printer. According to Joseph Grandet, Bourdoise wrote many pamphlets of this sort to distribute in the parish and circulate in the countryside, a practice continued by Claude de la Croix. See Joseph Grandet, *Les Saints prêtres français du XVIIe siècle, ouvrage publié pour la première fois, d'après le manuscrit original*, edited by G. Letourneau, vol. 2 (Angers: Germain et G. Grassin; A. Roger et F. Chernoviz, 1897), 258n1. Regarding the parish church's doorkeeper, see "Registre dans lequel sont contenus les reglemens des officiers de l'Autel," fols. 143r–145v.

114. Cosandey, *Le Rang*, chap. 5, loc. 2963.

115. Henri François Simon de Doncourt, *Remarques historiques sur l'église et la paroisse de Saint Sulpice: Pièces justificatives*, vol. 2 (Paris: Chez Nicolas Crapart, Libraire, rue de Vaugirard, près de la place S. Michel, 1773), 117.

116. Doncourt, *Remarques historiques sur l'église et la paroisse de Saint Sulpice*, 2:212.

117. Doncourt, *Remarques historiques sur l'église et la paroisse de Saint Sulpice*, 2:86–87.

118. "Puis ayant fait derechef inclination ou genuflexion, il encense de trois coups, dans une égale distance, le dessus de l'Autel vers la partie derriere": *Manuel des cérémonies romaines*, 221, emphasis mine.

119. "Registre dans lequel sont contenus les reglemens des officiers de l'Autel," fol. 25.

120. "En passant devant les Eglises, Croix ou Images des S[aint]s ou devant les Prestres ou Religieux, leur faire la reverence": *Reglemens et matieres des catechismes qui se font en la paroisse de S. Nicolas du Chardonnet*, 35.

121. *Manuel des cérémonies romaines*, 8–10.

122. "Il se faut mettre à genoux devant quelque devote Image": *La Journée chrétienne* (Paris: Pierre Trichard, n.d.), 1–2. This is the twenty-second pamphlet in the same collection as the *Instruction familiere pour bien entendre la Sainte Messe* (BN D-49744).

123. "En quelque estat particulier"; "Allant faire un Baptesme, l'adorer dans le Jordain; Allant entendre les Confessions, comme celuy qui s'est fait peché pour les hommes, & comme leur Medecin; Donnant la saincte Eucharistie, comme souverain Prestre & victime tout ensemble; Appliquant les saintes Huiles en l'Extreme-Onction, comme la vertu du Pere Eternel, & la force es Chrestiens, Celebrant un Mariage; comme l'Espoux de l'Eglise": Beuvelet, *Instruction sur le manuel*, 1:8.

## CHAPTER 4

1. Pierre Le Brun, *Discours sur la comédie, où on voit la réponse au théologien qui la deffend, avec l'histoire du théâtre, et les sentimens des docteurs de l'Eglise depuis le premier siecle jusqu'à présent* (Paris: Loüis Guerin, 1694), 8; "Entretiens des ordinands sur les matières de dévotion (Tome II)" (n.d.), fol. 17v, Ms. 158, SS.

2. "Étant les personnes publiques et qui sont choisis pour . . . rendre à DIEU par leur religion les devoirs de tout le monde. Ils sont engagés par leur condition à renfermer dans leurs prières toute la religion et <à> en avoir, eux seuls, autant que tous les hommes ensembles": Jean-Jacques Olier, "Mystères de N.S. Jésus-Christ" (n.d.), fols. 79–81, Ms. 147, SS; published in Gilles Chaillot, Paul Cochois, and Irénée Noye, eds., *Traité des Saints Ordres (1676), compare aux écrits authentiques de Jean-Jacques Olier (†1657)* (Paris: Procure de la Compagnie de Saint-Sulpice, 1984), 288. As I discuss in Chapter 3, the term "religion" here has a strongly ceremonial connotation.

3. On Tronson's probable authorship, see Chaillot, Cochois, and Noye, *Traité des Saints Ordres*, ix–x.

4. "Les Ecclésiastiques sont ceux qui font publiquement ces fonctions extérieures, et qui sont établis de DIEU pour lui rendre ces devoirs publics de la part et au nom de tous les fidèles": Chaillot, Cochois, and Noye, *Traité des Saints Ordres*, 45.

5. "Empoisonneurs publics qui font couler leur venin par les yeux et par les oreilles": "Du Carnaval, contre les desbauches qui s'y passent" (n.d.), fol. 41, MS 317, SS. The folios are not numbered, so I have counted each recto and verso separately, starting from the first page of the first sermon in the volume. The author of this sermon, although referring to performers, seems to have read either Pierre Nicole's *L'Hérésie imaginaire*, in which Nicole calls playwrights "public poisoners," or Racine's response, see Jean Racine, "Lettre à l'auteur des Hérésies imaginaires et des deux Visionnaires (1666)," in *Traité de la comédie, et autre pièces d'un procès du théâtre*, edited by Laurent Thirouin (Paris: Honoré Champion, 1998), 225–32.

6. Benedetto Ojetti, "The Roman Congregations," in *The Catholic Encyclopedia* (New York: Robert Appleton, 1912), http://www.newadvent.org/cathen/13136a.htm. The Congregation for Divine Worship and the Discipline of the Sacraments now directs the liturgy. See "Rites, Congregation of Sacred," in *Oxford Reference*, accessed May 21, 2021, https://www.oxfordreference .com/view/10.1093/oi/authority.20110803100422710. See also "Congregation for Divine Worship and the Discipline of the Sacraments," accessed May 21, 2021, https://www.vatican.va /content/romancuria/en/congregazioni/congregazione-per-il-culto-divino-e-la-disciplina-dei -sacrament.index.html.

7. Jean Dubu, *Les Églises chrétiennes et le théâtre (1550–1850)* (Grenoble: Presses Universitaires de Grenoble, 1997), 71–72.

8. Dubu, *Les Églises chrétiennes et le théâtre (1550–1850)*, 73; Paul V, *Rituale romanum, Pauli V. Pont* (Antwerp: Ex Officina Plantiniana, Apud Balthasarem et Joannem Moretos, 1617), 70.

9. Dubu, *Les Églises chrétiennes et le théâtre (1550–1850)*, 75.

10. "Quelles sont les personnes ausquelles on doit differer, ou refuser l'absolution, pour estre engagées dans les occasions prochaines du peché, jusques à ce qu'elles s'en soient éloignées?": Nicolas Pavillon, *Les Instructions du rituel du diocese d'Alet*, 4th ed. (Paris: Guillaume Desprez, 1678), 132.

11. "A cela se reduisent aussi certaines personnes publiques, comme sont les curez; les juges, les medecins, les apotiquaires, les chirurgiens, qui notoirement ne sont pas capables de leurs charges & de leurs emplois; ce qui fait qu'ils sont exposez à un danger continuel de faire des fautes, & des injustices notables, & qu'ils sont par consequent dans l'occasion prochaine du peché": Pavillon, *Les Instructions du rituel du diocese d'Alet*, 133.

12. Jostein Gripsrud et al., "Editors' Introduction," in *The Idea of the Public Sphere: A Reader*, edited by Jostein Gripsrud et al. (Lanham: Lexington Books, 2010), 7. Emphasis in original.

13. Norbert Elias, *The Court Society*, trans. Edmund Jephcott (New York: Pantheon Books, 1983); Jürgen Habermas, *The Structural Transformation of the Public Sphere: An Inquiry into the Category of Bourgeois Society* (Cambridge, MA: MIT Press, 1989); Ralph E. Giesey, *Cérémonial et puissance souveraine: France, XVe–XVIIe siècles* (Paris: Armand Colin, 1987); Richard A. Jackson, *Vive le Roi! A History of the French Coronation from Charles V to Charles X* (Chapel Hill: University of North Carolina Press, 1984); Sarah Hanley, *The Lit de Justice of the Kings of France: Constitutional Ideology in Legend, Ritual, and Discourse* (Princeton, NJ: Princeton University Press, 1983); Lawrence M. Bryant, *The King and the City in the Parisian Royal Entry Ceremony: Politics, Ritual, and Art in the Renaissance*, Travaux d'humanisme et renaissance (Geneva: Librairie Droz, 1986).

14. Habermas, *The Structural Transformation of the Public Sphere*, 8.

15. Habermas, *The Structural Transformation of the Public Sphere*, 7.

16. For more on éclat, see Chapter 3.

17. Habermas, *The Structural Transformation of the Public Sphere*, 7.

18. Habermas, *The Structural Transformation of the Public Sphere*, 8, 13.

19. Habermas, *The Structural Transformation of the Public Sphere*, 8.

20. Habermas, *The Structural Transformation of the Public Sphere*, 8.

21. Habermas, *The Structural Transformation of the Public Sphere*, 8–9.

22. My tripartite classification of types of publicness is just one way of thinking about the problem and could be further nuanced in a longer treatment. For a more complete list of the various relations between public and private, many of which have roots stretching back at least through early modernity, see Michael Warner, *Publics and Counterpublics* (New York: Zone Books, 2005), 29. See also Hélène Merlin's analysis of seveneenth-century definitions of "public" in *Public et littérature en France au XVIIe siècle*, Histoire (Paris: Les Belles Lettres, 1994), 35–38.

23. "Public, publique, adj. Connu, manifeste. [Son crime est public & l'on en peut parler. La chose n'est pas encore publique, mais elle le sera bientôt.] Public, publique. Prostitué à tout le monde. De mauvaise vie. Ce mot de public en ce sens se dit des filles & des femmes. [En droit les servantes de cabaret passent pour publiques . . .]": César-Pierre Richelet, "Public," in *Dictionnaire françois* (Genève: Jean Herman Widerhold, 1680), http://gallica.bnf.fr/ark:/12148/bpt6k509323 /f814. Brackets and emphasis in the original.

24. "Publiquement, adv. En public. A la vuë du monde": Richelet, "Public" (1680).

25. "Ce qui est connu & manifesté à tout le monde": Antoine Furetière, "Public," in *Dictionnaire universel* (La Haye: Arnout et Renier Leers, 1690).

26. "Injurieux, & signifie celle qui se prostitue à tous venans"; "lors qu'elle tient boutique ouverte, & qu'elle s'oblige pour raison des choses dont elle fait commerce": Furetière, "Public" (1690).

27. "Il faut avoir de la hardiesse pour paroistre en public. Les Advocats parlent en public. Les Predicateurs preschent en public. Ce President a donné une audience publique. On dit aussi, qu'un Auteur donne ses ouvrages au public, quand il les fait imprimer. Autrefois il suffisoit de les faire courir en manuscrit": Furetière, "Public" (1690).

28. The parterre, or pit, was especially associated with judgment. See Pierre Mélèse, *Le Théâtre et le public à Paris sous Louis XIV, 1659–1715* (Paris: Librairie Droz, 1934), 215–17.

29. Merlin, *Public et littérature en France au XVIIe siècle*, 35–40.

30. Furetière, "Public" (1690).

31. "Quelque décrié que soit le public, il n'y a pas de Juge plus incorruptible, & tôt ou tard il rend justice": Antoine Furetière, "Public," in *Dictionnaire universel*, ed. Basnage de Bauval (La Haye: Arnout et Renier Leers, 1702), 625. The citation is from Boileau.

32. "Si vôtre Ouvrage est bon le public lui rendra justice": Furetière, "Public" (1702), 625.

33. "Le public est un juge inexorable, qu'il faudroit menager plus qu'on ne fait": Furetière, "Public" (1702), 625. The dictionary attributes the citation to an author named Bell.

34. Merlin, *Public et littérature en France au XVIIe siècle*, 385: "personne fictive renvoyant à l'ensemble viriuel des lecteurs et spectateurs d'une ouvre littéraire."

35. See the title of Claude de la Croix, *Le Parfaict ecclesiastique ou diverses instructions sur toutes les fonctions clericales* (Paris: Pierre de Bresche, 1666). "Le Prestre est un miroir & une lumiere en laquelle les peuples doivent se mirer": Jean Avila, *Discours aux prestres contenant une doctrine fort necessaire à tous ceux lesquels estans élevez à cette haute dignité desirent que Dieu leur soit propice au dernier jugement*, 3rd ed. (Paris: Pierre Trichard, 1658), 12.

36. For an overview of clerical vestments see Louis Trichet, *Le Costume du clergé: Ses origines et son évolution en France d'après les règlements de l'église* (Paris: Les Éditions du Cerf, 1986); Robert Alexander Stewart Macalister, *Ecclesiastical Vestments: Their Development and History* (London: Elliot Stock, 1896).

37. *The Council of Trent: The Canons and Decrees of the Sacred and Oecumenical Council of Trent*, edited and translated by J. Waterworth, Hanover Historical Texts Projects (London: Dolman, 1848), 51, http://history.hanover.edu/texts/trent.html.

38. Waterworth, *The Council of Trent*, 50–52.

39. "J'eusse eu honte de manquer à bien faire": "Dix conferences aux confesseurs" (n.d.), fols. 35–36, Ms. 316, SS. The folios are not numbered, so I have counted each recto and verso separately, starting from the first page of the first conference.

40. "J'ay trouvé du depuis que cette mesme tentation en avoit travaillé d'autres": "Dix conferences aux confesseurs," fol. 35.

41. "Je me suis trouvé souvent tenté d'avoir de beaux ornemens, de dire la messe aux autels mieux parés, et mesmes quand c'estoit devant les grilles de Religieuses. Ô Monseigneur, combien de fois ay-jeu eu tentation de retracer sur ma voix, sur mon geste, sur ce que je faisois quelque Ceremonie particuliere, m'Imaginant que ces filles me verroient ce qui n'estoit pas, et je n'avois pas honte de ne pas estre attentif à vous": "Dix conferences aux confesseurs," fols. 45–46.

42. "Une autre faute est le mespris qu'on faict de la practique des autres, et celle cy ô Mon Seigneur est grande . . . jamais on est à la Messe qu'avec distraction, en regardant avec Condamnation celuy qui dit mal la Messe, et en le mesprisant, la tentation mesme donne du chagrin, quelque fois elle va sans raison jusques à l'audace d'aller dans la sacristie accuser celuy qui a dict la Messe mal à n[ot]re gré. O Mon Dieu, j'ay failly autrefois en cela": "Dix conferences aux confesseurs," fols. 39–41.

43. "On devient Indevot et Irreligieux": "Dix conferences aux confesseurs," fol. 40.

44. "La practique des autres": "Dix conferences aux confesseurs," fol. 39.

45. "D'autres fois on s'absente de l'office divin, à cause qu'on le faict mal. . . . J'aymois mieux aller ailleurs perdre mon temps, au lieu que vostre Intention est qu'on aille vo[u]s loüer interieurement comme il faut encores pl[u]s volontiers dans les lieux où vous estes mal honnoré du culte exterieur": "Dix conferences aux confesseurs," fols. 41–2.

46. Karen E. Carter, *Creating Catholics: Catechism and Primary Education in Early Modern France* (Notre Dame, IN: University of Notre Dame Press, 2011), 28.

47. Carter, *Creating Catholics,* 29–32.

48. Carter, *Creating Catholics,* 32.

49. Carter, *Creating Catholics,* 5.

50. Carter, *Creating Catholics,* 5.

51. Carter, *Creating Catholics,* 5.

52. Jeanne Ferté, *La Vie religieuse dans les campagnes parisiennes (1622–1695)* (Paris: Librarie Philosophique J. Vrin, 1962), 158–59.

53. Pasté, *Abrégé du reglement du seminaire paroissial de S. Nicolas du Chardonnet, pour l'usage des seminaristes* (Paris: Pierre Trichard, 1672), 6; "Livre dans lequel sont escrits tous les Reglemens de chaque office, et Exercice du Seminaire desquels le Prestre doit avoir une parfaite connoissance" (n.d.), fols. 124r, 125v, AN MM 475.

54. "Plus pour l'exercice et instruction des ecclesiastiques du seminaire, que pour l'instruction des enfans": "Livre dans lequel sont escrits tous les Reglemens de chaque office," fol. 124r.

55. *Reglemens et matieres des catechismes qui se font en la paroisse de S. Nicolas du Chardonnet, dressez par l'ordre de Monsieur le Curé dudit lieu pour servir à ceux qui sont employez de sa part à faire le catechisme dans son eglise et autres.* (Paris: Gabriel Targa, 1668), 14. In extremely hot or cold weather, the classes were reduced to thirty minutes.

56. *Reglemens et matieres des catechismes qui se font en la paroisse de S. Nicolas du Chardonnet,* 1–9. According to the manuscript version of the rules for catechists, they divided the children into six or seven classes. See "Livre dans lequel sont escrits tous les Reglemens de chaque office," fols. 122r–123v. See also Ferté, *La Vie religieuse dans les campagnes parisiennes,* 158–59.

57. "Il prendre garde qu'aux habits des enfans, il n'y ait point de mondanitez, superfluitez, ny de nuditez, pour les en advertir doucement": *Reglemens et matieres des catechismes qui se font en la paroisse de S. Nicolas du Chardonnet,* 12.

58. "Pour donner de l'emulation aux enfans & les tenir en modestie"; "plus modestes": *Reglemens et matieres des catechismes qui se font en la paroisse de S. Nicolas du Chardonnet,* 17.

59. "On n'usera pas de ces termes, ny de mon fils, ny de ma fille, bien moins encore de Monsieur ny de Mademoiselle, mais on les appellera simplement par leur propre nom, ou sur-nom": *Reglemens et matieres des catechismes qui se font en la paroisse de S. Nicolas du Chardonnet,* 16.

60. "N'ayant point d'égard aux riches plus qu'aux pauvres, mais les aymant tous également": *Reglemens et matieres des catechismes qui se font en la paroisse de S. Nicolas du Chardonnet,* 30.

61. "L'estime que Dieu fait des ames, & en particulier de celle du plus pauvre & plus abject des enfans que l'on va enseigner; disant en son coeur: O Jesus mon Seigneur! que vous aimiez cette ame lors que vous épanchiez vostre Sang precieux pour elle": Matthieu Beuvelet, *Conduites pour les exercices principaux qui se font dans les séminaires ecclesiastiques, dressées en faveur des clercs demeurans dans le Seminaire de S. Nicolas du Chardonnet* (Lyon: Hierosne de la Garde, 1660), 232.

62. "De la façon de l'entendre [la messe], & avec combien de modestie il y faut assister": *Reglemens et matieres des catechismes qui se font en la paroisse de S. Nicolas du Chardonnet,* 35.

63. "Ne permettant jamais que les enfans luy touchent les mains, ny la sottane, ny le surpelis, ny le regardent fixement, sur tout les filles": *Reglemens et matieres des catechismes qui se font en la paroisse de S. Nicolas du Chardonnet,* 31.

64. "Les reprenant aigrement, & leur monstrant un visage plustost severe & austre que trop doux": *Reglemens et matieres des catechismes qui se font en la paroisse de S. Nicolas du Chardonnet*, 31.

65. "Ne les regardera jamais qu'en passant autant que la necessité requerra, il ne s'entretiendra avec elles familierement": *Reglemens et matieres des catechismes qui se font en la paroisse de S. Nicolas du Chardonnet*, 31.

66. "En passant devant les Eglises, Croix ou Images des S[aint]s ou devant les Prestres ou Religieux, leur faire la reverence": *Reglemens et matieres des catechismes qui se font en la paroisse de S. Nicolas du Chardonnet*, 35.

67. "Parler avec respect & humilité, respondant tousjours quand on les interroge, ouy mon Pere, ouy Monsieur, nenny Monsieur": *Reglemens et matieres des catechismes qui se font en la paroisse de S. Nicolas du Chardonnet*, 35.

68. "Sans bruit & avec modestie": *Reglemens et matieres des catechismes qui se font en la paroisse de S. Nicolas du Chardonnet*, 33.

69. "La Messe Paroissiale est une assemblée legitime des Chrestiens, laquelle a coustume de se faire en certains jours dans une Eglise publique, & destinée a cela, sous la conduite d'un Pasteur Hierarchique": Matthieu Beuvelet, *Instruction sur le manuel par forme de demandes et réponses familieres pour servir à ceux qui dans les séminaires se préparent à l'administration des Sacremens, où se voyent recüeillies les choses les plus remarquables qui se trouvent dans la pluspart des Manuels quis sont en usage dans l'Eglise, et la resolution de plusieurs difficultez de pratique*, 4th ed., vol. 2 (Paris: Georges Josse, 1659), 154–55.

70. Joseph Bergin, *Church, Society and Religious Change in France, 1580–1730* (New Haven: Yale University Press, 2009), 208.

71. Beuvelet, *Instruction sur le manuel* (1659), 2:157–72.

72. Bergin, *Church, Society and Religious Change in France*, 208.

73. Bergin, *Church, Society and Religious Change in France*, 208.

74. Bergin, *Church, Society and Religious Change in France*, 208.

75. "Pour distinguer les Paroisses (qui sont appellées les Eglises maistresses, baptismales, ou matrices, Cathedrales, basiliques, plus anciennes & venerables) d'avec les Eglises des Reguliers, qui estoient seulement nommées Chappelles, Oratoires ou Monasteres. . . . Les Religieux n'ayans jamais eu permission d'edifier des Eglises, pour y recevoir les peuples ou Paroissiens; mais seulement pour le propre usage de leur maison": Beuvelet, *Instruction sur le manuel* (1659), 2:155.

76. "Nous defendons sous peine de suspense, à tous Prêtres qui ne sont point de nôtre Diocése, & qui n'y ont ni titre Ecclesiastique ni employ approuvé de Nous, d'y dire la Messe, ni d'y faire aucunes fonctions de leurs Ordres sans en avoir obtenue la Permission par écrit de Nous, ou de nos Vicaires géneraux, ou des Directeurs du Seminaire de S. Nicolas du Chardonnet, que Nous avons commis pour les examiner": Louis Antoine de Noailles, *Ordonnance de Monseigneur l'archevesque de Paris, portant défenses de laisser dire la messe, ni de faire aucunes fonctions dans le diocése, aux prêtres étrangers tant séculiers que réguliers, sans permission écrit* (Paris: Louis Josse, 1697), 3–4.

77. "Des services que nous recevons de la paroisse en santé & en maladie": Beuvelet, *Instruction sur le manuel* (1659), 2:173.

78. See Adrian Fortescue, "Jerusalem (A.D. 71–1099)," in *The Catholic Encyclopedia* (New York: Robert Appleton, 1910), https://www.newadvent.org/cathen/08355a.htm.

79. "Quelles raisons ont eu les Conciles pour obliger les Paroissiens par tant de Canons, tant de fois renouvellez à frequenter leurs Paroisses?" "Car c'est en la paroisse que nous sommes conceus en la grace, que nous prenons une nouvelle naissance, que nous sommes faits enfans de Dieu,

& regenerez sur les Fonds du Baptesme, c'est-là que nous sommes eslevez comme entre les bras de nostre Mere, dans l'esprit du Christianisme, par le moyen des instructions familieres: c'est là que nous prenons nos repas dans la saincte Eucharistie, & que nous devons prendre nostre repos apres la mort; c'est là que l'on nous releve de nos cheutes par le Sacrement de penitence, & qu'on nous fortifie contre la recidive; c'est-là que nous sommes obligez de prendre le saint Viaticum pour faire ce grand voyage de cette vie en l'autre. C'est-là comme d'un arsenal spirituel, que nous recevons les armes de l'Extreme-Onction pour combattre à la fin de la vie contre nos ennemis invisibles; c'est-là que nous trouvons ces Anges visibles, lesquels apres nous avoir receus en la famille de Jesus-Christ, nous enfante à l'éternité": Beuvelet, *Instruction sur le manuel* (1659), 2:172, 173.

80. Louis Antoine de Noailles, *Ordonnance de Monseigneur l'archevesque de Paris touchant l'habit et la conduite exterieure des ecclesiastiques* (Paris: Louis Josse, 1697), 6.

81. "À condition toutefois que leur conduite soit non seulement sans reproche, mais aussi édifiante": Noailles, *Ordonnance de Monseigneur l'archevesque de Paris touchant l'habit et la conduite exterieure des ecclesiastiques,* 6.

82. "Où il n'y ait ni filles ni de femmes": Noailles, *Ordonnance de Monseigneur l'archevesque de Paris touchant l'habit et la conduite exterieure des ecclesiastiques,* 6.

83. Noailles, *Ordonnance de Monseigneur l'archevesque de Paris touchant l'habit et la conduite exterieure des ecclesiastiques,* 6; "Coûtumier ou registre des usages plus ordinaires de la Communauté et du Séminaire de St. Nicolas du Chardonnet par ordre Alphabetique" (n.d.), fol. 133v, MM 476, AN.

84. Matthieu Beuvelet, *Instruction sur le manuel par forme de demandes et réponses familieres pour servir à ceux qui dans les séminaires se préparent à l'administration des Sacremens, où se voyent recüeillies les choses les plus remarquables qui se trouvent dans la pluspart des Manuels quis sont en usage dans l'Eglise, & la resolution de plusieurs difficultez de pratique,* 4th ed., vol. 1 (Paris: Georges Josse, 1659), 190, 204–5.

85. "On ne doit pas entendre leurs Confessions dans des lieux retirez, ou dans des Chappelles obscures; mais en des lieux exposez à la veüe de tout le monde": Beuvelet, *Instruction sur le manuel* (1659), 1:180.

86. "Personnes de ce sexe"; "ayans commencé par l'esprit ont finy miserablement par la chair": Beuvelet, *Instruction sur le manuel* (1659), 1:180.

87. In the way Jesus uses the term "flesh" or body at the Last Supper, it referred to "a human being as transient creature on earth." See Leonhard Goppelt, *Theology of the New Testament,* edited by Jürgen Roloff, translated by John E. Alsup, vol. 1 (Grand Rapids, MI: William B. Eerdmans, 1981), 218. In Paul's writing, "flesh" takes on the connotation of sin. See Leonhard Goppelt, *Theology of the New Testament,* edited by Jürgen Roloff, translated by John E. Alsup, vol. 2 (Grand Rapids, MI: William B. Eerdmans, 1982), 74.

88. "Reglement général du Séminaire de S. Sulpice" (1682), fols. 112v, 114r–114v, MS Fr. 11760, BN.

89. "Reglement général du Séminaire de S. Sulpice," fols. 124r, 125r.

90. "Afin de garder la gravité et la modestie écclésiastique, on doit s'abstenir de se toucher les uns les autres même par jeu": "Reglement général du Séminaire de S. Sulpice," fol. 125r.

91. "Mais il faut éviter avec soin de contracter de ces amitiés particulieres qui ne sont fondées que sur l'inclination naturelle et non pas sur la charité et le désir de la perfection, et dont les suites les moins mauvaises sont la dissipation, la perte du temps, le mépris des autres, l'infraction des reglez et la défiance à l'égard de ceux qui nous conduisent": "Reglement général du Séminaire de S. Sulpice," fol. 112v.

92. Beuvelet, *Instruction sur le manuel* (1659), 2:252.

93. "La série à peu près complète": Théodore Meignan, "Une Nouvelle source d'informations historiques: Les Anciens registres paroissiaux de l'état-civil," *Revue des questions historiques* 25 (1879): 134–35.

94. Beuvelet, *Instruction sur le manuel* (1659), 2:36.

95. "Tout nouveau-né doit être immédiatement (sauf cas de danger) porté à l'église, souvent dans les vingt-quatre heures, et son acte de baptême constituera la seule base de son existence: qui n'est pas baptisé n'existe pas, même civilement": Pierre Goubert and Daniel Roche, *Les Français et l'ancien régime: La Société et l'etat*, vol. 1 (Paris: Armand Colin, 1984), 80.

96. "Passer par sa memoire chaque famille: voir comme on s'y comporte; & s'il s'y trouve quelque desordre, chercher les moyens d'y remedier": *Les Principaux devoirs d'un bon curé* (Paris: Pierre Trichard, 1657), 25.

97. "Il doit particulierement prendre garde sur ceux qui menent une vie mauvaise & scandaleuse, & tascher de les convertir à Dieu: Que s'ils sont pecheurs publics, ou notoirement dans l'occasion prochaine du peché, leur refuser l'usage & l'administration des Sacremens, desquels ils sont indignes": *Les Principaux devoirs d'un bon curé*, 15–16.

## CHAPTER 5

An earlier version of Chapter 5 was published as "Actors, Christian Burial, and Space in Early Modern Paris," *Past and Present* 232, no. 1 (August 2016): 127–63, https://doi.org/10.1093/pastj /gtwo10. Adapted and reprinted by permission of Oxford University Press on behalf of the Past and Present Society.

1. "Nous défendons sous peine de suspense à tous Ecclesiastiques, de se trouver aux Comedies, Bals, Opera, Assemblées de jeu & tous autres spectacles prophanes. . . . Le tumulte, les entretiens & les représentations de tous ces lieux étant entierement opposez à la sainteté que demandent des Clercs leur profession & leurs emplois": Louis Antoine de Noailles, *Ordonnance de Monseigneur l'archevesque de Paris touchant l'habit et la conduite exterieure des ecclesiastiques* (Paris: Louis Josse, 1697), 7.

2. Graham A. Runnalls, ed., *Études sur les mystères: Un Recueil de 22 études sur les mystères français, suivi d'un répertoire du théâtre religieux français du Moyen Âge et d'une bibliographie* (Paris: Honoré Champion, 1998), 87–89; Donnalee Dox, "Ceremonial Embodiment: The Problem of 'Liturgical Drama,'" *Ecumenica: Journal of Theatre and Performance* 3, no. 2 (2010): 31, 35–37; Edith A. Wright, "The Dissemination of the Liturgical Drama in France" (Bryn Mawr, PA: Bryn Mawr College, 1935), 9–16.

3. Raymond Lebègue, *La Tragédie religieuse en France: Les Débuts (1514–1573)*, Bibliothèque littéraire de la renaissance (Paris: Librairie Ancienne Honoré Champion, 1929), 5; Runnalls, *Études sur les mystères*, 93.

4. Sophie Wilma Deierkauf-Holsboer, *Le Théâtre de l'Hôtel de Bourgogne: I, 1548–1635*, vol. 1 (Paris: A.-G. Nizet, 1968), 29–30.

5. The sacramental exclusion of actors belongs to the larger system of inclusion through baptism and exclusion through excommunication or ritual withholding through which the Catholic Church establishes boundaries between insiders and outsiders, believers and nonbelievers. See Henry Phillips, *Church and Culture in Seventeenth-Century France* (Cambridge: Cambridge University Press, 1997), 1.

6. See "Variations sérieuses," in Jonas Barish, *The Antitheatrical Prejudice* (Berkeley: University of California Press, 1981), 191–200.

7. Jean Dubu, "L'Église catholique et la condamnation du théâtre en France au XVIIe siècle," *Quaderni francesi* 1 (1970): 319–49.

8. Jean Dubu, *Les Églises chrétiennes et le théâtre (1550–1850)* (Grenoble: Presses Universitaires de Grenoble, 1997), 88. As explained in this book's Introduction and Chapters 3 and 4, the Ritual is the book of the Roman Rite that contains the sacraments and ceremonies not given in the Missal or the Breviary. Many dioceses issue their own versions. See Adrian Fortescue, "Ritual," in *The Catholic Encyclopedia* (New York: Robert Appleton, 1912), http://www.newadvent.org/cathen/13088b.htm, accessed 3 April 2011.

9. "Sur la reverence qui est deüe aux lieux saincts, & sur l'immunité des Eglises, & la saincteté, qui ne permet dans son enclos, que ceux que l'on presume estre decedez dans une foy vive": Matthieu Beuvelet, *Instruction sur le manuel par forme de demandes et réponses familieres pour servir à ceux qui dans les séminaires se préparent à l'administration des Sacremens, où se voyent recüeillies les choses les plus remarquables qui se trouvent dans la pluspart des Manuels quis sont en usage dans l'Eglise, et la resolution de plusieurs difficultez de pratique*, 4th ed., vol. 2 (Paris: Georges Josse, 1659), 125.

10. "Communauté de Sepultures": Beuvelet, *Instruction sur le manuel* (1659), 2:125. In addition to public sinners, the handbook specifies that, among others, pagans, Jews, Protestants, duelists, and those who did not receive Communion at Easter without good cause should all be denied Christian burial.

11. On parish registers, see Christiane Demeulenaere-Douyere, *Guide des sources de l'état civil parisien* (Paris: Imprimerie municipale, 1982). The seventeenth century awaits a study like Lauren Clay's *Stagestruck: The Business of Theater in Eighteenth-Century France and Its Colonies* (Ithaca, NY: Cornell University Press, 2013).

12. For a detailed table, see Dubu, *Les Églises chrétiennes et le théâtre (1550–1850)*, 86–93.

13. Georges Monval, *Lettres de Adrienne Le Couvreur, réunies pour la première fois et publiées avec notes, étude biographique, documents inédits tirés des archives de la Comédie, des minutiers de notaires et des papiers de la Bastille* (Paris: Librairie Plon, 1892), 40–66.

14. Leonor Jean Christine Soulas Allainval abbé de, "Lettre à mylord *** sur Baron et la Dlle Le Couvreur par George Wink (l'Abbé d'Allainval)," in *Lettre a mylord *** sur Baron et la Dlle Le Couvreur par George Wink (l'Abbé d'Allanval), Lettre du souffleur de la comédie de Roüen au garçon de caffé (par du Mas d'Aigueberre)*, edited by Jules Bonnassies (Paris: L. Willem, 1870), 18.

15. Allainval, "Lettre à mylord," 56–58n.

16. On Languet de Gergy, see Charles Hamel, *Histoire de l'Église Saint-Sulpice*, 2nd ed. (Paris: Librairie Victor Lecoffre, J. Gabalda, 1909), 187–225.

17. "Accompagnés d'une escouade du guet," "comme un paquet," "dans un terrain vague ou sur le bord de la rivière": Monval, *Lettres de Adrienne Le Couvreur*, 62–63; Allainval, "Lettre à mylord," 77n.

18. "Ce triste tombeau": Monval, *Lettres de Adrienne Le Couvreur*, 295; Allainval, "Lettre à mylord," 72n3.

19. "Fait unique dans l'histoire du théâtre!": Monval, *Lettres de Adrienne Le Couvreur*, 62.

20. "Plus grande punition": Beuvelet, *Instruction sur le manuel* (1659), 2:126.

21. Although she was the most famous, Lecouvreur was not the only actor to suffer a total sacramental exclusion. Thirty years earlier Languet de Gergy's predecessor, Henri Baudrand, had imposed a similar posthumous punishment upon Charles Chevillet, Sieur de Champmeslé, an actor and author from the Comédie-Française best known as the widower of the famous Marie Desmares, for whom Racine wrote such roles as Phèdre. See Georges Monval, "Documents inédits

sur les Champmeslé," in *Revue d'art dramatique: Tome XXVIII, octobre-décembre 1892* (Geneva: Slatkine Reprints, 1971), 138–39, http://gallica.bnf.fr/ark:/12148/bpt6k16452z.

22. For the documents pertaining to this case, see Georges Mongrédien, *Recueil des textes et documents du XVIIe siècle relatifs à Molière* (Paris: Éditions du Centre national de la recherche scientifique, 1965), 435–44.

23. *Resolutions de plusieurs cas importans pour la morale, et pour la discipline ecclesiastique, par un grand nombre de docteurs en Theologie de la Faculté de Paris* (Paris: Charles Savreux, 1666). In relation to Protestants, the refusal to bury the dead was also a way of establishing confessional boundaries. See Keith P. Luria, "Separated by Death? Cemeteries, Burials, and Confessional Boundaries," in *Sacred Boundaries: Religious Coexistence and Conflict in Early-Modern France* (Washington, DC: Catholic University of America Press, 2005), 103–42.

24. "'Suivant la doctrine des saints Peres, & de tous les Théologiens apres saint Thomas, on est obligé de refuser les sacremens aux pecheurs publics: Que l'on appelle un pecheur public, celuy qui persevere dans la volonté d'un péché mortel, lequel est manifeste, ou par l'evidence du fait, ou par ce qu'il le confesse publiquement, ou parce qu'il en est declaré atteint & convaincu en justice ecclesiastique ou seculiere": *Resolutions de plusieurs cas importans pour la morale*, 4.

25. Gaston Maugras, *Les Comédiens hors la loi*, 2nd ed. (Paris: Calmann Lévy, 1887), 137.

26. Jan Clarke, *The Guénégaud Theatre in Paris (1673–1680): Founding, Design and Production*, vol. 1, Studies in Theatre Arts 5 (Lewiston, NY: Edwin Mellen Press, 1998), 58; Maurice Albert, *Les Théâtres de la Foire (1660–1789)*, 2nd ed. (Geneva: Slatkine Reprints, 1969), 1–2.

27. For Bérulle's influence on Olier's thought, see Yves Krumenacker, *L'École française de spiritualité: Des Mystiques, des fondateurs, des courants et leurs interprètes* (Paris: Les Éditions du Cerf, 1998), 423–53. On the difference between regular and secular priests, see Arthur Vermeersch, "Religious Life," in *The Catholic Encyclopedia* (New York: Robert Appleton, 1911), http://www.newadvent.org/cathen/12748b.htm; Antoine Furetière, "Seculier, iere," in *Dictionnaire universel* (La Haye: Arnoud et Reinier Leers, 1701).

28. Henri François Simon de Doncourt, *Remarques historiques, sur l'église et la paroisse de S. Sulpice, tirées du premier volume des instructions et prieres à l'usage de ladite paroisse*, vol. 1, 3 vols. (Paris: Nicolas Crapart, 1773); M. Baudrand, "Mémoire sur la vie de M. Olier et sur le séminaire de Saint-Sulpice," in *Bibliothèque sulpicienne ou histoire littéraire de la Compagnie de Saint-Sulpice*, edited by L. Bertrand, vol. 3 (Paris: Alphonse Picard et Fils, 1900), 402n.

29. Pierre Boisard, *La Compagnie de Saint Sulpice: Trois siècles d'histoire*, vol. 1 (Paris: La Compagnie de Saint Sulpice, 1959), 16; Gwénola Hervouët, "Le Séminaire de Saint-Sulpice, 1642–1700: Étude sociologique et religieuse" (Mémoire de maîtrise sous la direction de M. le Professeur Bely, Paris, Université de Paris IV—Sorbonne, 1999). For information on the founding of the Communauté, see Doncourt, *Remarques historiques*, 1:203–4.

30. Boisard, *La Compagnie de Saint Sulpice*, 1:28–29. The "twelve," as they were sometimes called, also traveled to other dioceses to help bishops found seminaries in the provinces.

31. Clarke, *The Gunénégaud Theatre in Paris (1673–1680)*, 1:47, 58.

32. Clarke, *The Gunénégaud Theatre in Paris (1673–1680)*, 1:59.

33. For a brief overview of the Hôtel de Bourgogne's role in France's theatre history, see W. L. Wiley, *The Early Public Theatre in France* (Cambridge, MA: Harvard University Press, 1960), 133–57. On the fusion of the troupe from the Hôtel de Bourgogne with the troupe at the Théâtre Guénégaud, see Pierre Mélèse, *Le Théâtre et le public à Paris sous Louis XIV, 1659–1715* (Paris: Librairie Droz, 1934), 43–44.

34. The actors from the Comédie-Française were forced out of the Théâtre Guénégaud in 1687 by royal order when the founders of a new school across the street from the theater, the

Collège des Quatre-Nations, requested that the king require the actors to find another location. See Mélèse, *Le Théâtre et le public à Paris sous Louis XIV*, 48–51.

35. See, for example, the way Charles Varlet, Sieur de La Grange, and Molière describe themselves in the parish registers reproduced in Auguste Jal, *Dictionnaire critique de biographie et d'histoire, errat et supplément pour tous les dictionnaires historiques d'après des documents authentiques inédits* (Paris: Henri Plon, 1876), 157.

36. *Mercure galant, dédié à Monsieur le Dauphin: Mars 1692* (Paris: G. de Luyne, 1692), 227. The parish's modernized name is Saint-André-des-Arts.

37. One of Olier's early collaborators, Jean du Ferrier, records the encounter with a seasonal performer in Jean du Ferrier, "'Memoires [ecclésiastiques] de feu Mr [Jean] du Ferrier'" (n.d.), fols. 116r–118r, MS 1480, BSG; Étienne-Michel Faillon dates this incident to 1647. See *Vie de M. Olier, fondateur du séminaire de Saint-Sulpice*, 4th ed., vol. 2 (Paris: Poussielgue frères, 1873), 372–74.

38. F. Hillemacher and Revérend Du Mesnil, "L'Acte de renonciation de Brécourt," edited by Georges Monval, *Le Moliériste* 5, no. 57 (December 1883): 277–78; Jal, *Dictionnaire critique de biographie et d'histoire*, 279.

39. "Enterré sans Clergé, sans luminaire & sans aucune priere dans un endroit du Cimetiere de S. Sulpice, où l'on met les enfans morts sans Batême": Pierre Le Brun, *Discours sur la comedie: Ou traité historique et dogmatique des jeux de théatre et des autres divertissemens comiques soufferts ou condamnés depuis le premier siécle de l'Eglise jusqu'à présent. Avec un discours sur les pieces de théatre, tirées de l'Ecriture Sainte. Seconde edition, augmenté de plus de la moitié*, 2nd ed. (Paris: La Veuve Delaulne, 1731), 259. Note that Le Brun gives the wrong date for Rosimond's death, listing it as 1691.

40. François Parfaict and Claude Parfaict, *Histoire du théâtre françois, depuis son origine jusqu'à présent, avec la vie des plus célèbres poëtes dramatiques, un catalogue exact de leurs pièces, et des notes historiques et critiques*, vol. 13 (Paris: P. G. Le Mercier, 1748), 128–29; Jal, *Dictionnaire critique de biographie et d'histoire*, 723.

41. Jal, *Dictionnaire critique de biographie et d'histoire*, 1034.

42. Jal does not provide information about a renunciation but does record that the priests of Saint-Sulpice ensured that the godmother of Vondrebeck's third daughter was not a performer, which makes it likely that Vondrebeck, too, renounced the stage before his death when he wanted to receive the sacraments. A renunciation is even more likely given that, as I discuss later in the chapter, the priests of Saint-Sulpice had many encounters with Vondrebeck's troupe. See Jal, *Dictionnaire critique de biographie et d'histoire*, 164–65.

43. "Que Racine avait formée": Adolphe de Feuardent and P. de Feuardent, *Histoire d'Auteuil depuis son origine jusqu'à nos jours* (Paris-Auteil: Imprimeria des Apprentis Catholiques, 1877), 98; François Parfaict and Claude Parfaict, *Histoire du théâtre françois, depuis son origine jusqu'à présent, avec la vie des plus célèbres poëtes dramatiques, un catalogue exact de leurs pièces, et des notes historiques et critiques*, vol. 14 (Paris: P. G. Le Mercier, 1748), 520.

44. Monval, "Documents inédits sur les Champmeslé," 138–39. After Lecouvreur, sacramental refusals and reabsorptions in the parish of Saint-Sulpice include Catherine-Jeanne Dupré, known as Mademoiselle Dufresne, who in 1732 signed an act renouncing her profession but then regained her health and returned to the stage. See Maugras, *Les Comédiens hors la loi*, 203. Louis Paulin, who played both kings and peasants, renounced his profession, died, and was buried at Saint-Sulpice in 1770. See Pierre David Lemazurier, *Galerie historique des acteurs du théâtre français, depuis 1600 jusqu'à nos jours*, vol. 1 (Paris: Joseph Chaumerot, 1810), 437–41. Finally, in 1790 François Talma, who played leading tragic and comic roles, wanted to marry, but Saint-Sulpice's curate refused to publish the wedding banns. Talma took his case to a court and then to the National Assembly, to no avail. The following year he solved his problem by marrying at

the church of Notre-Dame de Lorette, where the vicar agreed to publish his banns. See Jal, *Dictionnaire critique de biographie et d'histoire*, 1171–72.

45. According to La Grange, the Orator of Molière's former troupe, the Comédie-Française had enough players to produce plays both in the city and at court simultaneously. See Mélèse, *Le Théâtre et le public à Paris sous Louis XIV*, 43–44.

46. For the most comprehensive history of France's seminaries, see Antoine Degert, *Histoire des séminaires français jusqu'à la Révolution*, 2 vols. (Paris: Gabriel Beauchesne, 1912).

47. On the key figures among the first three generations of Sulpicians, see Louis Bertrand, *Bibliothèque sulpicienne ou histoire littéraire de la Compagnie de Saint-Sulpice*, vol. 1 (Paris: Alphonse Picard et Fils, 1900), 51, 59–60, 124. For one example of the way the third generation formalized and enforced techniques developed under Olier, see Émile Goichot, *Les Examens particuliers de M. Tronson: Essai sur la formation du prêtre "classique,"* edited by René Heyer (Strasbourg: Presses Universitaires de Strasbourg, 2005).

48. Étendu expresses the Council of Trent's understanding of the church as a "totalizing force" that "could not envisage itself being excluded from any imaginable space and its aspiration could be nothing less than 'filling the space.'" See Phillips, *Church and Culture in Seventeenth-Century France*, 3, 5.

49. "Le Diacre donc qui chante l'Évangile pour le pr[ê]tre, le sousdiacre qui lit les propheties et les Ép[î]tres, les Acolythes qui portent les flambeaux devant l'Evangile . . . tout cela sont des Estendües du pr[ê]tre et co[mm]e la multiplication de sa seule personne. Par eux il est tout ensemble en divers endroits": "'Marques de vocation à l'estat ecclesiastique'" (n.d.), fols. 243–44, MS 163, SS. On the provenance of this manuscript and for a reproduction of the pages cited here, see Gilles Chaillot, Paul Cochois, and Irénée Noye, eds., *Traité des Saints Ordres (1676), compare aux écrits authentiques de Jean-Jacques Olier (†1657)* (Paris: Procure de la Compagnie de Saint-Sulpice, 1984), xiv–xv, 317–20.

50. "Les Prêtres sont les étendues de JÉSUS-CHRIST": Chaillot, Cochois, and Noye, *Traité des Saints Ordres*, 201.

51. "Et ainsy les Ap[ô]tres et les p[rê]tres sont les successeurs de son esprit pour honorer et glorifier D[ieu] à la place de tout le monde et pour cela la soutane est si ample representant la rondeur et l'estendüe de la terre": "'Marques de vocation à l'estat ecclesiastique,'" fol. 17. Chaillot, Cochois and Noye believe this manuscript summarizes Olier's texts and teachings; see *Traité des Saints Ordres*, xv, 76.

52. "Il [le curé] doit avoir un cœur de mere envers tous": *Les Principaux devoirs d'un bon curé* (Paris: Pierre Trichard, 1657), 12.

53. Jean Avila, *Discours aux prestres contenant une doctrine fort necessaire à tous ceux lesquels estans élevez à cette haute dignité desirent que Dieu leur soit propice au dernier jugement*, 3rd ed. (Paris: Pierre Trichard, 1658), 20.

54. "Il doit en temps & lieu visiter avec adresse chaque famille de sa Paroisse, & converser discrettement avec les particuliers, afin que connoissant plus certainement tout ce qui se passe, il puisse avec prudence & opportunement remedier aux maux, tant generaux que particuliers": *Les Principaux devoirs d'un bon curé*, 16–17.

55. *Les Principaux devoirs d'un bon curé*, 17.

56. "La joye des Mysteres," "les cloches servent de supplément au Prestre, pour exciter les peuples à leur devoir": Jean-Jacques Olier, *Explication des cérémonies de la grande messe de paroisse* (Paris: Jacques Langlois, 1656), 9–10.

57. "En fait rejaillir les operations [de l'Esprit de Notre Seigneur] par tout luy-mesme, usant des ceremonies": Olier, *Explication*, 8.

58. For a list of activities priests were supposed to avoid, see *Miroir des prestres et autres ecclesiastiques* (Paris: Pierre Trichard, 1659).

59. "Le Curé doit avoir un grand soin de la netteté & entretien de son Eglise, & pourvoir qu'elle soit bien close & fermée de tous costez": *Les Principaux devoirs d'un bon curé*, 17.

60. The altar space could be fruitfully analyzed as what Jonathan Z. Smith calls a "focusing lens" that clarified for priests what should and should not be important both inside the church and outside in parish spaces. See "The Bare Facts of Ritual," *History of Relgions* 20, nos. 12 (1980): 113. By including and excluding actors through liturgical ceremonies, parish clergymen positioned themselves as what Jenn Cianca calls "power brokers" in relation to the sacred space of the altar, while processions and the purity regulations they attempted to impose upon parishioners outside the architecturally bounded space of the church could be said to create what Cianca calls spaces of "graded sanctity." See *Sacred Ritual, Profane Space: The Roman House as Early Christian Meeting Place* (Montreal: McGill-Queen's University Press, 2018), 146–47.

61. "Que la porte en soit fermée à clef," "Qu'ils ne soient labourez ny ensemencez d'aucune chose," "Qu'on n'y fasse ny foires, ny marchez, ny danses, ny manufactures, ny Comedies, &c": Beuvelet, *Instruction sur le manuel* (1659), 2:123.

62. Francisci de Harlay, *Synodicon ecclesiae parisiensis* (Paris: Apud Franciscum Muguet Regis et illustrissimi Archiepiscopi Parisiensis Typographum, 1674), 408–9; *Du Respect deu aux eglises* (Paris: Pierre Trichard, n.d.), 13. This pamphlet was published during Pierre Trichard's activity as printer, sometime between 1634 and 1694.

63. Beuvelet, *Instruction sur le manuel* (1659), 2:209–16, 224–26. On burial inside the church, see Adrien Bourdoise, *L'Idée d'un bon ecclésiastique ou les sentences chrétiennes et cléricales de Messire Adrien Bourdoise, d'heureuse mémoire, prestre de la Communauté de Saint Nicolas du Chardonnet* (Paris: Jacques de Laize de Bresche, 1684), 78–79. On confession, see *Advis aux confesseurs, et demandes à faire aux pénitens* (Paris: Pierre Trichard, 1657). Alms were supposed to be received outside the church; see *Du Respect deu aux eglises*, 13.

64. Baudrand, "Mémoire sur la vie de M. Olier," 455n.

65. Doncourt, *Remarques historiques*, 1:10.

66. Doncourt, *Remarques historiques*, 1:10–11. See also Hamel, *Histoire de l'Église Saint-Sulpice*, 142–58.

67. Jal, *Dictionnaire critique de biographie et d'histoire*, 279; Hillemacher and Mesnil, "L'Acte de renonciation de Brécourt."

68. Doncourt, *Remarques historiques*, 1:14, 156.

69. Henri Malbois, "Histoire de l'Eglise Saint-Sulpice" (unpublished book manuscript, Paris, twentieth century), chap. 1, non-catalogued manuscript, SS.

70. See *Instruction familiere des processions de l'eglise* (Paris: Pierre Trichard, n.d.).

71. "Pourquoy dans la procession les fidelles vont-ils, & retournent-ils ensemble, & en la compagnie de leur pasteur? Pour nous apprendre qu'un chrestien doit vivre & mourir dans la foy & la communion de l'Eglise, & sous la conduite de son pasteur": Nicolas Pavillon, *Les Instructions du rituel du diocese d'Alet*, 4th ed. (Paris: Guillaume Desprez, 1678), 622.

72. "Quand vous rencontrez le S. Sacrement par les rües . . . vous vous mettrez à genous, & direz: 'Je vous adore, mon Seigneur Jesus-Christ'": *La Journée chrétienne* (Paris: Pierre Trichard, n.d.), 2.

73. "Le long du chemin, il prend garde de faire mettre à genoux ceux qui sont dans la rüe": Matthieu Beuvelet, *Instruction sur le manuel par forme de demandes et réponses familieres pour servir à ceux qui dans les séminaires se préparent à l'administration des Sacremens, où se voyent*

*recüeillies les choses les plus remarquables qui se trouvent dans la pluspart des Manuels quis sont en usage dans l'Eglise, et la resolution de plusieurs difficultez de pratique*, 4th ed., vol. 1 (Paris: Georges Josse, 1659), 230.

74. Doncourt, *Remarques historiques*, 1:145; For more on Doncourt, see Bertrand, *Bibliothèque sulpicienne*, 1:8n.

75. "Joueurs de Marionnettes, danseurs de corde & autres baladins": Doncourt, *Remarques historiques*, 1:145.

76. "[Ils] s'étaient fait admirer d'abord par leurs danses et leurs sauts, leurs postures à l'italienne, leurs tours, leurs voltiges et leurs équilibres périlleux": Albert, *Les Théâtres de la Foire (1660–1789)*, 5–7. Allard and Vonderbeck's troupe does not seem to have had marionette players, although a marionette player named Alexandre Bertrand erected a theater in the rue des Quatre-Vents in 1689. Doncourt might have confused two troupes, and he quite possibly blurred together several distinct incidents. The birth and death dates for Charles Allard are unknown.

77. "Depuis quelques temps . . . ils avaient eu l'ingénieuse idée d'encadrer leurs exercices dans de petites scènes dialoguées, qui servaient aux sauts et aux danses d'introduction et de commentaires": Albert, *Les Théâtres de la Foire (1660–1789)*, 6.

78. Jal, *Dictionnaire critique de biographie et d'histoire*, 164.

79. "Cette rue étoit celle de tout le fauxbourg où passoit le plus souvent le très-auguste S. Sacrement pour le porter aux malades": Doncourt, *Remarques historiques*, 1:145.

80. "Il [Olier] se mit à catéchiser de l'autre côté de la rue et eut bientôt plus d'auditeurs que le bouffon qui, à la fin, se voyant avandonné, vint l'écouter comme les autres et se convertit": Joseph Grandet, *Les Saints prêtres français du XVIIe siècle, ouvrage publié pour la première fois, d'après le manuscrit original*, edited by G. Letourneau, vol. 2 (Angers: Germain et G. Grassin; A. Roger et F. Chernoviz, 1897), 287.

81. Doncourt, *Remarques historiques*, 1:145–46. On La Reynie, see Holly Tucker, *City of Light, City of Poison: Murder, Magic, and the First Police Chief of Paris* (New York: W. W. Norton, 2017), 18–25.

82. Doncourt, *Remarques historiques,* 1:146.

83. "Comment peut-il y avoir des spectateurs dans un lieu qui n'est séparé du cimetiere que par une légere cloison?": Doncourt, *Remarques historiques,*1:146.

84. Doncourt, *Remarques historiques,*1:149.

85. Doncourt, *Remarques historiques,*1:149–50; See also Mélèse, *Le Théâtre et le public à Paris sous Louis XIV*, 50.

86. "N'est-il pas scandaleux qu'on ne puisse qu'avec la plus grande peine porter le S. Viatique aux malades, par la multitude des voitures qui entourent l'Eglise & occupent les rues où il faut nécessairement passer?": Doncourt, *Remarques historiques*, 1:147.

87. "Des amas de gens sans aveu, Filoux & autres canaille, qui s'y attroupoient & y causoient avec eux [les baladins] de très-grands désordres": Doncourt, *Remarques historiques,*1:145.

88. Maugras, *Les Comédiens hors la loi*, 165.

89. "& depuis ce tems, on ne fait plus le Reposoir, & ni la procession de la Fête-Dieu, ni aucune autre ne passe plus dans cette rue": Doncourt, *Remarques historiques*, 1:150.

90. "On fait aussi en sorte de ne jamais y [la Comédie-Française] passer lorsqu'on porte le St. Sacrement ou l'Extrême-Onction aux malades & lorsqu'on fait les convois & sépultures, à moins que les malades ou les morts ne soient de cette rue, & pour lors on vient à la maison du malade ou du défunt, par le chemin le plus court, & on ne traverse point la rue, mais on s'en retourne sur ses pas": Doncourt, *Remarques historiques,*1:150.

91. Beuvelet, *Instruction sur le manuel* (1659), 1:227–28.

92. See, for example, the many actors and musicians who participated in the various sacraments received by the actor Pierre Le Messier, stage name Bellerose, in the parish of Saint-Sauveur between 1630 and 1640 in Jal, *Dictionnaire critique de biographie et d'histoire*, 190.

93. Beuvelet, *Instruction sur le manuel* (1659), 1:159–60, 231.

94. "Toute autre peinture des-honneste": Beuvelet, *Instruction sur le manuel* (1659), 1:226–27.

95. "Que le lit du malade soit tout couvert de linge blanc, en sorte que rien de sale ne paroisse, qu'il y ait une serviette blanche devant luy, & une autre autour du col, qui le couvre entierement pardevant": Beuvelet, *Instruction sur le manuel* (1659), 1:227.

96. "Qu'il y ait une table, s'il se peut, en veuë du malade; couverte d'une belle nappe blanche seulement, un Crucifix au milieu, deux chandeliers aux deux costez, avec deux cierges blancs, un benistier, avec un aspersoir à droite, derrier la Croix un tableau, ou du ligne blanc, où on peut attacher des bouquets": Beuvelet, *Instruction sur le manuel* (1659), 1:227.

97. This is especially true after the 1630s and 1640s. See Sabine Chaouche, *L'Art du comédien: Déclamation et jeu scénique en France à L'âge classique (1629–1680)* (Paris: Honoré Champion, 2001), 9–25. See also Georges Forestier, *Introduction à l'analyse des textes classiques: Éléments de rhétorique et de poétique du XVIIe siècle*, 4th ed., Kindle book (Paris: Armand Colin, 2012), 18–44.

98. Chaouche, *L'Art du comédien*, 17–20.

99. Eugène Green, *La parole baroque*, Texte et voix (Paris: Desclée de Brouwer, 2001), 135–63.

100. Chaouche, *L'Art du comédien*, 28–80.

101. "Estant prest de recevoir la sainte Hostie, il faut tenir le corps droit & arresté, sans pancher la teste, ny devant ny apres la reception de la sainte Hostie": Beuvelet, *Instruction sur le manuel* (1659), 1:205.

102. "Couchées en croix l'une sur l'autre": Beuvelet, *Instruction sur le manuel* (1659), 1:206.

103. Beuvelet, *Instruction sur le manuel* (1659), 1:206.

104. Beuvelet, *Instruction sur le manuel* (1659), 1:206.

105. Beuvelet, *Instruction sur le manuel* (1659), 1:267.

106. Beuvelet, *Instruction sur le manuel* (1659), 1:267–68.

107. "En ce Sacrement de l'Extreme-Onction, on y reçoit la grace à proportion des prieres qu'on y fait": Beuvelet, *Instruction sur le manuel* (1659), 1:276.

108. For the classic essay on performance's disappearance, see Peggy Phelan, "The Ontology of Performance: Representation Without Reproduction," in *Unmarked: The Politics of Performance* (London: Routledge, 1993), 146–66.

109. On the notion of repertoire in performance studies, see Diana Taylor, *The Archive and the Repertoire: Performing Cultural Memory in the Americas* (Durham, NC: Duke University Press, 2003), esp. 1627. For a sociological discussion, see Ann Swidler, "Culture in Action: Symbols and Strategies," *American Sociological Review* 51, no. 2 (1986): 273–86.

110. Ngũgĩ wa Thiong'o proposes a similar idea in "Enactments of Power: The Politics of Performance Space," *TDR: The Drama Review* 41, no. 3 (1997): 11–30. See also Jon McKenzie's definition of performance as a "formation of knowledge and power" in *Perform or Else: From Discipline to Performance* (London: Routledge, 2001), 18.

111. Paul Friedland, *Political Actors: Representative Bodies and Theatricality in the Age of the French Revolution* (Ithaca, NY: Cornell University Press, 2002), 6.

112. Friedland argues that theatrical representation in the seventeenth century belonged to the same incarnational paradigm as the Eucharist and that actors re-presented real passions for otherwise invisible characters much the way the Eucharist re-presented Christ's invisible body. At the level of spatial practices, however, playgoing behavior interrupted the ceremonial foundations

of the church's corpus mysticum much earlier than the 1750 turning point identified by Friedland, when acting theory shifts from what he calls re-presentation as transubstantiation to representation as imitation. See Friedland, *Political Actors: Representative Bodies and Theatricality in the Age of the French Revolution*, 17–21.

113. Bertrand, *Bibliothèque sulpicienne*, 1:293.

114. Doncourt, *Remarques historiques*, 1:12; Henri François Simon de Doncourt, *Remarques historiques sur l'église et la paroisse de Saint Sulpice: Pièces justificatives*, vol. 2 (Paris: Chez Nicolas Crapart, rue de Vaugirard, près de la place S. Michel, 1773), 356.

115. Doncourt, *Remarques historiques*, 1:14.

116. Doncourt, *Remarques historiques*, 1:15: "suffisamment close."

117. Gaston Lemesle, *L'Eglise Saint-Sulpice* (Paris: Librairie Bloud et Gay, 1931), 26–46.

118. "Véritables lieux d'enseignement de la philosophie et de la théologie": Dominique Julia, "L'Éducation des ecclésiastiques en France aux XVIIe et XVIIIe siècles," in *Problèmes d'histoire de l'éducation: Actes des séminaires organisés par l'École française de Rome et l'Università di Roma—La Sapienza (janvier–mai 1985)*, Collection de l'École française de Rome 104 (Rome: École française de Rome, 1988), 147–49. Seminaries created the first chairs in philosophy in 1720 and began to try, unsuccessfully, in the 1740s to secure academic recognition from universities for courses taught at seminaries.

119. This shift away from ceremonial distinction toward abstract forms of legitimization reflects the broad transformation Friedland traces in the eighteenth century away from modes of representation modeled on the incarnation and toward abstract modes, such as the political representative. See Friedland, *Political Actors: Representative Bodies and Theatricality in the Age of the French Revolution*, 21–28, 52–80.

120. [Charles-Louis de Lantages], *Instruction ecclesiastiques, où l'on tache de faire connoître l'essence, la dignité et la sainteté du clergé* (Puy: Les Veuves Delagarde, 1692), 1. On the attribution of this text to Lantages, see Bertrand, *Bibliothèque sulpicienne*, 1:99–100.

121. "Reçoivent d'eux [les Evêques] leur députation," "pour aider les Evêques à instruire, gouverner & sanctifier le Peuple Chretien": Lantages], *Instruction ecclesiastiques*, 9.

122. [Lantages], *Instruction ecclesiastiques*, 7: "Ministres inferieurs", "par la Subordination qu'on voit des inferieurs aux Superieurs dans l'état Ecclesiastique."

## CONCLUSION

1. "Un petit couloir ayant son ouverture dans une rue voisine et correspondant aux baignoires": François-Joseph Talma, *Mémoires de J.-F. Talma (1849), écrits par lui-même et recueillis et mis en ordre sur les papiers de sa famille par Alexandre Dumas*, edited by Alexandre Dumas (Montreal: Éditions Le Joyeux Roger, 2006), 109, https://numerique.banq.qc.ca/patrimoine/details/52327/1564089?docpos=109.

2. "C'est par ce couloir, que les prêtres de Saint-Sulpice, qui voulaient, sans être vus, voir *Tartuffe* et *Mahomet*, faisaient leur entrée et leur sortie": Talma, *Mémoires*, 109.

3. "Déguisé le personnage sous l'ajustement d'un homme du monde; j'ai eu beau lui doner un petit chapeau, de grands cheveux, un grand collet, une épée, et des dentelles sur tout l'habit": Molière, "Second placet présenté au roi dans son camp devant la ville de Lille en Flandre," in *Oeuvres complètes*, edited by Georges Couton, vol. 1 (Paris: Éditions Gallimard, 1971), 891.

4. "Les Ecclesiastiques qui contre l'ordre de l'Eglise & l'authorité des sacrez Canons, nourissent leurs Chevalures, qui paroissent ordinairement sans Tonsure . . . & ceux qui se mettent

presque tousjours en Habit court, meriteroient avec justice le honteux surnom de Dégradez": *Des Clercs desguisez, ou de l'habit clerical, selon les saints canons* (Paris: Pierre Trichard, n.d.), 1.

5. "Ces Messieurs disent par tout qu'ils peuvent se coëffer & s'habiller selon la bienseances du Siecle, & qu'estans engagez à hanter le beau monde & à y voir les precieuses compagnies, ils y seroient incommodes d'y paroistre en bons Ecclesiastiques, & qu'aussi-tost on les prendroit pour des devots & des reformateurs": *Des Clercs desguisez*, 2.

6. See, for example, statements made about actors in a sermon against plays given during Carnival in the parish of Saint-Sulpice during the second half of the seventeenth century in "Du Carnaval, contre les desbauches qui s'y passent" (n.d.), fols. 38–41, MS 317, SS. The folios are not numbered, so I have counted each recto and verso separately from the first page of the first sermon. See also the reasons given by Jean du Ferrier, a priest in the parish of Saint-Sulpice during the 1640s, for refusing to administer the viaticum to an actor in his "'Memoires [ecclésiastiques] de feu Mr [Jean] du Ferrier'" (n.d.), fols. 116r–117v, MS 1480, BSG. On the continuity of antitheatrical arguments during the early modern period, see Moses Barras, *The Stage Controversy in France from Corneille to Rousseau* (New York: Institute of French Studies, 1933), 14–38.

7. M. du Ferrier, cited above, was under this impression and gave the aforementioned councils as evidence. In fact, an actor's legal and ecclesiastical status depended on how local authorities interpreted common law, Roman jurisprudence, and diocesan rituals. See Jean Dubu, *Les Églises chrétiennes et le théâtre (1550–1850)* (Grenoble: Presses Universitaires de Grenoble, 1997), 71–94. For a nuanced discussion of the relationship between excommunication and infamy, see Déborah Blocker, *Instituter un "art": Politiques du théâtre dans la France du premier XVIIe siècle* (Paris: Honoré Champion, 2009), 291–99.

8. See, for example, Jacques Benigne Bossuet, "Maximes et réflexions sur la comédie," in *L'Eglise et le théâtre: Maximes et réflexions sur la comédie précédés d'une introduction historique et accompagnées de documents contemporains et de notes critiques*, edited by Charles Urbain and Eugene Levesque (Paris: Bernard Grasset, 1930), 169–276. See also Pierre Nicole, *Traité de la comédie, et autres pièces d'un procès du théâtre*, edited by Laurent Thirouin (Paris: Honoré Champion, 1998); For an analysis of moralist concerns about love on stage, see Henry Phillips, *The Theatre and Its Critics in Seventeenth-Century France* (Oxford: Oxford University Press, 1980), 87–112.

9. "Empoissonneur publics qui font couler leur venin par les yeux et par les oreilles": "Du Carnaval," fol. 41. For another example of the poison metaphor, see Jean Racine, "Lettre à l'auteur des Hérésies imaginaires et des deux Visionnaires (1666)," in *Traité de la comédie, et autre pièces d'un procès du théâtre*, edited by Laurent Thirouin (Paris: Honoré Champion, 1998), 225–32.

10. For a list of works on French antitheatrical sentiment, see note 15 of the Introduction.

11. "Ce que nous connaissons ce ne sont que des épisodes (condamnations de comédiens, interruptions de comédies, démolitions de théâtres, interdictions aux femmes de jouer, etc.), des anecdotes . . . qui ne parviennent pas à former un tout cohérent": Ferdinando Taviani, *La fascinazione del teatro: La commedia dell'arte e la società barocca* (Rome: Bulzoni, 1969), xlii–xliii; quoted in Sylviane Léoni, *Le Poison et le remède: Théâtre, morale et rhétorique en France et en Italie, 1694–1758* (Oxford: Voltaire Foundation, 1998), 43.

12. For a list of scholarship on early modern French ceremonial, see Chapter 4, note 13.

13. John Bossy, "The Mass as a Social Institution 1200–1700," *Past and Present*, no. 100 (1983): 29–61.

14. Ségolène de Dainville-Barbiche, "Le Clergé paroissial de Paris à la fin de l'ancien régime (1789–1791)," *Bibliothèque de l'École des chartes* 147 (1989): 542; Joseph Bergin, *Church, Society and Religious Change in France, 1580–1730* (New Haven: Yale University Press, 2009), 215–16.

15. For a brief discussion of this annual guide, see Philippe Martin, *Le Théâtre divin: Une histoire de la messe, XVIe–XXe siècle* (Paris: CNRS Éditions, 2010), 178–79. For a list of the years for which the Almanac is known to have been published, see the notice provided by the Bibliothèque nationale de France: https://catalogue.bnf.fr/ark:/12148/cb32690181n.

16. Martial du Mans, *Almanac spirituel de l'an de grace 1667. Pour la ville, faux-bourgs et és environs de Paris. Où sont marquées les festes, confrairies, indulgences pleniere, predications, assemblées, et conferences de pieté, qu'il y aura chaque jour de cette année dans les eglises, metropolitaine et collegiales, dans les paroisses et monasteres de Paris. A l'usage des personnes devotes. Reveu et corrigé par le P. Martial du Mans religieux penitent.* (Paris: Georges Josse, 1667), 3.

17. "En la pluspart des paroisses," "en plusieurs paroisses & monasteres": Martial du Mans, *Almanac spirituel de l'an grace 1667*, 3–6.

18. Pierre Mélèse, *Le Théâtre et le public à Paris sous Louis XIV, 1659–1715* (Paris: Librairie Droz, 1934), 34.

19. W. L. Wiley, *The Early Public Theatre in France* (Cambridge, MA: Harvard University Press, 1960), 224–25.

20. Mélèse, *Le Théâtre et le public à Paris sous Louis XIV*, 70.

21. Wiley, *The Early Public Theatre in France*, 225; Mélèse, *Le Théâtre et le public à Paris sous Louis XIV*, 60.

22. Mélèse, *Le Théâtre et le public à Paris sous Louis XIV*, 60.

23. Mélèse, *Le Théâtre et le public à Paris sous Louis XIV*, 60.

24. See, for example, Martial du Mans, *Almanac spirituel de l'an de grace 1667*, 20–23.

25. "Du Carnaval." On the pagination of this manuscript, see note 6. The title given to the manuscript in the register for the Archives des prêtres de la Compagnie de Saint-Sulpice in Paris is actually the title of the first sermon in the volume. All the sermons concern entertainments characteristic of the Foire Saint-Germain, the seasonal fair located across the street from the Church of Saint-Sulpice. The title page bears the following note indicating that the manuscript had originally belonged to Louis Tronson: "Ex libris biblio Lauret, ex dono L. Tronson." It seems that Tronson gave the manuscript to a person by the name of Lauret. According to Joseph Grandet, Tronson gathered a large collection of comparable texts during his lifetime, donating them to the library of Saint-Sulpice; see *Les Saints prêtres français du XVIIe siècle, ouvrage publié pour la première fois, d'après le manuscrit original*, edited by G. Letourneau, vol. 2 (Angers: Germain et G. Grassin; A. Roger et F. Chernoviz, 1897), 325. The identity of "Lauret" remains uncertain. Louis Bertrand does not mention any Sulpicians by this name in his *Bibliothèque sulpicienne ou histoire littéraire de la Compagnie de Saint-Sulpice*, 3 vols. (Paris: Alphonse Picard et Fils, 1900);. One hypothesis is that "Lauret" was l'abbé de Laurent, a priest in the diocese of Viviers who collaborated with a Sulpician and well-known preacher of polemical sermons named Jean-Pierre de Couderc during a mission against the Huguenots in Vivarais. Tronson sent eight Sulpician priests from Paris to join Couderc after the revocation of the Edict of Nantes in 1685. L'abbé de Laurent preached alongside these Sulpician priests in April of that year. See Étienne-Michel Faillon, *Vie de M. Olier, fondateur du séminaire de Saint-Sulpice*, 4th ed., vol. 2 (Paris: Poussielgue frères, 1873), 418–19. See also the article on Couderc in Louis Bertrand, *Bibliothèque sulpicienne ou histoire littéraire de la Compagnie de Saint-Sulpice*, vol. 2 (Paris: Alphonse Picard et Fils, 1900), 83–87.

26. "Du Carnaval," fols. 33–55. The other sermons in the manuscript are entitled "Des Danseurs de corde" (fols. 56–63), "Contre le bal, danses, etc." (fols. 65–90), "Contre les danses aux chansons" (fols. 91–109), and "Des jeux ou divertissemens permis ou deffendus" (fols. 110–131).

27. "Vous avez fait donc un jeu et un passetemps de ce qui fut autrefois un acte d'Idolatrie, et apres avoir renoncé aux Idoles, vous faites encore reserve de ce culte extravagant et libertin": "Du

Carnaval," fols. 40–43. The sermons in the manuscript do not name the preacher(s) who delivered them; however, the preacher of "Contre les marionnettes" indicates that he had been away from the parish for many years and has recently returned "in this time of fairs and of Carnaval." He states, "I don't know how things are now, if there are still some of these charlatans in some corner of your suburb, but I remember that it was a pity a few years ago to see how a certain troupe of acrobats were popular less for their Diogenes than for a number of fools who entertain the populace with God knows what, and if the impudence of the words and the depravity of the postures and movements and the dirtiness of the plots of which they composed their farces were not the best part of the entertainment, after these [entertainers] others could succeed them, if others haven't already, who can cause as much disorder as the first." ("en ce temps cy de foire et de Carnaval," "Je ne scay pas comme vont maintenant les choses; s'il y a encore de ces charlatans a quelque coing de v[ôt]re faubourg, mais je me souviens que c'estoit une pitie il y a quelques années de veoir comme une Certaine troupe de basteleurs estoient suivis moins pour leurs Diogenes que pour un nombre de fols, qui divertissent la populace, Et D[ieu] scait de quoy, et si l'Impudence des paroles, et la dissolution des postures et des mouvements et la saleté des Intrigues dont ils Composent leurs farces, ne composent pas la meilleure partié du divertissement, a ceux cy en peuvent succeder d'autres, si d'autres ne les ont pas desja suivis, qui peuvent causer autant de desordres que les 1ers").

28. "Le faste du siècle de Louis XIV s'appuie lui-même sur l'art de la mise en scène, et le 'Roi-Soleil' est le premier de tous les acteurs, le plus fréquemment en representation": Mélèse, *Le Théâtre et le public à Paris sous Louis XIV*, 1.

29. Jean-Marie Apostolidès, *Le Prince sacrifié: Théâtre et politique au temps de Louis XIV* (Paris: Les Éditions de Minuit, 1985).

30. "Théâtre permanent": Frédérique Leferme-Falguières, *Les Courtisans: Une Société de spectacle sous l'ancien régime* (Paris: Presses Universitaires de France, 2007), 224; "théâtre" qui "se déplace avec [le Roi]": Ralph E. Giesey, *Cérémonial et puissance souveraine: France, XVe–XVIIe siècles* (Paris: Armand Colin, 1987), 69.

31. Martin, *Le Théâtre divin*. Martin discusses the Mass's royal and political functions only in passing.

32. For a discussion of the way the theater metaphor mediates our understanding of medieval religious ceremonies, see Donnalee Dox, "Ceremonial Embodiment: The Problem of 'Liturgical Drama,'" *Ecumenica: Journal of Theatre and Performance* 3, no. 2 (2010): 31–41.

33. "Spectacle politique," "chaque geste et chaque détail de la décoration devaient être visible et compris": Lucien Bély, *La Société des princes, XVIe–XVIIIe siècle* (Paris: Librairie Arthème Fayard, 1999), 134.

34. "Les grands seigneurs et les grandes dames avaient besoin d'une armée de domestiques": Norbert Elias, *La Société de Cour* (Paris: Flammarion, 1969), 22, 66; I preferred the French translation. See also Norbert Elias, *The Court Society*, translated by Edmund Jephcott (New York: Pantheon Books, 1983), 45, 80.

35. "Introduire la distance nécessaire avec les courtisans": Leferme-Falguières, *Les Courtisans*, 227.

36. "Séparaient ... les members de la société les uns des autres": Elias, *La Société de Cour*, 108. Indeed, Elias jumps directly from his discussion of proximity and distance to parallels between courtly life and classical French theater; See also Elias, *The Court Society*, 111–12.

37. For a description of the early modern French theater in these terms, see Apostolidès, *Le Prince sacrifié*, 37–38.

38. Barbara G. Mittman, *Spectators on the Paris Stage in the Seventeenth and Eighteenth Centuries* (Ann Arbor: UMI Research Press, 1984); Jeffrey S. Ravel, *The Contested Parterre: Public Theater and French Political Culture, 1680–1791* (Ithaca, NY: Cornell University Press, 1999).

39. Richard Schechner, *Performance Studies: An Introduction* (London: Routledge, 2002), 22.

40. Richard Schechner, *Between Theater and Anthropology* (Philadelphia: University of Pennsylvania Press, 1985), 35.

41. "Ainsi, tout le dessein d'un poète, toute la fin de son travail, c'est qu'on soit, comme son héros, épris des belles personnes, qu'on les serve comme des divinités; en un mot, qu'on leur sacrifie tout": Bossuet, "Maximes et réflexions sur la comédie," 177.

42. Nicholas Paige, "Proto-Aesthetics and the Theatrical Image," *Papers on French Seventeenth-Century Literature* 35, no. 69 (2008): 521.

43. "Se faisait lire par sa brièveté": Bossuet, "Maximes et réflexions sur la comédie," 170.

44. "Des réflexions courtes, mais pleines des grandes principes de la religion": Bossuet, "Maximes et réflexions sur la comédie," 170.

45. "Dieu veut estre servy et honnoré": Jean-Jacques Olier, *Explication des cérémonies de la grande messe de paroisse* (Paris: Jacques Langlois, 1656), 12.

46. "L'admiration qu'il a pour ces Mysters, & le profond estonnement qui l'oblige à s'abîmer & à s'aneantir devant la Majesté Divine": Olier, *Explication*, 2.

47. "Pour le connoistre, l'aimer, le servir;" "sert à la Messe:" Jacques Benigne Bossuet, *Catéchisme du diocèse de Meaux* (Paris: Sebastien Mabre-Cramoisy, 1687), 10, 34, 166; italics mine.

48. Bossuet, *Catéchisme du diocèse de Meaux,* 1–2, 35.

49. "Parmi ces commotions où consiste tout le plaisir de la comédie, qui peut élever son cœur à Dieu? . . . qui ne craint pas, dans ces folles joies et dans ces folles douleurs, d'étouffer en soi l'esprit de prière, et d'interrompre cet exercice, qui, selon la parole de Jésus-Christ, doit être perpétuel dans un chrétien . . . ?": Bossuet, "Maximes et réflexions sur la comédie," 206.

50. Diana Taylor, *The Archive and the Repertoire: Performing Cultural Memory in the Americas* (Durham, NC: Duke University Press, 2003), 6.

51. J. L. Austin, *How to Do Things with Words*, edited by J. O. Urmson and Marina Sbisà, 2nd ed. (Cambridge, MA: Harvard University Press, 1975), 6.

52. Austin, *How to Do Things with Words,* 5.

53. On what I am calling the performatic function of such gestures, see also Eve Sweetser, "Blended Spaces and Performativity," *Cognitive Linguistics* 11, nos. 3–4 (2000): 315, https://doi.org/10.1515/cogl.2001.018.

54. Michel Foucault, *The Archaeology of Knowledge and The Discourse on Language*, translated by A. M. Sheridan Smith (New York: Pantheon Books, 1972), 38.

55. Foucault, *The Archaeology of Knowledge and The Discourse on Language*, 38.

56. Foucault, *The Archaeology of Knowledge and The Discourse on Language*, 37–38.

57. Sociologists have been using the notion of repertoire in this way since the 1960s. See Ann Swidler, "Culture in Action: Symbols and Strategies," *American Sociological Review* 51, no. 2 (1986): 273–86. Swidler writes, "A culture is not a unified system that pushes action in a consistent direction. Rather, it is more like a 'tool kit' or repertoire (Hannerz, 1969: 186–188) from which actors select differing pieces for constructing lines of action" (277).

58. "Le prêtre ne sert que pour supplément à l'hostie qui ne se peut offrir elle-même sensiblement": Gilles Chaillot, Paul Cochois, and Irénée Noye, eds., *Traité des Saints Ordres (1676),*

*compare aux écrits authentiques de Jean-Jacques Olier (†1657)* (Paris: Procure de la Compagnie de Saint-Sulpice, 1984), 213. Emphasis mine.

59. "Le prêtre est pour suppléer à la religion et au respect de tout le peuple, meut aux louanges de DIEU et insensible à son devoir. Et pour cela il faut que le prêtre ou le <pasteur> se regarde contenent en lui tout seul toute la religion de son Peuple": Olier, "Mémoires IV, " 85–89, published as an appendix in Chaillot, Cochois, and Noye, *Traité des Saints Ordres,* 285.

60. "Les cloches sont les supplements de la parole et de la voix": Chaillot, Cochois, and Noye, *Traité des Saints Ordres,* 121. Adrien Bourdoise also considered priests and bells mutually supplementary. In a manuscript from the late seventeenth century that compiles his sayings, one finds the following maxim: "All the actions of a Parish Priest are so many ringings of the Bell that call all their parishioners to their duty" ("Toutes les actions d'un Curé sont autant de coups de Cloche qui appellent tous ses paroissiens à leur devoir"). See Adrien Bourdoise, "Les Sentences ou maximes chrestiennes et ecclesiastiques de Messire Adrien Bourdoise, premier prestre de la Communauté et Seminaire de Saint Nicolas du Chardonnet à Paris" (late seventeenth century), fol. 101, MS 460, SS.

61. Jean-Jacques Olier, "Autographes de M. Olier, fondateur du Séminaire de St. Sulpice: Divers écrits, tome I" (n.d.), fols. 113–14, Ms. 14, SS.

62. "Fonctions principales sont de louer [Dieu] assidûment par un office magnifique ... avec de grandes cérémonies": Olier, "Autographes de M. Olier, fondateur du Séminaire de St. Sulpice," fols. 114–117.

63. *The Jesuit Relations and Allied Documents: Travels and Explorations of the Jesuit Missionaries in New France, 1610–1791,* edited and translated by Reuben Gold Thwaites, vol. 64 (Cleveland, OH: Burrow Brothers, 1900), 237.

64. "Le canal par lequel découlent les Graces divines és Fideles": Nicolas Janvier, *Des Prestres et curez: De leur institution, puissance, droicts et devoirs en l'Eglise* (Paris: Pierre Trichard, n.d.), 4.

65. "Considerez les rapports qu'il y a entre les fonctions du Prestre, & l'office de Mere de Dieu: Si elle a conceu le Verbe incarné dans ses chastes entrailles, c'est ce mesme Verbe que produisent les Prestres à l'autel par les paroles de la consecration. ... Mais remarquez principalement le rapport de ces deux excellentes dignitez en cecy ... que comme pour produire & former le Corps du Fils de Dieu dans le ventre de la sacrée Vierge, le S. Esprit luy a esté donné, le mesme S. Esprit est donné au Prestre en l'ordination": Matthieu Beuvelet, *Meditations sur les principales veritez chrétiennes, et ecclesiastiques, prises dans leurs propres principes, c'est à dire, dans les obligations contractées par les clercs en la reception de chaque ordre en particulier, et sur le modele du souverain prêtre nôtre Seigneur Jesus-Christ,* vol. 2 (Lyon: Daniel Gayet, 1674), 254.

66. "Et en même temps il a plu à la bonté de DIEU de me dire: Je veux que tu tiennes la place du saint Esprit sur ces enfants; et en même temps me sentant remplir du saint Esprit depuis les pieds jusques à la tête, je ressentais qu'en me tournant vers eux pour dire 'Dominus vobiscum,' j'avais une certaine substance en moi capable de les nourrir, comme si de moi elle fût sortie sur eux": reproduced as Appendix R in Chaillot, Cochois, and Noye, *Traité des Saints Ordres,* 301. Emphasis mine.

67. See *Manuel des cérémonies romaines, tiré des livres romains les plus authentiques, et des ecrivains les plus intelligens en cette matiere, par quelques-uns des prêtres de la Congrégation de L.M.* (Lyon: Benoist Bailly, 1679), 24, 42, 46, 74, 92.

68. "Le prêtre ouvre les mains, lorsqu'il dit: Dominus vobiscum, parce qu'il désire que le Saint-Esprit ... soit dilaté et répandu sur tous en plénitude": Jean-Jacques Olier, *L'Esprit des cérémonies de la messe: Explication des cérémonies de la grand'messe de paroisse selon l'usage romain,* edited by Claude Barthe and Michèle Debaecker ([Perpignan:] Tempora, 2009), 180.

69. "Le Prêtre est un prodige de grâce, et si le mot de monstre se pouvait prendre en un bon sens, on pourrait dire que c'est un monstre de sainteté. Car dans la nature on appelle un monstre celui qui a cent têtes, cent pieds, ou cent yeux: Et le Prêtre en la grâce est celui qui a cent cœurs; et même il en doit avoir bien davantage: car il faut qu'il en ait des millions, et qu'il en ait tout autant qu'il y a de créatures raisonnables qui vivent sur la terre": Chaillot, Cochois, and Noye, *Traité des Saints Ordres*, 222.

70. "C'est une chose Magnifique qu'un p[êt]re; et l'estenduë de son esprit n'a point de bornes, il comprent en tous ces ordres inferieurs qui representent en partie quelque chose de ce qu'il est et de ce qu'il doit estre dans l'Eglise": "'Marques de vocation à l'estat ecclesiastique'" (n.d.), fols. 156–57, MS 163, SS. For information about this manuscript, see Chaillot, Cochois, and Noye, *Traité des Saints Ordres*, xiv–xv.

71. "Ce debordement des passions," "de mesme dans les Poëmes dramatiques, les passions bien representées, ayant premièrement atteint le Poëtte, passent de luy à l'Acteur qui recite, & de l'acteur au peuple qui l'escoute": Georges de Scudéry, *L'apologie du théâtre par M. de Scudery* (Paris: Augustin Courbé, 1639), 6–7. Later in the seventeenth-century, theater apologists did not share Scudéry's view that passion seized the writer, instead maintaining that the author was guided by reason. See John D. Lyons, *Kingdom of Disorder: The Theory of Tragedy in Classical France* (West Lafayette, IN: Purdue University Press, 1999), 44–48.

72. "Tristesse majestueuse": Jean Racine, *Bérénice*, edited by Marie-Henriette Bru, Bibliolycée (Paris: Hachette, 2003).

73. Nicholas Paige, "Racine, *Phèdre*, and the French Classical Stage," in *A History of Modern French Literature: From the Sixteenth to the Twentieth Century*, edited by Christopher Prendergast (Princeton: Princeton University Press, 2017), 207, https://doi-org.ezproxy.lib.ucalgary.ca /10.1515/9781400885046.

74. "Action mystérieuse": Jacques Scherer, *Racine et/ou la cérémonie* (Paris: Presses Universitaires de France, 1982), 12–17.

75. Paul Friedland, *Political Actors: Representative Bodies and Theatricality in the Age of the French Revolution* (Ithaca, NY: Cornell University Press, 2002), 19.

76. "La loi de la concentration": René Bray, *La Formation de la doctrine classique en France* (Paris: Libraire Nizet, 1957), 288.

77. "Une poche 'théâtrale'": Sabine Chaouche, "Les Spectateurs dans la lorgnette des anecdotiers: fait divers ou fait théâtral?" *Journal for Eighteenth-Century Studies* 32, no. 4 (2009): 517, https://doi.org/10.1111/j.1754-0208.2009.00224.x.

78. Virginia Scott, *Women on the Stage in Early Modern France: 1540–1750* (Cambridge: Cambridge University Press, 2010), 207.

79. "Vera e naturale": Elena Virginia Balletti Riccoboni, "Lettera della signora Elena Riccoboni al signor abate Antonio Conti gentiluomo viniziano, sopra la maniera di Monsieur Baron nel rappresentare le tragedie franzesi" (c. 1720), http://www.irpmf.cnrs.fr/IMG/pdf/Elenia _virginia_riccoboni.pdf. This letter was transcribed and translated into French by Valentina Gallo and posted online as part of "Les Savoirs des acteurs italiens," a digital collection edited by Andrea Fabiano as part of the interdisciplinary program "Histoire de Savoirs." I was not able to find the French translation. According to Gallo, the letter was first published as Elena Virginia Balletti Riccoboni, "Lettera della signora Elena Riccoboni al signor abate Antonio Conti gentiluomo viniziano, sopra la maniera di Monsieur Baron nel rappresentare le tragedie franzesi," in *Raccolta d'opuscoli scientifici e filologici*, edited by Angelo Colagerà, vol. 13 (Venice: Christoforo Zane, 1736), 495–501. Baron's acting style in the first decades of the eighteenth century foreshadowed the shift from incarnational re-presentation to representation as imitation that, according to Paul

Friedland, occured in French dramatic theory in 1750. See Friedland, *Political Actors: Representative Bodies and Theatricality in the Age of the French Revolution*, 21–23.

80. "Per un braccio e gli porterà replicatamente la mano sul petto ed al cuore per renderli sensibili alla grandezza de' suoi sentimenti": Riccoboni, "Lettera della signora Elena Riccoboni al signor abate Antonio Conti" (c. 1720). Emphasis mine.

81. "Grandezza delle azioni e l'altezza della nascita;" "natura maestosa e degna": Riccoboni, "Lettera della signora Elena Riccoboni al signor abate Antonio Conti" (c. 1720). I take this English translation from Scott, *Women on the Stage in Early Modern France: 1540–1750*, 237.

82. "[I]n tal caso mi rappresenterà egli la verità e la natura non di un eroe, ma di un cittadino, di un mercante o di un semplice fantaccino. . . . Io credo che un eroe dica lo stesso e con egual vigore lontano ancora sei passi dalla persona a cui parla, e con gli sguardi e il tuono adeguato della voce gli arrivi al cuore senza avvertirlo col tatto che è al suo cuore che ragiona": Riccoboni, "Lettera della signora Elena Riccoboni al signor abate Antonio Conti" (c. 1720). I take the English translation for this quote from Scott, *Women on the Stage in Early Modern France: 1540–1750*, 237.

# BIBLIOGRAPHY

## ARCHIVAL SOURCES

Bourdoise, Adrien. "Les Sentences ou maximes chrestiennes et ecclesiastiques de Messire Adrien Bourdoise, premier prestre de la Communauté et Seminaire de Saint Nicolas du Chardonnet à Paris." Late seventeenth century. MS 460. SS.

Bretonvilliers, Alexandre le Ragois de. "Vie de M. Olier par M. de Bretonvilliers, tome II." Vie manuscrite. N.d. Ms. 109. SS.

"Conférences épiscopales." Late seventeenth century. Ms. Fr. 14428. BN.

"Coûtumier ou registre des usages plus ordinaires de la Communauté et du Séminaire de St. Nicolas du Chardonnet par ordre alphabetique." N.d. MM 476. AN.

"Devises a la Gloire du Roy sur ses conquestes dans la Hollande." 1672. Salles des estampes M92731. BN.

"Dix conferences aux confesseurs." N.d. Ms. 316. SS.

"Du Carnaval, contre les desbauches qui s'y passent." N.d. MS 317. SS.

"Entretien du reglement des ecclesiastiques quant a l'exterieur." 1657. MS Fr. 14428. BN.

"Entretiens des ordinands sur les matieres de devotion (tome I)." N.d. Ms. 157. SS.

"Entretiens des ordinands sur les matières de dévotion (tome II)." N.d. Ms. 158. SS.

Ferrier, Jean du. "'Memoires [ecclésiastiques] de feu Mr [Jean] du Ferrier.'" N.d. MS 1480. BSG.

"Livre dans lequel sont escrits tous les Reglemens de chaque office, et Exercice du Seminaire desquels le prestre doit avoir une parfaite connoissance." N.d. AN MM 475.

Malbois, Henri. "Histoire de l'Eglise Saint-Sulpice." Unpublished book manuscript. Paris, twentieth century. Non-catalogued manuscript. SS.

"'Marques de vocation à l'estat ecclesiastique.'" N.d. MS 163. SS.

Olier, Jean-Jacques. "Autographes de M. Olier, fondateur du Séminaire de St. Sulpice: Divers écrits, tome I." N.d. Ms. 14. SS.

———. "Mystères de N.S. Jésus-Christ." N.d. Ms. 147. SS.

———. "Projet de l'establissement d'un séminaire dans un diocèse, où il est traité premierement de l'estat et de la disposition des sujets, secondement de l'esprit de tous leurs exercices, par un prestre du clergé." Printed document with handwritten notes and rough draft manuscript by Olier. Paris: Jacques Langlois, 1651. Ms. 20. SS.

"Recueil de la conduite d'un ecclesiastique pour vivre conformement a la saincteté de vie qu'il doit mener, reduit en examens composé et digeré par un tres scavant et pieux ecclesiastique d'une illustre communauté de Paris." Seminary of Saint-Sulpice, Paris, n.d. 906. SS.

"Registre dans lequel sont contenus les reglemens des officiers de l'Autel et du Choeur selon l'usage de Paris et de cette paroisse de St. N.D.C." N.d. MM 492. AN.

"Reglement général du Séminaire de S. Sulpice." 1682. MS Fr. 11760. BN.

"Règlement général du Séminaire de Saint-Sulpice." Paris, 1710. Ms. 1342. SS.

"Resolutions arrestees a Paris par messeigneurs les evesques, et quelques supérieurs de séminaires, avec Monsieur, mil six cens cinquante sept." Paris, 1657. Ms. Fr. 14428. BN.

Tronson, Louis. "Entretiens." Paris, n.d. Ms. 50. SS.


EARLY MODERN PRINT SOURCES

Abelly, Louys. *La Vie du venerable serviteur de Dieu Vincent de Paul, institueur et premier superieur general de la Congregation de la Mission.* 2nd ed. Vol. 1. 2 vols. Paris: Florentin Lambert, 1668.

*Abrégé de la tonsure.* Paris: Pierre Trichard, n.d.

*Abrégé du petit livre de la bourse cléricale,* 1654.

*Advis aux confesseurs, et demandes à faire aux pénitens.* Paris: Pierre Trichard, 1657.

Allainval, Leonor Jean Christine Soulas, abbé de. "Lettre à mylord *** sur Baron et la Dlle Le Couvreur par George Wink (l'Abbé d'Allainval)." In *Lettre a mylord *** sur Baron et la Dlle Le Couvreur par George Wink (l'Abbé d'Allanval), Lettre du souffleur de la comédie de Roüen au garçon de caffé (par du Mas d'Aigueberre),* edited by Jules Bonnassies, 17–87. Paris: L. Willem, 1870.

Aubignac, François Hédelin d', abbé. *La Pratique du théâtre.* Edited by Hélène Baby. Paris: Honoré Champion, 2011. First published 1657.

Aubignac, Hédelin François d', l'abbé. *La Pratique du theatre, oeuvre tres-necessaire a tous ceux qui veulent s'appliquer a la composition des poëmes dramatiques, qui pour profession de les reciter en publique, ou qui prennent plaisir d'en voir les representations.* Paris: Antoine de Sommaville, 1657.

Avila, Jean. *Discours aux prestres contenant une doctrine fort necessaire à tous ceux lesquels estans élevez à cette haute dignité desirent que Dieu leur soit propice au dernier jugement.* 3rd ed. Paris: Pierre Trichard, 1658.

Bary, René. *La Rhétorique française.* Amsterdam: J. de Ravenstein, 1679.

Baudrand, M. "Mémoire sur la vie de M. Olier et sur le séminaire de Saint-Sulpice." In *Bibliothèque sulpicienne ou histoire littéraire de la Compagnie de Saint-Sulpice,* edited by L. Bertrand, 3:369–466. Paris: Alphonse Picard et Fils, 1900.

Bérulle, Pierre de. *Les Oeuvres de l'eminentissime et reverendissime Pierre Cardinal de Bérulle, instituteur et premier superieur de la Congregation de l'Oratoire de Jesus-Christ Nostre Seigneur, augmentées de divers opuscules de controverse et de pieté, avec plusieurs lettres.* Edited by François Bourgoing. Paris: Antoine Estienne, 1644.

Beuvelet, Matthieu. *Conduites pour les exercices principaux qui se font dans les séminaires ecclesiastiques, dressées en faveur des clercs demeurans dans le Seminaire de S. Nicolas du Chardonnet.* Lyon: Hierosne de la Garde, 1660.

———. *Instruction sur le manuel par forme de demandes et réponses familieres pour servir à ceux qui dans les séminaires se préparent à l'administration des Sacremens, où se voyent recüeillies les choses les plus remarquables qui se trouvent dans la pluspart des Manuels quis sont en usage dans l'Eglise, et la resolution de plusieurs difficultez de pratique.* 4th ed. 2 vols. Paris: Georges Josse, 1659.

———. *Meditations sur les principales veritez chrétiennes, et ecclesiastiques, prises dans leurs propres principes, c'est à dire, dans les obligations contractées par les clercs en la reception de chaque ordre en particulier, et sur le modele du souverain prêtre nôtre Seigneur Jesus-Christ.* Vol. 2. 2 vols. Lyon: Daniel Gayet, 1674.

Bossuet, Jacques Benigne. *Catéchisme du diocèse de Meaux.* Paris: Sebastien Mabre-Cramoisy, 1687.

————. "Maximes et réflexions sur la comédie." In *L'Eglise et le théâtre: Maximes et réflexions sur la comédie précédés d'une introduction historique et accompagnées de documents contemporains et de notes critiques,* edited by Charles Urbain and Eugene Levesque, 169–276. Paris: Bernard Grasset, 1930.

Bourdoise, Adrien. *Le Désireux de parvenir salutairement à l'estat ecclesiastique, se faisant instruire des propres moyens d'y arriver. Premiere partie. Contenant la preparation requise pour recevoir la tonsure, ou clericature; et les devoirs clericaux de ceux qui sont tonsurez.* Paris: Pierre Menier et Jean Mestais, 1623.

————. *L'Idée d'un bon ecclésiastique ou les sentences chrétiennes et cléricales de Messire Adrien Bourdoise, d'heureuse mémoire, prestre de la Communauté de Saint Nicolas du Chardonnet.* Paris: Jacques de Laize de Bresche, 1684.

Brice, Germain. *Nouvelle description de la ville de Paris et de tout ce qu'elle continent de curieux et de plus remarquable.* 8th ed. Vol. 2. 2 vols. Paris: Julien Michel Gandouin, 1725.

*Briefve histoire de l'institution des ordres religieux, avec les figures de leurs habits, gravées sur le cuivre par Odoart Fialetti, Bolognois.* Paris: Adrien Menier, 1658.

Chaillot, Gilles, Paul Cochois, and Irénée Noye, eds. *Traité des Saints Ordres (1676), comparé aux écrits authentiques de Jean-Jacques Olier (†1657).* Paris: Procure de la Compagnie de Saint-Sulpice, 1984.

Chanut, L'abbé, trans. *Le Saint Concile de Trente oecumenique et general, celebré sous Paul III, Jule III et Pie IV, souverains pontifes, nouvellement traduit.* Paris: Sebastien Mabre-Cramoisy, 1674.

Chappuzeau, Samuel. *Le Théâtre françois par Samuel Chappuzeau, accompagné d'une préface et de notes.* Edited by Georges Monval. Paris: Jules Bonnassies, 1875.

Comédie-Française. *Registre de La Grange (1658–1685), précédé d'une notice biographique.* Archives de la Comédie-Française. Paris: J. Claye, 1876.

Conti, Armand de Bourbon, prince de. *Traité de la comédie et des spectacles, selon la tradition de l'Église, tirée des conciles et des saints pères.* Paris: Louys Billaine, 1666.

Croix, Claude de La. *Le Parfaict ecclesiastique ou diverses instructions sur toutes les fonctions clericales.* Paris: Pierre de Bresche, 1666.

*Des Clercs desguisez, ou de l'habit clerical, selon les saints canons.* Paris: Pierre Trichard, n.d.

Descourveaux, Philibert. *La Vie de Monsieur Bourdoise, premier prestre de la Communauté de S. Nicolas du Chardonnet.* Paris: François Fournier, 1714.

Doncourt, Henri François Simon de. *Remarques historiques, sur l'église et la paroisse de S. Sulpice, tirées du premier volume des instructions et prieres à l'usage de ladite paroisse.* Vol. 3 vols. Paris: Nicolas Crapart, 1773.

*Du Respect deu aux eglises.* Paris: Pierre Trichard, n.d.

*Éclaircissemens sur la vie de Messire Jean d'Aranthon d'Alex, évêque, et prince de Genève, avec de nouvelles preuves incontestables de la vérité de son zèle contre le jansénisme et le quiétisme.* Chambery: Jean Gorrin, 1699.

Furetière, Antoine. "Collet." In *Dictionnaire universel.* Vol. 1. La Haye: Arnout et Renier Leers, 1690.

————. "Curé." In *Dictionnaire universel.* Vol. 1. La Haye: Arnout et Renier Leers, 1690. Gallica.

————. "Miroir." In *Dictionnaire universel.* Vol. 2. La Haye: Arnout et Renier Leers, 1690.

————. "Orateur." In *Dictionnaire universel.* Vol. 2. La Haye: Arnout et Renier Leers, 1690.

———. "Public." In *Dictionnaire universel*. Vol. 3. La Haye: Arnout et Renier Leers, 1690.

———. "Public." In *Dictionnaire universel*, edited by Basnage de Bauval. Vol. 2. La Haye: Arnout et Renier Leers, 1702.

———. "Regulier, ere." In *Dictionnaire universel*. Vol. 3. La Haye: Arnout et Renier Leers, 1690. Gallica.

———. "Religieux, euse." In *Dictionnaire universel*. Vol. 3. La Haye: Arnout et Renier Leers, 1690. Gallica.

———. "Religion." In *Dictionnaire universel*. Vol. 3. La Haye: Arnout et Renier Leers, 1690.

———. "Seculier, iere." In *Dictionnaire universel*. Vol. 3. La Haye: Arnoud et Reinier Leers, 1701.

———. "Seculierement." In *Dictionnaire universel*. Vol. 3. La Haye: Arnout et Renier Leers, 1690. Gallica.

———. "Théâtre." In *Dictionnaire Universel*. Vol. 3. La Haye: Arnout et Renier Leers, 1690.

Gérard, Armand, l'abbé de. *Le Caractere de l'honneste-homme morale: Dédié au Roy par M. l'abbé de Gérard*. Paris: Chez Amable Auroy ruë Saint Jacques, attenant la Fontaine, S. Severin, 1688.

Harlay, Francisci de. *Synodicon ecclesiae parisiensis*. Paris: Apud. Franciscum Muguet Regis et illustrissimi Archiepiscopi Parisiensis Typographum, 1674.

*Instruction familiere des processions de l'eglise*. Paris: Pierre Trichard, n.d.

*Instruction familiere pour bien entendre la Sainte Messe*. Paris: Pierre Trichard, n.d.

Janvier, Nicolas. *Des Prestres et curez: De leur institution, puissance, droicts et devoirs en l'Eglise*. Paris: Pierre Trichard, n.d.

*La Journée chrétienne*. Paris: Pierre Trichard, n.d.

[Lantages, Charles-Louis de.] *Instruction ecclesiastiques, où l'on tache de faire connoître l'essence, la dignité et la sainteté du clergé*. Puy: Les Veuves Delagarde, 1692.

Le Brun, Pierre. *Discours sur la comédie, où on voit la réponse au théologien qui la deffend, avec l'Histoire du théâtre, et les sentimens des docteurs de l'Eglise depuis le premier siecle jusqu'à présent*. Paris: Loüis Guerin, 1694.

———. *Discours sur la comedie: Ou traité historique et dogmatique des jeux de théatre et des autres divertissemens comiques soufferts ou condamnés depuis le premier siécle de l'Eglise jusqu'à présent. Avec un discours sur les pieces de théatre, tirées de l'Ecriture Sainte. Seconde edition, augmenté de plus de la moitié*. 2nd ed. Paris: La Veuve Delaulne, 1731.

———. *Explication literale, historique et dogmatique des prieres et des ceremonies de la messe, suivant les anciens auteurs, et les monuments de la plupart des eglises, avec des dissertations & des notes sur les endroits difficiles, et sur l'origine des rites*. Paris: Florentin Delaulne, 1716.

Le Gendre, Pierre. *Declaration des papes, des conciles, des cardinaux, et des docteurs; touchant l'obligation d'entendre la messe paroissiale châcun en sa paroisse*. Paris: Guillaume Sassier, 1651.

*Les Principaux devoirs d'un bon curé*. Paris: Pierre Trichard, 1657.

L'Estoile, Pierre de. *Mémoires-Journaux de Pierre de L'Estoile (tome premier): Journal de Henri III, 1574–1580*. Edited by G. Brunet, A. Champollion, E. Halphen, Paul Lacroix, Charles Read, Tamizey de Larroque, and Ed. Tricotel. Vol. 1. 12 vols. Paris: Libraire des bibliophiles, 1875.

*Manuel des cérémonies romaines, tiré des livres romains les plus authentiques, et des ecrivains les plus intelligens en cette matiere, par quelques-uns des prêtres de la Congrégation de L.M.* Lyon: Benoist Bailly, 1679.

Martial du Mans. *Almanac spirituel de l'an de grace 1667. Pour la ville, faux-bourgs et és environs de Paris. Où sont marquées les festes, confrairies, indulgences pleniere, predications, assemblées, et conferences de pieté, qu'il y aura chaque jour de cette année dans les eglises, metropolitaine et collegiales, dans les paroisses et monasteres de Paris. A l'usage des personnes devotes. Reveu et corrigé par le P. Martial du Mans religieux penitent.* Paris: Georges Josse, 1667.

———. *Almanach spirituel, de l'an 1651, pour la ville et Fauxbourgs de Paris. Où sont marquées les festes, confrairies, indulgences pleniere, predications, assemblées, et conferences de pieté, qu'il y aura chaque jour de cette année dans les eglises, paroisses & monasteres de Paris, a l'usage des personnes devotes, par le P. Martial du Mans, religieux penitent.* Paris: Georges Josse, 1651.

*Mercure galant, dédié à Monsieur le Dauphin: Mars 1692.* Paris: G. de Luyne, 1692.

*Miroir des prestres et autres ecclesiastiques.* Paris: Pierre Trichard, 1659.

*Missel Romain selon le reglement du Concile de Trent, traduit en françois.* Cologne: Jean de la Pierre, 1692.

Molière. "Le Tartuffe ou l'imposteur." In *Oeuvres complètes*, edited by Georges Couton, 1:831–984. Paris: Éditions Gallimard, 1971.

———. "Premier placet présenté au roi sur la comédie du 'Tartuffe.'" In *Oeuvres complètes*, edited by Georges Couton, 1:889–91. Paris: Éditions Gallimard, 1971.

———. "Second placet présenté au roi dans son camp devant la ville de Lille en Flandre." In *Oeuvres complètes*, edited by Georges Couton, 1:891–93. Paris: Éditions Gallimard, 1971.

———. *Tartuffe: A Verse Translation.* Edited by Constance Congdon and Virginia Scott. Translated by Constance Congdon. New York: W. W. Norton, 2009.

Monval, Georges. "Documents inédits sur les Champmeslé." In *Revue d'art dramatique: Tome XXVIII, octobre-décembre 1892*, 129–41. Geneva: Slatkine Reprints, 1971. http://gallica.bnf.fr/ark:/12148/bpt6k16452z.

———. *Lettres de Adrienne Le Couvreur, réunies pour la première fois et publiées avec notes, étude biographique, documents inédits tirés des archives de la Comédie, des minutiers de notaires et des papiers de la Bastille.* Paris: Librairie Plon, 1892.

Nicole, Pierre. *Traité de la comédie, et autres pièces d'un procès du théâtre.* Edited by Laurent Thirouin. Paris: Honoré Champion, 1998.

Noailles, Louis Antoine de. *Ordonnance de Monseigneur l'archevesque de Paris, portant défenses de laisser dire la messe, ni de faire aucunes fonctions dans le diocése, aux prêtres étrangers tant séculiers que réguliers, sans permission écrit.* Paris: Louis Josse, 1697.

———. *Ordonnance de Monseigneur l'archevesque de Paris touchant l'habit et la conduite exterieure des ecclesiastiques.* Paris: Louis Josse, 1697.

Olier, Jean-Jacques. *Explication des cérémonies de la grande messe de paroisse.* Paris: Jacques Langlois, 1656.

———. *L'Esprit des cérémonies de la messe: Explication des cérémonies de la grand'messe de paroisse selon l'usage romain.* Edited by Claude Barthe and Michèle Debaecker. [Perpignan:] Tempora, 2009.

———. *Lettres de M. Olier, curé de la paroisse et fondateur du Séminaire de Saint-Sulpice.* Edited by Eugene Levesque. Paris: J. de Gigord, 1935.

———. *Lettres de M. Olier, fondateur du séminaire de Saint-Sulpice, nouvelle édition revue sur les autographes, considérablement augmenté, accompagné de notes biographiques et précédée d'un abrégé de la vie de M. Olier.* Paris: Libraire Victor Lecoffre, 1885.

———. "Projet pour l'établissement d'un séminaire dans un diocese." In Étienne-Michel Faillon, *Vie de M. Olier, fondateur du séminaire de Saint-Sulpice*, 551–614, 4th ed. Paris: Poussielgue frères, 1873.

Parfaict, François, and Claude Parfaict. *Histoire du théâtre françois, depuis son origine jusqu'à présent, avec la vie des plus célèbres poëtes dramatiques, un catalogue exact de leurs pièces, et des notes historiques et critiques.* Vol. 13. 15 vols. Paris: P. G. Le Mercier, 1748.

——. *Histoire du théâtre françois, depuis son origine jusqu'à présent, avec la vie des plus célèbres poëtes dramatiques, un catalogue exact de leurs pièces, et des notes historiques et critiques*. Vol. 14. 15 vols. Paris: P. G. Le Mercier, 1748.

Pasté. *Abrégé du reglement du seminaire paroissial de S. Nicolas du Chardonnet, pour l'usage des seminaristes*. Paris: Pierre Trichard, 1672.

Paul V. *Rituale romanum, Pauli V. Pont*. Antwerp: Ex Officina Plantiniana, Apud Balthasarem et Joannem Moretos, 1617.

Paul, Vincent de. *Correspondance, Entretiens, Documents: Correspondance (janvier 1640–juillet 1646)*. Edited by Pierre Coste. Vol. 2. 12 vols. Paris: Librairie Lecoffre. J. Gabalda, 1921.

——. *Correspondance, Entretiens, Documents: Entretiens aux missionnaires, tome 2*. Edited by Pierre Coste. Vol. 12. 12 vols. Paris: Librairie Lecoffre, 1924.

——. *Lettres de S. Vincent de Paul, fondateur des Prêtres de la Mission et des Filles de la Charité*. Vol. 1. Paris: Librairie de D. Dumoulin, 1882.

Pavillon, Nicolas. *Les Instructions du rituel du diocese d'Alet*. 4th ed. Paris: Guillaume Desprez, 1678.

Racine, Jean. *Bérénice*. Edited by Marie-Henriette Bru. Bibliolycée. Paris: Hachette, 2003.

——. "Lettre à l'auteur des Hérésies imaginaires et des deux Visionnaires (1666)." In *Traité de la comédie, et autre pièces d'un procès du théâtre*, edited by Laurent Thirouin, 225–32. Paris: Honoré Champion, 1998.

*Reglemens et matieres des catechismes qui se font en la paroisse de S. Nicolas du Chardonnet, dressez par l'ordre de Monsieur le Curé dudit lieu pour servir à ceux qui sont employez de sa part à faire le catechisme dans son eglise et autres*. Paris: Gabriel Targa, 1668.

*Resolutions de plusieurs cas importans pour la morale, et pour la discipline ecclesiastique, par un grand nombre de docteurs en Theologie de la Faculté de Paris*. Paris: Charles Savreux, 1666.

Riccoboni, Elena Virginia Balletti. "Lettera della signora Elena Riccoboni al signor abate Antonio Conti gentiluomo viniziano, sopra la maniera di Monsieur Baron nel rappresentare le tragedie franzesi." Circa 1720. http://www.irpmf.cnrs.fr/IMG/pdf/Elenia_virginia_riccoboni.pdf.

——. "Lettera della signora Elena Riccoboni al signor abate Antonio Conti gentiluomo viniziano, sopra la maniera di Monsieur Baron nel rappresentare le tragedie franzesi." In *Raccolta d'opuscoli scientifici e filologici*, edited by Angelo Colagerà, 13:495–501. Venice: Christoforo Zane, 1736.

Richelet, César-Pierre. "Public." In *Dictionnaire françois*, 229–30. Geneva: Jean Herman Widerhold, 1680. http://gallica.bnf.fr/ark:/12148/bpt6k509323/f814.

Roullé, Pierre. "Le Roi glorieux au monde ou Louis XIV le plus glorieux de tous les rois du monde." In Molière, *Oeuvres complètes*, edited by Georges Couton, 1:1143–44. Paris: Éditions Gallimard, 1971.

Saint-Simon, Louis de Rouvroy duc de. *Mémoires*. Vol. 1. Les Grands écrivains de la France. Paris: Hachette, 1951.

——. *Mémoires*. Vol. 2. Les Grands écrivains de la France. Paris: Hachette, 1951.

Schoonebeek, Adrien. *Histoire des ordres religieux de l'un et de l'autre sexe; ou l'on voit le temps de leur fondation, la vie abrégé, de leurs fondateurs, et les figures de leurs habits*. 2nd ed. Amsterdam: A. Schoonebeek, 1695.

Scudéry, Georges de. *L'apologie du théâtre par M. de Scudery*. Paris: Augustin Courbé, 1639.

Talma, François-Joseph. *Mémoires de J.-F. Talma (1849), écrits par lui-même et recueillis et mis en ordre sur les papiers de sa famille par Alexandre Dumas*. Edited by Alexandre Dumas. Montreal: Éditions Le Joyeux Roger, 2006. http://www.alexandredumasetcompagnie.com/images/1.pdf/MemoiresDeTalma.PDF.

Tellier, Charles Maurice le. *Rituel de la province de Reims, renouvellé et augmenté par Monseigneur l'Illustrissime et reverendissime Messire Charles Maurice le Tellier, archevêque, duc de Reims, premier pair de France, etc. Et publié dans son diocèze par son autorité.* Paris: Frederic Leonard, 1677.

Thiers, Jean-Baptiste. *Dissertations ecclésiastiques, sur les principaux autels des églises, les jubés des églises, la clôture du chœur des églises.* Paris: Antoine Dezallier, 1688.

Thwaites, Reuben Gold, ed. *The Jesuit Relations and Allied Documents: Travels and Explorations of the Jesuit Missionaries in New France, 1610–1791.* Translated by Reuben Gold Thwaites. Vol. 64. 73 vols. Cleveland, OH: Burrow Brothers, 1900.

Vantadour, Anne de Levy de. *Rituel de Bourges, fait par feu Monseigneur l'Illustrissime et reverendissime messire Anne de Levy de Vantadour, patriarche, archevêque de Bourges, primat des aquitaines: Publié par Illustrissime et reverendissime Monseigneur, Messire Jean de Montpezat de Carbon, patriarche, archevêque de Bourges, primat des Aquitaines.* Vol. 1. 2 vols. Bourges: Jean Toubeau, 1666.

Viret, Pierre. *Les Cauteles, canon et ceremonies de la messe.* Lyon: Pour Claude Ravot, 1564.

Waterworth, J., ed. *The Council of Trent: The Canons and Decrees of the Sacred and Oecumenical Council of Trent.* Translated by J. Waterworth. Hanover Historical Texts Projects. London: Dolman, 1848. http://history.hanover.edu/texts/trent.html.


SECONDARY SOURCES

Ackerman, Robert W. "The Knighting Ceremonies in the Middle English Romances." *Speculum* 19, no. 3 (1944): 285–313.

Ahaus, Hubert. "Holy Orders." In *The Catholic Encyclopedia.* Vol. 11. New York: Robert Appleton, 1911. http://www.newadvent.org/cathen/11279a.htm.

Albert, Maurice. *Les Théâtres de la Foire (1660–1789).* 2nd ed. Geneva: Slatkine Reprints, 1969.

Allier, Raoul. *La Cabale des dévots, 1627–1666.* Paris: Librairie Armand Colin, 1902.

Alston, G. C. "Hairshirt." In *The Catholic Encyclopedia.* New York: Robert Appleton, 1910. http://www.newadvent.org/cathen/07113b.htm.

Apostolidès, Jean-Marie. *Le Prince sacrifié: Théâtre et politique au temps de Louis XIV.* Paris: Les Éditions de Minuit, 1985.

Aubineau, Léon. *Notices littéraires sur le dix-septième siècle.* Paris: Gaume Frères et J. Duprey, 1859.

Aussedat-Minvielle, Annik. "Histoire et contenu des rituels diocesains et romains imprimés en France de 1476 à 1800: Inventaire descriptif des rituels des provinces de Paris, Reims et Rouen." Doctoral dissertation completed under the direction of Jean Delumeau, Université de Paris I, Panthéon-Sorbonne, 1987.

Austin, J. L. *How to Do Things with Words.* Edited by J. O. Urmson and Marina Sbisà. 2nd ed. Cambridge, MA: Harvard University Press, 1975.

Baby, Hélène, and Alain Viala. "Le XVIIe siècle ou l'institution du théâtre." In *Le Théâtre en France des origines à nos jours,* edited by Alain Viala, 153–230. Paris: Presses Universitaires de France, 1997.

Barish, Jonas. *The Antitheatrical Prejudice.* Berkeley: University of California Press, 1981.

Barras, Moses. *The Stage Controversy in France from Corneille to Rousseau.* New York: Institute of French Studies, 1933.

Barthe, Claude. "Introduction." In *L'Esprit des cérémonies de la messe: Explication des cérémonies de la grand'messe de paroisse selon l'usage romain,* 5–32. [Perpignan:] Tempora, 2009.

Baumal, Francis. *Tartuffe et ses avatars "de Montufar à Dom Juan": Histoire des relations de Molière avec la Cabale des Dévots.* Paris: Emile Nourry, 1925.

Beam, Sara. *Laughing Matters: Farce and the Making of Absolutism in France.* Ithaca, NY: Cornell University Press, 2007.

Beaumont, Keith. "Pierre de Bérulle (1575–1629) and the Renewal of Catholic Spiritual Life in France." *International Journal for the Study of the Christian Church* 17, no. 2 (2017): 73–92. https://doi.org/10.1080/1474225X.2017.1351085.

Bély, Lucien. *La Société des princes, XVIe–XVIIIe siècle.* Paris: Librairie Arthème Fayard, 1999.

Bénichou, Paul. *Morales du grand siècle.* Paris: Gallimard, 1984.

Bergin, Joseph. *Church, Society and Religious Change in France, 1580–1730.* New Haven: Yale University Press, 2009.

Bertrand, Louis. *Bibliothèque sulpicienne ou histoire littéraire de la Compagnie de Saint-Sulpice.* 3 vols. Paris: Alphonse Picard et Fils, 1900.

———. "L'Episcopat Sulpicien: Catalogue biographique des évêques de France élevés du séminaire de Saint-Sulpice aux XVIIe et XVIIIe siècles." *Bulletin trimestriel des anciens élèves de Saint-Sulpice*, no. 38 (August 1905): 425–48.

Block, Elaine C. "Liturgical and Anti-Liturgical Iconography on Medieval Choir Stalls." In *Objects, Images, and the Word: Art in Service of the Liturgy*, edited by Colum Hourihane, 161–79. Index of Christian Art 4. Princeton, NJ: Princeton University Press, 2003.

Blocker, Déborah. *Instituer un "art": Politiques du théâtre dans la France du premier XVIIe siècle.* Paris: Honoré Champion, 2009.

Boer, Wietse de. "Professionalization and Clerical Identity: Notes on the Early Modern Catholic Priest." *Nederlands Archief voor Kerkgeschiedenis / Dutch Review of Church History* 85, no. 1 (2005): 369–77.

Boisard, Pierre. *La Compagnie de Saint Sulpice: Trois siècles d'histoire.* Vol. 1. 2 vols. Paris: La Compagnie de Saint Sulpice, 1959.

Bossy, John. "The Mass as a Social Institution 1200–1700." *Past and Present*, no. 100 (1983): 29–61.

Bossy, John, and Marie-Solange Wane-Touzeau. "Essai de sociographie de la messe, 1200–1700." *Annales: Economies, sociétés, civilisations* 36, no. 1 (1981): 44–70. https://doi.org/10.3406/ahess.1981.282715.

Bourdieu, Pierre. *Outline of a Theory of Practice.* Translated by Richard Nice. Cambridge: Cambridge University Press, 1977.

Bray, René. *La Formation de la doctrine classique en France.* Paris: Libraire Nizet, 1957.

Bremond, Henri. *Histoire littéraire du sentiment religieux en France depuis la fin des guerres de religion jusqu'à nos jours.* Vol. 1. Paris: Bloud et Gay, 1916.

———. *Histoire littéraire du sentiment religieux en France depuis la fin des guerres de religion jusqu'à nos jours.* Vol. 3. Paris: Librairie Bloud et Gay, 1923.

Brian, Isabelle. "Catholic Liturgies of the Eucharist in the Time of Reform." In *A Companion to the Eucharist in the Reformation*, edited by Lee Palmer Wandel, 185–203. Leiden: Brill, 2014.

———. *Prêcher à Paris sous l'ancien régime: XVIIe–XVIIIe siècles.* Paris: Classiques Garnier, 2014.

Briggs, Robin. *Early Modern France: 1560–1715.* Oxford: Oxford University Press, 1977.

Brocher, Henri. *À la cour de Louis XIV: Le Rang et l'étiquette sous l'ancien régime.* Paris: Librairie Félix Alcan, 1934.

Broutin, Paul. *La Réforme pastorale en France au XVIIe siècle: Recherches sur la tradition pastorale après le Concile de Trente.* Vol. 2. 2 vols. Bibliothèque de théologie, série II: Théologie morale. Tournai, Belgium: Desclée, 1956.

Brundin, Abigail. "On the Convent Threshold: Poetry for New Nuns in Early Modern Italy." *Renaissance Quarterly* 65, no. 4 (2012): 1125–65.

Bryant, Lawrence M. *The King and the City in the Parisian Royal Entry Ceremony: Politics, Ritual, and Art in the Renaissance.* Travaux d'humanisme et renaissance. Geneva: Librairie Droz, 1986.

Burke, Peter. *The Fabrication of Louis XIV.* New Haven: Yale University Press, 1992.

Butler, Judith. *Gender Trouble: Feminism and the Subversion of Identity.* New York: Routledge, 1990.

———. *Undoing Gender.* London: Routledge, 2004.

Carlson, Marvin. *Performance: A Critical Introduction.* 2nd ed. New York: Routledge, 2004.

Carroll, Gérard. *Un Portrait du prêtre: Les Retraites de 10 jours pour les ordinands.* Vol. 1. 3 vols. Paris: Pierre Téqui, 2004.

Carter, Karen E. *Creating Catholics: Catechism and Primary Education in Early Modern France.* Notre Dame, IN: University of Notre Dame Press, 2011.

Chaouche, Sabine. *L'Art du comédien: Déclamation et jeu scénique en France à L'âge classique (1629–1680).* Paris: Honoré Champion, 2001.

———. "Les Spectateurs dans la lorgnette des anecdotiers: Fait divers ou fait théâtral?" *Journal for Eighteenth-Century Studies* 32, no. 4 (2009): 515–27. https://doi.org/10.1111/j.1754-0208 .2009.00224.x.

Chartier, Roger, and Lydia G. Cochrane. "Urban Reading Practices, 1660–1780." In *The Cultural Uses of Print in Early Modern France*, 183–239. Princeton, NJ: Princeton University Press, 1987.

Chédozeau, Bernard. *Chœur clos, chœur ouvert: De l'église médiévale à l'église tridentine (France, XVIIe–XVIIIe siècle).* Paris: Les Éditions du Cerf, 1998.

Chill, Emanuel S. "Tartuffe, Religion, and Courtly Culture." *French Historical Studies* 3, no. 2 (1963): 151–83.

Cianca, Jenn. *Sacred Ritual, Profane Space: The Roman House as Early Christian Meeting Place.* Montreal: McGill-Queen's University Press, 2018.

Clarke, Jan. *The Guénégaud Theatre in Paris (1673–1680): Founding, Design and Production.* Vol. 1. 2 vols. Studies in Theatre Arts 5. Lewiston, NY: Edwin Mellen Press, 1998.

Clay, Lauren. *Stagestruck: The Business of Theater in Eighteenth-Century France and Its Colonies.* Ithaca, NY: Cornell University Press, 2013.

Coleman, David. "Moral Formation and Social Control in the Catholic Reformation: The Case of San Juan de Avila." *Sixteenth Century Journal: The Journal of Early Modern Studies* 26, no. 1 (1995): 17–30.

Collinson, Patrick. *The Religion of Protestants: The Church in English Society, 1559–1625.* Oxford: Clarendon Press, 1982.

Comerford, Kathleen M. "Italian Tridentine Diocesan Seminaries: A Historiographical Study." *Sixteenth Century Journal* 29, no. 4 (1998): 999–1022.

Concha Sahli, Alejandra. "The Meaning of the Habit: Religious Orders, Dress and Identity, 1215–1650." Ph.D. dissertation, University College London, 2017.

"Congregation for Divine Worship and the Discipline of the Sacraments." Accessed May 21, 2021. https://www.vatican.va/content/romancuria/en/congregazioni/congregazione-per-il -culto-divino-e-la-disciplina-dei-sacrament.index.html.

Constant, G. "Les Maîtres de cérémonies du XVIe siècle: Leurs *Diaires.*" *Mélanges d'archéologie et d'histoire* 23 (1903): 161–229. https://doi.org/10.3406/mefr.1903.6295.

Coon, Lynda. *Dark Age Bodies: Gender and Monastic Practice in the Early Medieval West.* Philadelphia: University of Pennsylvania Press, 2010.

Corblet, Jules. *Histoire dogmatique, liturgique et archéologique du sacrement de l'eucharistie.* Vol. 2. 2 vols. Paris: Société Générale de Librairie Catholique, 1886.

Cosandey, Fanny. *Le Rang: Préséances et hiéarchies dans la France d'ancien régime.* Kindle Edition. Paris: Éditions Gallimard, 2016.

Cousinié, Frédéric. *Le Saint des saints: Maîtres-autels et retables parisiens du XVIIe siècle.* Aix-en-Provence: Publications de l'Université de Provence, 2006.

Couton, Georges. "Notice sur *Le Tartuffe ou l'Imposteur.*" In Molière, *Oeuvres complètes,* edited by Georges Couton, 833–81. Paris: Éditions Gallimard, 1971.

Crimando, Thomas I. "Two French Views of the Council of Trent." *Sixteenth Century Journal: The Journal of Early Modern Studies* 19, no. 2 (1988): 169–86.

Cullum, P. H., and Katherine J. Lewis, eds. *Religious Men and Masculine Identity in the Middle Ages.* Gender in the Middle Ages. Rochester, NY: Boydell Press, 2013.

"Cure, n.1." In *OED Online.* Oxford University Press, June 2020. https://www-oed-com.ezproxy .lib.ucalgary.ca/view/Entry/46000?rskey=PJZ9NQ&result=1&isAdvanced=false.

Dainville-Barbiche, Ségolène de. "Le Clergé paroissial de Paris à la fin de l'ancien régime (1789–1791)." *Bibliothèque de l'École des chartes* 147 (1989): 539–61.

Dauge-Roth, Katherine. *Signing the Body: Marks on Skin in Early Modern France.* London: Routledge, 2020.

Davy-Rigaux, C., B. Dompnier, and D.-O. Hurel, eds. *Les Cérémoniaux catholiques en France à l'époque moderne: Une Littérature de codification des rites liturgiques.* Église, liturgie et société dans l'Europe moderne. Turnhout, Belgium: Brepols, 2009.

"De Salignac de la Mothe-Fénelon." Prepared by Armorial Charentais de M. Ouvrard. Accessed May 11, 2021. http://jm.ouvrard.pagesperso-orange.fr/armor/fami/s/salignac_fenelon.htm.

Degert, Antoine. *Histoire des séminaires français jusqu'à la Révolution.* 2 vols. Paris: Gabriel Beauchesne, 1912.

Deierkauf-Holsboer, Sophie Wilma. *Le Théâtre de l'Hôtel de Bourgogne: I, 1548–1635.* Vol. 1. 2 vols. Paris: A.-G. Nizet, 1968.

Demeulenaere-Douyere, Christiane. *Guide des sources de l'état civil parisien.* Paris: Imprimerie municipale, 1982.

Diamond, Elin. *Unmaking Mimesis: Essays on Feminism and Theater.* London: Routledge, 1997.

Dox, Donnalee. "Ceremonial Embodiment: The Problem of 'Liturgical Drama.'" *Ecumenica: Journal of Theatre and Performance* 3, no. 2 (2010): 31–41.

Dubu, Jean. "Le Rituel romain et les rituels des diocèses de France au XVIIe siècle." In Jean Dubu, *Les Églises chrétiennes et le théâtre (1550–1850),* 71–94. Grenoble: Presses Universitaires de Grenoble, 1997.

——. "L'Église catholique et la condamnation du théâtre en France au XVIIe siècle." *Quaderni francesi* 1 (1970): 319–49.

——. *Les Églises chrétiennes et le théâtre (1550–1850).* Grenoble: Presses Universitaires de Grenoble, 1997.

Dujon, Fernand. *Les Livres à clefs: Études de bibliographie critique et analytique pour servir à l'histoire littéraire.* Vol. 1. 2 vols. Paris: Édouard Rouveyre, 1888.

Durkheim, Emile. *The Elementary Forms of Religious Life.* Translated by Karen E. Fields. New York: Free Press, 1995.

Elias, Norbert. *The Court Society.* Translated by Edmund Jephcott. New York: Pantheon Books, 1983.

——. *La Société de Cour.* Paris: Flammarion, 1969.

Elwood, Christopher. *The Body Broken: The Calvinist Doctrine of the Eucharist and the Symbolization of Power in Sixteenth-Century France*. New York: Oxford University Press, 1999.

Emminghaus, Johannes H. *The Eucharist: Essence, Form, Celebration*. Translated by Linda M. Maloney. Collegeville, MN: Liturgical Press, 1997.

Evans, G. R. *The I. B. Tauris History of Monasticism: The Western Tradition*. London: I. B. Tauris, 2016.

Evennett, H. Outram. *The Spirit of the Counter-Reformation: The Birkbeck Lectures on Ecclesiastical History Given in the University of Cambridge in May 1951*. Edited by John Bossy. Cambridge: Cambridge University Press, 1968.

Faillon, Étienne-Michel. *Vie de M. Olier, fondateur du Séminaire de Saint-Sulpice*. 4th ed. 3 vols. Paris: Poussielgue frères, 1873.

Fanning, William. "Cure of Souls." In *The Catholic Encyclopedia*. New York: Robert Appleton, 1908. http://www.newadvent.org/cathen/04572a.htm.

Faret, Nicolas. *L'Honnête homme, ou l'art de plaire à la cour*. Edited by Maurice Magendie. Geneva: Slatkine Reprints, 1970.

Feldt, Laura. "Reframing Authority: The Role of Media and Materiality." *Postscripts: The Journal of Sacred Texts, Cultural Histories, and Contemporary Contexts* 8, no. 3 (2018): 185–92. https://doi.org/10.1558/post.33710.

Ferreyrolles, Gérard. *Molière: Tartuffe*. Études littéraires. Paris: Presses Universitaires de la France, 1987.

Ferté, Jeanne. *La Vie religieuse dans les campagnes parisiennes (1622–1695)*. Paris: Librairie Philosophique J. Vrin, 1962.

Feuardent, Adolphe de, and P. de Feuardent. *Histoire d'Auteuil depuis son origine jusqu'à nos jours*. Paris-Auteil: Imprimeria des Apprentis Catholiques, 1877.

Forestier, Georges. *Introduction à l'analyse des textes classiques: Éléments de rhétorique et de poétique du XVIIe siècle*. 4th ed. Kindle book. Paris: Armand Colin, 2012.

Fortescue, Adrian. "Jerusalem (A.D. 71–1099)." In *The Catholic Encyclopedia*. Vol. 8. New York: Robert Appleton, 1910. https://www.newadvent.org/cathen/08355a.htm.

———. "Ritual." In *The Catholic Encyclopedia*. Vol. 13. New York: Robert Appleton, 1912. http://www.newadvent.org/cathen/13088b.htm.

Foster, Hal. "Preface." In *Vision and Visuality*, edited by Hal Foster, ix–xiv. Dia Art Foundation, Discussion in Contemporary Culture 2. Seattle, WA: Bay Press, 1988.

Foucault, Michel. *The Archaeology of Knowledge and The Discourse on Language*. Translated by A. M. Sheridan Smith. New York: Pantheon Books, 1972.

Friedland, Paul. *Political Actors: Representative Bodies and Theatricality in the Age of the French Revolution*. Ithaca, NY: Cornell University Press, 2002.

Fumaroli, Marc. "La Querelle de la moralité du théâtre au XVIIe siècle." *Bulletin de la Société française de philosophie* 84, no. 3 (1990): 65–97.

———. "La Querelle de la moralité du théâtre avant Nicole et Bossuet." *Revue d'histoire littéraire de la France* 70, nos. 5–6 (1970): 1007–30.

———. "Sacerdos sive rhetor, orator sive histrio: Rhétorique, théologie, et 'moralité du théâtre' en France de Corneille à Molière." In *Héros et orateurs: Rhétorique et dramaturgie cornéliennes*, 449–92. Geneva: Librairie Droz, 1990.

Gaines, James F. *Social Structures in Molière's Theater*. Columbus: Ohio State University Press, 1984.

Gennep, Arnold van. *The Rites of Passage*. Translated by Monika B. Vizedom and Gabrielle L. Caffee. Chicago: University of Chicago Press, 1960.

Giesey, Ralph E. *Cérémonial et puissance souveraine: France, XVe–XVIIe siècles*. Paris: Armand Colin, 1987.

"The Glory, Nimbus, and Aureola." *Art Amateur* 5, no. 1 (1881): 9.

Godard de Donville, Louise. *Signification de la mode sous Louis XIII*. Aix-en-Provence: EDISUD, 1978.

Goichot, Émile. *Les Examens particuliers de M. Tronson: Essai sur la formation du prêtre "classique."* Edited by René Heyer. Strasbourg: Presses Universitaires de Strasbourg, 2005.

Golder, John. "Molière and the Circumstances of Late Seventeenth-Century Rehearsal Practice." *Theatre Research International* 33, no. 3 (2008): 250–62. https://doi.org/10.1017/S0307883308003957.

Goppelt, Leonhard. *Theology of the New Testament*. Edited by Jürgen Roloff. Translated by John E. Alsup. Vol. 1. 2 vols. Grand Rapids, MI: William B. Eerdmans, 1981.

———. *Theology of the New Testament*. Edited by Jürgen Roloff. Translated by John E. Alsup. Vol. 2. 2 vols. Grand Rapids, MI: William B. Eerdmans, 1982.

Gordon, Stewart, ed. *Robes and Honor: The Medieval World of Investiture*. New Middle Ages. New York: Palgrave Macmillan, 2001.

Goubert, Pierre, and Daniel Roche. *Les Français et l'ancien régime: La Société et l'état*. Vol. 1. Paris: Armand Colin, 1984.

Grandet, Joseph. *Les Saints prêtres français du XVIIe siècle, ouvrage publié pour la première fois, d'après le manuscrit original*. Edited by G. Letourneau. Vol. 2. 3 vols. Angers: Germain et G. Grassin; A. Roger et F. Chernoviz, 1897.

Green, Eugène. *La Parole baroque*. Texte et voix. Paris: Desclée de Brouwer, 2001.

Grimes, Ronald L. *The Craft of Ritual Studies*. New York: Oxford University Press, 2014.

Gripsrud, Jostein, Hallvard Moe, Anders Molander, and Graham Murdock. "Editors' Introduction." In *The Idea of the Public Sphere: A Reader*, edited by Jostein Gripsrud, Hallvard Moe, Anders Molander, and Graham Murdock, 6–22. Lanham: Lexington Books, 2010.

Guttin, Geneviève, and Gisèle Caumont. "Rapport de restauration de la couche picturale 'Le Sacrifice de la messe': Maison de retraite des prêtres de Saint Sulpice 'La Solitude'-Issy-les-Moulineaux." Conseil Général, Hauts-de-Seine, 2007.

Habermas, Jürgen. *The Structural Transformation of the Public Sphere: An Inquiry into the Category of Bourgeois Society*. Cambridge, MA: MIT Press, 1989.

Hamel, Charles. *Histoire de l'Église Saint-Sulpice*. 2nd ed. Paris: Librairie Victor Lecoffre, J. Gabalda, 1909.

Hameline, Jean-Yves. "Introduction." In *Les Cérémoniaux catholiques en France à l'époque moderne: Une littérature de codification des rites liturgiques*, edited by Cécile Davy-Rigaux, Bernard Dompnier, and Daniel-Odon Hurel, 13–42. Église, liturgie et société dans l'Europe moderne. Turnhout, Belgium: Brepols, 2009.

Hanley, Sarah. *The Lit de Justice of the Kings of France: Constitutional Ideology in Legend, Ritual, and Discourse*. Princeton, NJ: Princeton University Press, 1983.

Hautecoeur, Louis. *Louis XIV: Roi-Soleil*. Paris: Librairie Plon, 1953.

Hervouët, Gwénola. "Le Séminaire de Saint-Sulpice, 1642–1700: Étude sociologique et religieuse." Mémoire de maîtrise sous la direction de M. le Professeur Bely, Université de Paris IV—Sorbonne, 1999.

Hillemacher, F, and Révérend Du Mesnil. "L'acte de renonciation de Brécourt." Edited by Georges Monval. *Le Moliériste* 5, no. 57 (December 1883): 277–78.

Howarth, W. D. *Molière: A Playwright and His Audience*. Cambridge: Cambridge University Press, 1982.

Hyland, Peter. *Disguise on the Early Modern English Stage.* Burlington, VT: Ashgate, 2011.

"Investiture." In *OED Online.* Oxford University Press, 2019. https://www-oed-com.ezproxy.lib
.ucalgary.ca/view/Entry/99050?redirectedFrom=investiture.

Jackson, Richard A. *Vive le Roi! A History of the French Coronation from Charles V to Charles X.*
Chapel Hill: University of North Carolina Press, 1984.

Jacob, P.-L., ed. *Observations sur le festin de Pierre par de Rochemont et réponses aux observations,*
*réimpressions textuelles des éditions originelles de Paris, 1665.* Geneva: J. Gay et fils, 1869.

Jal, Auguste. *Dictionnaire critique de biographie et d'histoire, errata et supplément pour tous les dic-*
*tionnaires historiques d'après des documents authentiques inédits.* Paris: Henri Plon, 1876.

Jones, Ann Rosalind, and Peter Stallybrass. *Renaissance Clothing and the Materials of Memory.*
Cambridge Studies in Renaissance Literature and Culture. Cambridge: Cambridge University Press, 2000.

Julia, Dominique. "L'Éducation des ecclésiastiques en France aux XVIIe et XVIIIe siècles." In *Pro-*
*blèmes d'histoire de l'éducation: Actes des séminaires organisés par l'École française de Rome*
*et l'Università di Roma—La Sapienza (janvier–mai 1985),* 141–205. Collection de l'École
française de Rome 104. Rome: École française de Rome, 1988.

Kostroun, Daniella. *Feminism, Absolutism, and Jansenism: Louis XIV and the Port Royal Nuns.*
Cambridge: Cambridge University Press, 2011.

Krumenacker, Yves. *L'École française de spiritualité: Des Mystiques, des fondateurs, des courants et*
*leurs interprètes.* Paris: Les Éditions du Cerf, 1998.

Lachaud, Frédérique. "Liveries of Robes in England, c. 1200–c. 1330." *English Historical Review*
111, no. 441 (1996): 279–98.

Larroumet, Gustave. "Molière et Louis XIV." *Revue des Deux Mondes (1829–1971)* 77, no. 1 (1886):
64–100.

Latour, Bruno. *We Have Never Been Modern.* Translated by Catherine Porter. Cambridge, MA:
Harvard University Press, 1993.

Lebègue, Raymond. *La Tragédie religieuse en France: Les Débuts (1514–1573).* Bibliothèque littéraire de la renaissance. Paris: Librairie Ancienne Honoré Champion, 1929.

Leferme-Falguières, Frédérique. *Les Courtisans: Une Société de spectacle sous l'ancien régime.* Paris:
Presses Universitaires de France, 2007.

Lemaître, Nicole. "Le Prêtre mis à part ou le triomphe d'une idéologie sacerdotale au XVIe siècle." *Revue d'histoire de l'Église de France* 85, no. 215 (1999): 275–89. https://doi.org/10.3406
/rhef.1999.1371.

Lemazurier, Pierre David. *Galerie historique des acteurs du théâtre français, depuis 1600 jusqu'à nos*
*jours.* Vol. 1. 2 vols. Paris: Joseph Chaumerot, Libraire, 1810.

Lemesle, Gaston. *L'Eglise Saint-Sulpice.* Paris: Librairie Bloud et Gay, 1931.

Léoni, Sylviane. *Le Poison et le remède: Théâtre, morale et rhétorique en France et en Italie, 1694–*
*1758.* Oxford: Voltaire Foundation, 1998.

Lévêque, André. "'L'Honnête homme' et 'l'homme de bien' au XVII siècle." *PMLA* 72, no. 4
(1957): 620–32.

Lincoln, Bruce. *Authority: Construction and Corrosion.* Chicago: University of Chicago Press,
1994.

Lublin, Robert I. *Costuming the Shakespearean Stage: Visual Codes of Representation in Early Mod-*
*ern Theatre and Culture.* Burlington, VT: Ashgate, 2011.

Luria, Keith P. "Separated by Death? Cemeteries, Burials, and Confessional Boundaries." In *Sa-*
*cred Boundaries: Religious Coexistence and Conflict in Early-Modern France,* 103–42. Washington, DC: Catholic University of America Press, 2005.

Lyons, John D. *Kingdom of Disorder: The Theory of Tragedy in Classical France.* West Lafayette, IN: Purdue University Press, 1999.

Macalister, Robert Alexander Stewart. *Ecclesiastical Vestments: Their Development and History.* London: Elliot Stock, 1896.

Magendie, Maurice. *La Politesse mondaine et les théories de l'honnêteté, en France, au XVIIe siècle, de 1600 à 1660.* Vol. 1. 2 vols. Paris: Librairie Félix Alcan, 1926.

Maloney, Robert. "Préface." In Gérard Carroll, *Un Portrait du prêtre: Les Retraites de 10 jours pour les ordinands,* 13–1. Paris: Pierre Téqui, 2004.

Marin, Louis. "Le Cadre de la représentation et quelques-unes de ses figures." In *De la représentation,* edited by Daniel Arasse, Alain Cantillon, Giovanni Careri, Danièle Cohn, Pierre-Antoine Fabre, and Françoise Marin, 342–63. Paris: Gallimard Le Seuil, 1994.

Marly, Diana de. *Costume on the Stage: 1600–1940.* London: B. T. Batsford, 1982.

Marshall, Douglas A. "The Ritual Production of Belonging and Belief." In *Understanding Religious Ritual: Theoretical Approaches and Innovations,* edited by John P. Hoffmann, 31–53. Routledge Advances in Sociology. London: Routledge, 2012.

Martin, Henri-Jean. *Livre, pouvoirs et société à Paris au XVIIe siècle, 1598–1701.* Vol. 2. HathiTrust. Geneva: Librairie Droz, 1969.

Martin, Philippe. *Le Théâtre divin: Une Histoire de la messe, XVIe–XXe siècle.* Paris: CNRS Éditions, 2010.

Martin, Victor. *Le Gallicanism et la réforme catholique: Essai historique sur l'introduction en France des décrets du Concile de Trente (1563–1615).* Geneva: Slatkine Reprints, 1975.

Maugras, Gaston. *Les Comédiens hors la loi.* 2nd ed. Paris: Calmann Lévy, 1887.

McCabe, S.J., William H. *An Introduction to the Jesuit Theater: A Posthumous Work.* Edited by Louis J. Oldani, S.J. St. Louis, MO: Institute of Jesuit Sources, 1983.

McClain, Hannah G. "Corporal Penance in Belief and Practice: Medieval Monastic Precedents and Their Reception by the New and Reformed Religious Orders of the Sixteenth Century." *Footnotes: A Journal of History* 2 (2018): 177–98.

McClure, Ellen. *The Logic of Idolatry in Seventeenth-Century French Literature.* Gallica. Cambridge: D. S. Brewer, 2020.

McKenzie, Jon. *Perform or Else: From Discipline to Performance.* London: Routledge, 2001.

Meignan, Théodore. "Une Nouvelle source d'informations historiques: Les Anciens registres paroissiaux de l'état-civil." *Revue des questions historiques* 25 (1879): 131–72.

Mélèse, Pierre. *Le Théâtre et le public à Paris sous Louis XIV, 1659–1715.* Paris: Librairie Droz, 1934.

Merlin, Hélène. *Public et littérature en France au XVIIe siècle.* Histoire. Paris: Les Belles Lettres, 1994.

Michael, Roberts, and Christine F. Salazar. "Prince's Mirror." In *Brill's New Pauly,* 2006. http://dx.doi.org.ezproxy.lib.ucalgary.ca/10.1163/1574-9347_bnp_e415580.

Miller, Maureen C. *Clothing the Clergy: Virtue and Power in Medieval Europe, c. 800–1200.* Ithaca, NY: Cornell University Press, 2014.

———. *Power and the Holy in the Age of the Investiture Conflict: A Brief History with Documents.* Bedford Series in History and Culture. New York: Palgrave Macmillan, 2005.

Mittman, Barbara G. *Spectators on the Paris Stage in the Seventeenth and Eighteenth Centuries.* Ann Arbor: UMI Research Press, 1984.

Moloney, Raymond. *The Eucharist.* Problems in Theology. Collegeville, MN: Liturgical Press, 1995.

Mongrédien, Georges. *Recueil des textes et documents du XVIIe siècle relatifs à Molière.* Paris: Éditions du Centre national de la recherche scientifique, 1965.

Morgan, David. *Sacred Gaze: Religious Visual Culture in Theory and Practice*. Berkeley: University of California Press, 2005. http://troy.lib.sfu.ca/record=b4586481~S1a.

Muir, Edward. *Ritual in Early Modern Europe*. 2nd ed. Cambridge: Cambridge University Press, 2005.

O'Day, Rosemary. *The English Clergy: The Emergence and Consolidation of a Profession, 1558–1642*. Leicester: Leicester University Press, 1979.

Ojetti, Benedetto. "The Roman Congregations." In *The Catholic Encyclopedia*. Vol. 13. New York: Robert Appleton, 1912. http://www.newadvent.org/cathen/13136a.htm.

Paige, Nicholas. "Proto-Aesthetics and the Theatrical Image." *Papers on French Seventeenth-Century Literature* 35, no. 69 (2008): 517–25.

———. "Racine, *Phèdre*, and the French Classical Stage." In *A History of Modern French Literature: From the Sixteenth to the Twentieth Century*, edited by Christopher Prendergast, 190–211. Princeton, NJ: Princeton University Press, 2017. https://doi-org.ezproxy.lib.ucalgary.ca/10.1515/9781400885046.

Palacios, Joy. "Actors, Christian Burial, and Space in Early Modern Paris." *Past and Present* 232, no. 1 (August 2016): 127–63. https://doi.org/10.1093/pastj/gtw010.

Phelan, Peggy. "The Ontology of Performance: Representation Without Reproduction." In *Unmarked: The Politics of Performance*, 146–66. London: Routledge, 1993.

Phillips, Henry. *Church and Culture in Seventeenth-Century France*. Cambridge: Cambridge University Press, 1997.

———. *The Theatre and Its Critics in Seventeenth-Century France*. Oxford: Oxford University Press, 1980.

Plante, Guy. *Le Rigorisme au XVIIe siècle: Mgr de Saint-Vallier et le sacrement de pénitence (1685–1727)*. Gembloux, Belgium: Éditions J. Duculot, Gembloux, 1970.

Postlewait, Thomas, and Tracy C. Davis. "Theatricality: An Introduction." In *Theatricality*, edited by Thomas Postlewait and Tracy C. Davis, 1–39. Cambridge: Cambridge University Press, 2003.

Ramsden, E. H. "The Halo: A Further Enquiry into Its Origin." *Burlington Magazine for Connoisseurs* 78, no. 457 (1941): 123–31.

Ravel, Jeffrey S. *The Contested Parterre: Public Theater and French Political Culture, 1680–1791*. Ithaca, NY: Cornell University Press, 1999.

Régent-Susini, Anne. *Bossuet et la rhétorique de l'autorité*. Paris: Honoré Champion, 2011.

Restif, Bruno. *La Révolution des paroisses: Culture paroissiale et réforme catholique en Haute-Bretagne aux XVIe et XVIIe siècles*. Rennes: Presses Universitaires de Rennes, 2006.

Reyff, Simone de. *L'Église et le théâtre: L'Exemple de la France au XVIIe siècle*. Paris: Cerf, 1998.

Richardson, Catherine, ed. *Clothing Culture, 1350–1650*. Aldershot: Ashgate, 2004.

"Rites, Congregation of Sacred." In *Oxford Reference*. Accessed May 21, 2021. https://www.oxfordreference.com/view/10.1093/oi/authority.20110803100422710.

Roche, Daniel. *The Culture of Clothing: Dress and Fashion in the "Ancien Régime."* Translated by Jean Birrel. Cambridge: Cambridge University Press, 1994.

Román, David. *Acts of Intervention: Performance, Gay Culture, and AIDS*. Bloomington: Indiana University Press, 1998.

Roure, H. "Le Clergé du sud-est de la France au XVIIe siècle." *Revue d'histoire de l'Église de France* 37, no. 130 (1951): 153–87. https://doi.org/10.3406/rhef.1951.3115.

Runnalls, Graham A., ed. *Études sur les mystères: Un Recueil de 22 études sur les mystères français, suivi d'un répertoire du théâtre religieux français du Moyen Âge et d'une bibliographie*. Paris: Honoré Champion, 1998.

Sanchez, Ruth Olaizola. "Les Jésuites au théâtre dans l'Espagne du siècle d'or: Théories et pratiques, 1588–1689." Dissertation, l'École des Hautes Études en Sciences Sociales, under the direction of Yves Hersant, 2005.

Schechner, Richard. *Between Theater and Anthropology*. Philadelphia: University of Pennsylvania Press, 1985.

———. *Performance Studies: An Introduction*. London: Routledge, 2002.

Scherer, Jacques. *La Dramaturgie classique en France*. Paris: Libraire Nizet, 1959.

———. *Racine et/ou la cérémonie*. Paris: Presses Universitaires de France, 1982.

———. *Structures de Tartuffe*. 2nd ed. Paris: Société d'Éditions d'Enseignement Supérieur, 1974.

Schneider, Rebecca. *Performing Remains: Art and War in Times of Theatrical Reenactment*. New York: Routledge, 2011.

Schneider, Robert A. *The Ceremonial City: Toulouse Observed, 1738–1780*. Princeton, NJ: Princeton University Press, 1995.

Schœnher, P. *Histoire du Séminaire de Saint-Nicolas du Chardonnet, 1612–1908, d'après des documents inédits*. Vol. 1. 2 vols. Quelques pages de l'histoire religieuse du diocèse de Paris. Paris: Société Saint Augustin, 1909.

Schorn-Schütte, Luise. "Priest, Preacher, Pastor: Research on Clerical Office in Early Modern Europe." *Central European History* 33, no. 1 (2000): 1–39.

Scott, Virginia. *Women on the Stage in Early Modern France: 1540–1750*. Cambridge: Cambridge University Press, 2010.

"Seminary, n.1." In *OED Online*, March 2012. http://www.oed.com/view/Entry/175684.

Smith, Jonathan Z. "The Bare Facts of Ritual." *History of Religions* 20, nos. 1–2 (1980): 112–17.

States, Bert O. "Performance as Metaphor." *Theatre Journal* 48, no. 1 (1996): 1–26.

Sturken, Marita, and Lisa Cartwright. *Practices of Looking: An Introduction to Visual Culture*. Oxford: Oxford University Press, 2001.

Swanson, Robert N. "Apostolic Successors: Priests and Priesthood, Bishops, and Episcopacy in Medieval Western Europe." In *A Companion to Priesthood and Holy Orders in the Middle Ages*, edited by Greg Peters and C. Colt Anderson, 62:4–42. Brill's Companions to the Christian Tradition. Leiden: Brill, 2016.

Sweetser, Eve. "Blended Spaces and Performativity." *Cognitive Linguistics* 11, nos. 3–4 (2000): 305–33. https://doi.org/10.1515/cogl.2001.018.

Swidler, Ann. "Culture in Action: Symbols and Strategies." *American Sociological Review* 51, no. 2 (1986): 273–86.

Taveneaux, René. *Le Catholicisme dans la France classique, 1610–1715: Première partie*. Vol. 1. 2 vols. Regards sur l'histoire: Histoire moderne. Paris: Société d'Éditions d'Enseignement Supérieur, 1980.

———. *Le Catholicisme dans la France classique, 1610–1715: Deuxième partie*. Vol. 2. 2 vols. Regards sur l'histoire: Histoire moderne. Paris: Société d'Éditions d'Enseignement Supérieur, 1980.

Taviani, Ferdinando. *La fascinazione del teatro: La commedia dell'arte e la società barocca*. Roma: Bulzoni, 1969.

Taylor, Diana. *The Archive and the Repertoire: Performing Cultural Memory in the Americas*. Durham, NC: Duke University Press, 2003.

Thibodeaux, Jennifer D. *The Manly Priest: Clerical Celibacy, Masculinity, and Reform in England and Normandy, 1066–1300*. Middle Ages Series. Philadelphia: University of Pennsylvania Press, 2015.

Thiong'o, Ngũgĩ wa. "Enactments of Power: The Politics of Performance Space." *TDR: The Drama Review* 41, no. 3 (1997): 11–30.

Thirouin, Laurent. *L'Aveuglement salutaire: Le Requisitoire contre le théâtre dans la France classique*. Paris: Champion, 1997.

Thompson, William M., ed. *Bérulle and the French School: Selected Writings*. Translated by Lowell M. Glendon. New York: Paulist Press, 1989.

Thurston, Herbert. "Missal." In *The Catholic Encyclopedia*. Vol. 10. New York: Robert Appleton, 1911. http://www.newadvent.org/cathen/10354c.htm.

Trichet, Louis. *La Tonsure: Vie et mort d'une pratique ecclésiastique*. Paris: Les Éditions du Cerf, 1990.

———. *Le Costume du clergé: Ses origines et son évolution en France d'après les règlements de l'église*. Paris: Les Éditions du Cerf, 1986.

Tucker, Holly. *City of Light, City of Poison: Murder, Magic, and the First Police Chief of Paris*. New York: W. W. Norton, 2017.

Turner, Victor. "Betwixt and Between: The Liminal Period in *Rites de Passage*." In *The Forest of Symbols: Aspects of Ndembu Ritual*, 93–111. Ithaca, NY: Cornell University Press, 1967.

Van Zanden, Jan L. "Wages and the Standard of Living in Europe, 1500–1800." *European Review of Economic History* 3, no. 2 (1999): 175–97.

Vermeersch, Arthur. "Religious Life." In *The Catholic Encyclopedia*. Vol. 12. New York: Robert Appleton, 1911. http://www.newadvent.org/cathen/12748b.htm.

Viéban, Anthony. "Ecclesiastical Seminary." In *The Catholic Encyclopedia*. New York: Robert Appleton, 1912. http://www.newadvent.org/cathen/13694a.htm.

Warner, Michael. *Publics and Counterpublics*. New York: Zone Books, 2005.

Weber, Max. "The Three Types of Legitimate Rule." Translated by Hans Gerth. *Berkeley Publications in Society and Institutions* 4, no. 1 (1958): 1–11.

Wiley, W. L. *The Early Public Theatre in France*. Cambridge, MA: Harvard University Press, 1960.

Worthen, W. B. "Drama, Performativity, and Performance." *PMLA* 113, no. 5 (1998): 1093–1107.

Wright, Anthony D. *The Divisions of French Catholicism, 1629–1645: "The Parting of Ways."* London: Routledge, 2016.

Wright, Edith A. "The Dissemination of the Liturgical Drama in France." Bryn Mawr, PA: Bryn Mawr College, 1935.

# INDEX

Figures are indicated by page numbers followed by fig.

# ACKNOWLEDGMENTS

Many people and institutions have helped this project arrive at its final form, and I am profoundly grateful for their support. My archival research was funded by a summer Foreign Language Area Studies (FLAS) fellowship, a yearlong FLAS fellowship, and a Marjorie M. Farrar Memorial Award from the Society for French Historical Studies. I owe a particular debt to the archivists at the Archives of the Society of Saint-Sulpice in Paris, Jean Longère and Irénée Noye, who gave me permission to consult and photograph every manuscript I requested, and to the librarians who administered the print collection, Marie Odile Appavou and Agnès Jauréguibéhère. Without them this project would not exist. Start-up grants from Simon Fraser University and the University of Calgary enabled me to return to Paris to gather additional materials and to present portions of my work at conferences. I thank my colleagues for the valuable feedback I received at the Society for Interdisciplinary French Seventeenth-Century Studies, the North American Society for Seventeenth-Century French Literature, the Modern Language Association, the Western Society for French History, the Renaissance Society of America, and the American Academy of Religion.

I want to extend especially warm thanks to my mentors Shannon Steen, Nicholas Paige, Michael Wintroub, and Shannon Jackson, who from the very beginning of this project encouraged my desire to do archival research and helped me transform my findings into arguments. Their generosity and patience allowed me to follow this project where it wanted to go. Déborah Blocker's guidance in the project's early phases was also irreplaceable, as was the warm welcome I received from Pierre-Antoine Fabre at what was then the Centre d'Anthropologie Religieuse Européenne in Paris. I also thank Mark Griffith, who provided advice in the early phases, Catherine Cole, who helped arrange departmental support for my first semester of archival research, and Steven Mullaney and Paul Yachnin, whose summer seminar "Making Theatrical Publics in Early Modern Europe" had a lasting influence on my project.

Throughout the writing process, I have been incredibly lucky to share drafts on a regular basis with Anna Rosensweig, who has read every version of the manuscript multiple times, helped me see at each stage how to continue refining it, and boosted my morale. Our regular meetings kept me going. My colleagues at Simon Fraser University and the University of Calgary provided encouragement throughout as well. I especially thank Lindsay Driediger-Murphy for her incredible support during the peer review process, and Catherine Black, Jorge Calderón, Luke Clossey, Susan Bennett, John Vanderspoel, Rachel Schmidt, Tinu Ruparell, Lisa Hughes, and Marica Cassis for their support and mentorship in relation to the book specifically and the academic path more broadly. I am thankful to Emine Fisek and James Coons for their comments on Chapter 5, to Geoffrey Turnovsky for comments on an early version of the manuscript at SE17, and to Scott Magelssen for the opportunity to present and receive feedback on part of my manuscript in his "Religion, Performance, and Antitheatricality" seminar at the University of Washington. When I had questions along the way, Ellen McClure, Holly Tucker, Hélène Bilis, Lauren Clay, and Joel Harrington all gave important advice at just the right moment, and to them I am grateful. My friends and colleagues through the Collectif d'Anthropologie et d'Histoire du Spirituel et des Affects have given me a sense of community and of the bigger conversation to which I hope to contribute (and helped me on more than one occasion with my French), especially Emmanuelle Friant, Anne Régent-Susini, Corinne Bayerl, and Arnaud Wydler. I am extremely grateful to my editor, Jerome Singerman, for guiding my manuscript to publication, and to the readers at the University of Pennsylvania Press, Katherine Ibbett and Daniella Kostroun, whose detailed feedback made this book better than it would have been. Their insights and questions were invaluable.

I lack sufficient words to thank my family, who cheered me every step of the way. My father, Joel Crosby, provided morale, research tools (like the camera I used in the archives), and, although neither of us realized it at the time, the research questions that gave rise to this project. Until I was sixteen, he was the pastor of a small Presbyterian Church in a low-income neighborhood of Spokane, Washington. Every summer, he wrote modern-day morality plays for the Vacation Bible School featuring superheroes like Batman and Robin, recast as Christians who used their faith to convert the villains. Children piled into the sanctuary to see Spiderman jump from the balcony or Wonder Woman run up the aisle. Some church members, however, thought the plays were too secular and worried that they replaced worship with entertainment. Why, I wondered? The church used other forms of performance—skits during the children's sermon on Sundays, a praise band—and the pastor's work involved at times a kind of acting. What made these plays offensive? Later, when I reflected on these experiences at the beginning of my scholarly journey, I realized that the controversy stirred up by my father's plays had roots stretching back to the Protestant Reformation, if not further, and I set out to understand antitheatrical sentiment's liturgical basis. Little did my father know he was setting my research direction.

My mother, Kathy Crosby, nourished my spirit with wisdom, comfort, and empathy, and visited frequently during the book phase to help with childcare. My sister, Betsy Lind, read my very first draft while on her maternity leave, which helped me start to get words onto the page. My brother, Jed Crosby, read the first full version of the manuscript, brainstormed with me extensively at all stages of the project, and drove me back and forth to the airport innumerable times. Ariane Ville, who is like family to me, provided unflagging friendship, shared my enthusiasm for questions relating church and theater, and helped me prepare to present part of my manuscript in French at the École des Hautes Études en Sciences Sociales. My mother- and father-in-law, María Mercedes Lleras and Hugo Palacios, made it possible for me to write during holidays and took sincere interest in the project. The biggest thanks, though, goes to my husband, Miguel Palacios, and our sons, Daniel and David, for supporting the writing process day in and day out. They fill my life with love and keep me laughing.

CPSIA information can be obtained
at www.ICGtesting.com
Printed in the USA
JSHW060511140722
27850JS00002BB/2

9 781512 822786